There have been few winners following the war to depose Saddam Hussein in Iraq in 2003: the Iraqi Kurds may however be one of them as Mohammed Shareef explains in this lucid volume. We shall now have to wait and see whether a fully independent Kurdistan can become what many thought it never could in the past – a source of stability in a region that continues to be plagued by tensions and conflicts. A must read book on a crucial geostrategic issue.

Michael Cox, *Professor of International Relations,*
London School of Economics, UK

The value of Dr Shareef's excellent new book on Iraq is not just in its discussion of the roots of the crisis, the extraordinary level of detail therein and the enlightening interviews, not only for its rich insights and extensive data collection, not simply for the valuable and textured commentary that it provides on American policy making, but equally importantly for the crisp analysis that it provides of the aftermath of the 2003 war on the body politics of Iraq, particularly on its substantial and often oppressed Kurdish communities. This is one for the reference collection!

Anoushiravan Ehteshami, *Professor of International Relations,*
University of Durham, UK

Shareef's study is a welcome and timely in-depth study of US foreign policy developments in Arab Iraq and Kurdistan Iraq especially after the US invasion of Kuwait in 1991 and invasion and occupation of Iraq in 2003. He embeds his study in three Grand Strategies: one, 1979–1990 influenced by the Cold War; two, 1991–2001, stresses the liberal international strategy and three, the War on Terror from 2002–2013. Diplomatic scholars will be particularly interested in phase three which analyses the role of the Kurds of Iraq in the formation of US policies toward the wider Middle East; a hitherto topic largely ignored by scholars. During phase three Shareef argues that for geopolitical and geostrategic interests the US pursued (and still does) policies of maintaining a unified Iraq even as developments in Kurdistan Iraq were/are moving toward self-determination. The eventuation of an independent Kurdistan would of course seriously affect US foreign policies toward Turkey, Iran and Syria all of whom oppose an independent Kurdish state in Iraq. This will result in the Kurdish question becoming even a more salient factor in the making of US foreign policies not just toward the Middle East but internationally. Shareef's study is one of only a few that uses Arab and Kurdish based source. I recommend it highly to scholars and policy makers.

Robert Olson, *Professor of Middle East History and Politics,*
University of Kentucky, USA

The United States, Iraq and the Kurds

This book provides a descriptive and analytical narrative of the evolution of US foreign policy towards Iraq at the supra-national (global), national (Arab Iraq) and sub-national (Iraqi Kurdistan) levels.

The book is unique in that it presents a sophisticated insight into the two major components of US Iraq policy. To achieve this, it addresses US foreign policy towards both Arab Iraq and an entirely original analysis on US policy towards the Iraqi Kurds as components of a larger US Iraq policy, dictated by the supreme US Grand Strategy. The book also examines whether US foreign policy towards Iraq has been one of continuity or change – a dimension that has not been illustrated in any other publication. The book deals intelligently and at great length with the events surrounding US Iraq policy in three distinct phases, going back to 1979 with regard to Arab Iraq, and 1961 in respect to the Kurdish liberation movement, covering all subsequent US administrations including the Obama presidency. It provides a thorough examination of US interests in Iraq and reasons for the 2003 invasion and its aftermath. It also engages with the intellectual roots of US foreign policy, presenting an intricate reaction of views, objectives and agendas.

This work will be of interest to students and scholars of Middle East studies, US Foreign Policy and Security studies.

Mohammed Shareef is a fellow of the Royal Asiatic Society (London). He has worked for the UN and is a lecturer in International Relations at the University of Sulaimani in the Kurdistan Region of Iraq. Mohammed completed his PhD in International Relations at the University of Durham and has an MSc in International Relations from the University of Bristol in the United Kingdom. His research interests range from US foreign policy towards Iraq and the Kurds to US policy towards the Middle East in general.

Routledge studies in US foreign policy

Edited by Inderjeet Parmar
University of Manchester
and
John Dumbrell
University of Durham

This new series sets out to publish high quality works by leading and emerging scholars critically engaging with United States Foreign Policy. The series welcomes a variety of approaches to the subject and draws on scholarship from international relations, security studies, international political economy, foreign policy analysis and contemporary international history.

Subjects covered include the role of administrations and institutions, the media, think tanks, ideologues and intellectuals, elites, transnational corporations, public opinion, and pressure groups in shaping foreign policy, US relations with individual nations, with global regions and global institutions and America's evolving strategic and military policies.

The series aims to provide a range of books – from individual research monographs and edited collections to textbooks and supplemental reading for scholars, researchers, policy analysts, and students.

United States Foreign Policy and National Identity in the 21st Century
Edited by Kenneth Christie

New Directions in US Foreign Policy
Edited by Inderjeet Parmar, Linda B. Miller and Mark Ledwidge

America's 'Special Relationships'
Foreign and domestic aspects of the politics of alliance
Edited by John Dumbrell and Axel R. Schäfer

US Foreign Policy in Context
National ideology from the founders to the Bush doctrine
Adam Quinn

The United States and NATO since 9/11
The transatlantic alliance renewed
Ellen Hallams

The United States, Iraq and the Kurds

Shock, awe and aftermath

Mohammed Shareef

Routledge
Taylor & Francis Group

LONDON AND NEW YORK

First published 2014 by Routledge

2 Park Square, Milton Park, Abingdon, Oxfordshire OX14 4RN
711 Third Avenue, New York, NY 10017

Routledge is an imprint of the Taylor & Francis Group, an informa business

First issued in paperback 2018

British Library Cataloguing in Publication Data
A catalogue record for this book is available from the British Library

Library of Congress Cataloging in Publication Data
Shareef, Mohammed.
  The United States, Iraq and the Kurds : shock, awe and aftermath / Mohammed Shareef.
  pages cm. – (Routledge studies in US foreign policy)
  Includes bibliographical references and index.
  1. United States–Foreign relations–Iraq. 2. Iraq–Foreign relations–United States. 3. Kurds–Government policy–United States. I. Title.
  E183.8.I57S527 2014
  327.730567–dc23

                                                                    2013035990

ISBN: 978-0-415-71990-2 (hbk)
ISBN: 978-1-138-35932-1 (pbk)

Typeset in Times New Roman
by Wearset Ltd, Boldon, Tyne and Wear

To my parents, Professor Jalal Shareef and Gashaw Shalli,
my wife Dr Rangeen Ibrahim,
and my daughters Gasha and Rozha

Contents

Acknowledgements

The writing of this book could not have been successfully completed without the invaluable contributions of two scholars I hold in great esteem.

To Professor John Dumbrell I owe a particular debt of gratitude. I am sincerely grateful for his continuous guidance throughout this demanding and extensive project. I found him an inspiration for both his vast knowledge and humility. I can never thank him enough for his willingness to support this interesting yet controversial and, at times, difficult endeavour.

My heartfelt thanks also go to Professor Anoushiravan Ehteshami who nurtured this book with insightful suggestions and encouraging comments. The depth and breadth of his knowledge is nothing short of astounding and his encouragement and guidance were invaluable throughout.

I would like to extend my personal gratitude to the Kurdistan Regional Government Representation in Washington, D.C. for their wonderful support during my three months in the United States researching this book. My special thanks go to Mr Qubad Talabani and the senior staff at the representation who provided unlimited assistance by helping to arrange a large number of invaluable interviews to enrich this project.

Moreover, I would like to recognise and express gratitude to my brilliant friends who read through early manuscripts of this book. I wish to thank Alan Rose, David Ogilvie, Dr Gillian Boughton, Iain Whitaker, Jacquie Evans, Judith Stevenson, Dr Noel Kingsbury, Dr Peter Scott, Ryan Phillips and Till Vere-Hodge for their invaluable suggestions and valid comments. I am indeed privileged to count them as my friends.

I am deeply obliged to my sister Roshin and brother Aram for their enduring support and unceasing encouragement from the very beginning of embarking on writing this book. They were instrumental in raising my spirits and helping to bring this project to a successful close.

Finally, I wish to honour and remember my beloved late grandmother Sabria Haji Hama Agha who passed away in 2009. I would like to express my limitless thanks for her unwavering love and support since my early days in high school and, most of all, for her constant encouragement to do well.

Acronyms

ABM	Anti-Ballistic Missile treaty
AEI	American Enterprise Institute
AWACS	Airborne Warning and Control System
CCC	Commodity Credit Corporation
CENTCOM	Central Command of the US armed forces
CIA	Central Intelligence Agency
CNTBT	Comprehensive Nuclear Test Ban Treaty
CPA	Coalition Provisional Authority
DDR	De-mobilisation, Disarming and Re-integration
FBI	Federal Bureau of Investigation
GMEI	Greater Middle East Initiative
IAEA	International Atomic Energy Agency
ICC	International Criminal Court
IGC	Iraqi Governing Council
IIA	Iraqi Interim Authority
ILA	Iraq Liberation Act
INA	Iraqi National Accord
INC	Iraqi National Congress
KDP	Kurdistan Democratic Party
KRG	Kurdistan Regional Government
NSA	National Security Advisor
NSC	National Security Council
NSD	National Security Directive
NSS	National Security Strategy
OFF	Oil for Food programme
OIF	Operation Iraqi Freedom
ORHA	Office for Reconstruction and Humanitarian Assistance
OSP	Office of Special Plans
PKK	Kurdistan Workers' Party
PNAC	Project for the New American Century
PUK	Patriotic Union of Kurdistan
SAIC	Science Applications International Corporation
SCIRI	Supreme Council for the Islamic Revolution in Iraq

SOF	Special Operations Forces
SOFA	Status of Forces Agreement
TAL	Transitional Administrative Law
UN	United Nations
UNMOVIC	United Nations Monitoring, Verification and Inspection Commission
UNSC	United Nations Security Council
UNSCOM	United Nations Special Commission
UNSCR	United Nations Security Council Resolution
USD	US Dollars
USIP	United States Institute for Peace
WINEP	Washington Institute for Near East Policy
WMD	Weapons of Mass Destruction

1   Introduction

> The current Iraqi regime has shown the power of tyranny to spread discord and violence in the Middle East. A liberated Iraq can show the power of freedom to transform that vital region, by bringing hope and progress into the lives of millions. America's interests in security, and America's belief in liberty, both lead in the same direction: to a free and peaceful Iraq.
>
> George W. Bush, 26 February 2003[1]

Since the United States assumed its role as a superpower it has never shied away from pronouncing the centrality of the Middle East as a national interest priority. By 1944, President Franklin Roosevelt had already described the region as a 'vital interest' to the US, and stressed that the 'maintenance of peace' in the Middle East was central to US and international concerns.[2] Several decades later, with the demise of the British Empire and later Britain's decision in 1968 to withdraw from the Persian Gulf, the US adopted the role of security guarantor in the Middle East. This US goal was initially achieved indirectly through proxies, only to evolve gradually into direct US military intervention. From its inception as a superpower, the US has taken its policing role seriously and assertively. It has insisted that peace be preserved, however, only on its own terms.

Throughout the Cold War, the US maintained its position at the helm of the Middle East by attempting to deny its nemesis, the Soviet Union, influence or authority over this strategically valuable region, and was largely successful in denying it a foothold. As part of America's view of interests in the region, the security of Israel and access of world markets to oil were secured during this period. At the height of the Cold War, US strategy was restricted to managing regional actors and dissuading them from Soviet influence. To this end, it became US strategy to maintain friendly relations with willing regional actors on the one hand, and on the other to discourage regional adversaries from engaging in relations with the Soviet Union. Throughout this time Iraq, which is the focus of this book, engaged in a fluctuating relationship with the United States, one dependent on the nature of government in Baghdad and the distinctive geopolitical context. Iraq, like other regional actors, was affected by the superpower rivalry for the region. With the absence of the Soviet Union after the Cold War's end, the American policy of blocking emergent regional hegemons and potential competitors to US hegemony in the Middle East region continued, relying on the strategies of deterrence and containment, and even military confrontation when necessary. Iraq, however, had discarded its colonial past with the overthrow of the pro-British monarchy in 1958; it had already embarked on a nationalistic dis- course, as it too aspired to reach regional power status. This aspiration in turn became an inconvenience for US interests, and as a consequence a challenge America was willing to confront.

The central theme and purpose of this book is to address change and con- tinuity in US Iraq policy. Hence it takes 1979 as its primary launching point for a major reason. For this year is of great significance, as it is the year in which Saddam Hussein gained ultimate power as Iraq's president and, ironically, the same year the United States considered reviving relations and tilting favourably towards Iraq. The Carter administration's desire for revived relations with Iraq was further strengthened with the Reagan administration's engagement with Saddam's regime. This was a policy later pursued by the George H. W. Bush administration, revised after Iraq's occupation of Kuwait and continued by Pres- ident Bill Clinton.

US foreign policy towards Iraq during President George W. Bush's adminis- tration is especially compelling, as Saddam Hussein's eventual demise came at the hands of the United States, under his administration and on his personal orders. The George W. Bush presidency provides an excellent platform from which to assess consistencies and departures in US Iraq policy. The attacks of 11 September 2001, perpetrated during the early months of the George W. Bush administration, provide a paradigm shift in America's attitude to the world, and a critical baseline from which this book gauges US policy towards Iraq. The administration of George W. Bush was undeniably rich in major events, some of which were external and outside his control, while many were a direct result of his own proactive foreign policy. Through analysis of this foreign policy and also of contemporary diplomatic history it is possible to gain a richer under- standing of America's policy perspective towards Iraq, and also towards Iraq's Kurds. This book will therefore provide both a descriptive and an analytical nar- rative of the evolution of US foreign policy towards Arab Iraq from 1979 and towards the Iraqi Kurds from 1961. It covers the George W. Bush administration that led the invasion and occupation of Iraq, and the major developments in Iraq during the Obama presidency including the withdrawal of the last US forces from that country and its aftermath.

Three interacting, yet distinct phases have occurred in US Iraq policy during the period studied in this book: The first phase starts with the overthrow in 1979 of the Shah of Iran, and his replacement with a theocratic regime hostile to the US. The dethroning of this strategic ally compelled the US to rethink its strat- egies in the Middle East and, as a result, choose to pursue a new role in the Gulf with a regional security strategy based, at heart, on the strategic balancing of regional actors. With this new strategy put into practice Iraq gradually gained a favoured status as a potential regional ally, and as a practical replacement to the valuable but now lost regional asset of Iran.

The second phase of US–Iraq relations was triggered by Iraq's occupation of Kuwait in 1990. As a result of this aggression, Iraq was seen as a hostile and irreconcilable actor in the region neither willing nor capable of acting within the confines of acceptable international behaviour. The US perceived Iraq as inherently adverse to its regional interests, and beyond moderation. As a result America changed its strategy and Iraq was reclassified as 'rogue' – a terrorism-sponsoring state that defied the possibility of achieving once hoped-for reform.

The third phase of US Iraq policy emerged in the immediate aftermath of the attacks on Washington, D.C. and New York on 11 September 2001. America's heightened international security fears which resulted from the attacks provided the necessary grounds for a third assessment in US strategy towards Iraq.

Focusing on consistencies and departures in US Iraq policy, this book observes three major levels of US interaction with Iraq. The first level of analysis is at the supra-national level, addressing US global strategy and its effects on US policy towards Iraq. US global strategy is guided by its Grand Strategy, defined as the overall vision of America's national security goals and a determination of the most appropriate means to achieve these goals.[3] At this highest level of US foreign policy consideration this book looks at whether there have been any changes in US Grand Strategy in response to changes in the global security order. In the end, it finds that there have indeed been transitions, from a Cold War Grand Strategy to that of the Liberal Internationalist Grand Strategy to the Grand Strategy of the Global War on Terror.

The second is US Iraq policy at the national level, where bilateral policy towards Iraq as a nation state will be observed. Using a detailed historical narrative, the political events and disturbances in Iraq and the Middle East that have affected and influenced US–Iraq relations since 1979 will be examined. This level can be defined as US policy towards Arab Iraq, as the country's Kurds – the second largest ethnic group in the country – are largely absent in this interaction.

The third level of analysis of this book is that of US Iraq policy at the sub-national level. This includes analysis of the second dimension of US Iraq policy from 1961, that of its policy towards Iraq's Kurds. US policy on the Kurdish nationalist movement in Iraq, and America's interests – at times avoiding and at other times engaging this relationship – will be discussed. This book contends that, while the US does have an Iraq policy, it also has a de facto policy towards Iraq's Kurds. And although America's policy towards Iraqi Kurds is not formally articulated, the very nature of US interaction with the Kurdish movement, having evolved over time from initial contacts to a now much more institutionalised relationship, makes US Kurdish policy a tangible and observable reality.

The consistencies in American policy, upon which this book is premised, are enlightening, as conventional wisdom and current scholarship primarily perceives the Bush Doctrine as unconventional in its approach and a dramatic shift in US foreign policy. A substantial amount of commentary has been dedicated to George W. Bush's policy towards Iraq, with many perceiving it as a departure from traditional US foreign policy practice towards this country – an assertion this book attempts to refute. Additionally, most of the existing literature in the field predominantly addresses US foreign policy towards Iraq within the larger context of the Middle East or, frequently, deals with US foreign policy more generally, of which Iraq is but one component. As such, little can be found focusing solely on US Iraq policy, a gap this book attempts to address. Furthermore, most scholarship and books currently available on US foreign policy (especially regarding the George W. Bush administration) deal with Iraq only within the confines and context of other issues, for instance the threat from terrorism, the War on Terror, pre-emption unilateralism, the role of the neoconservatives or US hegemony, and do not specifically address US Iraq policy.

Moreover, very little attention has been paid to the issue of Iraqi Kurds in US foreign policy. Modern scholarship fails heavily in describing accurately the highly significant and parallel US interaction with Iraq's Kurds. It is therefore necessary that US Iraq policy is described accurately and completely, encompassing both its Arab and Kurdish dimensions, as US policy towards Arab and Kurdish Iraq, though heavily linked, differ from each other.

The Kurdish issue has been largely neglected by scholars mainly due to the lack of a Kurdish nation state and the state-centric nature of the international system, but also for lack of skill amongst scholars in the Kurdish language. The Kurdish issue has been largely perceived as a nationalist movement, denying it the attention it deserves in International Relations scholarship. Having had a considerable impact on the international relations of the Middle East, the Kurds thus need to be addressed appropriately. Although US-Kurdish relations are an inseparable part of US Iraq policy they are distinct and elaborate. The Kurdish issue has been a critical issue for important neighbouring states, namely Iran and Turkey, and therefore has played a major role in America's policy towards those states as well. It has been a major issue affecting Turkish national security, Turkish relations with Iraq and US-Turkish relations. Since 1991, Iraqi Kurdistan has enjoyed de facto nationhood under US protection, changing to a de jure entity in 2005 after the new Iraqi constitution, recognising its federal status, was passed. This relatively new-found status seems to have changed international and regional perceptions for this newly emergent non-state actor from neglect to intrigue and consideration in contemporary international affairs. Yet still very little scholarship has been carried out on this important issue directly. To address this deficiency this book addresses a large and important gap in the understanding of US foreign policy and subsequently introduces a fresh understanding of the role and influence of the Kurds on Iraq and the region.

This book challenges the conventional notion that changes in Grand Strategy at the supra-national level and changes in strategies and tactics at the national and sub-national level are actual changes in US policy. Thus it is critical to our understanding of US foreign policy to make a distinction between policy and strategy. In a political environment where US foreign policy is predominantly a vision of American interests and goals, and strategy the framework for achieving these objectives, and the appropriate tactics the means to achieve these aims, it becomes apparent that policy objectives have remained largely the same. Essentially a

policy is the end goal served by different strategies and tactics. With this definition in mind we can observe that US Iraq policy is primarily one of continuity,
rather than change, as US interests regarding Iraq are defined by the same fundamental concerns, regardless of the nature of the American administration in
office. This book's conclusion finds that US Iraq policy for George W. Bush's
predecessors, his successor President Obama, and indeed the Bush junior administration itself, which ordered the military invasion of Iraq and managed US
actions in its aftermath, were all guided largely by the same considerations and
goals. However, different strategies and tactics were pursued, and certain policy
objectives amplified, gaining heightened attention based on US national security
concerns and the geopolitical circumstances of the moment.

Chapter 2 provides a detailed historical narrative of US policy towards Arab
Iraq, starting with the Carter administration and Saddam's accession to power in
1979. This chapter extends through the successive administrations up to the
George W. Bush administration, including his first eight months in office. This
chapter describes phases one and two of US–Iraq relations. Phase one begins
with US engagement with Iraq after the fall of the Shah in 1979; phase two sees
the review of US Iraq policy after Saddam Hussein's occupation of Kuwait, and
subsequent containment strategy. It is only through tracking these two phases
that the necessary grounds are set to fully assess change or continuity in US Iraq
policy during the George W. Bush presidency and Barack Obama's administration that followed.

Chapter 3 takes a comprehensive look at the different intellectual groupings
within the George W. Bush administration. In this chapter the different factions
and their respective intellectual roots that influenced US foreign policy after the
al-Qaeda attacks on 9/11 will be identified. This chapter aids in the understanding of ideologies and the various interpretations of the US role on the world
stage. This is a crucial chapter for our understanding of the Bush administration
as it challenges the assertion that it was an administration restricted by a neoconservative agenda. The chapter deals primarily with four major groups deemed
directly involved in the decision-making process: the neoconservatives, George
W. Bush (the compassionate Conservative), the assertive nationalists and the
defensive realists. Two external groups are also identified.

Chapter 4 comprises two major sections. The first section introduces the
actual decision-making process leading to the invasion of Iraq and the toppling
of Saddam's regime. It recalls the debates and discussions leading to military
action to overthrow Saddam. This chapter examines phase three of US Iraq
policy, which began as a result of the 9/11 terrorist attacks. The second section
of the chapter then studies the various objectives used to justify the US invasion
of Iraq. For simplification, this chapter makes use of a geological analogy, sub-
dividing the objectives of the invasion into crust, mantle and core. Such a cat-
egorisation allows all issues considered of vital importance to the Bush
administration to be highlighted systematically. This subdivision allows a thorough understanding of the visible and publicly stated reasons and also the underlying (largely unarticulated publicly) justifications for regime change in Iraq.

Chapter 5 proceeds with the aftermath of the Iraq invasion. Here, US actions will be examined, along with the mistakes made and dealings with the fall of the regime. This chapter describes the post-invasion era in US Iraq policy, and studies American management of the occupation and the events leading to the nominal handing over of sovereignty on 28 June 2004. This chapter follows US policy towards Arab Iraq until the end of the Bush administration and follows through to the Obama presidency, and forms a concluding picture on US Iraq policy at the national level and the US objectives for a Saddam-free Iraq.

Chapter 6 addresses the second major focus of this book: US policy towards Iraq's Kurds. Similarly to US policy towards Arab Iraq, this is also influenced by the same three distinct phases. This chapter, however, takes the first phase back to the unsuccessful Kurdish attempts to create a relationship with the US in 1961, when the Kurdish movement against Baghdad began in earnest. A brief covert engagement from 1972 to 1975 followed by an era of non-interaction until the 1991 Kurdish uprising is also discussed. This engagement was intensified with the Iraq Liberation Act in 1998 and further strengthened with the change in US mood after the attacks of 9/11. The final section of this chapter deals with the Kurds in post-Saddam Iraq and US policy towards Iraqi Kurdistan under the administrations of George W. Bush and Barack Obama.

The final chapter summarises and assesses continuity and change in US Iraq policy at the global supra-national, national and sub-national levels throughout the three phases covered. It addresses continuity and change during the two terms of the George W. Bush presidency and the Obama administration that followed, as well as the preceding administrations of presidents Clinton, George H. W. Bush, Reagan and Carter, all the way back to the Kennedy presidency. The chapter also addresses continuity and change with US foreign policy in general. In this chapter the consistencies and departures with regard to US policy towards Arab Iraq are identified, as is US policy towards Kurdish Iraq and US global policy. This chapter concludes that US policy towards Iraq is far more consistent than is often assumed.

Notes

1 George W. Bush. (2003c). *President Discusses the Future of Iraq.* [The White House] Available at: URL: http://georgewbush-whitehouse.archives.gov/news/releases/2003/02/20030226–11.html Access Date: 20 June 2008.
2 Franklin D. Roosevelt. (2005). *2005 Topical Symposium Prospects for Security in the Middle East April 20–21, 2005.* [National Defense University] Available at: URL: www.ndu.edu/inss/Symposia/Topical2005/Agenda.htm Access Date: 20 June 2009.
3 Brian Schmidt, 'Theories of US Foreign Policy', in *US Foreign Policy*, ed. Michael Cox and Doug Stokes (Oxford: Oxford University Press, 2008), p. 19.

2 US Iraq policy pre-September 11

Recognising a failing strategy

> We see no fundamental incompatibility of interests between the United States and Iraq ... we do not feel that American-Iraqi relations need to be frozen in antagonisms.
>
> Zbigniew Brzezinski, National Security Advisor, 14 April 1980[1]

Introduction

In order to better understand both the continuity and change in US foreign policy towards Iraq, it is first necessary to conduct an historical policy review of preceding US administrations. This chapter does so by taking US policy back to America's initial tilt towards Iraq, during the administration of President Jimmy Carter. In 1979, US Middle East strategy was forced to change. This was the year in which America's strategic ally, the Shah of Iran, was overthrown, and the same year that saw Saddam Hussein assume the presidency after forcing his predecessor, Ahmed Hassan al-Bakir, to step down. As this US tilt towards Iraq came during Saddam's reign, and as Saddam's own eventual demise came also at American hands, this chapter explains the full-circle evolution of US foreign policy discourse towards Saddam Hussein's Iraq. The chapter will pay close attention to US Iraq policy under the George W. Bush administration pre-9/11 – a brief period that serves as a benchmark upon which to measure consistencies and departures in US policy both before and after the 2003 invasion.

2.1 The tilt in US Iraq strategy: Jimmy Carter and Ronald Reagan

After the Algiers Agreement between Iraq and Iran in 1975 the US saw this as an opportunity to establish contact with Iraq and 'have a new relationship with Iraq'. In a meeting with the Iraqi Foreign Minster Saadoun Hammadi in Paris, on 17 December 1975, Henry Kissinger stressed that the US felt there was no 'basic clash of national interests between Iraq and the United States'. This attempt, however, failed as Iraq was suspicious of any genuine change in the US position, especially with regard to Israel and US support for the Kurdish movement, and as

Kissinger himself stressed they were willing to improve relations with Iraq but it was a relationship the US could 'live without'.[2] The US departed from its previous disposition with the accession to power of Islamic revolutionaries in Iran in 1979. As a consequence, the US strategic relationship with Iran ended and with it the Nixon Doctrine. The Nixon Doctrine relied primarily on the dependency of the US on its 'twin pillars' to maintain its interests in the Gulf: the Shah's Iran and the royal Saudi household. However, no longer, through the support of proxies, could the US maintain hegemony, balance of power and stability in the region. On 23 January 1980 this shift materialised, in response to the Islamic revolution and the Soviet invasion of Afghanistan. In a joint session of Congress Jimmy Carter stated:

> An attempt by any outside force to gain control of the Persian Gulf region will be regarded as an assault on the vital interests of the United States of America, and such an assault will be repelled by any means necessary, including military force.[3]

This declaration, known as the Carter Doctrine, was similar to the Truman Doctrine, only it stipulated the defence of friendly Arab Gulf states in the region instead of Turkey and Greece.[4] It appears that the US had no appetite for any other revolutionary regimes to emerge, and would not allow friendly client regimes to be toppled either. In a response to critics as regards the sale of weapons to Saudi Arabia, Reagan responded: 'We will not permit [Saudi Arabia] to become another Iran.'[5] Consequently, with the collapse of the Nixon Doctrine and subsequently the 'Twin Pillar' concept, the US became further engulfed in the politics of the region.

America was in a dilemma. A revolutionary regime in Iran was a disadvantage to US interests in the region. But so was a radical Arab nationalist regime in Iraq. So as the tension escalated between Iran and Iraq, leading eventually to the invasion of Iran by Iraq in 1980, the US response was mild. At the beginning of the Iran–Iraq war the United States declared neutrality.[6] The US showed no interest in taking sides. America took a neutral stance according to President Carter's National Security Advisor Zbigniew Brzezinski. It did, however, provide Airborne Warning and Control System (AWACS) to Saudi Arabia in response to a Saudi request, resulting from fear of Iranian attacks on their oil installations.[7] Former Carter official Gary Sick denies that Washington directly encouraged Iraq's attack, but instead let 'Saddam assume there was a US green light because there was no explicit red light'.[8] The purpose of this attitude was to contain the new revolutionary Iran and weaken Iraq. Henry Kissinger, in a 1980 meeting with the Jewish community in St Louis, Missouri, captured the US sentiment, 'It's too bad they both can't lose this war.'[9]

Testimony to this neutrality was United Nations Security Council Resolution (UNSCR) 479 passed on 28 September 1980, characterising the war as 'The situation between Iran and Iraq.' This so-called neutrality was in itself, however, a clear strategy of weakening both warring sides – another variety of containment.[10]

This strategy checked Iraq's and Iran's power by sustaining their involvement in a costly, lengthy and lethal war. This attitude was not too dissimilar to the 'Dual Containment' strategy pursued by the Clinton administration from 1993, which will be explained at greater length later in this chapter. US neutrality continued up to mid 1982 when Iran started to gain an upper hand in the war in May 1982. Amid growing concerns that an Iranian victory would damage US interests, Ronald Reagan issued a National Security Directive (number classified) in the June of that year to support Iraqi efforts.[11] Howard Teicher, a former National Security Council (NSC) official, described the US position in a testimony to a Florida District court as a dilemma between either 'maintaining strict neutrality and allowing Iran to defeat Iraq' or 'intervening and providing assistance to Iraq', which was on the 'brink of losing its war with Iran'.[12] Based on Reagan's approach of strategic balancing, Secretary of State George Shultz described the support to Iraq as 'a limited form of balance-of-power policy'.[13] It was clearly a strategy that helped maintain a balance of power between Iraq and Iran, leading to an eight-year-long war.

The Soviet Union had also denied Iraq all military supplies in 1980 in response to the Iraqi invasion of Iran. With these developments came the opportunity to divert Iraq from its alliance with the Soviet Union. And in turn came the opportunity for the United States to develop relations with Iraq which the US thought would replace its missed alliance with Iran as the future guarantor of US interests in the region.[14] Peter Galbraith, former US ambassador and senior Congressional staffer, argues that the Reagan administration's tilt towards Iraq early in the war was not merely to disallow an Iraqi defeat, but also to create out of Iraq a 'potential ally'.[15] Iraq, a founding member of the State Department's State Sponsors of Terrorism list in 1979 along with Libya, South Yemen and Syria, was removed from the list of countries supporting terrorism in 1982 to allow US support. A new tilt towards Iraq was born.[16] To permit this, a demand also made by Shultz, Iraq expelled the Abu Nidal terrorist group from its territory.[17]

Middle East envoy Donald Rumsfeld visited Iraq twice, in late December 1983 and March 1984, resulting in resumption of full diplomatic relations with Iraq in November 1984. Iraq had severed relations with the US as a result of US support to Israel during the Six-Day war of 1967. By this time, the US was already aware of Iraqi use and technological advancements in chemical weapons production.[18] The Iranian government in November 1983 had made an official request for a UN investigation into the Iraqi use of chemical weapons. And US intelligence had gained knowledge of Iraqi chemical warfare. This led the US to respond privately. On 21 November 1983 a démarche was sent to Baghdad in Secretary of State George Shultz's name to Foreign Minister Tariq Aziz to protest against the Iraqi use of chemical weapons and the potential damage it could do to their evolving relationship.[19] Although reports of Iraq's use of chemical weapons against Iran were confirmed by the Reagan administration in 1983, the United States did not wish to antagonise Iraq. During Rumsfeld's first visit to Baghdad in December 1983, little mention of Weapons of Mass Destruction

(WMD) was made. Rumsfeld only made it known to Iraqi Foreign Minister Tariq Aziz that the United States was concerned about chemical weapons as part of a list of issues concerning America.[20] Saddam Hussein told US ambassador to Iraq, April Glaspie, that the decision to establish relations with the US was taken in '1980 during the two months prior to the war between us and Iran'.[21] This reflected Saddam's knowledge of the change in US attitude towards Iran. For the US this was a healthy development, due to the changed regional circumstances.

The US tilt towards Iraq intensified after the failure of the Iran Contra initiatives, as it did not produce the required results. The US was persuaded by Iraq to provide support for its war efforts. The US allowed purchase of non-military technology as well as sharing military intelligence on the movements of Iranian forces obtained through American AWACS reconnaissance flights.[22] The State Department continued its strategy of engagement with Iraq, hoping it would allow influence on Saddam's regime. It even went so far as to contend: 'Human rights and chemical weapons aside, in many respects our political and economic interests run parallel with those of Iraq.'[23] However with the escalation of the Iran–Iraq war and oil tankers being targeted in the gulf, the UN Security Council intervened on 20 July 1987 by passing a mandatory resolution to create a cease-fire between both countries: this time to put an end to the war.[24] On 20 August 1988, Iran and Iraq signed an armistice to end their bloody struggle. During this period the United States continued to believe that Iraq's behaviour could be moderated. Haywood Rankin, a US embassy official in Baghdad, stressed that the US believed that if Saddam no longer had to fight Iran, he could become the 'man we wished he could be'.[25]

2.2 The tilt and untilt in US Iraq strategy: George H. W. Bush

President George H. W. Bush signed a national security directive 26 (NSD-26) in October 1989 declaring 'normal relations between the United States and Iraq would serve our longer-term interests and promote stability in both the Gulf and the Middle East'. He also continued to believe that Iraq could 'moderate its behavior' if provided with sufficient incentives.[26] Before that in January 1989 Bush's foreign policy team prepared a report entitled 'Guidelines for US Iraq Policy'. The guidelines established Iraq as a potentially helpful ally in containing Iran and helping advance the Middle East process.[27] April Glaspie, who had been appointed as US ambassador to Iraq in 1989, had instructions to broaden cultural and commercial contacts with the Iraqi regime in hopes of 'civilising' it.[28] This was an implicit recognition of the brutal nature of the regime. US Senator Bob Dole in a visit to Iraq told Saddam on 12 April 1990 that President Bush had assured him that 'he wants better relations, and that the US government wants better relations with Iraq'.[29] From 1983 until 1988 the United States had provided annual credit to Iraq worth 500 million US dollars (USD) under a programme called the Commodity Credit Corporation (CCC). When Bush senior came to office he doubled the CCC to over one billion.[30] However, in the spring of 1990 the US congressional efforts to impose sanctions against Saddam's regime resumed, this time in response to Saddam's threats in a speech to use chemical weapons against Israel. A Senate bill titled 'Iraq International Law Compliance Act'[31] was passed regardless of strong opposition from the Bush senior administration to halt financial and military assistance to Iraq until the president could provide evidence that Iraq was in 'substantial compliance' with the provisions of human rights conventions. The bill passed on 25 July 1990 a week before Saddam's occupation of Kuwait.[32]

However, the US government's taming strategy totally changed with the Iraqi occupation of Kuwait on 2 August 1990. President Bush senior made the US position clear on 11 September 1990:

> An Iraq permitted to swallow Kuwait would have the economic and military power, as well as the arrogance, to intimidate and coerce its neighbors – neighbors who control the lion's share of the world's remaining oil reserves. We cannot permit a resource so vital to be dominated by one so ruthless. And we won't.[33]

Saddam's miscalculations in Iraq's annexation of Kuwait rested on several assumptions. First, that the US would need Iraqi and Kuwaiti oil. Iraq also assumed that it was the leading Arab nation and that it was an important counterweight to revolutionary Iran.[34] Saddam Hussein tried in vain to deal with the consequences of his strategic miscalculation of occupying Kuwait; he sought to invoke the now defunct language and logic of the Cold War. Up to the very last moment of the crisis, prior to the liberation of Kuwait by the allied forces, the Iraqi regime was hoping that the USSR would extricate Iraq from its situation, through mediation or deterrence.[35] Saddam, however, was not totally naïve; in a speech he made in early 1990 he acknowledged that the old 'balance' between the superpowers had now disappeared, giving the US unmatched power.[36] The Soviet Union was on the brink of collapse at the time, giving the United States greater freedom of action, that Iraq had not fully considered in its calculations. On 6 August, the UN Security Council adopted resolution 661 (1990), imposing comprehensive economic sanctions under Chapter VII of the UN Charter. This was followed by a US-led military campaign to eject the Iraqi army from the country. President Bush senior on 15 February 1991 in a speech called on the Iraqi people and military to topple Saddam's regime.[37] His intention was to encourage a coup, not an uprising. However, when the preferred agent for the US government (the Iraqi army) failed to topple Saddam's regime immediately after the liberation of Kuwait, the Iraqi uprising went unsupported due to US fear of the potential instability it could create. President Bush, however, signed a 'lethal finding' in October 1991 to authorise the Central Intelligence Agency (CIA) to create conditions for regime change. To this end, forty million USD were allocated for this operation.[38] Moreover, the US put forward UNSCR 687 on 3 April 1991, continuing the rigorous economic sanctions imposed on Iraq and conditioning the ceasefire upon Iraq's complete compliance with its disarmament mandate.[39]

However, the disarmament was only a vehicle to destabilise Saddam and achieve the US objective of regime change.[40] The Bush senior administration stated that sanctions against Iraq would not be lifted, regardless of Iraq's compliance with its disarmament stipulated in UNSCR 687.[41] Secretary of State James Baker told a Senate Hearing on 23 May 1991 that the US would 'never normalise relations with Iraq so long as Saddam remained in power', stressing that UN sanctions would be maintained as long as Saddam was in power.[42] The lethal finding President George H. W. Bush forwarded to Congress stated that the United States would undertake efforts to promote a military coup against Saddam Hussein.[43] It was for this reason, even after Saddam's invasion of Kuwait, that the US refused to interact with the Iraqi opposition, hoping Saddam's overthrow would come through a coup. It was only when the ban on official US contacts with the Iraqi opposition became publicly known in late March 1991, three weeks after the Iraqi uprising had started, that it was reversed the next day. The reversal was too late and the White House took the decision to let Saddam crush the post-war rebellions.[44]

Reports in July 1992 of a serious but unsuccessful coup attempt suggested that the US strategy might ultimately succeed. However, there was disappointment within the George H. W. Bush administration that the coup had failed, and it appears a decision was made to shift the US approach from promotion of a coup to supporting the diverse opposition groups that had led the post-war rebellions.[45] Following the failed uprising and the immaterialised coup, the CIA helped create a united Iraqi front, culminating in supporting and sponsoring a conference of Iraqi oppositionists in Vienna from 16 to 19 June 1992 which led to the creation of the Iraqi National Congress (INC).[46] The CIA recruited the Rendon Group, a public relations firm to conduct the job.[47] This was followed by the first opposition conference on Iraqi soil in the Kurdish north on 28 October 1992. During this period it appears that the US objective was to create a viable united Iraqi opposition. However, no evidence exists to suggest that the US felt it could rely on such a weak and divided opposition and a coup was always deemed the most appropriate answer to Saddam's regime.[48]

2.3 From dual containment to regime change: Bill Clinton

Shortly afterwards the presidency changed and Bill Clinton became president. In May 1993, Al Gore, the new vice president, received the INC in Washington, giving the struggle against Saddam further recognition. According to Elaine Sciolino, the Clinton administration maintained the 1991 lethal finding while denying it the necessary resources to succeed. The Clinton administration scaled back the programme from a high of 40 million USD in 1992 to less than 20 million USD a year, after it concluded that the programme had failed to weaken the Iraqi leader.[49] According to a CIA source, it was, 'How much can you get along on?' in the Clinton administration as opposed to, 'How much do you need?' under the Bush senior.[50] Many in and outside the Clinton administration believed that a coup could produce a more favourable regime without risking the fragmentation of Iraq. Many observers maintained that Shiite and Kurdish groups, if they succeeded in ousting Saddam, would divide the country into warring ethnic and tribal groups, and open Iraq to political and military influence from neighbouring Iran, Turkey and Syria.[51]

To this end, the Clinton administration devised the 'Dual Containment' strategy, first made public by Martin Indyk, then senior director of Near East and South Asian Affairs at the NSC, on 18 May 1993 at a speech to the Washington Institute for Near East Policy (WINEP). Indyk emphasised that a particular focus on Iraq would only strengthen Iran. He also stressed that the older strategy of sustaining the balance of power between both Iran and Iraq would not be pursued, as the US had enough regional allies to be able to succeed and to sustain its interests.

However, the strategy of 'Dual Containment' was aimed at weakening, but not specifically overthrowing, Saddam Hussein, as well as keeping together an anti-Iraq coalition at the United Nations, and strangling Iran's economy as it tried to rebuild its military muscle.[52] The objective of this strategy was to isolate Iraq and Iran, economically, politically and militarily. Secondary attention was paid to Iraqi opposition groups. No longer was the requirement the traditional balance of power concept, where either Iran or Iraq was favoured to keep the other in check.[53] Under the Clinton administration there was no intention of putting teeth into overthrowing the regime. The administration was willing to do some things. Its strategy was to contain Saddam and give some support to the opposition. Phebe Marr, Iraq expert and advisor to the Iraq Study Group,[54] stated, 'If the opposition could do it, fine. But few really expected the opposition to overthrow him on their own without military support.'[55]

The Clinton administration, however, was still in pursuit of the lethal finding and regime change. In September 1994, following an inspection tour to Iraqi Kurdistan, the Senate Intelligence Committee cleared the CIA to establish a semi-permanent base.[56] In late January 1995 CIA operatives set up base in Iraqi Kurdistan. They believed supporting resistance fighters in the north of Iraq might lead to a successful insurrection and spread south towards Baghdad.[57] The CIA officers had wanted gradually to strengthen the 'liberated' zone in the country's Kurdish north.[58] Robert Baer was the chief CIA officer responsible for this attempt. He and three other CIA officers had arrived in Iraqi Kurdistan to set up the clandestine CIA base in northern Iraq. The purpose of the four-man base was to assist Iraqi dissidents overthrow Saddam.[59] Baer states that the premise of this base was to take care of an 'unfinished war'.[60] He asserts that his order was to support any serious movement to get rid of Saddam.[61] Upon arrival a defecting Iraqi general had approached Baer and informed him of a coup plot by a group of cousins.[62] The INC's Ahmed Chalabi had also devised an 'End Game' plan to be executed on 3 March 1995. The coup would coincide with Chalabi's plan. The 'End Game' plan was composed of a Kurdish attack on Iraqi lines in the north, combined with a Kurdish fifth column creating disturbances in Kirkuk and Mosul. The Shiite groups would also attack the Iraqi army and consequently the army would revolt, leading to the end of the regime.[63]

In the end, Washington had not supported nor committed to the venture. The US preferred to maintain the status quo.[64] Washington refused to acknowledge both the diversion and coup and Robert Baer was recalled for a criminal invest-igation.[65] This demonstrated that US faith in the Iraqi opposition to achieve change was minimal, in addition to the administration's wariness of the burden and difficulties such a shake-up would bring. Democratic promotion seems to have had little impetus as well. The possibility of an independent Kurdistan, and an emerging Shiite satellite state in the south as a result of the weakening of a Sunni constituent, was a concern. Hoshyar Zebari, a member of the INC execu-tive council, had expressed his frustration with this US attitude: 'But surely after nearly four years of waiting for this coup, they must know that it is almost impossible to arrange.' He went so far as to suggest that the West supported a coup over any other alternative since he believed it 'would leave the country in safe, autocratic, Sunni hands' because the West opposed 'the democratic solu-tion ... in which the majority Shiites find influence proportionate to their number' for 'fear that the Shiites would fall prey to fundamentalist, expansionist Iran'.[66]

Kurdish leader Jalal Talabani stated that the INC had started with great poten-tial and that it could have brought together all the major and minor parties in Iraq. But it failed due to two major reasons. The first was an ambiguous Amer-ican policy. The Iraqis had initially believed that establishing the INC meant the United States would take a more active step to bring change to Iraq. According to Talabani, the Iraqi opposition soon discovered that the United States wanted the INC to be just a 'propaganda organisation'. Second, the opposition groups had not found consensus since they had different ideas about how to change the regime. Talabani asserted that Ahmed Chalabi was not in complete compliance with CIA policy. The United States proposed that Chalabi be the main actor not the leader in the INC. Moreover, Chalabi had favoured an armed struggle inside Iraq, and to do this, he wanted to establish an INC army. Meanwhile the CIA wanted the INC to organise a military coup and not develop any kind of military forces to fight against the Iraqi army. As a result the US government changed its mind about Chalabi and began to loathe him. According to Talabani he was ini-tially 'beloved' inside the CIA, then he was 'hated' there.[67]

Pressure within the Clinton administration to proceed with overthrowing Saddam accelerated when John Deutch, Deputy Secretary of Defense, moved from the Defense Department to become CIA director in May 1995, and intensified as the 1996 presidential election campaign moved nearer.[68] The US again opted for a 'quick coup' option mostly due to lack of faith in the external Iraqi opposition.[69] The internal Kurdish fighting spanning May 1994 to November 1997 was a major reason why the Iraqi opposition lost weight. Both the Kurdistan Democratic Party (KDP) and the Patriotic Union of Kurdistan (PUK), the 'two main pillars' of INC were heavily fighting each other.[70] In early 1996 Ayad Allawi's Iraqi National Accord (INA) with the CIA's support attempted a coup through claimed contacts in the senior officer corps. Clinton even gave 6 million USD to support this opera-tion. The attempt failed, Saddam infiltrated this operation and in June 1996 executed some 100 of those involved.[71] The CIA's Iraq Operations Group (a division within the CIA's Directorate of Operations) plotted the coup against Saddam Hussein. The 'Silver Bullet' coup, as it became known, was approved by the White House, ordering CIA director John Deutch to press forward. The coup was scheduled for June 1996 before the US presidential elections.[72] The coup was to incorporate the United Nations Special Commission (UNSCOM). An Iraqi non-cooperation with the inspectors would create a crisis prompting US military strikes against Iraqi Special Republican Guards. This distraction would permit the coup plotters to take action.[73] Scott Ritter, chief UN weapons inspector in Iraq, describes it as 'sanctions-assisted regime change'.[74]

Throughout this time the UN inspections were in process. Scott Ritter states that the US had reservations about any inspection designed to 'close the file' on missile disarmament issues.[75] When UNSCOM 45 (14th ballistic missiles team) was over Ritter was satisfied enough to confirm that Iraq had been 'disarmed of ballistic missiles'. However, these assessments were not recognised in Washington and considered flawed.[76] The US intelligence community was interested in maintaining the perception that Iraq was not telling the truth.[77] Essentially it was a strategy of refusing to allow Iraq to be disarmed to maintain the sanctions.[78] Madeleine Albright, in a speech on 26 March 1996, stressed that sanctions against Iraq would not be lifted as long as Saddam remained in power.[79] Anthony Lake, National Security Advisor during the first Clinton administration, had explained that the problem at the time was that the administration could not explicitly state that the purpose of US policy was the overthrow of the regime. To explicitly state the US goal of regime change would have blown apart the coalition and was not in the mandate of the UN resolutions. Lake argued that the very mention of full compliance with all the resolutions passed in the wake of the First Gulf War was essentially calling for Saddam Hussein's overthrow because, if 'he observed the provisions calling for an end to repression, then his regime would fall'.[80]

Nevertheless, a change of strategy emerged in 1998. It became obvious that coups would not succeed. Republican and neoconservative voices of discontent were also rising in this respect. The US government knew that it had to reinforce its posture on Iraq as it seemed that Iraq was winning its war. In an effort to regroup the Iraqi opposition after many years of poor performance, in May 1998 President Clinton signed a bill giving 5 million more USD to the Iraqi opposition. According to this provision the funds would help the training, organising and promoting the unity of the democratic Iraqi opposition.[81] Additionally, the sanctions were already eroding. Iraq was already illegally exporting petroleum through Jordan and Turkey, a trade which provided substantial revenues to the regime. International support was constantly corroded with Russian and Chinese interests opposed to its continuation. Furthermore, due to increased reports on the humanitarian situation in Iraq, the UN Security Council, on 14 April 1995, adopted Resolution 986 to address this issue which came to be known as the Oil for Food Programme that went into effect on 10 December 1996.

The situation deteriorated further following Executive Chairman of UNSCOM Richard Butler's visit to Iraq in January 1998, reporting Iraq's refusal to allow access to presidential sites. After this incident the Clinton administration embarked on an effort to gain congressional support for a military strike against Iraq.[82] However, the major thrust came in the summer of 1998. On 3 August, during a visit to Baghdad, Richard Butler was told by Iraqi Deputy Prime Minister Tariq Aziz that he must certify to the Security Council that the requirements of section C of resolution 687 (1991) had been met.[83] The Chairman responded that he was not in a position to do so, and the Deputy Prime Minister suspended the talks. On 5 August 1998, Iraq halted cooperation with UNSCOM and the International Atomic Energy Agency (IAEA) pending Security Council agreement to lift the oil embargo, reorganise the Commission and move it to either Geneva or Vienna. In the interim, Iraq maintained it would, on its own terms, permit monitoring under resolution 715 (1991). However, after increased international pressure and the passing of UN Security Council resolution 1194, on 9 September 1998 the Commission reported to the Council that it was satisfied that it has been able to exercise its full range of activities, including inspections. Again on 31 October 1998 Iraq announced that it would cease all forms of interaction with UNSCOM and its Chairman and halt all UNSCOM's activities inside Iraq, including monitoring in response to the signing into law of the Iraq Liberation Act (ILA).[84]

The recognition of failing US policies towards Iraq had gained momentum. On 26 January 1998 the Project for the New American Century (PNAC), a Washington, D.C. (neoconservative) organisation, signed an open letter to President Clinton emphasising that the containment of Iraq was eroding and that regime change should be pursued vigorously. This was followed by a second open letter on 19 February 1998 to President Clinton sponsored this time by the Committee for Peace and Security in the Gulf also requesting regime change.[85] However, the Clinton administration had no intention of using its own forces to bring about regime change. Also aware of the opposition's abilities, Secretary of State Albright, on 26 February 1998, in testimony before a Senate Appropriations subcommittee, stated that the opposition is fragmented and that it would be 'wrong to create false or unsustainable expectations' about what US support for the opposition can accomplish.[86]

On 29 September 1998 Congressman Benjamin Gilman (R-NY) introduced H.R.4655, a bill 'To establish a program to support a transition to democracy in Iraq'. It was co-sponsored by Congressman Christopher Cox (R-CA). The bill ultimately known as 'The Iraq Liberation Act of 1998' was passed in both houses of Congress.[87] On 5 October, the House passed the ILA by an overwhelming majority and the Senate passed it unanimously on 7 October. The Act declared that it was the policy of the United States to support 'regime change' in Iraq. US President Bill Clinton signed the bill into law on 31 October 1998, which also authorised 97 million USD in assistance to Iraqi opposition groups.[88] The publicly declared policy of regime change was a stark contrast to the previously pursued 'Dual Containment' strategy.[89] On the day of signing President Clinton explained:

> Today I am signing into law H.R. 4655, the 'Iraq Liberation Act of 1998'.
> This Act makes clear that it is the sense of the Congress that the United

States should support those elements of the Iraqi opposition that advocate a very different future for Iraq than the bitter reality of internal repression and external aggression that the current regime in Baghdad now offers.[90]

Following Iraq's refusal to cooperate with UNSCOM with B-52 bombers in the air on 14 November 1998 and within about 20 minutes of attack, Saddam Hussein agreed to allow UN monitors back in. The bombers were recalled and weapons inspectors returned. However, on 8 December 1998 Richard Butler reported that Iraq was still impeding inspections. Cooperation ended again between Iraq and the inspectors when the country demanded the lifting of the UN oil embargo. UNSCOM and the IAEA pulled their staff out of Iraq in anticipation of a US-led air raid on Iraqi military targets. On 16 December 1998 the United States and United Kingdom began a four-day air campaign against targets in Iraq codenamed Operation Desert Fox. Some opponents of Clinton charged that the attacks were a diversion as it was only three days before the House of Representatives impeached President Clinton. The stated mission: 'to strike military and security targets in Iraq that contribute to Iraq's ability to produce, store, maintain and deliver weapons of mass destruction'. On the day of the bombing Clinton stated publicly that ending the Iraqi threat would only come thorough regime change in Baghdad. He stressed US commitment to strengthen engagement with the full range of Iraqi opposition forces and 'work with them effectively and prudently'.[91] These events further led to the continuation of the deteriorating status quo. This time Iraq refused the return of weapons inspectors permanently.[92]

President Clinton signed the appropriation bill into law on 29 November 1999. Congress had allocated 10 million USD to support efforts to bring about political transition in Iraq, of which no less than 8 million USD would be made available to Iraqi opposition groups designated under the 'Iraq Liberation Act (Public Law 105–338)'.[93] The Clinton administration gave further recognition to the opposition and sponsored a major Iraqi opposition conference in New York. After the official ending in a speech before the assembly on the conference's closing day, 29 October 1999, Undersecretary of State for Political Affairs, Thomas Pickering, pledged that the United States 'will actively support you not only until you are free, but also thereafter in rebuilding a new, democratic Iraq'.[94]

2.4 The failing Iraq strategy: George W. Bush

Iraq was never far down on the Bush foreign policy agenda. During his presidential campaign Bush asserted he would be firm with regimes like North Korea and Iraq.[95] In his campaign Bush also stated that if it was discovered that Saddam Hussein was pursuing WMD he would 'take him out'.[96] Bush believed that the Iraqi WMD programme was still active. Bush explained 'Iran has made rapid strides in its missile program, and Iraq persists in a race to do the same'.[97] During the campaign in 2000 Condoleezza Rice described Bush's foreign policy towards

Iraq as a clear case of deterrence, writing, 'if they do acquire WMD, their weapons will be unusable because any attempt to use them will bring national obliteration'.[98] She also referred to Iraq's isolation and described Saddam as having 'no useful place in international politics'. Rice made it clear that regime change was not off the table. She stated that 'nothing will change until Saddam is gone'; it should be US policy to 'mobilise whatever resources it can, including support from his opposition, to remove him'.[99] As a candidate, however, Bush saw Iraq as a containable threat; on 16 February 2000 he proposed to 'keep them isolated in the world of public opinion and to work with our alliances to keep them isolated'.[100]

About a week before President Bush's inauguration, CIA Director George Tenet and Deputy for Operations James Pavitt met with President-elect George W. Bush, Vice President-elect Richard Cheney and the incoming National Security Advisor Condoleezza Rice. He told them that al-Qaeda was one of the three gravest threats facing the United States and that this 'tremendous threat' was 'immediate'. The other two grave threats were the proliferation of weapons of mass destruction and China's rising power.[101] This gave the Bush presidency three major US National Security focuses.[102] The second point directly associated with the potential threats of the Iraqi regime.

When Bush was elected, Cheney also asked for a security briefing for the president-elect. William Cohen, Clinton's Secretary of Defense, was told that the session should focus on Iraq.[103] Moreover, when President-elect Bush met with Clinton a month before his inauguration, Clinton made clear to Bush that he had observed from his campaign that his major concern was National Missile Defense and Iraq; Bush confirmed this fact. However, Clinton advised that his priorities should be: al-Qaeda, Middle East diplomacy, North Korea, nuclear competition in South Asia, and only then Iraq.[104]

After his inauguration and on 6 February 2001, President George W. Bush announced that the US would resume funding opposition efforts inside Iraq for the first time since the Iraqi army overran opposition bases in 1996.[105] On 16 February 2001 US aircraft targeted areas around Baghdad. The attacks were to send a warning to the Iraqi regime and also degrade Iraq's ability to shoot at pilots flying over the No-fly zones. The attacks were the first outside the No-fly zones in the north and south of the country since December 1998.[106] This was only to indicate to the Iraqi regime that there was no shift of focus or relaxation in the United States' hostile attitude to Iraq. However, this did not mean or bring any significant change of US strategy towards Iraq. Even the *Washington Post* described a joint US-British attack on Iraqi installations on 10 August 2001 as minimal, affirming that 'yesterday's strikes appeared to continue the Clinton era pattern of hitting Iraqi air defences every six months or so'.[107]

After February 2001, allied forces continued strikes against Iraqi air defence installations, including an Iraqi mobile early warning radar in southern Iraq on 19 April, an air defence site in northern Iraq on 20 April, an air defence installation 180 miles south-east of Baghdad on 18 May, and an air defence site in northern Iraq on 7 August and another on 10 August. The airstrike on 10 August

2001 was the most lethal since February. US and British aircraft hit three installations: a surface-to-air missile battery 170 miles south-east of Baghdad, an associated long-range mobile radar system and a fibre-optic communications station
70 miles south-east of Baghdad. Before this strike, on 29 July, US National
Security Advisor Condoleezza Rice had told CNN that the administration was
contemplating the use of 'military force in a more resolute manner' and said that
'Saddam Hussein was on the radar screen for the administration'.[108]

Before 9/11 the Bush administration did not focus on the Iraq problem at the
Principals' level.[109] All discussion regarding Iraq was at the Deputies' level.[110] In
late Spring of 2001 Condoleezza Rice's staff prepared a document entitled
'Freeing the Iraqi People'. It encompassed three steps to confront the Iraq threat.
The first step was to provide immediate training and military assistance to the
Iraqi opposition as stipulated in the ILA. The second step would be to arm the
Iraqi opposition to enable effective action against Saddam's regime and finally
to take action against the Iraqi regime by US forces.[111] In a meeting on 22 June
2001, the Deputies discussed the proposal and the first measure they agreed upon
for a new US Iraq strategy was the 'lethal training'[112] of the Iraqi opposition.[113]
In a 13 July 2001 meeting, the Deputies returned to the Iraq issue particularly
the No-fly zones and the constant attacks against US and UK patrols. Paul Wolfowitz, Deputy Secretary of Defense, argued that Iraqi targets should be hit
severely to induce Saddam to stop 'shooting'.[114] The Deputies had different
assessments of the Iraq threat pre-9/11. Richard Armitage, Deputy Secretary of
State, and John McLaughlin, Deputy CIA Director, tended to downplay the
threats posed by Saddam Hussein although they recognised them. Wolfowitz and
Scooter Libby, Chief of Staff to Vice President Cheney, stressed that the Iraq
threat had not been contained and if the sanctions were removed Saddam would
pose a greater threat that would be even more difficult to handle.[115] In early 2001
Wolfowitz proposed a strategy for regime change that would not necessarily
entail a US invasion. It would include, however, the broadening of international
cooperation against Iraq, strengthen the Iraqi democratic opposition through US
training and also economically enhance the Iraqi opposition through the exclu-
sion of the Kurdish northern region from the ongoing sanctions.[116] Deputy Secretary of Defense Paul Wolfowitz asked if the US might create an autonomous
area in southern Iraq similar to the autonomous Kurdish region in the north, with
the goal of making Saddam little more than the 'mayor of Baghdad'. US officials
also discussed whether a popular uprising in Iraq should be encouraged, and how
the US could best work with free Iraqi groups that opposed the Saddam
regime.[117] In a Principals' Committee meeting on 1 June four options were set
on the table. First, to continue with the containment strategy. Second, to continue containment while actively supporting Saddam's opponents. Third, setting
up a safe haven for insurgents in southern Iraq. Finally, to plan a US invasion.[118]

However, in the early months of the Bush administration there was no clear
Iraq policy. Donald Rumsfeld acknowledges this in his memoirs: 'US policy
remained essentially what it had been at the end of the Clinton administration –
adrift.'[119] Douglas Feith, Under Secretary of Defense for Policy, argues that

President Bush and Rumsfeld had no set direction on US policy towards Iraq as late as the summer of 2001. He states that Rumsfeld's position on Iraq was war as a last resort, but with no effective alternative.[120] However, the intention of a more radical approach to Iraq could be seen. Drifts and clashes of opinion were already to take hold between the realists at the State Department and hawks at the Pentagon, with further funds released to opposition groups and a more forceful air campaign against Iraqi anti-aircraft positions.[121] When the Bush administration officials came to office they were thinking of either maintaining the containment strategy or revising it with a replacement.[122]

Pre-9/11, the debate focused on containment versus regime change.[123] Before 9/11 CIA officials had floated the possibility of a coup, though they knew Saddam was far better at undoing coup plots than the CIA was at engineering them.[124] Before 9/11 the CIA's Iraq Operations Group chief thought there was a clear contradiction in the Bush Iraq policy; the administration's approach was irrational. On the one hand it was containing and deterring the Iraqi regime through the UN; on the other it had a standing order to the CIA advising their support to topple Saddam's regime. In their minds, the only way to succeed was a full US military invasion of Iraq.[125] The real focus, however, was on how to pressure Saddam's regime through the instruments of economic sanctions, WMD inspections and the No-fly zones. The differences amongst administration officials on how to deal with Saddam were deep. For regime change advocates the debate was between a military coup or a change of the Baathist government. Discussions also included the suspension of the No-fly zone patrols that were being shot at on a daily basis.[126]

Paul O'Neill, the US Treasury Secretary, indicated that the first NSC meeting in the Bush White House in January 2001 considered the Iraq threat and the possibility of the removal of Saddam.[127] This clearly shows that Iraq was always considered a US national security threat, but in no way suggests that the Bush presidency was mentally fixed on removing the Baath regime. Henri Barkey, former member of the Policy Planning Staff at the US State Department, stressed that the US believed the French were breaking the sanctions and the coalition was crumbling. To him, O'Neill had only confirmed an obvious concern. Barkey asserted that the attention paid to Iraq was only normal as it was considered the first threat and the most important threat to the US at the time. The fact that Saddam was evading the sanctions was a troublesome sign in US circles. There were all kinds of American attempts at devising and creating new and smarter sanctions.[128] Richard Clarke, the anti-terrorism official on the NSC, also recalled the first meeting on terrorism in April 2001 where the Iraq issue was given far more significance than al-Qaeda especially by Paul Wolfowitz.[129] Saddam was considered a threat to US interests and the region, and it had been so for more than a decade pre-9/11 since Iraq invaded Kuwait.[130] Feith asserted that Saddam's threat was multi-faceted. Saddam had used his WMD domestically and internationally. He was harbouring and training terrorists, rewarding Palestinian suicide bombers, thus encouraging anti-Israel extremism – blocking a possible peace settlement to the Palestinian–Israeli peace.[131]

Although the debate was intense as regards Iraq, before 9/11 Secretary of State Colin Powell was managing the US foreign policy portfolio and had no interest in nation-building; concerning Iraq, his focus was on containment and on new, better targeted, so-called 'smart' sanctions.[132] Wolfowitz was pushing a policy of regime change, but not getting anywhere with it.[133] Pre-9/11 the only Iraq strategy the US adopted was to revise the terms of the sanctions imposed on Iraq. They introduced 'smart sanctions' that would have less of an immediate effect on the general Iraqi public, but with a stricter flow on dual use equipment and material.[134] In late February 2001, Colin Powell started a tour of the Middle East to start his new course to deal with Iraq. His intention was to create a new set of sanctions. Feith argues, 'in the months before the 9/11 attack, Secretary of State Colin Powell advocated diluting the multinational economic sanctions, in the hope that a weaker set of sanctions could win stronger and more sustained international support'.[135] Lawrence Wilkerson, Colin Powell's Chief of Staff, emphasised that US Iraq policy in the first eight months of the Bush administration before 9/11 could be 'summed up in one word, containment'. It was to make sure Saddam Hussein was kept from being a major threat to his neighbours, did not violate UN sanctions to the point where WMD did not become a problem for the region, and ensure that oil from the Strait of Hormuz flowed into world markets.[136] The US frustration with the collapse of the sanctions was becoming evident. In a memo dated 27 July to the Principals, Rumsfeld suggested that they could publicly acknowledge that sanctions did not work over extended periods and stop the pretence of having a policy that is keeping Saddam 'in the box', when he had actually 'crawled a good distance out of the box'. The new Powell proposals would, in fact, aim to take away what money the regime had made by shutting down an oil-smuggling operation worth about 2 billion USD a year. The revised embargo attempt appeared to be the dovish answer to an internal US power struggle about how to deal with Iraq.[137] On 1 June 2001 the United Nations Security Council (UNSC) passed resolution 1352 unanimously to ensure a thirty-day extension of the Oil for Food (OFF) programme to allow a possible revision of the sanctions regime, rather than the usual six months. The United Nations Security Council adopted the resolution signalling a possible reform of the decade-old sanctions on Iraq.[138] Even then British officials said 'it is very unlikely that London and Washington will give President Saddam Hussein control of his oil revenues again'.[139] However, the 'smart sanctions' approach eventually failed due to lack of support from China, Russia and France. The attempts ended with no real results. At the end of the 30 days revision period, the Security Council deferred action yet again, by extending the program for another five months.[140] On 29 November 2001 the Security Council extended the programme for another six months, the status quo being maintained this time however, with 9/11 specifically in mind.[141]

This Bush administration had come to power thinking that something had to be done about Saddam. On 31 October 2000, Barkey, who had worked for the State Department less than one year earlier, had organised an International Institute for Strategic Studies and United States Institute of Peace (USIP) sponsored meeting in Paris between American, British, French, German, Italian and

Turkish former officials and think tankers. He stressed that the whole point of the meeting was 'no matter who won the elections, Gore or Bush, the US would have a conflict with Iraq of some sort'. The only perceived way to avoid this conflict was for the Europeans and Americans to start devising a method of forcing Saddam through all kinds of sanctions, smart sanctions and new initiatives. Barkey believed that the US was on a conflict course. Saddam was getting rid of the sanctions by slowly eroding them and the mood in the region had changed dramatically against the United States.[142]

The Iraq policy debate remained unresolved when the 11 September attacks occurred.[143] Vice President Cheney agreed there was a lack of focus on the Middle East before the 9/11 attacks. In a Camp David meeting on 15 September 2001, he acknowledged that the position and role of the US before the attacks were quite unknown in the region. However, he asserted that with the attacks less than a week old 'an opportunity for US action has arisen with the Turks, Saudis all on their side'.[144] President Bush expressed his frustration of the pre-9/11 period where he had no clear plan or authority to change Saddam Hussein's behaviour. Three years after 9/11, Bush explained 'I was not happy with our policy'. He also made clear the transformation in attitude to perceived or potential threats, 'prior to September 11, however, a president could see a threat and contain it or deal with it in a variety of ways without fear of that threat materialising on your own soil'.[145] This all changed with 9/11.

This chapter highlighted the urgency and consistent primacy of the Iraq issue in US national security debates even before the attacks of 9/11 in the George W. Bush and the preceding administrations, starting primarily after Saddam's invasion of Kuwait. Additionally, it stressed the strategy with which the US dealt with Iraq, based on extensive and intensive multilateral diplomacy largely led and dominated by the State Department's doves and Secretary Powell in the junior Bush's administration. The following chapter attempts to identify the major ideological factions that dominated the George W. Bush administration and the influence they had on shaping and making US Iraq policy and the effect they had on changing the nature of the US national security debate after 9/11.

Notes

1 Zbigniew Brzezinski quoted in Larry Everest. (n.d.). *1980–1988, Iran-Iraq: Helping Both Sides Lose the War.* Available at: URL: http://coat.ncf.ca/our_magazine/links/issue51/articles/51_30–31.pdf Access Date: 20 June 2007.

2 Henry Kissinger. (1975). *Discussion with Iraqi Foreign Minister Saadoun Hammadi: Secret, Memorandum of Conversation, December 17, 1975.* [The National Security Archive: The George Washington University] Available at: http://gateway.proquest.com/openurl?url_ver=Z39.88–2004&res_dat=xri:dnsa&rft_dat=xri:dnsa:article:CKT01856 Access Date: 1 December 2008.

3 Jimmy Carter. (1980). *State of the Union Address 1980.* Available at: URL: www.jimmycarterlibrary.org/documents/speeches/su80jec.phtml Access Date: 14 December 2009.

4 Majid Khadduri and Edmund Ghareeb, *War in the Gulf, 1990–91: The Iraq-Kuwait Conflict and Its Implications* (New York: Oxford University Press, 1997), p. 92.

5 Ibid., p. 93.
6 Ibid.
7 Zbigniew Brzezinski, *Power and Principle: Memoirs of the National Security Advisor 1977–1981* (London: Weidenfeld and Nicolson, 1983), pp. 451–4.
8 Gary Sick quoted in Larry Everest. (2003). *Four Questions for Saddam – and the US*. [New America Media] Available at: URL: http://news.pacificnews.org/news/view_article.html?article_id=c33335175cc184e56416dbb1d1ebc595 Access Date: 20 June 2009.
9 Henry Kissinger quoted in Robert Cohn. (2008). *Best of Bob: Presidents and Precedents*. [jewishinstlouis.org] Available at: URL: www.jewishinstlouis.org/page.aspx?id=125519&page=8 Access Date: 20 June 2009.
10 Peter Galbraith, *The End of Iraq: How American Incompetence Created a War Without End* (New York: Simon and Schuster, 2006), p. 17.
11 Howard Teicher. (1995). *United States District Court Southern District of Florida.* [The National Security Archive: The George Washington University] Available at: URL: www.gwu.edu/~nsarchiv/NSAEBB/NSAEBB82/iraq61.pdf Access Date: 20 December 2007.
12 Ibid.
13 Samantha Power, *A Problem from Hell: America and the Age of Genocide* (New York: Basic Books, 2002), p. 176.
14 Galbraith (2006), op. cit., p. 17.
15 Ibid., p. 20.
16 Ibid., p. 19.
17 Steven Hurst, *The United States and Iraq since 1979: Hegemony, Oil, and War* (Edinburgh: Edinburgh University Press, 2009), p. 46.
18 Lawrence Freedman, *A Choice of Enemies: America Confronts the Middle East* (New York: PublicAffairs, 2008), p. 162.
19 Ibid.
20 Ibid., p. 163.
21 Saddam Hussein, 'The Glaspie Transcript: Saddam Meets the US Ambassador' in *The Iraq War Reader: History, Documents, Opinions*, ed. Micah Sifry and Christopher Cerf (New York: Touchstone, 2003), p. 61.
22 Khadduri and Ghareeb (1997), op. cit., p. 94.
23 Power (2002), op. cit., p. 221.
24 Khadduri and Ghareeb (1997), op. cit., p. 94.
25 Haywood Rankin quoted in Power (2002), op. cit., p. 200.
26 George H. W. Bush. (1989). *National Security Directive 26*. [Federation of American Scientists: Intelligence Resource Program] Available at: URL: www.fas.org/irp/offdocs/nsd/nsd26.pdf Access Date: 20 December 2007.
27 Power (2002), op. cit., p. 233.
28 *Knowledgerush:* April Glaspie. (2005). Available at: URL: www.knowledgerush.com/kr/encyclopedia/April_Glaspie/ Access Date: 17 December 2008.
29 Bob Dole, 'US Senators Chat with Saddam' in *The Iraq War Reader: History, Documents, Opinions*, ed. Micah Sifry and Christopher Cerf (New York: Touchstone, 2003), p. 61.
30 Power (2002), op. cit., p. 173.
31 The first defeated Congressional attempt at imposing US sanctions on Iraq was stipulated in the 'Prevention of Genocide Act of 1988'. This is explained at greater length in Chapter 6.
32 Galbraith (2006), op. cit., p. 36.
33 George H. W. Bush. (1990). *Address Before a Joint Session of the Congress on the Persian Gulf Crisis and the Federal Budget Deficit*. Available at: URL: http://bushlibrary.tamu.edu/research/public_papers.php?id=2217&year=1990&month=9 Access Date: 15 December 2009.

34 Galbraith (2006), op. cit., p. 39.
35 Charles Tripp, 'Iraq' in *The Cold War and the Middle East*, ed. Yezid Sayigh and Avi Shlaim (Oxford: Oxford University Press, 2003), p. 215.
36 Ibid.
37 Khadduri and Ghareeb (1997), op. cit., p. 191.
38 Jim Hoagland. 'How CIA's Secret War on Saddam Collapsed; A Retired Intelligence Operative Surfaces with Details and Critique of US Campaign', *The Washington Post* (1997, 26 June), p. A21.
39 Scott Ritter, *Iraq Confidential: The Untold Story of America's Intelligence Conspiracy* (London: I.B. Tauris, 2005), p. 4.
40 Ibid., p. 4.
41 Ibid., p. 5.
42 James Baker. (1991). *Congressional Testimony: Hearing of the Subcommittee of the Committee on Appropriations on Foreign Operations, Export Financing and Related Agencies Appropriations for Fiscal Year 1992:* Washington, D.C.
43 Patrick Tyler. 'Congress Notified of Iraq Coup Plan', *The New York Times*, (1992, 9 February). p. FD1.
44 Laurie Mylroie. (2001). *The United States and the Iraqi National Congress.* Available at: URL: www.mail-archive.com/ctrl@listserv.aol.com/msg78634.html Access Date: 15 January 2009.
45 Kenneth Katzman. (2000). *Iraq's Opposition Movements* (Order Code 98–179 F). Washington, D.C.: Congressional Research Service.
46 Gareth Stansfield. (2003). *Can the Iraqi Opposition Unite?* [Royal Institute of International Affairs] Available at: URL: www.guardian.co.uk/world/2003/mar/23/iraq.theworldtodayessays Access Date: 20 June 2007.
47 *Events Leading up to the 2003 Invasion of Iraq.* (n.d.). [History Commons] Available at: URL: www.historycommons.org/timeline.jsp?timeline=complete_timeline_of_the_2003_invasion_of_iraq&startpos=100 Access Date: 17 December 2008.
48 Bob Woodward, *Plan of Attack* (London: Simon and Schuster, 2004), p. 70.
49 Elaine Sciolino. 'C.I.A. Asks Congress for Money to Rein in Iraq and Iran', *The New York Times* (1995, 12 April), p. FD8.
50 Hoagland (1997), op. cit.
51 Katzman (2000), op. cit.
52 Sciolino (1995), op. cit.
53 Ali Allawi, *The Occupation of Iraq: Winning the War, Losing the Peace* (USA: Yale University Press, 2007), p. 48.
54 The Iraq Study Group was a bipartisan panel appointed on 15 March 2006 by the US Congress to assess the situation in Iraq. It released its findings on 6 December 2006.
55 Phebe Marr, Interview with Author, 19 June 2008, Washington, D.C.
56 Hoagland (1997), op. cit.
57 Evan Thomas, Christopher Dickey and Gregory Vistica, 'Bay of Pigs Redux', *Newsweek* (1998, 23 March), Vol. 131, No. 12, pp. 36–44.
58 Hoagland (1997), op. cit.
59 Robert Baer, *See No Evil: The True Story of a Ground Soldier in the CIA's War on Terrorism* (London: Arrow Books, 2002), p. 260.
60 Ibid., p. 256.
61 Ibid., p. 296.
62 Ibid., p. 275.
63 Ibid., pp. 285–6.
64 Ibid., p. 304.
65 Ibid., p. 307.
66 Hoshyar Zebari quoted in Michael Gunter, *The Kurdish Predicament in Iraq: A Political Analysis* (Pennsylvania: Macmillan, 1999), p. 43.
67 Jalal Talabani. (2002). *Jalal Talabani: 'No Grounds for a Relationship with*

Baghdad'. [Middle East Forum] Available at: URL: www.meforum.org/126/jalal-talabani-no-grounds-for-a-relationship-with Access Date: 20 June 2007.
68 Hoagland (1997), op. cit.
69 Ibid.
70 Hoshyar Zebari quoted in Gunter (1999), op. cit., p. 43.
71 Gunter (1999), op. cit., p. 51.
72 Ritter (2005), op. cit., p. 163.
73 Ibid., p. 153.
74 Ibid., p. 168.
75 Ibid., p. 64.
76 Ibid., p. 72.
77 Ibid., p. 73.
78 Ibid., p. 223.
79 Ibid., p. 151.
80 Anthony Lake quoted in Steven Wright. *Analysing United States Foreign Policy Towards the Middle East 1993–2003: Origins and Grand Strategies.* PhD thesis, University of Durham, 2005.
81 Gunter (1999), op. cit., p. 62.
82 Ritter (2005), op. cit., p. 269.
83 Section C of UNSCR 687 is the article of the resolution demanding the Iraqi destruction of all WMD-related materials and programmes.
84 *UNSCOM Chronology of Main Events.* (1999). Available at: URL: www.un.org/Depts/unscom/Chronology/chronologyframe.htm Access Date: 19 February 2009.
85 Douglas Feith, *War and Decision: Inside the Pentagon at the Dawn of the War on Terrorism* (New York: Harper Collins Publishers, 2008), p. 195.
86 Madeleine Albright quoted in Kenneth Katzman. (2003). *Iraq: U.S. Regime Change Efforts, the Iraqi Opposition, and Post-War Iraq* (Order Code RL31339). Washington, D.C.: Congressional Research Service.
87 *A Brief History of a Long War (Iraq, 1990–2003).* (2006). Available at: URL: www.mudvillegazette.com/2006_09.html Access Date: 22 February 2009.
88 *Iraq Liberation Act of 1998 (Enrolled Bill (Sent to President)).* (n.d.). [Iraq Watch] Available at: URL: www.iraqwatch.org/government/US/Legislation/ILA.htm Access Date: 17 December 2008.
89 Allawi (2007), op. cit., p. 67.
90 Bill Clinton. (1998a). *Statement on Signing the Iraq Liberation Act of 1998.* Available at: URL: http://findarticles.com/p/articles/mi_m2889/is_45_34/ai_53414246/ Access Date: 15 January 2009.
91 Bill Clinton. (1998b). *Statement by the President: The Oval Office.* [The White House] Available at: URL: http://clinton2.nara.gov/WH/New/html/19981216–3611. html Access Date: 20 June 2008.
92 *A Brief History of a Long War (Iraq, 1990–2003)*, op. cit.
93 *Public Law 106–113 106th Congress.* (1999). Available at: URL: http://frwebgate. access.gpo.gov/cgi-bin/getdoc.cgi?dbname=106_cong_public_laws&docid=f:publ113. 106.pdf Access Date: 17 December 2008.
94 Thomas Pickering quoted in Judy Aita. (1999). *US Pledges Support for Iraqi Opposition.* Available at: URL: www.fas.org/news/iraq/1999/11/991101-iraq-usia. htm Access Date: 20 June 2008.
95 George W. Bush. (1999a). *A Period of Consequences.* Available at: URL: http://www3.citadel.edu/pao/addresses/pres_bush.html Access Date: 20 June 2009.
96 Kerim Yildiz, *The Kurds In Iraq: The Past, Present and Future* (London: Pluto Press, 2004), p. 89.
97 Bush (1999a), op. cit., *A Period of Consequences.*
98 Condoleezza Rice, 'Campaign 2000: Promoting the National Interest', *Foreign Affairs* Vol. 79, No. 1 (2000): p. 61.

99 Ibid., p. 60.
100 Stefan Halper and Jonathan Clarke, *America Alone: The Neo-Conservatives and the Global Order* (Cambridge: Cambridge University Press, 2004), p. 204.
101 Ivo Daalder and James Lindsay, *America Unbound: The Bush Revolution in Foreign Policy* (Maryland: The Brookings Institution, 2003), p. 75.
102 Bob Woodward, *Bush at War* (London: Simon and Schuster, 2002), p. 35.
103 Michael Gordon and Bernard Trainor, *Cobra II: The Inside Story of the Invasion and Occupation of Iraq* (London: Atlantic Books, 2007), p. 15.
104 Ibid.
105 Nicholas Arons. (2001). *US-Supported Iraqi Opposition.* [Washington, D.C.: Institute for Policy Studies] Available at: URL: www.iraqwatch.org/perspectives/for-pol-in-focus-iraqoppo.pdf Access Date: 20 December 2009.
106 Yildiz (2004), op. cit., p. 90.
107 Woodward (2004), op. cit., p. 23.
108 Alfred Prados. (2002). *Iraq: Former and Recent Military Confrontations with the United States* (Order Code IB94049). Washington, D.C.: Congressional Research Service.
109 The Principals are the heads of the major national security-related US governmental departments. The Deputies are the second in command of the major national security-related US governmental departments.
110 Feith (2008), op. cit., p. 199.
111 Ibid., p. 206.
112 Lethal Training means training for lethal operations.
113 Feith (2008), op. cit., p. 206.
114 Ibid.
115 Ibid., p. 203.
116 Ibid., p. 204.
117 Douglas Feith. 'Why We Went to War in Iraq', *The Wall Street Journal*, (2008, July 3), p. 13.
118 Gordon and Trainor (2007), op. cit., p. 16.
119 Donald Rumsfeld, *Known and Unknown: A Memoir* (New York: Sentinel, 2011), p. 419.
120 Feith (2008), op. cit., p. 212.
121 Allawi (2007), op. cit., p. 79.
122 Feith (2008), op. cit., p. 198.
123 Ibid., p. 238.
124 Feith (2008), op. cit., *The Wall Street Journal*.
125 Woodward (2004), op. cit., p. 71.
126 Feith (2008), op. cit., p. 199.
127 George Packer, *The Assassins' Gate: America in Iraq* (New York: Farrar, Straus and Giroux, 2005), p. 39.
128 Henri Barkey, Interview with Author, 21 August 2008, Washington, D.C.
129 Packer (2005), op. cit., p. 40.
130 Feith (2008), op. cit., p. xi.
131 Ibid., p. 203.
132 Carole O'Leary, Interview with Author, 8 August 2008, Washington, D.C.
133 Phebe Marr, Interview with Author, 19 June 2008, Washington, D.C.
134 Woodward (2004), op. cit., p. 13.
135 Feith (2008), op. cit., *The Wall Street Journal*.
136 Lawrence Wilkerson, Interview with Author, 26 August 2008, Washington, D.C.
137 Barbara Plett. (2001). *Analysis: Will 'Smart' Sanctions Work?* [Amman: BBC] Available at: URL: http://news.bbc.co.uk/1/hi/world/middle_east/1366201.stm Access Date: 20 September 2008.
138 *UN Approves Iraq Sanctions Review.* (2001). [BBC News] Available at: URL: http://news.bbc.co.uk/1/hi/world/middle_east/1364434.stm Access Date: 17 June 2008.

139 Barnaby Mason. (2001). *Powell's New Plans for Iraq.* [BBC News] Available at: URL: http://news.bbc.co.uk/1/hi/world/middle_east/1192815.stm Access Date: 20 September 2008.

140 Edward L. Rubinoff, Wynn H. Segall and Heidi L. Gunst Akin. (2001). *New UN Debate on Iraq: The 'Smart' Sanctions Approach.* [The Metropolitan Corporate Counsel] Available at: URL: www.akingump.com/files/Publication/2dbd5b91–6cda-40e5-b6c4-f34cff9b8c9b/Presentation/PublicationAttachment/19872f31–1584–4a1 d-8524-f629ce3bdbf0/236.pdf Access Date: 20 December 2008.

141 *Office of the Iraq Programme: Oil for Food.* (2010). Available at: URL: www. un.org/Depts/oip/background/scrsindex.html Access Date: 11 March 2008.

142 Henri Barkey, Interview with Author, 21 August 2008, Washington, D.C.

143 Feith (2008), op. cit., *The Wall Street Journal.*

144 Woodward (2002), op. cit., p. 90.

145 George W. Bush quoted in Woodward (2004), op. cit., p. 12.

3 Intellectual roots of the Bush foreign policy

The power of ideas

America must maintain our moral clarity. I've often spoken to you about good and evil, and this has made some uncomfortable. But good and evil are present in this world, and between the two of them there can be no compromise. Murdering the innocent to advance an ideology is wrong every time, everywhere. Freeing people from oppression and despair is eternally right.

George W. Bush, 15 January 2009[1]

Introduction

In order to comprehend US foreign policy during the administration of George W. Bush it is first necessary to understand the ideas of the major actors of his presidency. This chapter will therefore introduce the key groups and their respective ideologies, which were central to guiding foreign policy during the Bush administration. Conventional wisdom asserts that those known as the neoconservatives were the dominant faction during the Bush administration. This chapter, however, identifies three additional streams of thinking that contributed to the administration's foreign policy stance. One of these influential groups was indeed the neoconservatives: This group of individuals believed in the necessity of America's use of power in order to achieve long-term interests by changing the very nature of regimes. They were, however, far from a uniform and unified faction. Rather, they held a range of disparate ideas and contributed a number of approaches. The second element in the Bush administration was President George W. Bush himself. Bush was an idealist who believed American values were right for all peoples, and grounded his foreign policy rationale on his Christian faith. Critically, he believed he had a mission from God to confront evil. The third important element was a collection of assertive nationalists. These individuals focused specifically on the maintenance of US dominance, security and global hegemony. The fourth element, which however lost influence after the 9/11 attacks, was that of the defensive realists. Being broadly Realist, this group was therefore similar to the nationalists in orientation, but by nature cautious to the application of US power and reluctant to take on extensive military engagements. The US media and the liberal hawks which were two external groups that exerted considerable influence are also discussed. This chapter discusses these various contributing – and indeed sometimes competing – approaches, and provides an understanding of the various motivations that led to the toppling of Saddam in 2003. As will become evident, while a firm grasp of neoconservative ideas and ambitions is essential for understanding the administration's foreign policy, it is not sufficient to gain a complete picture of foreign policy under the Bush administration. Instead, US policy under George W. Bush was an intricate reaction of views, objectives and agendas.

3.1 The neoconservatives

During the Clinton administration the neoconservatives found themselves in the margins, generally visible on the pages of publications such as the *Weekly Standard* and the *National Interest* as well as in certain think tanks. The American Enterprise Institute (AEI) became a centre for neoconservative thought and publication. In the pages of conservative publications and think tanks, neoconservatives advocated for a transformation of the Middle East, a forward leaning assertive and aggressive approach to contain and undermine rogue regimes. Throughout the 1990s, however, they had little clout. The foreign policy establishment during the Clinton administration was led by career professionals and practitioners, primarily pragmatists, not ideologues. They were focused on US national interests, preserving American power and dealing with problems as they came up.[2]

The influence of the neoconservatives in foreign policy making increased after the 9/11 attacks. When George W. Bush came to office, neoconservatives saw an opportunity for change. In a sign of what was to come Charles Krauthammer stated in June 2001,

> An unprecedentedly dominant United States ... is in the unique position of being able to fashion its own foreign policy. After a decade of Prometheus playing pygmy, the first task of the new [Bush] administration is precisely to reassert American freedom of action.[3]

Krauthammer stated,

> After eight years during which foreign policy success was largely measured by the number of treaties the president could sign and the number of summits he could attend, we now have an administration willing to assert American freedom of action and the primacy of American national interests.[4]

Krauthammer was critical of the Clinton administration attitude to international treaties and agreements. He described the Chemical and Biological Weapons treaties signed by the Clinton administration as useless, but nevertheless signed to build good will for future needs. In 1997 the Senate had passed a Chemical

Weapons Convention Krauthammer argues largely because of the argument that everyone else had signed it, and failure to ratify would leave the US isolated and the Kyoto Treaty was signed because the rest of the world supported it.[5]

Neoconservatives were also appointed to senior positions in the George W. Bush administration. Richard Perle was made Chairman of the Defense Policy Board at the Pentagon. In his position, Perle directed the Pentagon on defence and military planning issues. The leading neoconservative in the administration, however, was Paul Wolfowitz, in the office of Deputy Secretary of Defense, with Douglas Feith in the number three job.

Although neoconservativism is built around the idea that having a 'good offence is a good defence' and a common belief in the universal applicability of US ideals,[6] they are frequently erroneously described as a monolithic group. There is, however, no one single neoconservative viewpoint[7] as it includes different strands of thinking.[8] In an interview, Adam Garfinkle, speechwriter to Secretaries of State Colin Powell and Condoleezza Rice, stressed, 'The idea that this one homogenous group that all has the same view of everything, this is an exaggeration, this is not true'.[9] Indeed, the neoconservatives present during the Bush years – both inside and outside the administration – can be best characterised by dividing them into two subgroups.

The first group can be described as *Reagan Democrats/Daniel Patrick Moynihan Style Centrists*. The leading member of this group was Richard Perle, Chairman of the Defense Policy Board Advisory Committee. This is a subgroup of the second generation of neoconservatives. These were pragmatically inclined foreign policy professionals and activists, advocating use of American power. They were motivated by Reagan's rhetoric, to use American power to secure US interests.[10] Richard Perle himself better described his position:

> I don't think there is a single answer. People who call themselves neoconservatives hold different views on these things. For example I am thought of as a neoconservative, but I think of myself as pragmatic in these regards, sort of looking at each situation case by case and making some judgment about what is in the best interest of the United States which is what you expect an American to do.[11]

This group went on to add to their ranks the likes of Douglas Feith, Under Secretary of Defense for Policy, John Bolton, Undersecretary of State for Arms Control and International Security, I. Lewis 'Scooter' Libby Jr, Chief of Staff to the vice president, and Robert Kagan (a prolific writer for several conservative publications such as the *Weekly Standard* and *Commentary*), Michael Rubin, of the Office of Special Plans and later resident scholar at the AEI, Danielle Pletka of the AEI, and academics like Bernard Lewis and Fuad Ajami among others.[12] These neoconservatives wanted to remake the Middle East and to put an end to Arab tyranny characterised by the totalitarian Arab regimes. In their view, this would benefit both the US and Israel. The neoconservatives perceived Arab totalitarianism as equivalent to communism. Demolition of these totalitarian regimes would eventually lead to a stable Middle East at peace with itself, and no threat to US, Israel and Western interests.[13] Regarding their position on Israel these neoconservatives believe that by protecting Israel they protect freedom. They secure democracy in a part of the world which is alien to the concept. To this group, the protection of Israel meant the protection of democracy, and anything that threatened democracy was a threat to the US and its interests. Norman Podhoretz argues that many believe the neoconservatives' defence of Israel is mainly because these intellectuals are mostly of Jewish birth. Rather, their support of Israel was mostly because Israel was anti-communist during the Cold War.[14] Irving Kristol argues: 'The United States will feel obliged to defend, if possible, a democratic nation against undemocratic forces ... that is why we feel it necessary to defend Israel today.'[15]

The second subgroup can be called *Straussian/Nietzchean Conservatives*. These students of Leo Strauss, also second generation neoconservatives, included the likes of Allan Bloom, Harvey Mansfield, Deputy Secretary of Defense Paul Wolfowitz, Special Assistant to US President George W. Bush Elliot Abrams, and later William Kristol. The Straussians, of which Wolfowitz is a perfect example, have almost a religious belief in natural rights – a belief in the universal sameness of humanity and God-given inalienable rights. Having a religious zeal or commitment to these rights provided a substitute for the surety that revelation gives.[16] Wolfowitz was a romantic Wilsonian who believed in the spread of democracy, as well as in the idea that there was nothing innate in Islam that would impede Muslims from embracing democracy. His goal was to transform the Middle East region through regime change. Wolfowitz believed that democracy is transformative, and that Iraq deserved better. He believed that Iraq could be transformed like Indonesia.[17] Wolfowitz believed democracy was a universal idea, deserving to be enjoyed by all peoples. He had influenced democratic change in the Philippines and South Korea and thus believed any democratic change to be in US interests. He once stated, 'I think democracy is a universal idea ... and I think letting people rule themselves happens to be something that serves American's and America's interests.'[18] Wolfowitz genuinely believed in democracy and was passionate about giving democracy to the Middle East.[19] For Wolfowitz it was less ideological and more of a humanitarian operation.[20] They embraced two major concepts as their guiding rule: 'moralism' and the 'underdog'. The idea was to use US power to help others who cannot help themselves.[21] Wolfowitz and William Kristol were conservative ideologues, idealists and nation builders.[22]

The neoconservatives generally were not particularly influential in the first nine months of the Bush administration. It was only after 9/11 that they gained greater influence.[23] Previously, the foreign policy portfolio was run through the State Department by Colin Powell and career diplomats. In response to the attacks, the State Department's control over foreign policy shifted dramatically. Early after the terrorist attacks the neoconservatives started advancing their case. Richard Perle called David Frum, speechwriter to President Bush, at the White House on 11 September 2001 and pressed that the failure to impose a penalty on states harbouring terrorists meant that terrorists would be able to operate far more effectively as a result. Perle stated that if global terrorism is to be taken 'seriously', the US had to consider action against the states harbouring them.[24] On 19 September 2001, Perle chaired a Defense Policy Board meeting that concentrated predominantly on Iraq.[25]

The disintegration of the 'criminal justice approach to terrorism' after 9/11 was fully exploited by the neoconservatives to implement their long articulated plans and perceptions of how to deal with the world.[26] The Iraqi issue had been discussed for many years among the architects of the war. But it was only with 9/11 and the political context it provided that it turned into operational policy. The Iraq war was the point in which neoconservative ideology became fully operational.[27]

In late November 2001 at the time of the Afghan war, Paul Wolfowitz contacted the director of the American Enterprise Institute, asking for ideas and a strategy to deal with the 9/11 crisis.[28] The American Enterprise Institute formed a group named 'Bletchley II' made up of twelve members, mainly neoconservatives.[29] The ensuing report was named by AEI director DeMuth 'Delta of Terrorism'. The group concluded that this was not an isolated incident requiring a criminal preventive response, but rather this was a war with Islam, most probably a two-generation war with radical Islam. To them Iraq was an easy target, weak and vulnerable. The group also concluded that Baathism was an Arab form of fascism, and that the only way to transform the region was to get rid of Saddam's regime first then address the question of radical Islam.[30] Zalmay Khalilzad explained how 9/11 allowed the rethinking of the situation:

> Very few people thought at that time [after the end of the Cold War] that 9/11 would happen and yet again the world would change, and we had to then develop approaches for how do you deal with the problems of the Middle East, because the dysfunctionality of that region, the challenges of that region, replaced, in a sense, the Soviet challenge – they were different challenges but replaced it as the most important geopolitical issues facing the world. And very quickly, in response to the 9/11 attack we had to deal with the issue of Afghanistan because that's where al-Qaeda was present, and had cooperated and supported the Taliban, the Taliban supported it, and then with the longer-term strategy of how you make the Middle East region a more functional region of the world.[31]

Neoconservatives like Robert Kagan and William Kristol pressed for US assertiveness in the international system. They claimed, 'It is past time for the United States to step up and accept the real responsibilities and requirements of global leadership.'[32] Charles Krauthammer advocated a 'new unilateralism' that defined American interests far beyond a narrow based realism. It focused on two major global elements: first, extending peace by advancing democracy, and second, preserving the peace by acting as a global balancer.[33] Daniel Pipes, Director of the Middle East Forum, defending the neoconservative point of view with relation to Iraq explained:

In this context of Iraq policy it is a robust interpretation of America's role in the world, having to do with the sense that the US is an exceptional country, has had an exceptional historical role, has a message, a model that others can learn from. This effort to spread the American way such as: democracy, human rights, capitalism are to be engaged in with energy, it is a good investment to make these efforts. As opposed to the realist model, is leave them alone and we are not particularly special! It is based on a great appreciation of the US ... And it is truly unique ... I am sympathetic to the approach ... The US has worked things out, we've got certain successes and certain understandings that others can learn from.[34]

In the wake of the 9/11 attacks, Paul Wolfowitz affirmed that the US would create a new order in the Middle East with democracy promotion as its premise.[35] Though democracy promotion has been credited to neoconservatives primarily, it does not seem to be restricted to that group. Many officials within administration circles believed in democracy. A National Security Council official, interviewed by the author, asserted 'I think there is almost a core American belief that where democracy is we have friends and allies and generally there is peace, rightly or wrongly, so I'm not sure that is a neoconservative viewpoint.'[36]

The events of 9/11 had indeed changed the presidency. It brought different calculations to bear. It also narrowed policy circles to a very small group, close to the president.[37] However, when George W. Bush took office the neoconservatives were already in relatively important positions. 9/11 had only affirmed that their assumptions were right and that it was clear that there was something wrong with the Middle East and its culture.[38] The neoconservative agenda of a new world order, made operational after 9/11, was merely the PNAC's 1997 statement of principles.[39] The statement's chief objective was to shape a new century favourable to American principles and interests. Even Joseph Biden, the ranking Democratic member of the Senate Foreign Relations Committee at the time, said in July 2003 in response to the influence neoconservatives were playing: 'They seem to have captured the heart and mind of the president, and they're controlling the foreign policy agenda.'[40] The State Department was suspicious of the neoconservatives' new role and Richard Perle in particular.[41]

Without the events of 9/11 which amplified the sense of threat among the assertive nationalists and President Bush and without the strong intellectual presence of neoconservatives in the administration, it would have been highly improbable that the US administration would have jumped into an unprovoked Iraq war.[42]

The neoconservatives defend their position. According to Robert Kagan the US has played the role of the benign hegemon and has held no imperial aspiration but rather the desire to restore world order and provide leadership in favour of all mankind.[43] Kristol and Kagan turn to Theodore Roosevelt for justification, concurring his view that 'the defenders of civilisation must exercise their power against civilisation's opponents'. They feel that the US represents civilisation and the opponents of the West are barbaric. They urge the US to stand against the forces of evil, the proponents of backwardness and opponents of liberal values.[44] The neoconservative movement was a combination of Theodore Roosevelt's military imperialism and Woodrow Wilson's idealistic imperialism.[45]

3.2 George W. Bush: the president

The second contributing ideological factor was the president himself. Neoconservative columnist John Podhoretz argues that Ronald Reagan was a neoconservative. Like other neoconservatives, he too had started his political life as a member of the Democratic Party and only at the age of 51 did he become a Republican.[46] Bush was attracted to Reagan's beliefs and ideas. On one occasion, Senator John McCain (R-AZ) told Brent Scowcroft that President Bush has told him that he aspires to Ronald Reagan and not to his father President Bush senior.[47] Bush, however, was not a neoconservative, but he had neoconservative tendencies due to his preoccupation with democracy.[48]

Bush had come to office envisioning a fusion of idealism and realism, one he phrased as 'American Internationalism'. It was based on 'Idealism, without illusions. Confidence, without conceit. Realism, in the service of American ideals.'[49] Robert Kagan argued in 1999 that Bush's calls for American Internationalism were a strong and clear articulation of a policy of American global leadership not articulated by a major political figure since the collapse of the Soviet Union. It was a call for renewed American strength, confidence and leadership and a return to the Ronald Reagan style of leadership.[50]

Bush believed he had a personal mission, a duty to perform. Asserting this to Andrew Card, White House Chief of Staff, he said, 'I'm here for a reason, and this is going to be how we're going to be judged.'[51] Bush had a new vision for reordering the world to reduce suffering and promote peace internationally. Bush believed that the US had a unique position as a worldly leader to provide leadership and action for the sake of humanity.[52] President Bush wanted to promote democracy and human rights, and defend women's rights in the Muslim world. He wanted to reform these societies which perceived the US and the West as the enemy.[53] Bush may have had an inward-looking agenda, a clear focus on domestic politics before 9/11. Bush had always portrayed himself as a 'compassionate conservative' with a clear domestic agenda to tackle: patients' bill of rights, education reform, tort reform, tax cuts, medicare reform and support for faith-based programs. This appears to have come mostly from the influence of Karl Rove, Deputy White House Chief of Staff, who helped Bush translate his resentment of the political elite who he blamed for the 1960s social obsession of self that had ended in a rejection of community and volunteerism.[54] This aspect of Bush's beliefs paralleled to a large extent the neoconservative disgust for counter-culture and its rejection of selfish individualism. It also helped Bush shape his views and his role as the leader of the free world and his views on US foreign policy post 9/11. It became his duty to help those who could not help themselves.

Bush's faith was an influential factor in developing his perceptions of the world. When asked if he thought faith would be an important part of being a good president, he replied 'Yes, I do.'[55] Bush's religiosity was unusual as it had no theological content. It was a form of Methodist self-help with God giving the gift of freedom to man, and humans having the ability to do good.[56] Bush had his own ideas on religiosity and essentially believed there was no distinction between the Declaration of Independence and Christianity. Bush was also an admirer and reader of Abraham Lincoln due to his use of force for moral purposes, reading fourteen Lincoln biographies in total during his presidency.[57] Bush's views were also highly influenced by his speechwriter Michael Gerson, a born-again Christian and idealist, and Natan Sharansky, former Russian dissident, advocating a moral foreign policy based on belief in the universality of freedom and human rights.[58] Bush even denied categorically any consultation with his father (Bush senior) as regards his decision to invade Iraq and stressed his father would be the 'wrong father to appeal to in terms of strength. There is a higher father that I appeal to.'[59] Moreover, for Bush, as a reformed alcoholic, he had reason to believe in transformation. It was possible for people on a wayward path to become stable and prosperous and so could Iraq.[60] The very belief in democracy as the 'natural order' for all mankind was a 'faith-based foreign policy'.[61] Paul Pillar, National Intelligence Officer for the Near East and South Asia during the Bush administration, explained that attacks on 9/11 gave Bush a direction as president he had been missing. Pillar described this as more of 'psychological need' as it is not easy to explain things mainly in terms of rationale as opposed to driving beliefs.[62] President Bush was open about his religious convictions, he noted:

> in our grief and anger we have found our mission and our moment. Freedom and fear are at war. Freedom and fear, justice and cruelty, have always been at war, and we know that God is not neutral between them.[63]

George W. Bush's religiosity helped outline his new strategy through a clear definition of 'evil'. This time evil had a new definition; it was no longer about retaliation for 9/11 and punishing its perpetrator al-Qaeda, and the Taliban regime which had harboured it. The new principal objective was to prevent the next attack through combating possible threats and potential dangers. The Bush administration decided after 9/11 on a new basis for its interactions with hostile powers. Michael Gerson, President Bush's chief speechwriter, thought the old phrase 'rogue state' previously used to describe hostile states was no longer valid, as it understated the potential threat states of such nature posed to US interests. So the phrase 'Axis of Evil' was deemed to hit the right tone.[64] On 29 January 2002 Bush delivered his famous State of the Union address, where he had declared Iraq, Iran and North Korea formed an 'Axis of Evil'.[65] No longer would the US wait for its enemies to strike, it would strike first. Bush's foreign policy philosophy was based on the United States aggressively going abroad in search of evil to destroy. This logic was behind the Iraq war, and it animated the administration's efforts to deal with other rogue states.[66]

Bush asserted in late 2001, 'We wage a war to save civilisation itself. We did not seek it, but we must fight it and we will prevail.'[67] The mission that Bush envisioned went well beyond defending America's national interests. Bush's freedom agenda was more fundamentally a struggle between good and evil that touched all the world's peoples. The notion of evil had always figured prominently in Bush's thinking, as it had in the thinking of the president he often sought to emulate, Ronald Reagan.[68] Jervis stresses that no other US administration since Reagan's has been willing to sacrifice stability for the sake of democracy. As such the Bush administration does show resemblance to that of Ronald Reagan in refusing détente with the Soviet Union and also emphasising human rights issues in their discussions with the Soviet regime.[69] For years the US had sacrificed democracy at the expense of autocratic stability, hence favouring various economic and security interests. For this reason, Bush can be understood as having promoted a neo-Reaganite foreign policy, where the promotion of democracy became an overriding objective.[70] Bush said, 'My administration has a job to do and we're going to do it. We will rid the world of the evil-doers.' In the aftermath of the 9/11 attacks Bush was adamant about his new role and his mission. This was clearly reflected in his National Cathedral speech on 14 September. He affirmed, 'But our responsibility to history is already clear: To answer these attacks and rid the world of evil.'[71] When President Bush said 'You're either with us or against us' he was referring to two worlds, one that was 'good' and the other that was 'evil'. To make his argument the president argued: 'Our enemies believed America was weak and materialistic, that we would splinter in fear and selfishness. They were as wrong as they are evil.'[72] Bush's speech echoed Reagan's declaration in 1983 that the Soviet Union was an 'evil Empire'.[73] In addition to drawing on the ideas of Reagan, Bush drew liberally on the ideas of other US presidents. In a speech at the Heritage Foundation on 11 November 2003, Bush compared his policies to those of Truman in thwarting communism.[74] He told an audience at the Heritage Foundation: 'The will and resolve of America are being tested in Afghanistan and in Iraq. We are not only containing the terrorist threat, we are turning it back.'[75]

Bush's repeated statements that the spread of freedom, democracy and free enterprise would make the world 'not just safer but better' paralleled Woodrow Wilson's notion that the values of powerful states were universal values and they would benefit mankind as a whole.[76] The Reagan administration's attempts at bringing democracy to Latin America through its anti-communism are comparable to Bush's attempts in the Middle East and its War on Terror.[77] On 1 May 2003 Bush gave a speech on board the *USS Abraham Lincoln*, drawing his speech from previous presidents. He referred to Franklin Roosevelt's Four Freedoms, the Truman Doctrine and Reagan's challenge of the evil empire.[78]

3.3 The assertive nationalists

The third group of Bush administration insiders was the assertive nationalists. They were the 'national-interest realists'.[79] This group believed that US military primacy had to be maintained and US threats neutralised and defeated. The two prominent members of this group were Vice President Richard Cheney and

Defense Secretary Donald Rumsfeld. Both were very conscious of threats to US interests and national security. In 1998, Rumsfeld had led the Commission to Assess the Ballistic Missile Threat to the United States. His final report in July 1998 claimed grave and serious threats emanating from hostile states on the verge of developing missile technology. Cheney and Rumsfeld desired more military engagement and were persuaded that US military capabilities could achieve greater political purposes and were usable on a whole variety of contingencies.[80] To them US national security should not be restricted simply to the protection of American power but had to include pre-emptive action, making it clear that no such attack would be countenanced again. They also had no interest in nation-building.[81] It was an assertive stance to defend US national security and satisfy American interests with no interest in democracy promotion.[82] Cheney and Rumsfeld were not neoconservatives. They were instead assertive nationalist traditional hard-line conservatives, willing to use American military power to defeat threats to US security but reluctant as a general rule to use American primacy to remake the world in its image.[83]

Rumsfeld had initially defined his mission to create a US military ready for the twenty-first century. Rumsfeld wanted to develop a smaller, leaner lethal force, using new technology to its maximum.[84] The war for Cheney and Rumsfeld was about projecting US power. Both were less concerned about remaking the politics of the Middle East but more about focused on asserting American power. To them the US was the sole superpower and thus had to assert its might. Their attitudes was a 'we use it or lose it' mentality.[85] Tommy Franks, US CENTCOM[86] commander, describes Rumsfeld as a 'New Frontier cold warrior' willing to 'pay any price, bear any burden' to confront any adversary to assure America's survival. Rumsfeld had whole-heartedly agreed with Bush's 'either you are with us, or you are with the terrorists' concept and as a result his major focus was winning the global War on Terror.[87]

Rumsfeld emphasised from his experience as US presidential envoy to the Middle East that the US could not and should not stay the conventional course of defence, but rather take up a new offensive position and pre-empt US adversaries. Rumsfeld believed that terrorists could not be stopped as they had the advantage in their ability to change tactics. These fundamental beliefs of the assertive nationalists had important consequences for the practice of American foreign policy post 9/11. In addition to the preference for pre-emption, Rumsfeld and Cheney believed in unilateralism. Unilateralism was appealing because it was often easier and more efficient, at least in the short term, than multilateralism. Clinton's efforts as regards the task of coordinating the views of all NATO members in the Kosovo war, were perceived by Bush advisers as greatly complicating the war effort, as opposed to the Afghanistan war, where Pentagon planners did not have to subject any of their decisions to foreign approval. This group had not flatly ruled out working with others. Rather, their preferred form of multilateralism was building ad hoc coalitions of the willing. This was clearly reflected in Donald Rumsfeld's statement that the mission defines the coalition rather it being the other way round.[88]

3.4 The defensive realists

The fourth group involved in the Bush administration was the defensive realists. These were a group that believed that 'America goes not abroad in search of monsters to destroy', as US President John Quincy Adams had once advised. David Mack, former Deputy Assistant Secretary of State, has stated their view thus: 'the most we can do for the rest of the world is wish them well and be a good example'.[89] Powell was the leading figure of this group, followed by his deputy and close friend Richard Armitage, as well as Richard Haass, Director of Policy Planning at the State Department and Peter Rodman (Assistant Secretary of Defense) and many other career diplomats and Arabists at the State Department. This group was leading and winning the US foreign policy debate before the attacks on 9/11. However, their influence declined considerably after the attacks. Consequently, this led to enormous tensions between different US departments, especially between the Departments of State and Defense. Powell was concerned about the way the administration's policy was going forward. Powell was less ideological and 'hates ideology', hated Wolfowitz as he 'sees him as an ideologue'. Powell was more of a practical official and opposed to much of the administration policy.[90]

Lawrence Wilkerson, who was a close observer of events in the State Department as Colin Powell's Chief of Staff, insisted that Powell and Armitage were not totally against the war in Iraq. Both had understood that sixteen Security Council resolutions had been defied by Saddam, including the sanctions regime, and the US air force was still involved in patrolling the two No-fly zones in northern and southern Iraq. The opinion was that if it became necessary to use force to topple Saddam Hussein 'Powell and Armitage were not necessarily opposed to it' as long as it was done 'smartly and wisely'. Powell had told the president that the timing was poor. Powell thought that before engaging Iraq in a military conflict, 'Afghanistan should be wrapped up'. Powell and Armitage both thought Saddam was already contained and, if force had to be used, it could wait. They preferred to continue with the containment policy and a year-long inspections regime. They thought that the best approach was to do it later when all other possibilities were exhausted.[91] However, once the president made clear he was going to war, Wilkerson insisted that Powell and Armitage were good soldiers and followed Bush.[92]

This group also defined as 'conservative realists' are humble and passive, more sceptical about and distrust 'grand abstractions' and 'grand social engineering enterprises'. This group distrusted grand abstractions but after 9/11 the president stopped 'listening to them'.[93] The neoconservatives and assertive nationalists like Cheney and Rumsfeld also worked to marginalise Powell. They wanted to undermine him particularly with regard to US policy towards the 'Axis of Evil', Iran, Iraq and North Korea.[94]

Powell remembered very vividly what had happened in the Gulf War in 1991 when he had been Chairman of the Joint Chiefs of Staff. The question for him was not how to get in, but how to get out. As a result his worry was not the war but what would happen after the war. Powell was worried about the US responsibility for 26 million Iraqis. Powell indeed believed that getting rid of Saddam was good, but it was not urgent. Powell had told the president that without exhausting diplomacy the US would not get the coalition of 1991 and as a result make things expensive by not being able to spread responsibilities. Powell advised the president that the US should go to the UN, even if it did not get final authorisation as it would help create a much broader coalition and consequently spread the risk. At the time, however, Powell had thought the US could get a second resolution and did not anticipate the French intention to veto the resolution.[95]

Walter Russell Mead describes Colin Powell as a Hamiltonian. Hamiltonians, according to Mead, value international alliances and organisations. However, they do not think these organisations should have power over the United States, to veto a desired US course of action or for that matter be able to compel the US to do something it does not want to do.[96] Colin Powell wanted the US to act as a global citizen and equal to the rest in obligations and rights. Powell, however, was interested in US leadership to create international networks to ease tensions in the Middle East, to fight AIDS and drugs, lower trade barriers, promote human rights and combat global terrorism. He had put great faith in international organisations and partnerships like the UN and NATO.[97] President Bush, Cheney, Rumsfeld and Rice tended to see the world differently from Powell. Feith describes Powell was a here and now man, a crises manager. Powell disagreed with the rest of the Principals who were more inclined to see in US leadership the possibility to change the world landscape and make difficult goals achievable.[98]

Essentially the invasion of Iraq in 2003 was influenced by four major groups within the administration: the neoconservatives (idealist and realist strands), the president, the assertive nationalists (offensive realists) and finally the cautious nationalists (defensive realists). The first three major groups were in harmony as regards their perception of urgency as regards the nature of Iraq's perceived threat and willingness to de-throne Saddam's regime. The fourth group was not. External groups outside the administration played a highly significant role as well.

Major external groups were highly influential in providing the intellectual rationale or at least little opposition for the invasion. The first was the US media. The media played a highly important role in making the invasion of Iraq possible. They followed the administration's line in supporting the War on Terror. This happened mainly due to the media's awareness of the strengthened sentiments of patriotism among the US public and their heightened fear from threats of WMD and further terrorist attacks. They were responding to their viewers' needs and perceptions. Second, the smooth and relatively easy nature of the Afghanistan military operation was a factor. The negative attitude the media showed at the outset of the Afghan campaign, echoing messages of quagmires, was not an embarrassment they were willing to afford for the Iraq invasion. The Afghanistan operation went smoothly and quickly as opposed to the messages they were initially broadcasting at the inception of the kinetic action. Third, the media later became impartial as they were embedded with the actual military invasion, removing a sense of detachment and impartiality.

The second external group which played a significant role in the drum beat leading up to the war were the liberal hawks. This included people like David Brooks of the *New York Times*, Jim Hoagland of the *Washington Post*, Judi Miller of the *New York Times*, Thomas Friedman of the *New York Times*, George Packer of the *New Yorker*, Christopher Hitchens and Peter Galbraith among others. All participated in making the case for war possible. All were liberal hawks who saw in the removal of Saddam a humanitarian intervention and a moral obligation to remove evil. To this end, among many other public pronouncements, a group of liberal hawks signed three public statements advancing the case for the removal of Saddam Hussein from power and the rebuilding of Iraq based on human rights and democracy. The first was on 19 March 2003 (the day before the US invasion) and the second on 28 March 2003. The first two letters were prepared by the PNAC and included several prominent neoconservative signatories as well. A third open letter issued by the Social Democrats USA and signed by a large group of liberal hawks, in support of the invasion, was sent on 25 February 2003 to President George W. Bush. To them it was another case of necessity to remove a brutal regime liberating a people from oppression and tyranny. To them the invasion of Iraq was similar in its objectives to the 1995 war in Bosnia and the Kosovo war of 1999.[99]

These various influences and opinions helped motivate the invasion of Iraq. Accordingly the Bush Doctrine was the doctrine of the Bush administration as a whole. It accumulated and unified the views and objectives of the different factions of the administration. The chapter that follows attempts to narrate the actual decision-making process, and puts forward the publicly declared and underlying reasons and purposes used to advance the decision to invade Iraq.

Notes

1 George W. Bush. (2009). *President Bush Delivers Farewell Address to the Nation.* [The White House] Available at: URL: http://georgewbush-whitehouse.archives.gov/news/releases/2009/01/20090115–17.html Access Date: 20 June 2009.
2 Sam Parker, Interview with Author, 21 July 2008, Washington, D.C.
3 Charles Krauthammer, 'The New Unilateralism', *The Washington Post* (2001, 8 June), p. A29.
4 Ibid.
5 Charles Krauthammer, 'The Unipolar Moment Revisited: America, The Benevolent Empire', *The National Interest* Vol. 70 (Winter 2002): p. 15.
6 Sam Parker, Interview with Author, 27 June 2008, Washington, D.C.
7 Henri Barkey, Interview with Author, 21 August 2008, Washington, D.C.
8 Phebe Marr, Interview with Author, 19 June 2008, Washington, D.C.
9 Adam Garfinkle, Interview with Author, 7 August 2008, Washington, D.C.
10 Sam Parker, Interview with Author, 27 June 2008, Washington, D.C.
11 Richard Perle, Telephone Interview with Author, 24 September 2008.
12 Carole O'Leary, Interview with Author, 8 August 2008, Washington, D.C.
13 Ibid.

14 Norman Podhoretz, 'Neoconservatism: A Eulogy', *Commentary* Vol. 101, No. 3 (1996), p. 22.
15 Irving Kristol quoted in Ann Norton, *Leo Strauss and the Politics of American Empire* (USA: Yale University Press, 2004), p. 208.
16 Sam Parker, Interview with Author, 27 June 2008, Washington, D.C.
17 Carole O'Leary, Interview with Author, 8 August 2008, Washington, D.C.
18 Paul Wolfowitz quoted in Thomas Ricks, *Fiasco: The American Military Adventure in Iraq* (London: Penguin Press, 2007), p. 17.
19 Henri Barkey, Interview with Author, 21 August 2008, Washington, D.C.
20 Former Senior Congressional Staffer, Interview with Author, 8 August 2008, Washington, D.C.
21 Ayal Frank, Interview with Author, 11 June 2008, Washington, D.C.
22 Phebe Marr, Interview with Author, 19 June 2008, Washington, D.C.
23 James Goldgeier, Interview with Author, 10 July 2008, Washington, D.C.
24 Richard Perle. (2003). *Truth, War & Consequences: Interview Richard Perle.* [Frontline] Available at: URL: www.pbs.org/wgbh/pages/frontline/shows/truth/interviews/perle.html Access Date: 20 December 2008.
25 Michael Gordon and Bernard Trainor, *Cobra II: The Inside Story of the Invasion and Occupation of Iraq* (London: Atlantic Books, 2007), p. 15.
26 Ian Shapiro, *Containment: Rebuilding a Strategy Against Global Terror*, (Princeton: Princeton University Press, 2007), p. 120.
27 Stefan Halper and Jonathan Clarke, *America Alone: The Neo-Conservatives and the Global Order* (Cambridge: Cambridge University Press, 2004), p. 230.
28 Bob Woodward, *State of Denial: Bush at War, Part III* (London: Simon and Schuster, 2006), p. 83.
29 Ibid., p. 84.
30 Ibid., pp. 84–5.
31 Zalmay Khalilzad. (2009). *Conversations with History: Responding to Strategic Challenges of the Post 9–11 World.* [University of California, Berkeley: Institute of International Studies] Available at: URL: http://globetrotter.berkeley.edu/people9/Khalilzad/Amb%20Khalilzad%20transcript.pdf Access Date: 15 July 2009.
32 Robert Kagan and William Kristol. 'What To Do About Iraq', *The Weekly Standard* Vol. 7, No. 18 (2002, January), pp. 23–6.
33 Krauthammer (2002), op. cit., p. 15.
34 Daniel Pipes, Interview with Author, 23 July 2008, Washington, D.C.
35 Norton (2004), op. cit., p. 209.
36 National Security Council Official, Interview with Author, 11 July 2008, Washington, D.C.
37 Phebe Marr, Interview with Author, 19 June 2008, Washington, D.C.
38 Sam Parker, Interview with Author, 21 July 2008, Washington, D.C.
39 Halper and Clarke (2004), op. cit., p. 230.
40 Ivo Daalder and James Lindsay, *America Unbound: The Bush Revolution in Foreign Policy* (Maryland: The Brookings Institution, 2003), p. 15.
41 Lawrence Wilkerson, Interview with Author, 26 August 2008, Washington, D.C.
42 Joshua Marshall, 'Remaking the World: Bush and the Neoconservatives', *Foreign Affairs* Vol. 82, No. 6 (2003): p. 146.
43 Robert Kagan, 'America's Crisis of Legitimacy', *Foreign Affairs* Vol. 83, No. 2 (2004): p. 74.
44 Norton (2004), op. cit., p. 197.
45 Chalmers Johnson quoted in John Dumbrell, 'The Neoconservative Roots of the War in Iraq', in *Intelligence and National Security Policymaking on Iraq: British and American Perspectives*, ed. James Pfiffner and Mark Phythian (Manchester: Manchester University Press, 2008a), p. 30.
46 Podhoretz (1996), op. cit., p. 22.

47 Woodward (2006), op. cit., p. 419.
48 Ariel Cohen, Interview with Author, 7 August 2008, Washington, D.C.
49 George W. Bush. (1999b). Governor George W. Bush, 'A Distinctly American Internationalism', Ronald Reagan Presidential Library, Simi Valley, California, 19 November 1999. Available at: URL: www.mtholyoke.edu/acad/intrel/bush/wspeech. htm Access Date: 20 December 2009.
50 Robert Kagan. (1999). *Distinctly American Internationalism.* [Carnegie Endowment for International Peace] Available at: URL: www.carnegieendowment.org/publications/index.cfm?fa=view&id=237 Access Date: 20 June 2008.
51 Bob Woodward, *Plan of Attack* (London: Simon and Schuster, 2004), p. 91.
52 Bob Woodward, *Bush at War* (London: Simon and Schuster, 2002), p. 341.
53 Woodward (2004), op. cit., p. 89.
54 Richard Melanson, *American Foreign Policy Since the Vietnam War: The Search for Consensus from Richard Nixon to George W. Bush* (New York: M.E. Sharpe, 2005), pp. 295–7.
55 George W. Bush. (2010). *George W. Bush Quotes.* [BrainyQuote] Available at: URL: www.brainyquote.com/quotes/authors/g/george_w_bush.html Access Date: 18 January 2011.
56 The Methodist tradition of holiness presupposes that God gives humans both the grace and the freedom to be able to do good and to grow in habits of doing good.
57 Adam Garfinkle, Interview with Author, 7 August 2008, Washington, D.C.
58 Ibid.
59 Woodward (2004), op. cit., p. 421.
60 Paul Pillar, Interview with Author, 15 July 2008, Washington, D.C.
61 Robert Jervis, 'Understanding the Bush Doctrine', *Political Science Quarterly* Vol. 118, No. 3 (2003): p. 367.
62 Paul Pillar, Interview with Author, 15 July 2008, Washington, D.C.
63 George W. Bush. (2001). *Address to a Joint Session of Congress and the American People.* [The White House] Available at: URL: http://georgewbush-whitehouse. archives.gov/news/releases/2001/09/20010920–8.html Access Date: 20 June 2009.
64 Michael Gerson quoted in Woodward (2002), op. cit., p. 89.
65 Dumbrell (2008a), op. cit., p. 33.
66 Daalder and Lindsay (2003), op. cit., p. 13.
67 George W. Bush quoted in Caroline Kennedy-Pipe, 'American Foreign Policy After 9/11', in *US Foreign Policy*, ed. Michael Cox and Doug Stokes (Oxford: Oxford University Press, 2008), p. 408.
68 Daalder and Lindsay (2003), op. cit., p. 87.
69 Jervis (2003), op. cit., p. 367.
70 Thomas Carothers, 'Promoting Democracy and Fighting Terror', *Foreign Affairs* Vol. 82, No. 1 (2003): p. 91.
71 George W. Bush quoted in Woodward (2002), op. cit., p. 48.
72 George W. Bush. (2002a). *President Delivers State of the Union Address.* [The White House] Available at: URL: http://georgewbush-whitehouse.archives.gov/news/ releases/2002/01/20020129–11.html Access Date: 20 June 2009.
73 George W. Bush quoted in Woodward (2002), op. cit., p. 89.
74 Woodward (2004), op. cit., p. 93.
75 George W. Bush. (2003f). *President Bush: Address to The Heritage Foundation.* [The Heritage Foundation] Available at: URL: www.heritage.org/Press/Commentary/ bush111103.cfm Access Date: 20 March 2008.
76 Jervis (2003), op. cit., p. 366.
77 Carothers (2003), op. cit., p. 95.
78 Woodward (2004), op. cit., p. 412.
79 Adam Garfinkle, Interview with Author, 7 August 2008, Washington, D.C.
80 Ibid.

81 Phebe Marr, Interview with Author, 19 June 2008, Washington, D.C.
82 Sam Parker, Interview with Author, 27 June 2008, Washington, D.C.
83 Daalder and Lindsay (2003), op. cit., pp. 15–16.
84 Adam Garfinkle, Interview with Author, 7 August 2008, Washington, D.C.
85 Paul Pillar, Interview with Author, 15 July 2008, Washington, D.C.
86 The United States Central Command (USCENTCOM) is a theatre-level Unified Combatant Command unit of the US armed forces. Its area of responsibility is in the Middle East, including Egypt, and Central Asia.
87 Tommy Franks with Malcolm McConnell, *American Soldier* (New York: Harper-Collins, 2004), p. 374.
88 Daalder and Lindsay (2003), op. cit., p. 14.
89 David Mack, Interview with Author, 27 August 2008, Washington, D.C.
90 James Goldgeier, Interview with Author, 10 July 2008, Washington, D.C.
91 Lawrence Wilkerson, Interview with Author, 26 August 2008, Washington, D.C.
92 Ibid.
93 Adam Garfinkle, Interview with Author, 7 August 2008, Washington, D.C.
94 Lawrence Wilkerson, Interview with Author, 26 August 2008, Washington, D.C.
95 Adam Garfinkle, Interview with Author, 7 August 2008, Washington, D.C.
96 Walter Russell Mead. (2003). *US Foreign Policy and the American Political Tradition.* [University of California, Berkeley: Institute of International Studies] Available at: URL: http://globetrotter.berkeley.edu/people3/Mead/mead-con4.html Access Date: 15 March 2008.
97 Franks (2004), op. cit., p. 374.
98 Douglas Feith, *War and Decision: Inside the Pentagon at the Dawn of the War on Terrorism* (New York: HarperCollins Publishers, 2008), p. 60.
99 Marc Lynch, Interview with Author, 24 June 2008, Washington, D.C.

4 Invading Iraq

One decision, various reasons

Prior to September the 11th, we were discussing smart sanctions. We were trying to fashion a sanction regime that would make it more likely to be able to contain somebody like Saddam Hussein. After September the 11th, the doctrine of containment just doesn't hold any water, as far as I'm concerned ... My vision shifted dramatically after September the 11th, because I now realise the stakes. I realise the world has changed.

George W. Bush, 31 January 2003[1]

Introduction

This chapter illustrates the core debates and discussions that eventually led to the decision to topple Saddam Hussein. It contends that the objective of removing Saddam from power was almost unanimously accepted in Washington across both parties and throughout the key government agencies. An understanding had been reached that Saddam would neither fall in a military coup from inside the regime, nor was the Iraqi opposition sophisticated or strong enough to achieve this goal through its own means. Direct US military intervention became the answer for achieving this political objective, as several coup attempts against the regime, encouraged and assisted by the US, had all failed. The head of the CIA's Iraq Operations Group, Luis Rueda, confirmed this in a meeting with the vice president on 3 January 2002. As will be seen through the various reasons used by different factions to justify America's pursuit of this goal, motivation was based on divergent ideas and expectations to what regime change could achieve.

4.1 Decision for war: a creeping evolution

There was an evolution in the decision to invade Iraq. Threat tolerance and risk acceptance had disappeared since conventional thinking had changed as a result of the attacks of 9/11. US policy had elevated actions of terrorist organisations (non-state actors) from acts of criminal activity, to acts of war. As a result, the distinction between these terrorist groups and their sponsors (state actors) that had hitherto been considered when pursuing terrorist organisations was removed. When the president on the evening of 9/11 addressed the nation and spoke about a war against terrorism, it was a profound shift. Detectives, judges and jails had been deployed in the past. Intelligence agencies and military forces had not been involved. This all changed on 9/11. The use of military Special Operations Forces (SOF) in Afghanistan showed that the United States was prepared to use military force.[2] The attacks on 9/11 brought a paradigm shift. Wolfowitz explained that the threat against the United States was 'not going to stop if a few criminals are taken care of'.[3]

Donald Rumsfeld was the first person to float the idea of attacking Saddam Hussein, at 2:40 pm in the Pentagon on 11 September 2001. The next day when Bush's war cabinet came together, Rumsfeld again raised the possibility of exploiting the opportunity and launching an attack on Iraq.[4] Colin Powell insisted in the 12 September NSC meeting that any action required public support and therefore any action against Iraq before defeating al-Qaeda would not enjoy public as well as international support.[5] On 13 September 2001 President Bush in another NSC meeting raised a question about Iraq and its possible involvement in the 9/11 attack. Iraq had already been discussed as a serious threat by the administration in the previous months. Iraq had managed to frustrate the inspections regime, breach sanctions and had been shooting constantly at US and UK planes patrolling the northern and southern No-fly zones.[6] At the 13 September NSC meeting, however, President Bush stressed that any military action against Iraq would have to bring about regime change.[7] On 13 September Rumsfeld had also sent a short memo to his Pentagon staff known internally as a 'snowflake', asking for the previous Iraq plan to be revisited and even asking for a scheme to seize Iraq's southern oil fields if necessary. The idea was to show to the world that an attack on the US would have serious consequences, and that merely an affiliation with a terrorist group would be fatal.[8] Rumsfeld mentioned Iraq as a major threat to the US and the region in that 13 September NSC meeting. He stated that Saddam supported terrorism (acts of random killing of innocent civilians) and that Iraq had Weapons of Mass Destruction (WMD) that it could provide to terrorists to use against the US. Rumsfeld asserted that inflicting costly damage on Iraq might also make terrorist-supporting regimes rethink their policies.[9] Saddam's terrorist activities included among many other things a cash reward of 25,000 USD to families of Palestinian suicide bombers.[10]

The mention of a possible attack on Iraq came again at the Camp David meeting of 15–16 September 2001. Rumsfeld outlined his opinions on the nature of this new threat but left it to Wolfowitz to expand on the necessity of confronting Saddam Hussein. However, the president chose to defer Iraq and focus on Afghanistan.[11] Even after the 9/11 attacks and Bush's decision to leave Iraq and commence military action in Afghanistan, some members of the war cabinet, specifically Cheney and Rumsfeld, managed to keep the invasion of Iraq on the agenda.[12] Condoleezza Rice had devised a three-option proposal to confront the new threat prepared for the NSC meeting in Camp David. Option three was to consider eliminating the Iraq threat in addition to al-Qaeda and the Taliban. When the Deputies' Committee had met to discuss Rice's proposal on 13 September, Paul Wolfowitz was unhappy with the options put forward by Rice.

He suggested that US military action should not be designed to punish the 9/11 perpetrators but rather to attack those who could launch the next 9/11.[13] This was a departure in US strategy as previous retaliatory attacks were punitive rather than preventative. Colin Powell thought there was a clear fixation on the Iraq issue, and the toppling of its regime. To Powell, Cheney was in a fever, no longer a cool detached thinker as he was during the First Gulf War. Cheney, Wolfowitz, Libby and Feith were always looking for a link between Saddam and the 9/11 attacks.[14]

Paul Wolfowitz, in a 13 September press briefing, made it known that the newly declared War on Terror would be a campaign and 'not a single action'. He also stressed that the administration would pursue the perpetrators and the 'people who support them until this stops'. The new approach would not simply be a matter of capturing people and holding them accountable. The new policy would involve removing the sanctuaries, removing the support systems, 'ending states who sponsor terrorism', Wolfowitz stressed. The strategy would be to sustain a broad and long-term campaign.[15]

Bush told Bob Woodward, a respected journalist at the *Washington Post*, that the US objective was to 'rout out terror wherever it may exist' and it did not matter how long this would take. The new Bush Doctrine was effectively, 'if you harbour them, feed them, you're just as guilty', and you will be held to account. It was a dramatic departure from previous reactions. It was a war to be fought on many fronts, including the intelligence, financial, diplomatic, as well as military fronts.[16] 'Deterrence – the promise of massive retaliation against nations – means nothing against shadowy terrorist networks with no nation or citizens to defend.' Containment was no longer deemed possible when 'unbalanced dictators with weapons of mass destruction can deliver those weapons on missiles or secretly provide them to terrorist allies'.[17] In a memo dated 20 September 2001, Rumsfeld made clear to the president that Iraq should be a major consideration in the new War on Terror. The reason was the nexus between Baghdad's alleged sponsoring of terrorism and its WMD development ambitions:

> The president has stressed that we are not defining our fight narrowly and are not focused only on those directly responsible for the September 11 attacks.... It would drive this point home if the initial military strikes hit [targets] in addition to al-Qaeda. That is one of the reasons why I still favour an early focus on Iraq as well.[18]

On 21 November 2001 President Bush made his intention known for an invasion of Iraq and the removal of Saddam Hussein. After an NSC meeting he asked Rumsfeld 'what kind of a war plan do you have for Iraq? How do you feel about the war plan for Iraq?'[19] Bush asked Rumsfeld to update him on plans for future military action in the region. He told Rumsfeld, 'Let's get started on this', and 'get Tommy Franks looking at what it would take to protect America by removing Saddam Hussein if we have to.'[20] Franks says Rumsfeld had asked him for an update of the Iraq war plan on 27 November 2001.[21] It was obvious that President Bush wanted to develop his Iraq policy within the new understanding of the potential dangers that state supporters of terrorism can bring.[22] A special Pentagon intelligence unit was established by Rumsfeld and Wolfowitz, headed by Feith, to gather intelligence in the wake of the 9/11 attacks and to find Iraq's links to the attack.[23] This unit, established a few weeks after 9/11, was named the Policy Counter Terrorism Evaluation Group.[24]

On 29 September 2001, Rumsfeld had already asked General Myers, Chairman of the Joint Chiefs of Staff, to prepare a military plan for Iraq. The plan requested from CENTCOM was to be two-fold. One, it would find the WMD and then destroy them. The second priority was regime change with the stipulation that it would take a few months and no more than 250,000 troops.[25] On 24 January 2003, General Franks delivered his final version of the Iraq invasion named the 5–11–16–125-day Hybrid Plan.[26]

In early 2002, Deputies meetings were held twice a week to discuss Iraq policy specifically.[27] By January 2002 the US had emerged victorious from its military operations in Afghanistan, having apparently achieved its objective of defeating al-Qaeda and the Taliban. In his 2002 State of the Union speech, President Bush expressed this sentiment.[28] The now infamous address served two purposes. First, it was a clear, bold and strong message to the world; no president since Reagan had been so aggressive. Second, it helped distract people from the actual Iraq war which was being planned.[29] The main concerns he reiterated in his 28 January 2003 State of the Union address were the Iraqi government's behaviour towards UN inspectors, the unaccounted WMD in Iraq and the regime's attempts to purchase uranium from Africa.[30]

Secretary of State Colin Powell, on 6 February 2002 gave testimony before a House Committee, following President Bush's State of the Union address. He stated that they had not ruled out other options with respect to Iraq. 'We still believe strongly in regime change in Iraq', Powell stressed. He also confirmed the United States' desire for an Iraq that was democratic, representative, at peace with its neighbours and prepared to rejoin the family of nations.[31] On a second hearing in the Senate on 12 February, Powell asserted that with respect to Iraq it has 'long been, for several years now', the policy of the United States that regime change would be in the best interests of the region and the Iraqi people.[32]

In the spring of 2002 Bush publicly declared his objective of regime change in Iraq after a meeting with British Prime Minister Tony Blair.[33] 'I explained to the prime minister that, you know, that the policy of my government is the removal of Saddam, and that all options are on the table', Bush said on 6 April 2002.[34] On 26 May 2002 at a Press Conference with President Chirac, Bush stated:

> Let me start with the Iraqi regime. The stated policy of my government is that we have a regime change. And as I told President Chirac, I have no war plans on my desk. And I will continue to consult closely with him. We do view Saddam Hussein as a serious, significant – serious threat to stability and peace.[35]

On 14 August 2002 the NSC Principals met without the president and agreed that a UN cover was needed if the war with Iraq was to become reality. However, they also agreed that, once they took the issue to the UN, it would become an endless process of debate, discussion and compromise.[36] On 9 August Rice had presented a paper entitled 'Liberation Strategy for Iraq' for the Principals Committee meeting. This stipulated that the US 'create' a unified and democratic Iraq, strategic partner to America and a model of 'good governance'. Rumsfeld saw it as promising democracy to Iraq, something the US could not guarantee and beyond the objective of regime change in Iraq.[37] In the 14 August 2002 meeting Rice submitted a revised edition of the 9 August paper for regime change in Iraq as a result of Rumsfeld's dissatisfaction with the promise of democracy for Iraq. It was titled 'Iraq: Goals, Objectives and Strategy'. This time the tone was more sober. The objective would be to maintain Iraq's unity and territorial integrity; and liberate the Iraqi people from tyranny and 'assist them in creating a society based on moderation, pluralism and democracy'.[38]

Feith argues that there was 'no actual meeting of the minds' on how to formulate US objectives for the post-Saddam Iraqi government. This version, however, was approved by the Principals and later in the month by the president.[39] However, in another modification to Rice's 14 August 'Goals, Objectives and Strategy' paper, on 29 October another version was presented due to the Pentagon's and Rumsfeld's reservations about the paper. It replaced US goals in Iraq from a 'society based on moderation, pluralism, and democracy' to one that 'encourages the building of democratic intuitions'. The new version also replaced 'establish a broad-based democratic government' with 'establishes an interim administration in Iraq that prepares for the transition to an elected Iraqi government as quickly as practicable'.[40] This was mostly a result of Rumsfeld's lack of interest in nation-building which led to the constant diluting of US objectives in Iraq, discussed at greater length in the next chapter.

In the summer of 2002 the Office of Special Plans (OSP) was established at the Pentagon by Douglas Feith. Until that date only two civilian staffers were working full time on Iraq. This office was designed to focus on Iraq, with extra staff to deal with the overwhelming material related to Iraq. The OSP had a substantial role in gathering evidence against Saddam's regime. It relied heavily on Iraqi opposition groups to collect material rather than on the CIA and the Defense Department's very own Defense Intelligence Agency.[41] In terms of intelligence, Paul Pillar, National Intelligence Officer for the Near East at the CIA, stated that 'nobody asked me for any input'. The policy makers had not asked for intelligence input which could impact on decision making or have strategic ramifications in relation to Iraq in the run-up to the war. According to Pillar they had 'no role'. And according to Pillar the OSP was only an extension of a speech writing office with the single purpose of providing scary material to be used in speeches, especially in relation to links between Saddam and al-Qaeda.[42]

Michael Rubin, who worked at the OSP, refutes this claim. He said the OSP did not have any intelligence gathering duties and that it was a corollary to the

State Department's Office of North Gulf Affairs. As such it would meet with the exact same Iraqis whom the State Department met. He asserted that often Iraqis would come from Detroit or Dearborn or London or Kurdistan and do the rounds: go to State Department, the Pentagon, the NSC, and perhaps the CIA in order to meet officials working the Iraqi issue in each of those.[43] Douglas Feith also states that the name 'Office of Special Plans' was only an effort to avoid undermining the US diplomatic efforts at the time and was no more than the office of the Northern Gulf affairs.[44]

Rumsfeld sent a memo to President Bush on 5 October 2002, stating that a new UN resolution was not a requisite for a military confrontation with Iraq. In it he cited article 51 of the UN charter as regards self-defence and Saddam's breaches of the multiple UNSCR that had been the basis for the 1991 ceasefire with Iraq.[45] Moreover, the White House claimed that the Iraq Liberation Act of 1998 provided full authority to the administration to use military force in Iraq to topple the regime.[46] On 17 March 2003, President Bush met with a group of members from Congress and told them that they would not be able to get a second UN resolution authorising military action because of the French position, and referred to the congressionally mandated 1998 Iraq Liberation act.[47] Bush had already gained congressional support. On 10 and 11 October 2002, both the House and Senate voted overwhelmingly to give full backing to President Bush if he took the decision to attack Iraq unilaterally.[48] To achieve this the president had already invited eighteen key Senate and House leaders on 4 September 2002 to mandate congressional support and authority for the war. Bush reminded the members of Congress present that Congress had passed a law in 1998 for regime change in Iraq. The president stated that his administration had embraced that policy even more in light of the events of 9/11.[49]

The Iraqi opposition was also further revived, following from the last Iraqi opposition conference in October 1999 in New York. A meeting was held at the State Department in August 2002 with six major Iraqi opposition groups. The groups invited were deemed as the Iraqi democratic opposition, as listed in the Iraq Liberation Act of 1998. After considerable delay a US-sponsored opposition conference was held in London from 13 to 16 December 2002. The meeting resulted in the election of a leadership council of sixty-five members and a final political statement. A decision was reached to meet again in Iraqi Kurdistan within a few weeks.[50] The next meeting followed from 24 to 28 February 2003 in Iraqi Kurdistan where a six-member leadership council was elected, serving as the Iraqi point of contact after Saddam's overthrow.

Diplomacy was also revived; President Bush wanted Saddam to prove to the international community that he no longer possessed weapons of mass destruction, and that he should let the inspectors return.[51] He made this diplomatic gesture in a speech to the UN General Assembly on 12 September 2002. Iraq responded positively allowing the return of inspectors under UNSCR 1441. On 18 December 2002 at a NSC meeting President Bush discussed the 7 December 2002 Iraqi declaration of WMD. Powell explained that members of the UN Security Council, as well as Hans Blix, Head of the United Nations Monitoring,

Verification and Inspection Commission (UNMOVIC), saw gaps in the declaration. Powell described it as a material breach. President Bush asked Powell if that meant Saddam was not cooperating, to which Powell replied 'that's right'. President Bush responded 'that's a significant statement'. He then stated 'it means it's the beginning of the end for the guy'.[52] Feith argues that President Bush made up his mind on the necessity of using power to overthrow Saddam when the UN inspectors had declared the Iraqi cooperation as insufficient in December 2002.[53] In January 2003 Condoleezza Rice established that Iraq was not trustworthy, indicating that twelve chemical war heads discovered by inspectors were not mentioned in the declaratory report. She continued 'Iraq is proving not that it is a nation bent on disarmament, but it is a nation with something to hide'.[54]

Bush was not comfortable with the continuation of Hans Blix's inspections, as it would be difficult to maintain the military presence in the Gulf. Bush was worried it could drag on for a year. The president was concerned that Saddam would 'play games with the inspectors'.[55] Condoleezza Rice, however, told Bush that if he were to carry out coercive diplomacy, he would have 'to live with that decision'.[56] Bush felt Saddam was getting more confident in early January 2003. Bush told Rice that they were probably going to have to take military action.[57] In Rice's mind, this was the period the president decided the United States would go to war with Iraq.[58] Military planning had been under way for more than a year even as Bush sought a diplomatic solution through the United Nations. He would continue those efforts, at least publicly, for ten more weeks, but he had reached a point of no return.[59] In his 27 January 2003 examination report on the content of Iraq's voluminous 12,000-page declaration report, Hans Blix stated that it 'regrettably' does not provide sufficient information to 'eliminate the questions or reduce their number'. Blix also stated that, although Iraq was cooperating on some fronts, it had not seemed to come to a 'genuine acceptance' of the disarmament it has been ordered to carry out.[60] After these events the United States no longer had the patience, nor the intention, to carry on with inspections. The countdown to war had begun. All four leaders – Bush, Blair, Aznar of Spain and Barroso of Portugal – convened in the Azores on 16 March 2003. This was after attempts to gain a second resolution to mandate war were withdrawn due to French, Russian and German opposition. The group agreed that, according to UNSCR 1441, Iraq had not complied with the obligations prescribed in the resolution, and therefore there was legal authority to act upon the 'serious consequences' Iraq would face by failure to submit to the resolution.[61]

Richard Haass, Director of Policy Planning, told Lawrence Wilkerson that it was a 'creeping decision'.[62] One of the most baffling things for future historians is that there is no one meeting or single paper the president signed where it can be said 'that's the decision'.[63] The process of planning and preparation was already under way in the first half of 2002, and by summer 2002 there was no going back. The White House in summer 2002 started major efforts to sell the decision to go to war which they unveiled in September of that year.[64] Andrew Card on 6 September said 'From a marketing point of view you don't introduce new products in August.'[65] The immediate inclination to go to war after 9/11 effectively progressed to a decision by spring 2002.[66] Colin Powell explained that there was never a moment when the Principals made recommendations followed by a presidential decision.[67] Rice concurred with this view: 'there's no decision meeting'.[68] After 9/11 an 'established policy of regime change' was given heightened attention to the degree US military power could be used to achieve the goal.[69] Michael Rubin asserts that the invasion of Iraq was talked about seriously in 2002, even talked about in 2001. But the final decision was not made until US fire power 'kinetic' action was used, in essence a day or two before the Shock and Awe strikes commenced. Military planning and consideration were conducted thoroughly in 2002. Phase I, the preparation phase, which involved deployments, build-up and putting everything in the theatre of operation was under way in 2002 and early 2003.[70] The military build-up accelerated in March and accelerated further from June 2002.[71] Tommy Franks explains that his official request for 'Pre-N-Day' force, the regional force build-up (Phase I of operations) was submitted on 22 November 2002. This would be only the first request for pre-war build-up that would bring 128,000 soldiers to the Gulf by 15 February 2003.[72]

4.2 Saddam Hussein: the serial gambler

Saddam's rhetoric allowed him to be perceived as a threat. He constantly expressed his disdain for US imperialism and for Israel. Saddam told April Glaspie, US ambassador to Iraq, on 25 July 1990, 'We too can harm you. Everyone can cause harm according to their ability and their size. We cannot come all the way to you in the United States, but individual Arabs may reach you.'[73] This seems to have happed on 9/11 although it was not, apparently, Iraqi sponsored. In interrogations conducted by Federal Bureau of Investigation (FBI) agent George Piro after his capture, Saddam Hussein acknowledged that Iraq accepted UNSCR 687. However, Saddam further acknowledged that Iraq had made a 'mistake' by destroying some weapons without UN supervision. In Saddam's view, UN inspectors wanted generous expenses, including accommodations, travel and other costs paid for by Iraq. Instead of waiting for the inspectors and bearing these expenses, Iraq commenced destruction of the weapons unilaterally. Saddam stated during his interrogation with the FBI that Iraq did not hide these weapons. UN inspectors later requested documentation of the destruction of the weapons and visited various places taking samples for review.[74] Scott Ritter also stresses that the Iraqis claimed that the bulk of Iraqi WMDs were decommissioned unilaterally in July 1991. However, this issue remained the cause of continuous tension with inspectors, as formerly recorded weapons could not be accounted for and verified.[75]

Another reason for Saddam's defiance was that he believed that Iraq could not appear weak to its enemies, especially Iran. Saddam believed Iraq was being threatened by others in the region and must appear able to defend itself. Saddam stated that Iran was Iraq's major threat, due to their common border. He believed

Iran intended to annex Southern Iraq. Such an attempt by Iran was viewed in Baghdad as the most significant threat facing Iraq. Even though Saddam claimed Iraq did not have WMD, the threat from Iran was the major factor dissuading him from supporting the return of the UN inspectors after the events of 1998. Saddam stated he was more concerned about Iran discovering Iraq's weaknesses and vulnerabilities than the repercussions for the United States for his refusal to allow UN inspectors back into Iraq.[76] The declassified FBI interrogation documents suggest that Saddam and his regime perceived Iran to pose a greater and more immediate threat than the US. His plan was to deter Iran and his adversaries in Iraq by doubt, but in doing so he overlooked the implications of an emergent pre-emption doctrine in the US.[77]

Although Saddam had not expected a US invasion of Iraq, he felt US hostility had evolved before his invasion of Kuwait. He told his FBI interrogator: 'I ask you as an American, when did the United States stop shipments of grain to Iraq?' He also asked: when did the United States contact European countries to boycott sales of technological equipment to Iraq? He responded, '1989'. Saddam believed the US was planning to destroy Iraq, a desire pushed by a Zionist political agenda in the United States. Moreover, he attributed the invasion to Israel itself, a regional neighbour which saw Iraq as a major threat after the end of the Iran–Iraq war.[78] However, in 1989, as mentioned previously in Chapter 2, the US government, namely the Bush senior administration, had a policy of engagement contrary to congressional attempts at sanctions which Saddam seems to have confused.

Moreover, according to the Iraqi Survey Group's 960-page report (known as the Duelfer Report), Saddam was convinced that the Central Intelligence Agency (CIA) had thoroughly penetrated his regime and thus would know not only that he had dismantled his WMD (which the CIA apparently did not), but would also know about his plans for important intelligence operations.[79] Saddam had also inadvertently confirmed to the US the existence of his WMD in a speech given in June 2002. In the speech he had stated that you cannot expect Iraq to give up the rifle and live with a sword when his neighbour Iran had a rifle.[80] Additionally, Saddam believed the United States was a paper tiger. He even told Glaspie on 25 July 1990: 'I do not belittle you. But I hold this view by looking at the geography and nature of American society into account. Yours is a society which cannot accept 10,000 dead in one battle.'[81] Michael Rubin states that 'Saddam was bluffing, he thought the US was bluffing as well.'[82] For this reason he saw no significance in taking the US invasion seriously. Saddam also believed that France and Russia would prevent war. Even if hostilities began, a ceasefire would be declared under enormous international pressure.[83] Saddam Hussein probably assumed that an attack on Iraq was unlikely to happen in the absence of a unanimous vote at the UN Security Council, which would be most likely vetoed by France and Russia.[84]

Saddam seems to have constantly misinterpreted US policy. Veteran British left-wing politician Tony Benn stated that he wrote to Saddam Hussein in 1990 after he had invaded Kuwait and had taken British hostages. He later visited

Saddam in Baghdad to try to persuade him to release all the British hostages. Benn said he had a three-hour talk with Saddam, and was struck by his sense of utter betrayal by the United States. Saddam had said that the US had armed and supported him. He even stated 'the American ambassador in Baghdad said you can go into Kuwait, and now they've turned on me'.[85]

Saddam also maintained the image that he had WMD stockpiles to deter his domestic enemies: the Iraqi Kurds and the Shiite.[86] Bush asked David Kay, Head of the Iraq Survey Group, why Saddam had not been open about his lack of WMD. Kay responded believing that Saddam had found the invasion of the Iraq by the US a highly unlikely scenario. For this reason, he wanted to use the doubt to deter his internal population, especially the Kurds and Shiites. Kay continued telling Bush that totalitarian regimes tend to fear the domestic populations more than external threats.[87]

4.3 Reasons for war: different people, different agendas

As early as September 2001 Douglas Feith had prepared a memo for 15 September NSC Camp David meetings concerning the purpose of a possible Iraq invasion. Feith listed several points: to de-throne a regime which supported terrorism; that actively pursued WMD; that attacked US forces on a daily basis and threatened US interests in the region. And, finally, invasion would make it easier to confront other state supporters of terrorism through coercive diplomacy.[88] In August 2002 Condoleezza Rice's staff prepared the rationale for war in a paper titled 'Ultimatum to Saddam Hussein and the Iraqi Regime'. It provided four main reasons for invasion going beyond the CIA assessment that Saddam had WMD stockpiles: first, Iraq's WMD capability and infrastructure; second, its support for terrorism; third, threats to neighbours; and finally its tyrannical nature. Essentially what Feith describes as the WMD plus three Ts.[89] In the 14 August 2002 top-secret document 'Iraq: Goals, Objectives and Strategy' (mentioned earlier) the Bush administration also listed the reasons why Iraq's regime should be toppled. In this document it asserted six major points: first, eliminating the WMD threat; second, the means to deliver them; third, to prevent Saddam from breaking out of containment; fourth, to eliminate Iraq's threats to its neighbours; fifth, liberate Iraqi people from tyranny; and, finally, to prevent Baghdad supporting terrorists.[90] The problem with tyranny, Feith explains, was not merely the fact that Saddam was a threat to his own Kurdish and Shiite population, but the fact that in tyrannies there tended to be a lack of transparency, meaning diplomacy and agreements were hard to verify. Second, tyrannical regimes lacked any domestic checks or balances that could restrict the tyrant's freedom of action.[91]

Thus, the end of Saddam's regime became an ideal target in President Bush's War on Terror. Saddam Hussein was an unpredictable and ruthless dictator who could attack the US without any hesitation, therefore his removal was elevated to the top of the agenda.[92] Prevention was thus born from this form of thinking. The National Security Strategy (NSS) of September 2002 reflected this thinking. 'The greater the threat, the greater is the risk of inaction' – and the more 'compelling the case for taking anticipatory action' to defend America.[93]

In many respects, President Bush understood the danger of war, and wanted to avoid it as much as possible. This was particularly evident in his approach to North Korea and Iran. But when it came to Iraq, he felt that all channels had been spent for more than a decade. These channels included sixteen Security Council resolutions that Saddam had defied.[94] Iraq was considered in a class of its own when compared to other 'rogue nations'. In his State of the Union address the president made it clear that Iraq holds the potential to bring great harm to the US. The difference between Iraq and the two other Axis of Evil powers was that the US believed it had exhausted all means short of war to deal with the Iraqi threat.[95]

In this respect two different decisions were taken in the aftermath of 9/11. One was about the actual purpose of the war with Iraq and the other concerning Iraq after Saddam. As regards the first issue of regime change, Rubin stated among all US agencies there was 'almost unanimous agreement'[96] and asserted that the 'broad swath of the policymaking community agreed at the time'.[97] It was a decision that was supported across the board by republicans and influential democrats and public opinion. David Pollock, senior fellow at the Washington Institute for Near East Policy, stated that it is 'a serious error to look for some kind of small group'.[98] A National Security Council official explained that there were several camps that backed the decision to invade Iraq. The military camp (Pentagon) was arguing that US planes were being attacked on a daily basis, the intelligence camp (CIA) thought Iraq had weapons of mass destruction and Saddam supported terrorism. There were some people that believed a democratic Iraq would help the Middle East.[99] The majority of policy makers thought Iraq was a threat and dangerous, 'the risks were so great, not worth taking the risk'.[100] As regards the reason for the war there were a variety of motivations. Wilkerson asserted, 'different groups had different agendas' and 'different people had different motivations'.[101] Adam Garfinkle also believed that there was not one reason, but a host of people that had different reasons.[102] Pillar reiterated this sentiment. As far as motives were concerned there were 'different individual motives'. The president wanted something, the vice president something and Rumsfeld something else.[103]

As American financier J. P. Morgan once famously asserted, 'A man generally has two reasons for doing a thing. One that sounds good, and a real one.' The next section of this chapter addresses the various motivations and interests that led to the invasion of Iraq. It makes sense to look at the various reasons for war and the priority and place each reason held in terms of the decision-making process. For this reason a geological analogy is well suited to portraying this process by categorising the reasons into different layers: a crust (visible), mantle and core (underlying) may be used to express the various layers of reasons and the variety of motivations that helped drive the war on Iraq.

4.3.1 Pronounced 'sounds good' reasons: the crust

4.3.1.1 Weapons of mass destruction

The major reason the administration focused on WMD as a *casus belli* was because it would be 'easier to get attention that way' a National Security Council official told the author.[104] When it came to providing justification for war Rice believed it would be impossible to gain international support on Iraq's human rights records. The National Security Advisor also asserted that the terrorism issue was considered 'weak or unprovable'.[105] Thus, in light of Iraq's breach of numerous Security Council resolutions and its development of WMD it was considered the most reasonable channel to seek international support for a possible campaign in Iraq. Wolfowitz declared in 2003 that for bureaucratic reasons the administration had to settle on weapons of mass destruction, because it was the one reason everyone could agree on.[106] In an interview with *Vanity Fair* in May 2003, Wolfowitz stated:

> The truth is that for reasons that have a lot to do with the US government bureaucracy we settled on the one issue that everyone could agree on which was weapons of mass destruction as the core reason, but ... there have always been three fundamental concerns. One is weapons of mass destruction, the second is support for terrorism, the third is the criminal treatment of the Iraqi people.[107]

Pillar stated that policy makers did not ask him for anything resembling strategic input in relation to Iraq at all before the war.[108] According to Pillar, the policy makers did not ask questions, sought no intelligence and did not seek assessments. Even the Weapons Estimate was not requested by the administration but by the Democrats in Congress.[109] George Tenet, CIA Director, states in his memoirs that policy makers were not showing much curiosity as regards requests for new reports on Iraqi WMD and the implications of conflict in Iraq.[110] Even before the war General Franks made it clear to the president that there was a lack of evidence on WMD. He stated, 'Mr President, we've been looking for Scud missiles and other weapons of mass destruction for ten years and haven't found any yet.'[111]

The National Security Council official explained to the author that there had certainly been times when the US had involved itself in regional conflicts not because it had felt threatened itself but because international security had been at risk. But he also stressed that the Bush administration thought that the US was at risk from Iraq. The official was unequivocal: 'I have no doubt that they felt that Iraq was a threat, no doubt, it was a threat on homeland security.'[112] Senior Congressional staffer, Richard Kessler, stated that the key purpose, even prior to 9/11, was that Iraq was considered a centre for WMD production and had links to terrorism. Kessler affirmed, 'they did not make it up. They believed it sincerely.'[113]

In an interview with British journalist Trevor McDonald, President Bush stated, 'I made up my mind that Saddam needs to go'. He added,

> The worst thing that could happen would be to allow a nation like Iraq, run by Saddam Hussein, to develop weapons of mass destruction, and then team up with terrorist organisations so they can blackmail the world. I'm not going to let that happen.[114]

Post 9/11 there was a real feeling that America was going to be attacked again. It was not a matter of when but how bad and how soon. The administration was doing everything it possibly could to find threats and neutralise them quickly.[115] There was a genuine belief that Iraq had WMDs.[116]

The deeper root of the conflict was the US assumption that Saddam could not be deterred from using WMD.[117] George Tenet stresses that there was never a 'serious debate' about the imminence of a threat from Iraq before the war. It was, however, about acting before Saddam did.[118] Vice President Cheney was always a strong advocate of the war. He made his point clearly on *USS John C. Stennis*. 'The United States will not permit the forces of terror to gain the tools of genocide.' Frederick Kagan, Resident Scholar at AEI, asserted that the 'purpose was to eliminate WMD. We were wrong. There would not have been invasion if Saddam complied.'[119] Richard Perle echoed this view: 'If Saddam had convinced us that he didn't have WMD we wouldn't have gone in.'[120]

President Bush feared that Saddam might use his nuclear weapons when acquired to 'blackmail the United States'.[121] Former Congressman and marine Lieutenant Colonel James Longley stressed that it was universally understood that Saddam had WMD.[122] The most important incident advancing the Iraq invasion was a week after 9/11, when five anthrax-laden letters stopped Congress from working. With five letters the perpetrator managed to freeze the administration. The US suspected that it was far too sophisticated an operation for an individual or organisation to provide and orchestrate. And it was perceived as a message to the rest of the world that the US was weak. Saddam was well documented to have these anthrax spores, and was considered capable of doing this.[123] An exercise conducted a few weeks before 9/11 named 'Dark Winter' had already brought home the horrors of a possible smallpox attack on the US.[124]

American knowledge about Iraqi WMD went back to 1973. Republican Congressman Robert Huber of Michigan told Congress of Soviet supplies of poison gas to Iraq to suppress its Kurdish minority on 6 November of that year.[125] Moreover, mention of Iraqi WMD and chemical weapons, as discussed earlier in Chapter 2, specifically was made during Rumsfeld's first visit to Baghdad in 1983 when meeting with Tariq Aziz. But this issue was only mentioned in the context of a range of issues relevant to US–Iraq relations.[126]

In the aftermath of the 9/11 attacks, the US revised all the threats to its national security. All vulnerabilities overlooked prior to the attack were viewed in a different light. All threats whether or not directly related to al-Qaeda were explored. Iraq having been a concern before the attacks seemed graver and more serious.[127] The CIA reports stressed that Saddam's regime possessed chemical and biological weapons stockpiles.[128] This turned out to be incorrect. However, Saddam had retained the expertise and facilities to resume a WMD programme.[129] The Iraq Survey Group report findings after the invasion explicitly stated that Iraq had dual-use capabilities to resume its programmes if it wished. It also had the scientific know-how to achieve this goal after sanctions were removed.[130]

The nature of the 9/11 attacks and the amount of carnage was unprecedented. It was perceived as a case of 'terrorism of mass destruction', a departure from previous acts of attention-seeking political theatre. To this end the US found it utterly unacceptable to risk allowing WMD to fall in the hands of terrorist organisations, leading to focused attention on WMD-acquiring, terrorist-supporting, states.[131] Rumsfeld had argued that the chief strategic danger was that an extremist group would obtain WMD. And considering Saddam had a track record of WMD production and terrorism sponsorship, he was seen as a potential supplier. Thus Rumsfeld stated that the Iraq campaign should 'focus on WMD'.[132] Donald Rumsfeld also defended regime change in Iraq as a message to countries pursuing WMD 'that having them ... is attracting attention that is not favourable and is not helpful'.[133]

The Bush administration was genuinely concerned about a combination of WMD and terrorists. It represented the next potential danger it wanted to deal with. The policy essentially was to deal with the threat of WMD possessed by Saddam Hussein. Richard Perle explained that after 9/11 'We didn't know the full scope of the attack.' The Bush administration thought WMD would fall to al-Qaeda, so attention was turned immediately to this issue. The US had intelligence that al-Qaeda was attempting to acquire WMD. The administration had asked itself whether it had to expect others to come and, if so, how to prevent them. The US made a list of potential WMD suppliers to terrorists and Iraq was high on the list. The concern was 'not that Saddam would attack America directly'. The concern was that Saddam would share his WMD with terrorists. The United States knew Saddam hated the US. Saddam was bitter about his defeat, 'he cheered 9/11. He approved 9/11.' Although it turned out to be factually wrong that Saddam had WMD and was a likely supplier thereof for terrorists, he did have the capacity to produce them even though he did not have a stockpile.[134]

4.3.1.2 Sponsoring terrorism

Bush asserted that terrorism was a state of mind that had to be defeated. The president affirmed to congressional leaders 'They hate Christianity. They hate Judaism. They hate everything that is not them.'[135] President Bush's broad concept of a War on Terror was shared by Rumsfeld. The secretary helped the president develop its premise and objectives and worldwide nature. Rumsfeld warned against restricting it to al-Qaeda and Afghanistan and failing to define it as a worldwide threat.[136]

The main factor which led to the US invasion of Iraq and the overthrow of Saddam was the potential threat of terrorist action. Cheney states in his memoirs that when they looked around the world in the first months after 9/11 there was 'no place more likely to be a nexus between terrorism and WMD capability than Saddam Hussein's Iraq'.[137] David Pollock stated that there was 'no ideological agenda' except to address fears and vulnerabilities exposed by 9/11. The event created a genuine concern that Saddam's regime might be inspired to attempt something of the kind. It created a different political atmosphere in Washington where such threats were perceived more likely and more politically acceptable to contemplate.[138]

Iraq was first placed on the State Department's list of state sponsors of terrorism in 1979 as a founding member. It was removed in May 1982 after it agreed to close down the Abu Nidal Organisation. It was re-included in 1990 after Saddam's occupation of Kuwait.[139] Iraq was perceived as connected heavily with terrorist groups. It had resumed refuge to Abu Nidal. Iraq had provided a safe haven to Abdul–Rahman Yasin, the Iraqi who was believed to have been associated with the World Trade Centre attacks in 1993. It had also provided sanctuary to Abu Abbas, the Palestinian who had hijacked the cruise ship *Achille Lauro* in 1985. The training of foreign fighters was also conducted in Iraq.[140] Saddam also allowed groups recognised as terrorist organisations in Washington, like the Mojahedin-e-Khalq, Kurdistan Workers' Party (PKK) and the Palestine Liberation Front to operate on Iraqi soil.[141] Before the war, on 26 February 2003, Bush stated that Saddam's removal 'will deprive terrorist networks of a wealthy patron' that funds terrorist training, and 'offers rewards to families of suicide bombers'. It would be a 'clear warning' that support for terror will 'not be tolerated'.[142] Within this context a major purpose of the War on Terror was to protect the American way of life. The policy makers at the Pentagon thought it would be a travesty to allow the threat of terrorism to curtail civil liberties in America.[143]

In his 2003 State of the Union address Bush outlined to the American people the threats posed by Saddam's regime and the potential damage his regime could do.[144] He stated that a brutal dictator, with a history of reckless aggression, with 'ties to terrorism', with great potential wealth would not be permitted to dominate a vital region and threaten the United States.[145] In response to a question by Bob Woodward on the president's expectations for the consequences of the Iraq war Bush replied that it was his responsibility to 'secure America'. Bush reiterated that his frame of mind was focused on 'the solemn duty to protect America'.[146] The Bush administration also had in mind the opportunity of fighting terrorism outside US territory. On 7 September 2003 Bush stated that the 'surest way to avoid attacks on our own people is to engage the enemy where he lives and plans'. He stressed that the US was fighting the enemy in Iraq and Afghanistan 'so that we do not meet him again on our own streets, in our own cities'.[147] Another US objective was to find in Iraq 'an ally on the War on Terror'.[148]

To the US government, law enforcement was a deterrent, a method to punish not prevent. America came to recognise that it could no longer treat terrorism as a law enforcement matter. War was considered a suitable method to prevent further attacks. This included other actors from a broader spectrum than those responsible for 9/11.[149] Douglas Feith had drafted a paper entitled 'Strategic Thoughts' on behalf of Rumsfeld which captured the concept of the US global War on Terror. The draft was edited by Rumsfeld and sent to the president on 30 September 2001. The core concept of this paper was the focus on 'state actors' as the sources of threat and potential danger to the national security of the US through the procurement of nuclear and biological weapons for terrorist organisations. It was the objective of this paper to suggest to the president that a rational course of action was to target some rogue states militarily, with the consequence of making other state sponsors change their policies on supporting terrorism. The overall enterprise was military action or diplomatic pressure to disrupt terrorist activities in the long run.[150]

The Defense Department was convinced that a war with Saddam Hussein was part of the War on Terror. Two other documents were established towards this end. The first, on 3 October 2001, was 'Strategic Guidance for the Defense Department' followed by the June 2002 'Political-Military Strategic Plan for Iraq'. Both documents defined the War on Terror as 'a confrontation with state and non-state supporters of terrorist groups, as well as the terrorist groups themselves'. The objective of this plan was to focus on states that supported terrorism as well as aspiring to WMD. The June 2002 document also stressed that a war with Iraq should not be for the sake of ending Saddam's threat per se but also to 'convince and compel other countries to renounce WMD and support to terrorism'.[151]

Pillar argued that Feith was creating impressions to advance the cause and sell the war. However, Pillar stressed that it was not about 'fabricating evidence', but rather stitching things together in a way to promote a perception that things were different from what they were. So much of it rendered false impressions to the American public; it was not a matter of fabricating one particular fact, partly drawing conclusions that were not justified, to convey there was an operational alliance between Iraq and al-Qaeda. Pillar emphasised that it was a matter of rhetoric with a constant drumbeat about 9/11 and Iraq, using the same two things in the same sentence.[152] According to Pillar, the intelligence community, despite being pushed, turned over every stone; the basic judgement being that there was no alliance between Saddam and al-Qaeda.[153]

Paul Wolfowitz firmly held the view that the invasion of Iraq was the right thing to do. After 9/11 Wolfowitz believed that terrorism was no longer a manageable evil. It had to be handled and dealt with even if at the expense of American lives. The networks had to be destroyed and the sponsoring states attacked. To Wolfowitz, Saddam's regime had long deserved to be overthrown, but 9/11 had only made this necessity more obvious.[154]

4.3.1.3 Liberation

Bush had a great interest in seeing the US being perceived as a liberator rather than an occupier, and he made this known to his war council before the start of the Afghan war. He wanted visible humanitarian assistance delivered to the Afghan people, emphasising the moral mission of the United States.[155] President Bush made his aspirations known to his aides after 9/11 when preparing his 2002 State of the Union speech:

> Let me make sure you understand what I just said about the role of the United States. I believe the United States is the beacon for freedom in the world. And I believe we have a responsibility to promote freedom that is as solemn as the responsibility is to protecting the American people, because the two go hand-in-hand. No, it's very important for you to understand that about my presidency.[156]

The 2002 State of the Union speech was never intended to be focused on the 'Axis of Evil', but rather to emphasise democratic liberties envisaged in a new Afghanistan. It was more of a message to the Muslim nations that all liberties supersede the power of the state.[157] Bush further asserted this: 'I say that freedom is not America's gift to the world. Freedom is God's gift to everybody in the world ... and I believe we have a duty to free people.'[158]

The Bush administration's ambition to promote democracy was as heavily linked to changing the domestic politics of Iraq and the region as it was about human rights concerns. Bush believed that action in Iraq was not merely about 'strategic purposes or defensive purposes' but also about the 'immense suffering' and 'the human condition that we must worry about'. President Bush had referred to starvations and hunger in North Korea and Iraq and his passion to attend to these phenomena.[159]

Bush explains in his memoirs 'how anyone could deny that liberating Iraq advanced the cause of human rights'.[160] Bush clearly indicated in his 2002 State of the Union address to the American nation that he had a new emphasis, asserting US commitment towards 'human dignity'. Rice thought this had never been so vividly expressed as a US objective in American history.[161] In his West Point address he conveyed the purpose of his new foreign policy: 'We have a great opportunity to extend a just peace by replacing poverty, repression and resentment around the world with hope of a better day.'[162] In his 2002 NSS Bush asserted 'we will extend the peace by encouraging free and open societies on every continent', expressing his intention to 'use this moment of opportunity to extend the benefits of freedom across the globe'. Bush was adamant about this cause; to him 'freedom is the non-negotiable demand of human dignity; the birthright of every person – in every civilisation'. Bush stressed that 'The United States welcomes our responsibility to lead in this great mission'.[163] On the evening of Operation Iraqi Freedom (OIF) Bush stated 'We will defend our freedom. We will bring freedom to others and we will prevail.' The liberation of Iraqis was a major part of his thinking.[164] Bush felt that the 'first to benefit from a free Iraq would be the Iraqi people, themselves'.[165]

4.3.2 Unpronounced underlying reasons: the mantle

4.3.2.1 Ending the threat to Israel

One of the reasons the US believed that Saddam's overthrow would be favourable was the threat Iraq posed to the region, especially towards US-friendly allies in the Middle East. The security of oil-rich Arab Gulf states and Israel especially was definitely a motive. However, contrary to conventional wisdom, pressure from Israel and the Jewish lobby was not a major factor behind the decision to attack Iraq in March 2003. Nonetheless, it was not insignificant. David Mack explained that he met with numerous members of the Israeli government and intelligence before the war. In their minds Iran was the real threat and Iraq a secondary issue. Israel played a part in US views, but not the most important part.[166] According to Mack, even for neoconservatives, Israel was not the major factor. Saddam's toppling would be better not only for the US but for all the people of the Middle East.[167] There were regular visits from members of Mossad, the Israeli Defence Force, the Israeli Likud Party and other representatives of Israeli society and government, initially to dissuade the US from the invasion of Iraq because they thought Iran was the principal target and the Iraq campaign would only lead to a disequilibrium in the balance of power in the Gulf. But once they concluded that the US was going to war in Iraq they were willing to help with intelligence and influence on the American Jewish community.[168]

The war, however, was motivated in good part by a desire to make Israel more secure. According to Philip Zelikow, a former member of President Bush's Foreign Intelligence Advisory Board, the executive director of the 9/11 Commission and a counsellor to Condoleezza Rice, the 'real threat' from Iraq was not a threat to the United States. The 'unstated threat' was the 'threat against Israel', Zelikow told an audience at the University of Virginia in September 2002. 'The American government', he added, 'doesn't want to lean too hard on it rhetorically, because it is not a popular sell.' Also within the US, a main driving force behind the war was a small band of neoconservatives, many Jewish, and many with ties to Likud. Mearsheimer and Walt argue it would be wrong to blame the war in Iraq on 'Jewish influence'. Rather, it was due in large part to the Israeli lobby's influence, especially that of the neoconservatives within it.[169] Sympathy for Israel played a role as Wolfowitz in particular had strong ties with Israel.[170] The rising influence of evangelicals also affected US foreign policy by increasing US support to Israel.[171] The neoconservatives' focus on the Middle East combined with Christian belief regarding the Second Coming of Christ to the land of Israel, created a sense of common purpose and unity with the Christian evangelicals, which advanced the neoconservative agenda.[172]

On 11 September 2002, Bush met with eleven House members and clearly told them, 'The biggest threat, however, is Saddam Hussein and his weapons of mass destruction. He can blow up Israel and that would trigger an international conflict.'[173] Bush also told a group of Congress members on 26 September 2002: 'Saddam Hussein is a terrible guy who is teaming up with al-Qaeda. He tortures his own people and hates Israel.'[174] And several weeks before the American invasion of Iraq in a speech to the largely pro-Israeli American Enterprise Institute, Bush explained that removing Saddam from power 'could also begin a new stage for Middle Eastern peace' by depriving Palestinians of a wealthy patron.[175]

In April 2004, after the Iraq invasion, President Bush advised the Palestinians that the 'realities on the ground and in the region have changed greatly over the last several decades'. The president wanted a Palestinian acknowledgment to 'take into account those realities'. The implication of Bush's overthrow of Saddam was the destruction of a major sponsor to Palestinian activities. With Saddam's departure this wealthy and radical Arab nationalist support structure would no longer exist. The president advised that 'in light of new realities on the ground', which included 'already existing major Israeli population centres', it was unrealistic for the Palestinians to expect that the outcome of final status negotiations would be a full and complete return to the armistice lines of 1949.[176]

4.3.2.2 Easy target

To the Bush administration, Iraq was the 'lowest hanging fruit'.[177] The relative ease in which the Afghanistan war had panned out further fuelled this perception. Scooter Libby believed, the war in Afghanistan going well, that it would be a good idea to sell a war on Iraq within the broader framework of the War on Terror.[178] The Bush administration believed that Iraq was an inviting target, not because it was an immediate threat in any way but a potential threat. Rather it was a strategic opportunity to deliver the US message of pre-emption.[179] The US perceived 9/11 as an opening window for the opportunity to take action. Iraq was a prime target belonging to the Axis of Evil group and having significant vulnerabilities; it was an ideal candidate for regime change.[180] Moreover, the US was convinced that Iraqi forces were no match for America. Perle in an article in the summer of 2002 doubted the Iraqi military's effectiveness and competence. Perle stated that the Iraqi forces were a third of what they had been in 1991 and '11 years closer to obsolescence'.[181] Iraq was still stuck with what it had remaining from its First Gulf War's 1970s Soviet arsenal while the US had taken military technology to unprecedented levels of sophistication, power and accuracy.[182] Rice had even clarified in her 2000 *Foreign Affairs* article that Iraq was internationally isolated, its 'conventional military power has been severely restricted'.[183]

Though the US felt Iraq was weak, it also had no concrete intelligence on Iraq's genuine lack of WMD. To US military commanders WMD was a major threat. The military campaign's swift nature and the 'Shock and Awe' strategy were most probably the major reasons for this course of action. Iraq's conventional army posed no serious challenge to the US military establishment. America feared Iraqi biological and chemical attacks. Tommy Franks, CENTCOM commander, had made available special protective suits in case of such attacks. All forces were prepared to respond to incidents involving biological and chemical weapons. On the eve of the war Franks had received intelligence that Iraqi frontline units and

Republican Guards had been armed with nerve and mustard gas, anthrax and *botu-linum* toxins.[184] CENTCOM had produced leaflets and dropped hundreds of thousands of them on Iraqi positions. The leaflets warned that Iraqi units will face 'severe retribution' and unit commanders will be 'held accountable' if WMD is used.[185] Franks was equally convinced that a speedy strike against Saddam's regime would decrease the chances of any successful Iraqi WMD attacks on the invading force. Franks had told his commanders that speed of advance would kill the enemy and disrupt the Iraqis' ability to react effectively.[186]

4.3.2.3 Democracy promotion

Bush's war to disarm Iraq, topple Saddam and rebuild a viable state is something that defied political reason, as the president was betting his whole presidency on it. Bush was 'a man on a mission'. Thomas Friedman describes it as something coming from his own belief as it was a war of choice.[187] Bush expressed his intentions on 26 February 2003: 'A new regime in Iraq would serve as a dramatic and inspiring example of freedom for other nations in the region.'[188] US foreign policy has always had a 'missionary streak'. It was based on the premise that the US has an obligation to 'spread our values and way of life', Mack stressed.[189]

Condoleezza Rice's paper prepared for the Principals' Committee meeting on 9 August 2002 titled 'Liberation Strategy for Iraq' (mentioned earlier) was one of the first documents prepared to this end. One of the points made was to create a democratic and unified Iraq that can be a model of good governance for the region and a strategic partner of the United States, as such Iraq would have a 'transforming effect on the region'.[190] The paper was testimony to Rice's own strong support for democracy promotion in the Middle East and also reflected the 'intensity of the president's commitment to the idea'.[191]

Cheney was concerned about the president's vision of a new Iraq, not just the replacement of Saddam Hussein, but creating a democracy. He knew neither the State Department nor its secretary were sympathetic nor envisaged a transformation in the region. They believed democracy was a step too far for a place like Iraq that had never experienced truly representative government.[192] Cheney himself had argued in meetings with other Principals that the US had an obligation to stand up a democracy in Iraq. He asserted that the United States had to give the Iraqi people a chance at those fundamental values 'we believe in'.[193] Cheney stated on 9 August 2002 that 'we should make it clear that we are intent on major democratic change'.[194]

After 9/11 the US became more interested in promoting democratic institutions as a method to tackle jihadist extremism.[195] Bush's Middle East policy to promote democracy came in part to counteract populace anger exploited by hardline Islamist groups.[196] The creation of a democratic Iraq would help counter political extremism in the Muslim world. This was something the US hoped for. Nevertheless, Feith also stresses that the US officials' main priority was to protect the National Security of the US and in no way to control Iraq in the long term or compel them to do things the US way.[197] The idea of promoting demo-cracy in the region as a whole was only incidentally connected with Iraq. The origins of democracy promotion lay in 9/11. Thus, democracy was to be a long-term solution to the problem of terrorism.[198]

The debate in Washington before the invasion was whether to replace Saddam with one of his generals or whether to try to set Iraq on a fundamentally demo-cratic path. That was when the neoconservatives chimed in.[199] Rubin stated that the debate's premise was, if there was a war, would the US replace Saddam with a 'General or establish democracy'; neoconservatives advocated democracy.[200] Perle stated that democracy was not a motivation in the war, 'but we didn't want another dictator'.[201]

The Bush Doctrine is vulnerable to criticism, not necessarily because it is a departure from previous policies, but rather due to the incompatibility of its means with the ends, and the difficulties of achieving those ends. Only when military power is reconciled with moral clarity can ends and means unite in a winning outcome. The democratisation of the Middle East required both preven-tive war and supporting authoritative regimes; both means were contradictory to the end result of democratisation.[202]

The spread of democratic institutions around the world in the twentieth century had benefited US security and freedom. The US knew it was proven that war between democratic states is highly unlikely.[203] President Bush urged Iraq to adopt democracy. But Feith argues that that was as far as US interests could stretch in terms of the future governance of Iraq. According to Feith, US inter-ests in a new Iraq were restricted to an Iraqi government that did not create the four problems of the previous regime: aggression towards neighbours, support for terrorism, killing its own citizens and WMD aspirations. Feith describes US interests as both national and humanitarian and all four covered core American interests in Iraq.[204]

The Bush administration has been criticised for thinking it could easily export democracy to Iraq. But Feith asserts that that was never the thinking for a country that lacked a democratic past. He explains that it was always considered a difficult task since Iraq lacked the cultural and institutional building blocks to adopt democracy easily. Though it was recognised as a complex task it was deemed possible as the history of democratic progress suggested.[205] President Bush believed that many positive things had occurred in Iraq. He also under-stood that Iraq would be a difficult and time-consuming issue, but asserted that he was optimistic of the outcome, 'it's just a matter of time, it's a matter of society evolving. It's a matter of a sovereignty issue evolving.' Bush believed the US intervention was 'changing a mentality'.[206] The president was adamant in his belief in the necessity of promoting democracy. Bush believed the world had a clear interest in the spread of democratic values, as stable and free nations do not breed the ideologies of murder. Free people 'encourage the peaceful pursuit of a better life'.[207]

4.3.2.4 A broader purpose: transforming a region

On 15 September 2001 President Bush made it clear that the intention of his campaign had a larger implication to the broader international community. To him the Afghan campaign against al-Qaeda and its Taliban host was a message to other countries like Iran who had supported terrorism to change their behaviour.[208] Bush's major attention was on the Persian Gulf, a targeted focus on Iraq, while keeping an eye on Iran as well. The US perceived Iraq as a ripe target in the Middle East.[209] Iraq was to play the role Poland had achieved in changing Eastern Europe in 1989, but this time in reforming the Middle East.[210] President Bush made it clear to his war cabinet that the Middle East had to be reformed. In a NSC meeting on 17 September 2001 he stressed that the defeat of the Taliban transmitted a vital message to rogue states: 'Let's hit them hard. We want to signal this is a change from the past. We want to cause other countries like Syria and Iran to change their views. We want to hit as soon as possible.'[211]

President Bush admired how Harry Truman had made the most of the political capital he had attained after America's Second World War victory and believed he too had to make the most of his newly found political capital after the US Afghan victory.[212] The president had made it clear that with his new War on Terror a new era was about to be born. He told a group of business leaders in New York that he truly believed that out of the War on Terror will come 'more order in the world' and 'real progress to peace in the Middle East, stability with oil-producing regions'.[213] Cheney knew Bush truly believed in the transformation of the Middle East, and knew that the president had faith that Iraq would be the stepping stone towards the promotion of freedom and democracy in the region.[214] On 14 April 2003 Cheney said 'Democracy in the Middle East is just a big deal for him. It's what's driving him.'[215]

Bush wanted to change the US foreign policy mindset, so he used his second inaugural speech to address this issue. He wanted his speech to reflect his ambitions for the spread of liberty as a requisite for the defence of the future of America and its security. It was intended to be the most dramatic shift since the beginning of the Cold War in the late 1940s with policies such as containment and deterrence.[216] The Greater Middle East had emerged as Bush's major foreign policy preoccupation with a solid scheme titled the GMEI (Greater Middle East Initiative) in 2004, endorsed in his January 2005 State of the Union speech. This geopolitical theatre included the entire Middle East, North Africa, Central Asia, Afghanistan and Pakistan.[217]

The motivation behind the use of American power to get rid of Saddam, in an important Middle East state was a desire to use regime change in Iraq as a catalyst to shake up the politics and economics in the entire Middle East. This was also very much a neoconservative objective.[218] Iran was considered as the obstacle and entrance to dramatic reform in the Middle East. However, Iraq had to be dealt with first. Rice stated that Iran presented major setbacks to US interests in the region. It was destabilising US allies in the region, it supported terrorism and was advancing its military capabilities, it was a major menace in the Middle

East hindering US interests, a region of great value to the US and its key ally Israel.[219]

Rice believed that as a result of the US invasion of Iraq the old authoritarian structure of the Middle East had been challenged and destroyed. A new order would emerge. It was the beginning of change for the region. However, this would require time, in the same way that both world wars had changed the geo-political structure of Europe.[220] The Bush administration believed that for sixty years the US had pursued stability at the expense of democracy in the Middle East, but had 'achieved neither'. This was stated unequivocally by Rice in Cairo in 2005; she continued: 'Now, we are taking a different course. We are support-ing the democratic aspirations of all people.'[221] In a speech to the American Enterprise Institute in February 2003, Bush argued for a democratic transforma-tion of Iraq that would eventually promote the political liberalisation of the Middle East. A free and liberated Iraq, according to his administration's calcula-tions, would serve as a model that would motivate and inspire people of the region to good governance.

> A new regime in Iraq would serve as a dramatic and inspiring example of freedom for other nations in the region. It is presumptuous and insulting to suggest that a whole region of the world or the one-fifth of humanity that is Muslim is somehow untouched by the most basic aspirations of life.[222]

The democratic crusade of the Bush administration was a clear triumph for many neoconservatives inside and outside the administration. They believed that democratic governance would favour US interests in the long run. However, realists outside the administration such as Scowcroft believed it was in the US interest, and a requisite of US foreign policy, to maintain friendly relations with authoritarian regimes that provided regional stability.[223]

In its 20 September 2001 letter to Bush, the PNAC stipulated that US policy must aim not only at finding the people responsible for 9/11, but must also target those 'other groups out there that mean us no good'.[224] There was a clear meeting of minds between the president, many of the Principals and the neoconservatives which made the venture possible. Robert Kagan and William Kristol asserted that the removal of Saddam Hussein from power will determine the 'contours of the emerging world order, perhaps for decades to come'. They envisaged two possible scenarios, one with, the other without Saddam. The world order without Saddam would be one in line with liberal democratic principles and US security. The alternative, however, a world order where 'tyrants are allowed to hold democracy and international security hostage'.[225] In their book, *The War Over Iraq*, William Kristol of the *Weekly Standard* and Lawrence Kaplan of the *New Republic* asserted that the war was 'so clearly about more than Iraq ... more even than the future of the Middle East'. It would allow 'what sort of role the United States intends to play in the world in the twenty-first century'.[226] The Iraq war, Jay Bookman argues, was to mark the emergence of a fully fledged global empire.[227]

The invasion of Iraq was thought would allow the creation of permanent military bases to dominate the region. The 2002 NSS asserted 'The United States will require bases and stations within and beyond Western Europe and Northeast Asia.'[228] However, Longley asserted that the United States did not necessarily want permanent bases, but what it wanted was to maintain stability.[229]

America's main concern was Iran which influenced US decisions towards Iraq, as Iran was perceived as a highly significant threat to the area and the West.[230] Some in the administration believed that, once the Iraqi regime was toppled, Iraqi Shiites would become US allies; especially with the holy cities of Karbala and Najaf situated in Iraq they would be able to undermine Iran.[231] Shiism would also become a viable ideological tool to promote denationalisation in much of the Sunni Middle East.[232] Neoconservatives were more sympathetic towards the Iraqi Shiite as the majority of the country. In this context there was a greater tendency among the neoconservatives to argue that not all Shiite are the same, and that the Iraqi Shiite and the Iranian government should not be seen as necessarily sympathetic to the same ideals.[233]

There were three potential advantages of democracy in Iraq. A liberal Iraq would exert further pressure on Iran's leaders to open up. Iraq could replace Saudi Arabia as the key US ally, and finally it would encourage other liberalising regimes in the region to advance on their path towards democracy.[234] The US believed it should use its unparalleled power to make strategic moves and fundamental alterations rather than small play. Their vision, as Rice described it, was one for an impact comparable to that of post Second World War in 1947 when it started to lead the free world.[235]

4.3.2.5 Oil

Iraq sat on the third largest proven oil reserves in the world, so it was hugely important to American interests that Iraq be stabilised.[236] A definite motivation for an interventionist foreign policy is material interests, and one that is relevant to US Middle East is oil.[237] The free flow of oil at reasonable prices from the Persian Gulf oil is a major US strategic objective of the United States in the Middle East.[238] It could be argued validly that despite recent developments in the Middle East, US goals in the region have been surprisingly clear and consistent. Oil has remained one of its three pillars. The others are Israel's security and intense opposition to the emergence of any other regional hegemon.[239] Hence, a US strategic objective in Iraq was to secure oil.[240] A major US consideration in the Middle East is regional control of oil reserves, its pricing and supply routes of the nearby Persian Gulf.[241] The Iraq war would 'allow the world to enjoy lower oil prices'.[242] Oil was a critical element but not in any way related to the US stealing Iraq's oil. A democratic regime would through necessity pump oil out on to the world markets for its own benefit, increasing world oil supplies. Second, Iraq would possibly use American oil companies to develop its existing oil fields and vast untapped oil reserves.[243]

Marcy Katpur, who is US House Member for Ohio (Democrat), argued in Congress that 'the driving force of this potential war on Iraq is oil'.[244] The toppling of Saddam would indeed guarantee a secure output of oil in the hands of a pro-Western regime in Baghdad.[245] However, the oil issue, though not trivial, was a secondary consideration in US policy making. The US believed that Iraqi oil would pay for the reconstruction of the country.[246] Paul Wolfowitz in a Congressional hearing a month before the war, stated: 'there is a lot of money there. To assume that we are going to pay for it is just wrong.'[247] Many in the Bush administration thought that, because of its oil wealth, Iraq would pay for itself.[248] Additionally, it would also potentially replace US dependency on Saudi oil.[249]

4.3.2.6 Personal grievance: the assassination attempt on George H. W. Bush

Part of Bush's attempt at running for the presidency seems to have been his wish to put the Bush name back into the White House. Perhaps a sense of injustice existed in his psyche because his father had not been elected for a second term in office. In Bush's encounter in 1997 with Prince Bandar, Saudi ambassador to Washington, it seemed to the Prince that the 'younger George Bush wanted to avenge his father's loss to Clinton'. Bandar saw that the son was trying to say, 'I want to go after this guy and show who is better.'[250] To them, President Clinton lacked the experience and integrity to fulfil this role. Clinton was a Vietnam War draft evader, while Bush senior was a Second World War hero in their minds. The same determination to seek justice seems to have repeated itself before the Iraq invasion; this time, however, for Saddam's attempt to assassinate his father. During a fund-raiser speech for a Republican Senate candidate in September 2002, Bush cited a number of reasons, in addition to alleged terrorist links and weapons of mass destruction about why Saddam was so dangerous to the US, noting, in particular that, 'after all, this is the guy who tried to kill my dad'.[251] In his speech to the UN in 2002 he stated: 'in 1993, Iraq attempted to assassinate the Emir of Kuwait and a former American president'.[252] Also during a visit to the White House by eleven House members on 19 September 2002, when advised to mention Saddam's gassing of his own people, by Richard Burr, a North Carolina Republican, he responded, 'I am well aware, he tried to kill my dad.'[253] Bush junior's family connection to Bush senior and his targeting by Iraqi interests were not lost on his son.[254] The assassination attempt by Iraqi agents seems to have shaken the Bush household. It was an event vividly remembered in the family creating in them a personal detestation of Saddam Hussein and his regime.

4.3.3 The primary reason: the core

4.3.3.1 The war that never ended

According to Richard Haass the principal rationale for attacking Iraq was to signal to the world that even after 9/11, the United States was not, in Richard

Nixon's words, a 'pitiful, helpless giant'.[255] This may be true. There was also, however, a prevailing sentiment in Washington that the First Gulf War had not ended. Iraq was perceived by many as unfinished business and a remaining US national security concern. Elevating this concern was US officials who were convinced that Saddam would terminate the sanctions sooner or later if left in power. This would allow Iraq's resumption of its weapons programmes. A regime with such a history would eventually resume its aggressive actions and once again oblige the US to engage militarily. Feith argues that a probable second attack on Kuwait would have invited US involvement albeit this time with a more dangerous and hostile Iraq.[256]

The Bush administration was also worried that the inspectors would go back and find nothing, subsequently the international community would ask for a lifting of the sanctions. Rice made this clear in a meeting with senior Congress members at the White House.[257] After the invasion, the second Head of the Iraq Survey Group, Charles Duelfer, described in his report the sanctions as considerably weakened and concluded that Saddam was actively designing a missile programme in 2000 and 2001 the components of which could be procured outside the sanctions regime.[258] A senior Congressional staffer stated that by the end of 2002 Iraq no longer had any limits on its oil production under the OFF programme. This was also a source of concern as Iraq could keep larger sums of its oil revenue.[259] The strongest argument for the war was that Saddam was getting out of his cage. Better to fight him when weak rather than strong.[260]

Even if Saddam were to give everything up but stayed in power, the administration was convinced that as soon as the world was preoccupied with other issues, Saddam would be back again rebuilding his biological and chemical capabilities, and reconstituting his nuclear programme. Cheney had explained that the problem was, as before, that Saddam would still be in power.[261] The mental mood of the administration was if Saddam admitted he had weapons of mass destruction, then 'he is violating United Nations resolutions' and had 'deceived the world'. If he said he had none, then he 'is once again misleading the world'.[262]

The anonymous National Security Council official interviewed for this book stated there was a big difference between how the war was sold and the 'real reasons' the US went in. The United Stated believed the sanctions and the No-fly zones weren't working. So the US felt it had to make a policy change. According to the NSC staffer the US war with Iraq had never technically ended. US planes were targeted by Iraqi defences and this was perceived as an 'act of war'.[263] Longley argued that it was a major failure of US action in respect to the Iraq invasion not explaining 'why we really did what we did'.[264]

The purpose of the US invasion of Iraq to remove Saddam Hussein's government was based on the threat that Saddam posed to United States forces and the difficulty of sustaining that force level indefinitely in the Persian Gulf. Within a short time after the fall of Baghdad, the US removed most the forces it had based in Saudi Arabia when Kuwait was invaded. This made an immediate change to America's strategic posture in the region. The US did not want to maintain large numbers of troops in the region simply to check Saddam's behaviour.[265]

The primary reason the US went to war was the strategic aftermath of the First Gulf War. America had lost patience. Saddam had failed to moderate his government and continued to pose a threat to the Middle East requiring vast expenditures of men and material from the US.[266] The invasion of Iraq was to a large extent related to Operation Southern Watch, first imposed in 1991, in part to protect the Iraqi Shiite population and to make possible the US containment strategy. Contingents of the US Air Force based in Saudi Arabia were conducting the patrols of the southern No-fly zone. Certain policy makers, the vice president in particular, believed that was why al-Qaeda was attacking the US.[267] There was an understanding that Bin Laden had instigated action against the US and because Saddam's actions had drawn the US into a lengthy commitment in Saudi Arabia.[268] Administration officials thought if America withdrew from Saudi Arabia it would deny al-Qaeda one of its primary reasons to attack the US, but in order to do this it would have to get rid of Southern Watch but to do that it had to get rid of Saddam first.[269]

According to Longley, the 'real reason' the US went to war in Iraq was primarily due to the history of the First Gulf War, the ceasefire, and Iraq's failure to comply with the terms of this ceasefire.[270] After 9/11 there was a feeling of frustration with Saddam Hussein that the US was constantly dealing with the same issues since 1991. US military commitments in the region were large and had to be continually modified in response to Saddam's constant acts of non-compliance. This required significant expense in terms of personnel, money and equipment. The US had invested heavily to enforce the No-fly zones to keep Saddam at bay.[271] Longley described it as a 'cat and mouse game'.[272]

The end of the Gulf War was a ceasefire, not a surrender, with conditions stipulating what Saddam could and could not do.[273] Frederick Kagan stressed that the Iraq invasion was undertaken on the basis of UNSCR resolutions that had been passed in the 1990s that had ended the First Gulf War. In Kagan's view the invasion of Iraq took place under the auspices of the UNSC resolutions. Kagan clarified that it was important to keep in mind that there was no formal peace agreement that ended the First Gulf War. The First Gulf War had ended in a ceasefire – it was a 'conditional ceasefire'. The conditions were that Iraq submit to the unfettered inspection regime of the IAEA and UNSCOM. In Kagan's opinion Saddam had very self-evidently failed to adhere to that condition which, from the standpoint of the US and international law, rendered the ceasefire void. And considering that the ceasefire was void, the original UN resolutions that authorised all necessary means to impose these inspections on Iraq came back into play in Kagan's words. From Kagan's view that was the 'international legal basis' for the invasion.[274] Lawrence Wilkerson was willing to state that 'Iraq was a different matter' and that 'there was really no stop to the First Gulf War' and that it was 'only a ceasefire'. Wilkerson emphasised that a case could be made in International Law that it was a continuation of US foreign policy.[275] The Bush administration's Iraq policy was a continuation of a policy that the Clinton administration had also articulated. It was to prevent Saddam Hussein from acquiring WMD and escape the international inspection verification regime that Saddam had signed up to, and a US willingness to use force to enforce this. Clinton had fired rockets in 1998 at Iraq and maintained the No-fly zones. In terms of the use of force this was a continuation of that policy. Kagan stressed that there was no departure in US Iraq policy and that there was a 'tremendous amount of policy continuity'. After 9/11 the Bush administration decided that the threat posed by an Iraq potentially in possession of WMDs was greater than had been previously imagined. The policy before the invasion had continued to be regime change. This remained a constant desire of the Clinton administration, as it was for Bush senior's administration. It was 'only a change in the method by which that strategy was going to be implemented'.[276] Regime change in Iraq was consistent in US policy but was given greater urgency because of the impact of 9/11 on the US mindset. The attacks on 9/11 had 'only amplified the sense of threat'.[277]

The decision to invade Iraq, motivated by different reasons and purposes and attributed to different motivations and ideological factions within the administration, eventually led to the invasion of Iraq on 19 March 2003. Saddam's regime fell in spectacularly speedy fashion in three weeks, testimony to US military supremacy and its unrivalled technological advancements. However, what technological advancements could not achieve nor address was the Phase IV post-hostilities period which is the backbone to success of any military venture involving the occupation of a foreign country. The following chapter attempts to address US Iraq policy in post-Saddam Iraq, the mistakes, changes of course and adjustments in US strategy in pursuit of US strategic goals for the new Iraq under the George W. Bush and Obama administrations.

Notes

1 George W. Bush. (2003b). *President Bush Meets with Prime Minister Blair.* [The White House] Available at: URL: http://georgewbush-whitehouse.archives.gov/news/releases/2003/01/20030131–23.html Access Date: 20 June 2008.
2 Daniel Pipes. (2004). *Conversations with History: Militant Islam.* [University of California, Berkeley: Institute of International Studies] Available at: URL: http://globetrotter.berkeley.edu/people4/Pipes/pipes-con4.html Access Date: 15 March 2008.
3 Paul Wolfowitz. (2001). *DoD News Briefing – Deputy Secretary Wolfowitz.* Available at: URL: www.dartmouth.edu/~govdocs/docs/iraq/dod.htm Access Date: 17 February 2008.
4 Bob Woodward, *Plan of Attack* (London: Simon and Schuster, 2004), p. 25.
5 Bob Woodward, *Bush at War* (London: Simon and Schuster, 2002), p. 49.
6 Douglas Feith, *War and Decision: Inside the Pentagon at the Dawn of the War on Terrorism* (New York: HarperCollins Publishers, 2008), p. 14.
7 Ibid., p. 15.
8 Michael Gordon and Bernard Trainor, *Cobra II: The Inside Story of the Invasion and Occupation of Iraq* (London: Atlantic Books, 2007), pp. 21–2.
9 Feith (2008), op. cit., p. 15.
10 Ken Layne. (2002). *Saddam Pays 25K for Palestinian Bombers.* [Fox News] Available at: URL: www.foxnews.com/story/0,2933,48822,00.html Access Date: 20 June 2009.
11 Feith (2008), op. cit., p. 52.
12 Woodward (2002), op. cit., p. 329.

13 Feith (2008), op. cit., pp. 48–9.
14 Colin Powell quoted in Woodward (2004), op. cit., p. 292.
15 Wolfowitz (2001), op. cit.
16 George W. Bush quoted in Woodward (2002), op. cit., p. 48.
17 George W. Bush. (2002d). *President Bush Delivers Graduation Speech at West Point.* [The White House] Available at: URL: http://georgewbush-whitehouse. archives.gov/news/releases/2002/06/20020601–3.html Access Date: 20 June 2008.
18 Donald Rumsfeld quoted in Feith (2008), op. cit., p. 66.
19 Woodward (2004), op. cit., p. 1.
20 Bob Woodward, *State of Denial: Bush at War, Part III* (London: Simon and Schuster, 2006), p. 33.
21 Tommy Franks with Malcolm McConnell, *American Soldier* (New York: Harper-Collins, 2004), p. 329.
22 Feith (2008), op. cit., p. 219.
23 John Dumbrell, 'The Neoconservative Roots of the War in Iraq', in *Intelligence and National Security Policymaking on Iraq: British and American Perspectives*, ed. James Pfiffner and Mark Phythian (Manchester: Manchester University Press, 2008a), pp. 32–3.
24 Feith (2008), op. cit., p. 116.
25 Ibid., p. 218.
26 Woodward (2004), op. cit., p. 287.
27 Feith (2008), op. cit., p. 237.
28 George W. Bush. (2002a). *President Delivers State of the Union Address.* [The White House] Available at: URL: http://georgewbush-whitehouse.archives.gov/news/releases/2002/01/20020129–11.html Access Date: 13 May 2009.
29 Woodward (2004), op. cit., p. 95.
30 George W. Bush. (2003a). *President Delivers 'State of the Union'.* [The White House] Available at: URL: http://georgewbush-whitehouse.archives.gov/news/releases/2003/01/20030128–19.html Access Date: 20 June 2009.
31 Colin Powell. (2002). *The President's International Affairs Budget Request for FY 2003.* [Committee on International Relations: House of Representatives] Available at: URL: www.globalsecurity.org/military/library/congress/2002_hr/77532.pdf Access Date: 20 December 2007.
32 Colin Powell quoted in Julian Borger. (2002). *US Big Guns Silent on 'Regime Change'.* [guardian.co.uk] Available at: URL: www.guardian.co.uk/world/2002/feb/13/worlddispatch.usa Access Date: 20 June 2007.
33 Woodward (2002), op. cit., p. 330.
34 George W. Bush. (2002b). *President Bush, Prime Minister Blair Hold Press Conference.* [The White House] Available at: URL: http://georgewbush-whitehouse. archives.gov/news/releases/2002/04/20020406–3.html Access Date: 20 June 2008.
35 George W. Bush. (2002c). *President Bush Meets with French President Chirac.* [The White House] Available at: URL: http://georgewbush-whitehouse.archives. gov/news/releases/2002/05/20020526–2.html Access Date: 20 June 2008.
36 Woodward (2002), op. cit., p. 335.
37 Feith (2008), op. cit., pp. 283–5.
38 Ibid., p. 288.
39 Ibid., p. 289.
40 Ibid., p. 319.
41 Ali Allawi, *The Occupation of Iraq: Winning the War, Losing the Peace* (USA: Yale University Press, 2007), p. 81.
42 Paul Pillar, Interview with Author, 15 July 2008, Washington, D.C.
43 Michael Rubin, Interview with Author, 7 July 2008, Washington, D.C.
44 George Packer, *The Assassins' Gate: America in Iraq* (New York: Farrar, Straus and Giroux, 2005), p. 105.

45 Feith (2008), op. cit., p. 313.
46 Louis Fisher, 'Deciding on War Against Iraq: Institutional Failures', *Political Science Quarterly* Vol. 118, No. 3 (2003): pp. 389–410.
47 Woodward (2004), op. cit., pp. 368–9.
48 Ibid., p. 351.
49 Ibid., p. 169.
50 Feith (2008), op. cit., pp. 378–9.
51 Woodward (2004), op. cit., p. 36.
52 Feith (2008), op. cit., p. 339.
53 Ibid., p. 223.
54 Condoleezza Rice, 'Why We Know Iraq Is Lying', *The New York Times*, (2003, 23 January), p. ED25.
55 George W. Bush quoted in Bob Woodward, 'Behind Diplomatic Moves, Military Plan Was Launched', *The Washington Post* (2004, 18 April), p. A01.
56 Condoleezza Rice quoted in ibid.
57 George W. Bush quoted in ibid.
58 Condoleezza Rice quoted in ibid.
59 Ibid.
60 Feith (2008), op. cit., p. 352.
61 Woodward (2004), op. cit., p. 358.
62 Lawrence Wilkerson, Interview with Author, 26 August 2008, Washington, D.C.
63 Paul Pillar, Interview with Author, 15 July 2008, Washington, D.C.
64 Ibid.
65 Andrew Card quoted in Elizabeth Bumiller, 'Traces of Terror: The Strategy; Bush Aides Set Strategy to Sell Policy on Iraq', *The New York Times* (2002, 7 September), p. ND1.
66 Paul Pillar, Interview with Author, 15 July 2008, Washington, D.C.
67 Colin Powell quoted in Lawrence Freedman, *A Choice of Enemies: America Confronts the Middle East* (New York: PublicAffairs, 2008), p. 398.
68 Condoleezza Rice quoted in ibid.
69 Freedman (2008), op. cit., p. 398.
70 Michael Rubin, Interview with Author, 7 July 2008, Washington, D.C.
71 Marc Erikson. (2002). *Iraq: In All but Name, the War's on.* [Asia Times Online] Available at: URL: www.atimes.com/atimes/Middle_East/DH17Ak03.html Access Date: 15 July 2008.
72 Franks (2004), op. cit., p. 409.
73 Saddam Hussein, 'The Glaspie Transcript: Saddam Meets the US Ambassador', in *The Iraq War Reader: History, Documents, Opinions*, ed. Micah Sifry and Christopher Cerf (New York: Touchstone, 2003), p. 64.
74 Saddam Hussein. (2004a). *Interview Session 4, Conducted by George Piro: Baghdad Operations Centre: Federal Bureau of Investigation.* [The National Security Archive: The George Washington University] Available at: URL: www.gwu.edu/~nsarchiv/NSAEBB/NSAEBB279/05.pdf Access Date: 20 December 2009.
75 Scott Ritter, *Iraq Confidential: The Untold Story of America's Intelligence Conspiracy* (London: I.B. Tauris, 2005), p. 38.
76 Saddam Hussein. (2004b). *Casual Conversation, June 11, 2004: Baghdad Operations Centre: Federal Bureau of Investigation.* [The National Security Archive: The George Washington University] Available at: URL: www.gwu.edu/~nsarchiv/NSAEBB/NSAEBB279/24.pdf Access Date: 20 December 2009.
77 Gordon and Trainor (2007), op. cit., p. 580.
78 Hussein (2004a), op. cit., *Interview Session 4.*
79 Jim Lobe. (2004). *So, Did Saddam Hussein Try to Kill Bush's Dad?* Available at: URL: www.commondreams.org/headlines04/1019–05.htm Access Date: 15 July 2008.

80 George Tenet with Bill Harlow, *At the Center of the Storm: My Years at the CIA* (New York: HarperCollins, 2007), p. 332.
81 Hussein (2003), op. cit., 'The Glaspie Transcript: Saddam Meets the US Ambassador'.
82 Michael Rubin, Interview with Author, 7 July 2008, Washington, D.C.
83 Freedman (2008), op. cit., p. 427.
84 Woodward (2002), op. cit., p. 355.
85 Tony Benn. (2007). *Documentary: 'I Knew Saddam'*. Available at: URL: www. youtube.com/watch?v=oEH4sBsazGg&feature=channel Access Date: 20 December 2008.
86 Feith (2008), op. cit., p. 331.
87 Gordon and Trainor (2007), op. cit., p. 279.
88 Feith (2008), op. cit., p. 52.
89 Ibid., p. 304.
90 Gordon and Trainor (2007), op. cit., p. 83.
91 Feith (2008), op. cit., p. 283.
92 Woodward (2002), op. cit., p. 60.
93 The White House. (2002). *The National Security Strategy of the United States of America: September 2002*. Washington, D.C.: The White House.
94 Feith (2008), op. cit., p. 233.
95 Ibid.
96 Michael Rubin, Interview with Author, 7 July 2008, Washington, D.C.
97 Ibid.
98 David Pollock, Interview with Author, 24 July 2008, Washington, D.C.
99 National Security Council Official, Interview with Author, 11 July 2008, Washington, D.C.
100 Adam Garfinkle, Interview with Author, 7 August 2008, Washington, D.C.
101 Lawrence Wilkerson, Interview with Author, 26 August 2008, Washington, D.C.
102 Adam Garfinkle, Interview with Author, 7 August 2008, Washington, D.C.
103 Paul Pillar, Interview with Author, 15 July 2008, Washington, D.C.
104 National Security Council Official, Interview with Author, 11 July 2008, Washington, D.C.
105 Condoleezza Rice quoted in Freedman (2008), op. cit., p. 408.
106 Stefan Halper and Jonathan Clarke, *America Alone: The Neo-Conservatives and the Global Order* (Cambridge: Cambridge University Press, 2004), p. 202.
107 Paul Wolfowitz quoted in Peter Galbraith, *The End of Iraq: How American Incompetence Created a War Without End* (New York: Simon and Schuster, 2006), p. 78.
108 Paul Pillar, Interview with Author, 15 July 2008, Washington, D.C.
109 Ibid.
110 Tenet (2007), op. cit., p. 322.
111 Woodward (2004), op. cit., p. 173.
112 National Security Council Official, Interview with Author, 11 July 2008, Washington, D.C.
113 Richard Kessler, Interview with Author, 2 July 2008, Washington, D.C.
114 George W. Bush quoted in Woodward (2004), op. cit., p. 120.
115 National Security Council Official, Interview with Author, 11 July 2008, Washington, D.C.
116 Carole O'Leary, Interview with Author, 8 August 2008, Washington, D.C.
117 John Mearsheimer and Stephen Walt, 'An Unnecessary War', *Foreign Policy*, (2003, Jan/Feb), p. 52.
118 Tenet (2007), op. cit., p. 305.
119 Frederick Kagan, Interview with Author, 25 July 2008, Washington, D.C.
120 Richard Perle, Telephone Interview with Author, 24 September 2008.
121 George W. Bush (2002a), op. cit., *President Delivers State of the Union Address*.

122 James Longley, Interview with Author, 22 July 2008, Washington, D.C.
123 Henri Barkey, Interview with Author, 21 August 2008, Washington, D.C.
124 Feith (2008), op. cit., p. 216.
125 Lokman Meho, *The Kurdish Question in US Foreign Policy: A Documentary Sourcebook* (Connecticut: Praeger Publishers, 2004), p. 29.
126 Freedman (2008), op. cit., p. 163.
127 Feith (2008), op. cit., p. 183.
128 Ibid., p. 224.
129 Ibid., p. 225.
130 Duelfer Report quoted in Feith (2008), op. cit., p. 326.
131 Feith (2008), op. cit., p. 214.
132 Ibid., p. 220.
133 Donald Rumsfeld quoted in Jay Bookman, 'The President's Real Goal in Iraq', *The Atlanta Journal-Constitution* (2002, 29 September), p. 1F.
134 Richard Perle, Telephone Interview with Author, 24 September 2008.
135 George W. Bush quoted in Woodward (2002), op. cit., p. 45.
136 Feith (2008), op. cit., p. 112.
137 Dick Cheney with Liz Cheney, *In My Time: A Personal and Political Memoir* (New York: Threshold Editions, 2011), p. 369.
138 David Pollock, Interview with Author, 17 July 2008, Washington, D.C.
139 Freedman (2008), op. cit., p. 160.
140 James Longley, Interview with Author, 22 July 2008, Washington, D.C.
141 Donald Rumsfeld, *Known and Unknown: A Memoir* (New York: Sentinel, 2011), p. 422.
142 George W. Bush. (2003c). *President Discusses the Future of Iraq.* [The White House] Available at: URL: http://georgewbush-whitehouse.archives.gov/news/releases/2003/02/20030226–11.html Access Date: 20 June 2008.
143 Feith (2008), op. cit., p. 10.
144 Woodward (2002), op. cit., p. 355.
145 George W. Bush (2003a), op. cit., *President Delivers 'State of the Union'.*
146 Woodward (2004), op. cit., p. 152.
147 George W. Bush. (2003e). *President Addresses the Nation.* [The White House] Available at: URL: http://georgewbush-whitehouse.archives.gov/news/releases/2003/09/20030907–1.html Access Date: 20 May 2008.
148 George W. Bush, *Decision Points* (New York: Crown Publishers, 2010), p. 257.
149 George W. Bush (2002a), op. cit., *President Delivers State of the Union Address.*
150 Feith (2008), op. cit., p. 81.
151 Ibid., p. 283.
152 Paul Pillar, Interview with Author, 15 July 2008, Washington, D.C.
153 Ibid.
154 Paul Wolfowitz quoted in Woodward (2004), op. cit., p. 426.
155 Woodward (2002), op. cit., p. 130.
156 George W. Bush quoted in Woodward (2004), op. cit., p. 88.
157 Robert Draper, *Dead Certain: The Presidency of George W. Bush* (New York: Free Press, 2007), p. 166.
158 George W. Bush quoted in Woodward (2004), op. cit., p. 89.
159 Woodward (2002), op. cit., pp. 339–40.
160 George W. Bush (2010), op. cit., p. 248.
161 Condoleezza Rice quoted in ibid., p. 93.
162 George W. Bush quoted in ibid., p. 132.
163 The White House (2002), op. cit.
164 George W. Bush. (2003d). *President Bush Addresses the Nation.* [The White House] Available at: URL: http://georgewbush-whitehouse.archives.gov/news/releases/2003/03/20030319–17.html Access Date: 20 June 2008.

165 George W. Bush (2002a), op. cit., *President Delivers State of the Union Address.*
166 David Mack, Interview with Author, 27 August 2008, Washington, D.C.
167 Ibid.
168 Lawrence Wilkerson, Interview with Author, 26 August 2008, Washington, D.C.
169 John Mearsheimer and Stephen Walt. (2006). *The Israel Lobby.* [London Review of Books] Available at: URL: www.lrb.co.uk/v28/n06/john-mearsheimer/the-israel-lobby Access Date: 20 June 2008.
170 Paul Pillar, Interview with Author, 15 July 2008, Washington, D.C.
171 Walter Russell Mead, 'God's Country?' *Foreign Affairs* Vol. 85, No. 5 (2006): pp. 24–43.
172 Ann Norton, *Leo Strauss and the Politics of American Empire* (USA: Yale University Press, 2004), p. 206.
173 Woodward (2004), op. cit., p. 186.
174 George W. Bush quoted in ibid., p. 188.
175 George W. Bush (2003c), op. cit., *President Discusses the Future of Iraq.*
176 George W. Bush. (2004). *Joint Press Conference: President Bush and PM Sharon.* [Israel Ministry of Foreign Affairs] Available at: URL: www.mfa.gov.il/MFA/Government/Speeches+by+Israeli+leaders/2004/Bush-Sharon+Press+Conference+14-Apr-2004.htm Access Date: 20 June 2007.
177 Henri Barkey, Interview with Author, 21 August 2008, Washington, D.C.
178 Woodward (2004), op. cit., p. 50.
179 Gordon and Trainor (2007), op. cit., p. 73.
180 Ibid., p. 150.
181 Richard Perle, 'Why the West Must Strike First Against Saddam Hussein', *The Daily Telegraph* (2002, 9 August), p. 22.
182 Stephen Tanner, *The Wars of the Bushes: A Father and Son as Military Leaders* (Pennsylvania: CASEMATE, 2004), p. 246.
183 Condolezza Rice quoted in ibid., p. 107.
184 Tommy Franks with Malcolm McConnell, *American Soldier* (New York: Harper-Collins, 2004), p. xiv.
185 Ibid., pp. 448–9.
186 Ibid., p. 466.
187 Thomas Friedman, 'The Long Bomb', *The New York Times* (2003, 2 March), p. ED13.
188 George W. Bush (2003c), op. cit., *President Discusses the Future of Iraq.*
189 David Mack, Interview with Author, 27 August 2008, Washington, D.C.
190 Feith (2008), op. cit., p. 284.
191 Ibid., pp. 283–5.
192 Richard Cheney quoted in Woodward (2004), op. cit., p. 284.
193 Ibid.
194 Richard Cheney quoted in Feith (2008), op. cit., p. 286.
195 Feith (2008), op. cit., p. 235.
196 Dennis Ross, 'The Middle East Predicament', *Foreign Affairs* Vol. 84, No. 1 (2005): pp. 61–74.
197 Feith (2008), op. cit., p. 457.
198 David Pollock, Interview with Author, 17 July 2008, Washington, D.C.
199 Michael Rubin, Interview with Author, 7 July 2008, Washington, D.C.
200 Ibid.
201 Richard Perle, Telephone Interview with Author, 24 September 2008.
202 Melvyn Leffler quoted in Robert Singh, 'The Bush Doctrine', in *The Bush Doctrine and the War on Terrorism: Global Responses, Global Consequences*, ed. Mary Buckley and Robert Singh (Oxford: Routledge, 2006), p. 29.
203 Feith (2008), op. cit., p. 235.
204 Ibid., p. 457.

205 Ibid., p. 409.
206 George W. Bush quoted in Woodward (2004), op. cit., p. 424.
207 George W. Bush (2003c), op. cit., *President Discusses the Future of Iraq.*
208 Woodward (2002), op. cit., p. 467.
209 Anoushiravan Ehteshami, 'The Middle East: Between Ideology and Geo-politics', in *The Bush Doctrine and the War on Terrorism: Global Responses, Global Consequences*, ed. Mary Buckley and Robert Singh (Oxford: Routledge, 2006), p. 107.
210 Peter Galbraith, Telephone Interview with Author, 8 August 2008.
211 George W. Bush quoted in Woodward (2002), op. cit., p. 98.
212 Draper (2007), op. cit., p. 166.
213 George W. Bush quoted in Woodward (2002), op. cit., p. 194.
214 Richard Cheney quoted in Woodward (2004), op. cit., p. 428.
215 Ibid., p. 412.
216 Woodward (2006), op. cit., p. 371.
217 Ehteshami (2006), op. cit., pp. 107–14.
218 Paul Pillar, Interview with Author, 15 July 2008, Washington, D.C.
219 Condoleezza Rice quoted in Ehteshami (2006), op. cit., pp. 107–14.
220 Woodward (2006), op. cit., p. 479.
221 Condoleezza Rice. (2005). *Condoleezza Rice's Remarks from her Cairo Speech at AUC.* [The Arabist] Available at: URL: www.arabist.net/blog/2005/6/20/condoleezza-rices-remarks-from-her-cairo-speech-at-auc.html Access Date: 15 July 2009.
222 George W. Bush (2003c), op. cit., *President Discusses the Future of Iraq.*
223 James Mann, *Rise of the Vulcans: The History of Bush's War Cabinet* (New York: Penguin Group, 2004), p. 352.
224 *Letter to President Bush on the War on Terrorism.* (2001). [Project For The New American Century] Available at: URL: www.newamericancentury.org/Bushletter. htm Access Date: 20 June 2009.
225 Robert Kagan and William Kristol, 'What To Do About Iraq', *The Weekly Standard* (2002, January), pp. 23–6.
226 Halper and Clarke (2004), op. cit., p. 206.
227 Bookman, op. cit.
228 Ibid.
229 James Longley, Interview with Author, 22 July 2008, Washington, D.C.
230 Ibid.
231 Peter Galbraith, Telephone Interview with Author, 8 August 2008.
232 Robert Olson, *The Goat and the Butcher: Nationalism and State Formation in Kurdistan-Iraq since the Iraqi War* (California: Mazda Publishers, 2005), p. 238.
233 Michael Rubin, Interview with Author, 7 July 2008, Washington, D.C.
234 Lawrence Kaplan and William Kristol quoted in Halper and Clarke (2004), op. cit., p. 220.
235 Draper (2007), op. cit., p. 166.
236 Woodward (2006), op. cit., p. 467.
237 David Garnham, *Clinton's Foreign Policy* (Nablus: Centre for Palestinian Research and Studies, 1994), p. 15.
238 Martin Indyk, 'The Postwar Balance of Power in the Middle East', in *After the Storm: Lessons from the Gulf War*, ed. Joseph Nye and Roger Smith *et al.* (Maryland: Madison Books, 1992), p. 83.
239 Richard Falk, 'The Global Setting: US Foreign Policy and the Future of the Middle East', in *The Iraq War and Democratic Politics*, ed. Alex Danchev and John Macmillan *et al.* (Oxford: Routledge, 2005), p. 23.
240 Ibid., p. 27.
241 Ibid., p. 28.
242 Michael Cox, 'Empire by Denial: The Strange Case of the United States', *International Affairs* Vol. 81, No. 1 (2005): p. 25.

243 Jason Gluck, Interview with Author, 27 June 2008, Washington, D.C.
244 Marcy Katpur quoted in John Dumbrell, 'Bush's War: The Iraq Conflict and American Democracy', in *The Iraq War and Democratic Politics*, ed. Alex Danchev and John MacMillan *et al.* (Oxford: Routledge, 2005), p. 35.
245 Ibid., p. 38.
246 Freedman (2008), op. cit., p. 397.
247 Paul Wolfowitz. (2003). *Department of Defense Budget Priorities for Fiscal Year 2004.* [Committee on the Budget: House of Representatives] Available at: URL: http://usiraq.procon.org/sourcefiles/WolfowitzTestimonyHBC.pdf Access Date: 20 December 2007.
248 Paul Pillar, Interview with Author, 15 July 2008, Washington, D.C.
249 Freedman (2008), op. cit., p. 397.
250 Woodward (2006), op. cit., p. 4.
251 George W. Bush. (2002f). *Bush Calls Saddam 'The Guy Who Tried to Kill My Dad'.* [CNN.com/Inside Politics] Available at: URL: http://archives.cnn.com/2002/ALL-POLITICS/09/27/bush.war.talk/ Access Date: 17 June 2008.
252 George W. Bush. (2002e). *President's Remarks at the United Nations General Assembly.* [The White House] Available at: URL: http://georgewbush-whitehouse.archives.gov/news/releases/2002/09/20020912–1.html Access Date: 20 June 2009.
253 Woodward (2004), op. cit., p. 187.
254 Ayal Frank, Interview with Author, 15 July 2008, Washington, D.C.
255 Richard N. Haass, 'The Irony of American Strategy: Putting the Middle East in Proper Perspective', *Foreign Affairs* Vol. 92, No. 3 (2013): p. 57.
256 Feith (2008), op. cit., p. 215.
257 Condoleezza Rice quoted in Woodward (2002), op. cit., p. 308.
258 Feith (2008), op. cit., p. 192.
259 Senior Congressional Staffer, Interview with Author, 2 July 2008, Washington, D.C.
260 Ibid.
261 Freedman (2008), op. cit., p. 421.
262 Ari Fleischer quoted in ibid., p. 417.
263 National Security Council Official, Interview with Author, 11 July 2008, Washington, D.C.
264 James Longley, Interview with Author, 22 July 2008, Washington, D.C.
265 Ibid.
266 Ibid.
267 Paul Hughes, Interview with Author, 29 July 2008, Washington, D.C.
268 Ibid.
269 Paul Hughes, Interview with Author, 29 July 2008, Washington, D.C.
270 James Longley, Interview with Author, 22 July 2008, Washington, D.C.
271 Ibid.
272 Ibid.
273 Ibid.
274 Frederick Kagan, Interview with Author, 25 July 2008, Washington, D.C.
275 Lawrence Wilkerson, Interview with Author, 26 August 2008, Washington, D.C.
276 Frederick Kagan, Interview with Author, 25 July 2008, Washington, D.C.
277 Michael Rubin, Interview with Author, 7 July 2008, Washington, D.C.

5 The war in Iraq

A planned war, an unplanned occupation

Washington isn't all that thought out. So much of it is improvisation. Too much rationality and planning can be attributed to it. Much of it is trying something, taking a pratfall, and then looking either bad or good when you do.

Fred Dutton, former advisor to John F. Kennedy[1]

Introduction

This chapter will review the aftermath of America's invasion of Iraq. It will provide an analytical look at the various phases of US Iraq policy under the Bush administration after major combat operations ended, and provide insight into Phase IV of post-conflict US operations in Iraq. The events included in this chapter provide a comprehensive overview of the evolution of US policy after the toppling of Saddam, during which it adapted to changing internal and external circumstances. The chapter addresses the numerous and costly mistakes made by the Bush administration during this period. It follows the transition phases of US influence in Iraq up to the conclusion of George W. Bush's presidency, and the developments in Iraq during the Obama administration. It addresses the US occupation of Iraq under ORHA and the CPA leading through to the interim government, describing US policy in the transitional government of Iraq and ending with the permanently elected Iraqi government. Iraq witnessed rapid changes following the overthrow of Saddam Hussein, transitioning first from total US occupation to joint control and, finally, to national sovereignty.

5.1 A dysfunctional administration

The military operation to overthrow the Saddam Hussein regime can be regarded as a success in strictly military terms. Iraq, a country of considerable size, fell to coalition forces in only twenty-one days. However, it was the aftermath that brought insecurity to the Iraqi people and the coalition. The differing opinions that dominated the actual purpose for the invasion were a major reason for this. It is fair to assert that different people had different agendas, leading to varying directions in managing the post-hostilities phase in Iraq.

Douglas Feith asserts that senior members of the Bush administration from the CIA and State Department were reluctant members of the Bush team. They disagreed with the policy decisions being made by the president, but also made no effort to challenge these policies openly in interagency discussions.[2] Richard Armitage believed that the foreign policy-making process that was supposed to be coordinated by Rice was not done effectively.[3] Rice had failed to bridge the gaps efficiently during her role as National Security Advisor (NSA). Rice was surrounded by very strong and assertive Principals, who had once even considered running for the presidency. This had made her job difficult. She was the first female NSA to take on this difficult role. One of the most damaging aspects of this dysfunction was the hostility and tension between the Pentagon and the Department of State, which could be considered as one of the major blows to the efforts in rebuilding Iraq. For example, the 'Future of Iraq Project', a 1000-page document of questionable value prepared by the State Department, was neglected by retired Lieutenant General Jay Garner, Director of the Office for Reconstruction and Humanitarian Assistance (ORHA)[4] and the first civilian administrator of Iraq, as a result of friction with the Pentagon.[5] Donald Rumsfeld contributed to this friction considerably. From the point of taking up the office of Secretary of Defense he was a forceful and strong character. His sense of purpose made him highly influential in designing and restricting US military operations for the invasion of Iraq and its aftermath. Rumsfeld had expressed discontent with the influence the Joint Chiefs of Staff had had in his early days as Secretary. He insisted they were not part of the chain of command and seemed adamant to reinvigorate the Goldwater-Nichols Act. Rumsfeld told the Pentagon 'I'm the Secretary of Defense … I'm in the chain of command' a month after he took office when the first attacks under the Bush administration against Iraqi targets were undertaken to enforce the No-fly zones in February 2001.[6]

State and CIA officials constantly delayed and opposed cooperation with the Iraqi exiles on all political, intelligence and military matters. Consequently, the US had to run and control Iraq after the toppling of the Baath regime.[7] The CIA and State Department were hostile to any involvement of the Iraqi opposition in the preparation stages of the war. Richard Armitage rejected any possibility of an interim government before or immediately after the invasion. These attitudes prevented any effective post-war planning in the pre-stages of the war.[8] The root of the tension between the various agencies of the government was in the supposition made by the State Department and CIA that there would be a rift between Iraqi internals and externals (oppositionists) post-Saddam. This prevented the administration from working sufficiently with the Iraqi externals before the war and to quickly transfer authority to the Iraqis immediately after the overthrow of the Baath regime.[9] Donald Rumsfeld attributes this blanket refusal of both American organisations to Iraqi exiles as a means to preventing a future role to Ahmed Chalabi in the new Iraq.[10] State Department and CIA officials constantly emphasised that the external Iraqi leadership lacked legitimacy and consequently had very little political support in Iraq. The idea of 'externals' versus 'internals' was crucial to the State Department's, CIA and CENTCOM's thinking on post-Saddam Iraq. The prime reason behind this was the State Department and CIA's animosity towards Chalabi and, second, the ruling regional Sunni elites' influence in shaping this idea. All of them were Sunni ruled and non-democratic, and feared the prospects of a democratically governed Shiite Iraq.[11]

In a Deputies Lunch meeting on 25 July 2002 Richard Armitage distributed two papers prepared by the State Department. The first argued against occupation. The second argued for a prolonged US occupation, as the Department's view was that the Afghanistan Bonn model (*loya jirga*) was inappropriate to Iraq. The justification was that the externals in the Bonn process had more weight than in Iraq's case. Meanwhile in Iraq the internals held more legitimacy than the externals.[12] In the second document the State Department emphasised that a 'multi-year transitional period to build democratic institutions' was necessary so as not to alienate internal constituencies and to lead Iraq to 'develop credible, democratic Iraqi leadership'.[13] The neoconservatives, however, opposed the occupation of Iraq. They argued for a constitution and bill of rights ahead of time.[14] Neoconservatives like Paul Wolfowitz, Richard Perle, Douglas Feith and Michael Rubin wanted to avoid an occupation. It is likely that the installation of Ahmed Chalabi as head of an interim government was their desire.

Additionally, after the war, the US failed to sustain a unity of effort. The idea behind the CPA was to create a unity of effort and leadership in Iraq: in practice that was not the case – CENTCOM and the CPA both pursued different agendas. CENTCOM reported to Rumsfeld, and Paul Bremer's CPA on paper had the same obligation, but did not do so. As a result there was no unity of leadership and subsequently no unity of effort between CENTCOM and the CPA.[15] Moreover, interagency disputes in Washington denied the reconstruction programme the efforts it required.[16]

Rubin, who worked for the OSP from the summer of 2002 until the summer of 2003, explained that until right before commencement of kinetic action there was no agreement within the NSC and interagency process about whether or not the US would occupy and control Iraq or hand over control of Iraq to a provisional government, i.e. the chosen group of the seven Iraqi opposition leaders mentioned in the Iraq Liberation Act. The indecision by Rice and Stephen Hadley (Deputy NSA) over the resolution of the issue as to whether the US would have more influence with boots on the ground or without boots on the ground, hampered the ability of planning the long-term future of Iraq.[17]

The other major problem was the absence of clear goals for Iraq after Saddam. General Garner summed up the core reason of the crisis as the lack of a 'comprehensive strategy other than a democracy'.[18] A former member of the Iraqi Governing Council (IGC) and Iraqi ambassador to the United States, Samir Sumaidaie echoed this view, 'there was never a clear statement of objectives apart from the general terms of bringing freedom for Iraq'.[19] As for the Principals Jay Garner explained, 'Bush wanted democracy, Rumsfeld wanted to pull out, Cheney expected open arms.' As a result a strategy was never developed for post-war Iraq that all the agencies understood: the administration, CENTCOM and all agencies had separate plans of their own.[20] Peter Galbraith described the

Bush administration as 'ill disciplined', thus making it difficult to attribute to it any kind of coherent policy. It could better be described more accurately as individual policies of the Defense Department, the State Department and the NSC 'rather than Bush policy'.[21]

Conrad Crane, an Army War College professor, had co-authored a study before the invasion which stipulated that thinking about the war now and the occupation later was unacceptable.[22] However, Bush administration officials did just that.[23] A major problem was the president himself, as he lacked curiosity and failed to give his objectives the necessary scrutiny they deserved. Bush wanted to be like Reagan, wanting to get the big picture right, believing that the details would take care of themselves as long as the big ideas were right.[24] Lawrence Wilkerson stressed that President Bush 'doesn't do details' and let advisors do everything else. His additional handicap was his little foreign policy experience, which was comparable to former presidents such as Calvin Coolidge and Herbert Hoover.[25]

Rumsfeld wanted to transform the military, but saw the Iraq conflict as an interruption, and that was why he was in favour of a short tenure in Iraq. Rumsfeld wanted 100–120 days maximum presence in Iraq, installing Chalabi and then leaving. Rumsfeld only became an advocate for Pentagon influence in Iraq as he realised how inadequate and minor the Pentagon's influence was in Afghanistan, since it had been primarily a CIA operation.[26] Rumsfeld wanted to leave Iraq after several months, then get back to the transformation of the military, having no desire to engage US forces in Iraq in the long term.[27] Rumsfeld wanted to use the military for war and opposed any other task being assigned to it. Former Principal Deputy Assistant Secretary of State Philip Wilcox described the operation as 'go in, remove Saddam, and leave; therefore there was no plan'. Consequently, there were no preparations for post-conflict stabilisation. The State Department asserted that the US must stay and rebuild Iraq, but this was rebuffed by the Pentagon. It was only with the US arrival that the administration realised it was trapped in a mess, with Garner's thinly staffed team making matters worse.[28]

Jay Garner added, 'the problem with the plans was they were developed rapidly'. Essentially there was not a lot of time to create effective plans.[29] Garner was not happy with the completeness of the plans since he did not have sufficient information on Iraq. Garner argued that 'the plans we had for post-war Germany we developed in 1942 for a 1945 problem, but plans for Iraq started in late 2002 for an early 2003 problem'. In Garner's opinion there was not enough time and intelligence to make complete plans.[30] Colonel Paul Hughes, senior staff officer of ORHA and later the CPA, stressed that post-war planning should have begun with the war plan. During the Second World War George Marshall established an office in January 1942 less than forty-five days after the attack on Pearl Harbor, in the then War Department, for the occupation of Germany and Japan. Hughes complained about the lack of time 'to pull it together'. Hughes stated: 'Marshall had two and half years to get it right! I had 59 days with ORHA, and then suddenly I was on the ground in Kuwait.' The same situation applied to the Joint Staff and CENTCOM efforts: they too began too late.

Hughes stressed 'this is not something that you can think about as an after-thought'.[31] According to Hughes even Tom Warrick's Future of Iraq Project (mentioned earlier) was not structured: 'it is a good doctoral dissertation, it's not a plan that is actionable'. The Departments of State and Defense, according to Hughes, if asked, would have said 'we don't have the resources or expertise'. The State Department was overwhelmed with the tasks, and Rumsfeld had a contract attitude.[32]

5.2 Mistakes made in Iraq

5.2.1 Unilateralism

US unilateralism had already increased with the end of the Cold War. Secretary Powell, however, was not comfortable with US unilateral tendencies for execut-ing the Iraq war, but thought Cheney and Rumsfeld's position in the war machine made war a likely resort.[33] The lack of faith in the United Nations was a major element of this unilateral trend, with Richard Cheney arguing that the president should tell the UN in his annual General Assembly speech 'Go tell them it's not about us. It's about you. You are not important.'[34] Nevertheless, the Bush administration was wary of going it totally alone on Iraq. It was their intention to support British Prime Minister Tony Blair to get a second UN Security Council resolution. Stephen Hadley was worried about what he called the 'Imperial Option'.[35]

However, after the damage inflicted on US diplomacy what could be described as a 'legitimacy deficit', in his June 2003 trip to Europe after the inva-sion, President Bush expressed a change of attitude on international issues – a clear shift in his approach to US foreign policy. He showed greater interest in multilateral institutions and international consensus. The Iraq invasion had most likely proved that superior military power itself was not enough to achieve the aspirations of a superpower. Bush started putting greater trust in the IAEA and European allies for a resolution to Iran's nuclear capabilities. On North Korea, he asked for a regional approach to confront the ongoing nuclear threat.[36] The UN involvement in Iraq with the Brahimi mission to select the new interim gov-ernment was a major shift in US cooperation with the UN. It came as part of the revised US policy on Iraq and the Middle East.[37]

5.2.2 Lack of understanding

Colin Powell tried to convey his message to the president about the aftermath of the Iraq invasion and its occupation. He explained that the Iraqis had a very complex history; in particular that they have never had a democracy.[38] The National Intelligence Council of the CIA cautioned that building a democracy in Iraq would be difficult, due to its authoritarian history, while the only way that the US could secure success was through three major channels: first, providing security to the Iraqi people; second, on the degree of progress in transferring power to Iraqis; and finally on the levels of reconstruction and of prosperity achieved.[39] During the post 9/11 world of policy, a lot of people around the president were very intelligent, but were not trained and did not have significant experience in dealing with the broader Middle East and with the challenges of the Islamic world. Many of the people in senior administration had been focused on the Soviet Union. But as the centre of gravity of problems shifted southward to the broader Middle East this according to Khailzad was a 'constraint that we faced, but you have to go forward with the team that you have'. The limitation was the availability of a lot of Soviet experts, European experts and not very many people who knew Iraq or the Middle East. Khalilzad stressed

> the sense of place, you know how a place feels – a strategist who doesn't have the innate sense about the area he's working on is going to get us in trouble. The US Government doesn't have enough people at the top who have that special sense about Iraq and the Middle East on their fingertips.

During the period immediately after 9/11, the US lacked expertise and regional proficiency, skills that require a long time to train in appreciating a society, understanding its complexity and learning its languages.[40] Ghassan Salame, political advisor to the UN Iraq mission, argues that the problem was not in Baghdad, but rather in Washington. It was a war decided, fought and won by a new breed of Americans – a group of ideologues who were different from the traditional brand of officials dealing with the Middle East over the past fifty years.[41]

John Stuart Mill was right to argue more than a century ago: 'If democracy is imposed on a country where there is insufficient indigenous support to achieve it, the strong likelihood is that it will collapse again into tyranny.'[42] The US failed to recognise that in a country with such a poor popular democratic tradition that it would be a long and tedious process. The Bush administration failed to recognise that democratic nation-building requires instilled legitimacy from domestic grassroots support.[43] The Bush administration consciously failed to provide the US occupation authorities with regional experts. Tim Carney, a former ambassador, argued the State Department's professional Arabists 'weren't welcome because they didn't think Iraq could be democratic'.[44] Iraqi Ambassador Sumaidaie stressed that the decisions and actions should have taken the realities on the ground into account. As a result of not doing so many opportunities were missed. He added: 'The Iraqis paid a heavy price. The Americans paid a price in their losses.'[45]

Additionally hampering the venture, the Washington Institute for Near East Policy (WINEP) had, in a three-day seminar before the invasion, advised the US agencies that there was a clear discrepancy and gap between the US rhetoric and its lack of commitment.[46] Alina Romanowski from the National Defense University argued at the WINEP seminar that democracy in Iraq would be difficult to adopt. She argued that Iraq had never had any form of centralised rule that enjoyed democratic legitimacy. The US force required to bring down the regime was not sufficient to keep up with US aspirations for that country.[47] The naïve idealistic and ideological analysis and prospects conducted from policy-making offices in Washington and London bore little resemblance to the facts and realities on the ground.[48] Iraq was tribal, communal and very locally focused, very much an agrarian farming country, where, as all over the world, farmers tend to be parochial and suspicious of strangers. Most Iraqis lived and died in the communities they were born in and gave their loyalty to kin and tribe.[49] Following the Iraq venture, according to Ariel Cohen, the US continued its mistakes, pressuring Egypt to hold elections, where 20 per cent was taken by the Muslim Brotherhood in 2005, and then Palestine elections in January 2006 won by Hamas. The same mistakes were made by the State Department under Rice. Cohen stressed that the US does not 'understand the realities of the people of the region, and lack[s] knowledge of the Middle East; they are tribal and religious people, culturally very different than the modern and post-modern American, European citizens of industrial and post-industrial societies'.[50]

The US also at times used excessive force, which reflected negatively on its overall strategy to secure and rebuild Iraq. On many occasions this led to Iraqi distrust and a feeling of inferiority. It has even been recalled that an army commander went as far as to say 'the only thing these sand niggers understand is force and I'm about to introduce it to them'.[51] From 2003 to 2006 US military strategy was focused predominantly on force protection, attacking the enemy and treating the Iraqi civilian populace as the playing field on which this violence occurred.[52] The tactic pursued was one of a 'kill and capture' mindset.[53] US tactics failed to realise the actual end result target was to win 'hearts and minds'. Acting responsibly would inevitably have led to a strategic victory, namely the political support of the Iraq populace.[54] When Bremer sought to expand the political spectrum by delaying the handing over of sovereignty, Iraqi exiles disapproved of the approach. Ahmed Chalabi told Bremer 'by slowing down this political process, you risk giving the impression that America intends to stay a long time in Iraq. That is not a good signal.' The chaotic aftermath in Iraq was not because the US did not have a plan, but rather because it adhered to the wrong plan.[55] The problem was entrenched in poor and inadequate planning and a lack of understanding of the realities on Iraq, in addition to the gap between different US agencies.[56] When Garfinkle entered the State Department in July 2003, people in the State Department were trying to understand what was going on in Iraq, as no one had much knowledge of Iraq since there had been no embassy there since 1990. Garfinkle suggested to Secretary of State Colin Powell that he could create a 'Green Cell' of outside experts who knew about Iraq which he approved. It was only then that the State Department could prepare specific assessment reports to Secretary Powell and the Bureau of Intelligence and Research on issues related to Iraq.[57]

5.2.3 The Iraqi opposition

The Iraqi opposition essentially was the group designated as the democratic Iraqi opposition stipulated in the Iraq Liberation Act. One rule of thumb is to be suspicious of expatriate groups claiming legitimate opposition unless there is demonstrable evidence to indigenous opposition with widespread support.[58]

The American transformers were not prepared for the Iraq they found: they were prepared for the Iraq Ahmed Chalabi told them would be there.[59] American academic and Iraq expert Carol O'Leary explained that the Iraqi opposition figures like Ahmed Chalabi 'told us what we want to hear. They never told us what Iraq was really like.' Iraq, under Saddam, was an incredibly brutalised place, as the US came to find out.[60] O'Leary stressed 'there were counter forces like myself who did not believe that Iraq was fully secular and detribalised, or that Iraqis will quickly embrace Israel and the West when freed of the Saddam regime'.[61] In response to the WMD controversy, Chalabi told London's the *Daily Telegraph* in February 2004,

> We are heroes in error. As far as we're concerned, we've been entirely successful. That tyrant Saddam is gone and the Americans are in Baghdad. What was said before is not important. The Bush administration is looking for a scapegoat.

5.2.4 WMD

During an 8 February 2004 interview, President Bush acknowledged that weapons were not found: 'I expected there to be stockpiles of weapons ... we thought he had weapons.'[62] The CIA had dramatically failed in intelligence gathering. It failed to identify a lack of WMD; more significantly it underestimated the significance and importance of the paramilitary Fidayeen and also the existence of tons of weapons scattered all around the country in caches.[63]

As explained in the previous chapter, WMD was the common denominator among US agencies and used as public justification for war. This became a source of great embarrassment. It damaged the US cause and legitimacy domestically and internationally. In his final days as president, Bush stated

> I don't know – the biggest regret of all the presidency has to have been the intelligence failure in Iraq. A lot of people put their reputations on the line and said the weapons of mass destruction is a reason to remove Saddam Hussein. It wasn't just people in my administration; a lot of members in Congress, prior to my arrival in Washington D.C., during the debate on Iraq, a lot of leaders of nations around the world were all looking at the same intelligence. And, you know, that's not a do-over, but I wish the intelligence had been different, I guess.

5.2.5 A non-existent appetite for nation-building

Bremer asserts that President Bush's message to him was that US involvement in Iraq was aiming beyond simple regime change and that 'a New Iraq' had to be created, free from brutality. President Bush believed that, regardless of the inherent difficulties, the US should put Iraq on the path of democracy after the Saddam threat had been removed. This had been the case with other US enemies in the twentieth century, where defeat followed by reconstruction had resulted in benefits to both sides.[64] In a meeting with Iraqi exiles (Kanan Makiya, Hatem Mukhlis and Rend Franke) on 10 January 2003, President Bush wanted to understand Iraqi sentiments towards the invasion. He foresaw the likelihood that Iraq would be seriously damaged during the military operations; he averred that he was planning for the worst. However, he made it clear that the US would take full responsibility for these incurred damages and would not abandon Iraq – referring to his father's failures in protecting Iraqis in 1991. He referred to two US armies: one to fight the regime, and the other to rebuild the country.[65] Before the Iraq war, and during the war against the Taliban in Afghanistan, Bush made it clear that US forces would be used to nation-build.[66] Even in his famous 1 May 2003 speech, Bush declared that a new phase in Iraq was beginning, a rebuilding phase, also emphasising that time and hard work would be required. He said:

> And we will stand with the new leaders of Iraq as they establish a government of, by, and for the Iraqi people. The transition from dictatorship to democracy will take time, but it is worth every effort. Our coalition will stay until our work is done. Then we will leave, and we will leave behind a free Iraq.[67]

However, rhetoric did not match reality. It was only as late as 3 September 2002 that Andrew Card gathered a group of senior staff which started off as the 'White House Iraq Coordination Meeting', later known as the 'White House Iraq Group', to effectively organise the war on Iraq.[68] And only in September 2002 was the OSP created to deal specifically with Iraq. The Bush administration was concerned that Saddam might use WMD in his last efforts to confront the invasion. It was US policy to convince Saddam that he was politically astute and that he could outmanoeuvre the administration accordingly.[69] This appears to have played a role in the US lack of assertive planning and preparation for the post-war period. This was a typical example of force-protection mentality. The other concern was coercive diplomacy. The US did not want to give the impression that war was inevitable.

Feith argues that during and after Operation Iraqi Freedom his office planned to avoid the military occupation of Iraq. An Iraqi Interim Authority (IIA) proposal was approved by President Bush on 10 March 2003. Feith describes this as a 'painful tale of a missed opportunity to empower an Iraqi authority'.[70] On 10 March 2003 Douglas Feith briefed the president at a National Security Council meeting on the IIA concept of developing an Iraqi authority. The idea was to avoid direct and full control of Iraq post-Saddam. The rationale of this proposal was that if the US were to pursue an occupation authority it would be defined as military rule and subsequently fail to gain support from the Iraqis, the UN and the international community in general. It would create a power vacuum that would be exploited by Iran and other outside powers, as well as creating an unhealthy outlet for Iraqi nationalism.[71] No US agency thought it would be a good idea to occupy an Arab capital. Everyone realised there would be an *intifada* if you had Western troops in Iraq, for a long time. The Departments of State and Defense and the CIA did not want to occupy Iraq and thus sought no budget share for that purpose. Garfinkle stressed 'a budget is the most political document in Washington' and if agencies do not have the necessary funds, they do not begin the process of planning.[72]

Another significant point was that senior administration officials not only paid little attention to the possible difficulties in Iraq after the war, but they also did not want others to do so either 'for fear that such attention might undermine the claim that a short, decisive victory could be achieved with remarkably few troops'.[73] Planning was disregarded by the Pentagon as it focused on the problems of the occupation. This was deemed harmful at a time when the decision to invade Iraq was not yet affirmed. Focus on such obstacles would have been an impediment to the war.[74] The Bush administration was so focused on making a case for war that they determined to undermine their political doubters at home. They were convinced that the Iraqis would embrace American-style democracy and were blinded by their ideology.[75]

Although the rhetoric was to rebuild Iraq, Bush had already had an established anti-nation-building mindset going back to his election campaign: 'The problem comes with open-ended deployments and unclear military missions.' Bush wanted clearly defined military goals and the pressing question to be asked was 'When do we leave?'[76] A day before the 2000 presidential elections, President Bush criticised Democratic opponent Al Gore, saying 'let me tell you what else I'm worried about: I'm worried about an opponent who uses nation building and the military in the same sentence'.[77] This mentality had a fateful impact on US preparations and attitude for post-invasion Iraq. Condoleezza Rice in her Bush campaign *Foreign Affairs* article clearly described the role and function of the US military. The US military was a 'lethal' instrument and by no means a 'civilian peace force'. Rice asserted that it is 'most certainly not designed to build a civilian society', but only as a tool to support 'clear political goals'.[78] Joseph Biden, who was a senator at the time, believed that the dominant senior members of the administration were Cheney and Rumsfeld, who were assertive nationalists, with no nation-building intentions at heart. For them the Afghanistan model was their way of doing business, which was a clear case of little US commitment to nation-building.[79] To make matters worse, Rumsfeld was not happy with the CIA's influence in the Afghan war: he had even complained at a Principals' meeting about this. In the meeting all, including the president, asserted that the Defense Secretary should be in charge. Rumsfeld therefore made sure he was fully in charge when assigned to prepare for the Iraq war.[80] This prevented active participation and debate and a sufficient joint effort with all other agencies for the post-invasion phase. In an August 2003 visit to Iraq, Donald Rumsfeld pressed for an accelerated programme to train Iraqis for the National Iraqi Army. Instead of the two battalions the Coalition was training,

Rumsfeld requested a twenty-seven battalion contingent.[81] This demand would create more Iraqi forces with less training to allow a speedy US withdrawal.

The Bush administration wanted to oust Saddam Hussein, shift the balance of power in the Middle East in the United States' favour, all without committing itself to a lengthy, costly and arguably exhausting peacekeeping and nation-building process, which the Clinton administration had committed itself to in both Bosnia and Kosovo. This 'enabling' (Iraqi self-dependency) approach in theory would be best both for Iraq and the US.[82] Moreover, neither the Bush administration nor its predecessors were prepared to handle wars of such nature. The US institutions and laws were not prepared to deal with post-invasion stability and reconstruction operations.[83] Rumsfeld had argued consistently that the US was not well suited to picking other countries' leaders.[84] Feith stresses that 'Rumsfeld was determined not to do "nation-building"'.[85] The US approach to the Afghanistan war was one opposing nation-building. In his briefing to Rumsfeld for an 11 October 2001 Principals' Committee meeting, Rumsfeld stated that 'creating a stable, post-Taliban Afghanistan is desirable, but not necessarily within the power of the US'. Rumsfeld also stressed that 'nation-building is not our key strategic goal'.[86] Rumsfeld was against nation-building, disagreeing with similar US engagements in the 1990s. His analogy was that of a kid whose dad never let go of his bicycle, which in turn created a forty-year-old man that could not ride a bike.[87] Rumsfeld made his position clear in a speech a month before the invasion: 'Iraq belongs to the Iraqis and we do not aspire to own it or run it. We hope to eliminate Iraq's weapons of mass destruction and to help liberate the Iraqi people from oppression.'[88]

Rumsfeld believed the Clinton administration had unnecessarily tied down US forces in the Balkans. This was clearly a continuation of the Bush 2000 presidential campaign message. He asserted that long deployments of US troops would create a 'culture of dependence', preventing the Kosovars from standing on their own feet. For them the Afghan war was the right way: help the Afghanis rebuild their own country and not involve a large US peacekeeping force there.[89] A wealth of contemporary expertise had been established. Experiences from the Panama invasion were taken to subsequent military invasions: Haiti in 1994, as well as to Bosnia, Kosovo and East Timor. These, however, had not created a 'nation-building doctrine' in America.[90] The US was wary of being perceived as expansionist. President Bush affirmed at West Point in June 2002 that America had no empire to extend.[91] The Bush administration's disapproval of his predecessor's involvement in nation-building in the Balkans was no more than wishful thinking. The Bush administration thought it could simply topple the regime, then leave the rebuilding process to the Iraqis.[92]

5.2.6 Low levels of US military presence: the manpower deficit

Rumsfeld influenced General Franks' war plans on keeping force levels low. He reminded Franks of the large excesses of force that had been used during Operation Desert Storm to expel Iraq from Kuwait in 1991.[93] Rumsfeld had a theory of transformational warfare and played out his theory on the real battlefield.[94] This was a continuation of the doctrine of military transformation Bush had promised during his campaign. During his election campaign, Bush had stated 'The Gulf War was a stunning victory. But it took six months of planning and transport to summon our fleets and divisions and position them for battle.'[95] The president too wanted to avoid a long open-ended war, telling General Tommy Franks, CENTCOM commander, 'It's really important for us that we don't leave ourselves open in the region.'[96] On 15 April 2003, Bush met with his senior staff to discuss possible troop withdrawals from Iraq.[97]

Garner's team complained they did not have enough resources to get the country functioning again. The US military was stretched very thin and could not therefore cover all necessities, especially security.[98] Apparently the Afghan operation had encouraged this approach. The number of US forces in Afghanistan had reached no more than 4000 troops throughout the whole process of overthrowing the Taliban and attacking al-Qaeda.[99] Bremer stressed that 'Washington provided only enough troops to topple the old regime, not enough to deter the emergence of violent resistance, or to counter and defeat the resultant insurgency'. Bremer complains in his book that 'the United States thus went in to Iraq with a maximalist reform agenda and a minimalist application of money and manpower'. Bremer attributed the subsequent difficulties encountered to the 'disjunction' between the scope of its ambitions and the scale of its initial commitment.[100]

Ironically Rumsfeld had developed a memo, dubbed a 'Parade of Horribles', on 15 October 2002 on the potential dangers the US faced in Iraq as a result of an invasion. His rationale for a smaller force developed from these expectations and the fact that a smaller force would provide 'speed and surprise' that could not be guaranteed with a larger invasion force that could potentially elongate the war.[101] On 11 May 2002, Tommy Franks presented his plan to the Bush war cabinet at Camp David. Andrew Card and Condoleezza Rice expressed their concerns about a 'Fortress Baghdad' scenario, with Saddam resisting fiercely in Baghdad, creating an ugly urban warfare scenario.[102] These fears were avoided due to the speed of the operation.[103]

A senior Congressional staffer on the House Foreign Affairs Committee, interviewed by the author, stressed that going in with so few troops was a mistake.[104] Niall Ferguson has argued that the US military 'manpower deficit' in Iraq was a major source of its ineffectiveness. He makes a comparison between the British in 1917 and the US in 2003. In 1917, for every British soldier there were 20 Iraqis; however, in 2003, for every US soldier there were 210 Iraqis.[105] This was a stark contrast in numbers. Brian Gifford provides a comparison of the number of US forces of today at being only 1.4 million. This is at a time when US forces at the end of Second World War were close to 12 million active-duty personnel and 3.5 million at the peak of the Vietnam War.[106] The US was keen to not give an impression of expansionism. In a meeting with Rumsfeld, former Iraqi opposition figure Kanan Makiya expressed doubts at the nature of US dealing in the new Iraq. Makiya stated 'you're trying so hard not to be imperialists that you're not giving Iraqis a sense that you are in charge'. Democracy, he said, would not develop if the US did not direct it.[107] As Michael Cox has pointed out, the US is in 'denial about what it is' and thus has primarily been unwilling to pay the price or go anywhere to build a new world order under US leadership.[108]

In mid June 2003 Bremer was already getting anxious about the relatively small numbers of US troops on the ground. In a call to Condoleezza Rice, Bremer stressed 'the Coalition's got about half the number of soldiers we need here and we run a real risk of having this thing go south on us'.[109] Yet Rumsfeld visited Iraq in September 2003 to assess the options to reduce US forces in Iraq. Bremer affirms that he was putting increasing pressure on the military to make it happen.[110] Rumsfeld's doctrine of a small and swift US military had been an attractive concept to Bush, but on the ground, the practicalities of the concept in Iraq had proven otherwise. Both Philip Zelikow and Meghan O'Sullivan had anticipated the turn of events in Iraq mostly as a result of these manpower deficiencies giving greater freedom to the insurgency.[111]

On 25 February 2003, four months before the end of his term as Chief of Staff of the Army, Shinseki had told the Senate Armed Services Committee, in response to a question by Senator Carl Levin (D-MI) as regards force requirements for an occupation of Iraq following a successful completion of the war,

> something on the order of several hundred thousand soldiers are probably, you know, a figure that would be required. We're talking about post-hostilities control over a piece of geography that's fairly significant, with the kinds of ethnic tensions that could lead to other problems. And so it takes a significant ground-force presence.

Moreover, the contingency operating plan for an invasion of Iraq (OPLAN 1003–98) which had last been fully reviewed in 1996 and was updated in 1998, had envisioned an invasion force of more than 380,000 troops. Former CENTCOM commander General Anthony Zinni, who saw gaps in the plan particularly in regard to the post-war order, organised a war game named Desert Crossing in 1999 to examine additional contingencies.[112] Franks had not designed an overwhelming force similar to that which Colin Powell had put together to defeat Iraqi forces in Kuwait in 1991. Frank's invasion force did not exceed 170,000.[113]

Major General Spider Marks argued that they did not have enough troops to counter the insurgency. He summarised the weaknesses in two major points. First, the US did not have enough troops to conduct combat patrols in order to acquire solid intelligence and draw a proper picture of the enemy on the ground. Second, the US needed more troops to act on the intelligence generated. Consequently, the insurgency took advantage of the relatively few US numbers.[114] Sceptics of the US occupation were already emerging before the invasion. The Brookings Institution's Michael O'Hanlon, at an American Enterprise Institute meeting, warned of the immensity of this commitment and the dark realities it was likely to face. O'Hanlon argued for a possible indefinite US presence, 'five to ten years, at a minimum' and the engagement of 100–150,000 troops.[115]

Bush had no intention of keeping US forces in Iraq. This was a continuation of his attitude in Afghanistan. When Kabul fell, Bush asserted 'The US forces will not stay ... we don't do police work.'[116] Bush was determined that Iraq would not be a Balkans-like commitment – it would be a fast, forceful and targeted war with no long-term troop presence.[117] Matters were only made worse in terms of manpower deficit on 1 March 2003. The Turkish Parliament rejected the permission to establish a northern front in Iraq. This was greatly damaging, as it prevented a land invasion of the Fourth Infantry Division from the north.[118]

5.2.7 Dissolving the Iraqi army

Before the invasion William Luti's Office of Special Plans suggested possible plans for the reform or possible creation of a new army on 21 January 2003. Garner, however, produced his own proposal. This defined the role of the Iraqi army to reconstruction projects as an apolitical entity subordinate to civilian control.[119] General David McKiernan, land component commander during the Iraq invasion, also believed he could use the Iraqi army for security in post-war Iraq, while Garner wanted to use them as a cheap source of labour before retraining them for the new Iraqi army, mostly due to his shortage in personnel.[120] General Garner had briefed senior officials, including the president, on the retaining of the Iraqi army. This was approved by all, including the payment of salaries.[121] At a NSC meeting on 12 March 2003, Douglas Feith argued that the dissolution of the regular army be withheld. He believed that three to five army divisions could be used as the nucleus of the new Iraqi army. Feith's plan was 'not immediately to demobilise all the people and put them on the street, but use them as a construction force'.[122] Frank Miller, the NSC staff director for defence, proposed the Iraqi army be reduced in size but still functional enough to allow certain reconstruction projects.[123] There were a variety of things ORHA envisioned the old Iraqi military could have done under the generic name of 'reconstruction'. ORHA had planned to form work units of 100 soldiers under the command of Iraqi officers, but closely advised and supervised by Americans, which would have been put to use clearing rubble from the streets and public places, fire fighting, clearing canals, fixing water systems and performing other general engineering tasks. Eventually, these units would have been recycled into the de-mobilisation, disarming and re-integration (DDR) process as it matured.[124] Hughes, who served as an aide to Garner, said that dissolving the Iraqi Army 'was absolutely the wrong decision'. Hughes said 'we changed from being a liberator to an occupier with that single decision'. According to Hughes, by abolishing the army, the US destroyed in the Iraqi mind the last recognisable symbol of sovereignty, and as a result created a significant part of the resistance. The decree to dissolve the army all started when Bremer asked Senior CPA Advisor Walter Slocombe to request the opinion of US generals on the proposed disbanding. All the generals had agreed, providing that it be done fast and that personnel were recalled under a different name. Slocombe went back to Bremer and reported that the military were in favour of disbanding the army, but did not say that the army needed to be recalled.[125] One of the cardinal rules of soldiering is to make and retain contact with your enemy. This was disregarded as a result of the decree. Hughes made contact with Iraqi officers, stressing 'not one of them was a Baathist'. All they wanted to do was help the Iraqi soldiers get the 20 USD allowance. It was an attempt to help stabilise their lives and the lives of their families. When Bremer dismantled the army this process was stopped. The result was that the disbanded soldiers were angry and convinced that the US were liars. This mistake of denying soldiers the 20 USD allowance took eight weeks to correct. The soldiers had joined the insurgency by the time this mistake was corrected.[126]

Hughes stated that the US should have allowed Garner to continue with his activities, especially his attempt at creating the Arab equivalent of the *loya jirga*. Additionally, the US should also have kept the Iraqi army intact and then taken them through the DDR process. When de-mobilising a unit, the soldiers and staff parade, and then symbolically the unit ceases to exist. Hughes insists this could have been an easier process. Hughes had come back to Washington to sign the contracts to get the DDR started when Bremer made the announcement.[127] The disbanding of the Iraqi military was neither discussed with Garner or Hughes. This was at a time when Hughes was having the Iraqi military registered to keep it controlled.[128]

Ironically, Bremer makes exactly the same case with the benefit of hindsight in 2008. He argues that a better prepared and resourced programme for disarmament, de-mobilisation and re-integration would almost certainly have both attenuated the reaction to the army's 'disbandment' and made reconstitution of a new force somewhat easier. Bremer describes these programmes as routine components of most post-conflict reconstruction missions over the past twenty years. The 'failure to develop, fund and staff such a programme prior to the invasion proved a costly mistake', asserts Bremer.[129]

The Kurds also played a part in pushing the dismantling decree. Bremer affirmed this in his one and only interview with an Arabic media outlet – the *Sharq Al-Awsat* newspaper. The Kurdish leaders were unambiguous about this issue. They told Bremer that if Saddam Hussein's army was recalled, that would mean there would be no independent and democratic Iraq, and threatened to secede from the country. Bremer contended that his 'analysis was that if such a thing happened, it would precipitate a regional war involving Iraq's neighbours'.[130]

Sumaidaie did not believe the old Iraqi army was suitable for the new Iraq. 'The army was ramshackle, more generals in proportion to any army in the world. It was in a really bad shape', he insisted. The army needed deep reform and rebuilding on modern democratic terms. Sumaidaie believed that the transition from that army into a new army through a radical reform process was necessary with the proviso that some kind of stipend be allocated to prevent officers of the old army from becoming enemies of the new Iraq. The former Governing Council member thought 'the idea of disbanding the army was mishandled'.[131] In addition to the argument that it was a force detested due to its involvement in the oppression of the populace, the other argument was the dismantling of the Iraqi army due to its dysfunctional organisation. It had more than 11,000 general officers compared with 800 general officers in the US army.[132]

The insurgency was not unavoidable, but was mostly exacerbated by political and military blunders. The US failed to prepare for post-combat operations, after waging a war with the minimal acceptable level of force. The cancelling of badly needed deployments and reinforcements, disbanding of the Iraqi army putting more than 300,000 armed men on the streets and a denial of local elections in the initial stages effected considerably the post-invasion environment.[133] Garner described the mistakes made as follows. First, the US did not have enough military personnel to secure the post-invasion phase. Second, he described the decision to disband the army as a 'disastrous decision'. Third, the de-Baathification decree went far too deep. Fourth, the US should have immediately had an interim Iraqi government as the face of government. Garner insisted that he did not want the US to be the face of the government to the Iraqi people. Fifth, once the US found out how bad the infrastructure was, it should have immediately brought in sufficient generators to increase electricity capacity to provide a decent quality of life for the population. Sixth, Garner's plan was to write a constitution no later than July 2003 with the Iraqi interim government. This was suspended. Seventh, his plans to have elections for city government for towns and cities with a population larger than 100,000 was put on hold.[134]

5.2.8 De-Baathification: a cut too deep

With the attempts to create a representative and credible government for the transitional period, Bremer started alluding to the 'excesses of de-Baathification': it was a major implicit recognition of a change in US strategy, and also for more Sunni involvement in the government to come.[135] Both CPA's de-Baathification orders and the dissolution of the army were considered as the major instigators of the insurgency.[136]

After Condoleezza Rice gave up on the OSP, she gave post-invasion responsibilities to Frank Miller in March 2003. According to Miller, de-Baathification would only be implemented for 1 per cent of the Baath Party.[137] This did not materialise. Bremer argued that one of the lessons learnt from the German occupation was the Nazi eradication. A decontamination of Iraq through de-Baathification was the best approach. To him a speedy vetting process implemented in Iraq would allow the rebuilding of the institutions and then a handback to the Iraqis.[138]

Hughes, who was in Baghdad at the time working for the CPA, disagreed with the assumption. He described the de-Baathification as a mistake but not on a par with the military disbanding. Hughes argued that the cut made was too deep. The Iraqis knew who the Baathists were. They knew who the four top layers (levels of party membership) were. The local people knew them and 'would take them out'.[139] On 4 November 2003 Bremer issued 'CPA Memorandum Number 7' empowering the Governing Council to carry out the de-Baathification of Iraqi society consistent with CPA Order No. 1. This was done by the Higher National de-Baathification Commission led by Ahmed Chalabi. Bremer states that he responded to Iraqi demands for more authority over the process. To this the CPA empowered Iraqi politicians to implement the de-Baathification policy, which he defines as 'a mistake'.[140] Sumaidaie stated that the Baath Party was an evil organisation. It was right to banish the party as an organisation and ideology. But it was not right to banish and punish every Baathist who had simply wanted to survive. Sumaidaie asserts that the Governing Council should have been more forgiving to individuals unless they had committed crimes, and that it should have been done through a judicial rather than a political process.[141] Meghan O'Sullivan, Deputy National Security Advisor for Iraq, also asserted that the de-Baathification was badly implemented. O'Sullivan said that the CPA gave the Iraqis authority over the process. This turned out to be detrimental, as it far exceeded the original intention, becoming a political tool in the hands of the Iraqi elite. It was not implemented through the judiciary. She asserts that 'if the orders had been implemented a little more targeted' it would have minimised the political and economic consequences that contributed to the security problems.[142] However, O'Sullivan also argued that it is important to understand the strategic context of the moment. Both decrees (disbanding the army and de-Baathification) were viewed as important in overcoming the suspicions that 80 per cent of Iraqis harboured toward the US dating back to the First Gulf War. The US wanted to show it was serious in rebuilding a new Iraq, and not planning on installing a Saddam-like figure. The disbanding of the army was a gesture towards the Kurds, and the de-Baathification one of goodwill towards the Shiites. It was, in her own words, 'statements to show seriousness about rebuilding Iraq'.[143] This, however, was only one of the reasons for the de-Baathification of Iraqi society. De-Baathification was synonymous with the de-Sunnisation of political and religious life in Iraq. Since Sunnism was a major component of Baathisim, the de-Baathification of Iraq would limit Sunnism's usefulness as an expression of nationalism. Neoconservatives predominantly believed that Islamic extremism and terrorism were mostly legitimised by Sunnism, then de-Sunnisation would also deprive extremists from using it as a mobilising vehicle against Americans or Israel.[144]

5.3 Unexpected outcomes

5.3.1 Insurgency

As the Iraq war project was not thoroughly thought out, it was consequently ill-executed. The adversaries, as opposed to the executors, knew what they did not want from a new Iraq.[145] Dealing with the insurgency was a major dilemma for the Bush administration, as the chief premise of Republican foreign policy was to show no more weakness. They were not impressed with the Carter or Clinton administrations.[146] The insurgency in Iraq was composed primarily of four major factions, according to Deputy CIA Director John McLaughlin: the former Baathists, foreign fighters, Iraqi nationalists and tribal members.[147] Iran also had a large influence in Iraq. The Iranian Revolutionary Guard was behind a large proportion of the insurgency especially in the making of the roadside bombs that were responsible for many US casualties.[148] Tony Blair told the Iraq Inquiry in January 2010 that one aspect of Iraq post-Saddam that nobody had envisaged was that Iran would support al-Qaeda. The conventional wisdom was that the 'two would never mix'. However, what unexpectedly happened was that both had a common interest in destabilising Iraq.[149]

There was also a second axis to this alliance. Douglas Feith states that the Bush administration anticipated acts of revenge killings, looting, terrorist attacks, fuelling of violence by Iraq's neighbours and ethnic violence. However, what was not anticipated was a sustained insurgency financed and led by the toppled Baathists in alliance with foreign jihadists.[150] When Baghdad fell, members of the Baath regime decided Islam was the best slogan to rally support for continuing the insurgency. So a marriage of convenience developed between radical jihadist groups and the former members of the regime.[151] Another mistake was the US failure to recall Osama Bin Laden's *fatwa* in 1996, where he declared war on the US as a result of its military presence in the Arab peninsula and described it as a military occupation: a point that the Pentagon did not make and one which the CIA should have emphasised.[152] The insurgency in the form it took was never anticipated by either intelligence officers or policy makers. The Baathists, in coordination with the Jihadists, had managed to launch a damaging military campaign in Iraq.[153] However, Paul Pillar disputes this claim, as he himself had prepared two reports to this end. Pillar stated that the Pentagon policy makers did not ask questions, because 'neoconservatives hate intelligence officers'.[154] Pillar had prepared these reports on his own initiative which was released by the Senate in redacted form. The first was entitled 'Regional Consequences of Regime Change in Iraq'; the second 'Principal Challenges in Post-Saddam Iraq'.[155] Both reports lay out a very pessimistic view. It predicted sectarian and ethnic violence, slow democratic evolution, a lot of backsliding, and political extremism including terrorists who would find a lot of opportunities in Iraq.[156]

The reconstruction of Iraq suffered a devastating blow with the beginning of a bombing campaign in Iraq. The first was bombing of the Jordanian embassy in Baghdad on 7 August 2003 followed by the bombing on 19 August 2003 of the UN headquarters killing UN special representative to Iraq Sergio Vieira de Mello and other UN staff. The second was the assassination of Ayatollah Mohammed Baqir al-Hakim and a group of his followers on 29 August 2003. These bombings characterised the beginning of the insurgency in earnest.[157]

The Sunnis were a major part of the insurgency. In a conversation with a Sunni Arab leader, Robert Blackwill of the NSC gave his assurance, 'I want to reassure you that it's our intent that the Sunnis in the new Iraq have in every dimension a status and privileges consistent with their role and number in Iraqi society.' To which the Sunni leader replied: 'Mr Ambassador, you don't understand. We want to run Iraq.'[158] Army Colonel Derek Harvey told President Bush at a meeting, where he was briefing the president on the state of affairs in Iraq and the insurgency, that there was far too much focus on foreign fighters and less focus on the core of the insurgency which was the Arab Sunni oligarchy and their sense of 'religious nationalism'.[159] The future of Iraq and the post-invasion period was primarily based on the way Iraqis perceived the new order and their subsequent losses and gains. The violence that occurred in Iraq was partly a rejection of foreign presence, but mostly a fear of the uncertainty of a new power structure in Iraq. No longer were the Sunnis the unrivalled power holders and the Shiite subjugated peoples.[160] Moreover, the desired outcome of the Bush rhetoric may have been to promote democracy and peace in the Middle East, but this resonated little with Iraqis and even with the liberals and secularists in their midst. This objective was seen as a by-product of the Iraq invasion and not a sincere attempt for change. The Iraqis predominantly believed that the US invasion was for four primary reasons. First, control of Iraq's vast oil wealth; second, using Iraq to intimidate and check Iran; third, breaking up Iraq to create a fragmented and weak Middle East; and finally removing Iraq's threat to Israel.[161] The insurgency which Saddam had himself participated in in its earlier stages had devised a fourfold plan. It was their intention to, first, expel US occupiers; second, to weaken Iraqi institutions; third, to create dissatisfaction among the Iraqis on the new order; and fourth, to maintain the influence of the Sunni base.[162]

In April 2003, a directive from Iraq's intelligence agency was found. It provided guidance to the Baath Party, Saddam Fidayeen, and Intelligence members, in the event of Saddam's toppling, what they were supposed to do in the event of 'God forbid, of the fall of our beloved leader'. It included assassinating collaborators, burning the ministries, looting, burning public documents, doing everything possible to create further chaos in Iraq. It was essentially advising all members of the Baath regime to raise hell if Saddam were toppled.[163] In another *Mukhabarat* memo dated 23 January 2003 directed to 'All Offices and Sections', orders on what to do if Iraq were invaded were included. It advocated a policy of sabotage and looting, requesting that electric power stations be destroyed, as well as infiltrating Shiite holy places.[164]

Bremer was frustrated at the lack of attention from the Pentagon to the mounting insurgency in Iraq as early as July 2003. In June he had told Bush that he was worried that the US was 'drawing down' its forces too soon. Bremer felt that the US military, Rumsfeld included, wanted to get the forces home.[165] On his way back to Washington the insurgency was gaining momentum. Bremer felt the US military was 'struggling to find effective means to combat the enemy'.[166]

On 31 March 2004, with the insurgency on the rise and in the wake of the start of the Faluja crisis, President Bush delivered a speech at the Marriot Wardman Park Hotel in Washington. He asserted, 'We still face thugs and terrorists in Iraq who would rather go on killing the innocent than accept the advance of liberty.' He stressed the US resolve to confront the issue: 'This collection of killers is trying to shake our will. America will never be intimidated by thugs and assassins. We are aggressively striking the terrorists in Iraq.'[167] The US tactics, though successful in the short run at quelling the insurgency, were deeply flawed with regards to strategy. The US military failed to see the end objective and focused on temporary tactics to deal with daily crises. At the time the insurgency was regarded as composed of a small minority of hostile remnants of the previous regime.[168] James Schlesinger, a former Defense Secretary, who led one of the many official inquiries into the *Abu Ghraib* scandal, concluded two major errors were made by Pentagon officials due to erroneous assumptions: first, failing to plan for a possible insurgency; and second, failing to react to the insurgency once it erupted.[169]

With the ongoing insurgency and the instability in Iraq, Steve Herbits told Rumsfeld about an op-ed written in the *New York Times* by Senator Joseph Biden and Leslie Gelb, the former president of the Council on Foreign Relations. The article proposed a possible timetable with the objective of setting up three autonomous regions (Kurdish, Sunni and Shiite) with a loose federal structure existing in Baghdad. The borderlines were already de facto developing, and this seemed like a reasonable solution. Rumsfeld neither agreed nor disagreed.[170] Senator Biden supported dividing Iraq into three major Kurdish, Sunni and Shiite enclaves with a weak central government in Baghdad controlling certain issues such as foreign policy and oil revenues. The Bush administration wanted to stick to a united Iraq, although some observers said that the three-part division should still be kept on the table.[171]

5.3.2 Shock and Awe: the sudden collapse of the regime

The joint ground and air campaign designed to 'Shock and Awe' and provide a prompt fall of Baghdad would be fatal to the post-war reconstruction process in Iraq and in maintaining order. Some command and control would be essential in the rebuilding process of Iraq. This would get the military and police forces back in action. The very actions taken by the military would be detrimental to their strategic interests in post-war Iraq.[172]

Bush administration officials did not expect the government of Iraq to fall as quickly as it did.[173] This was the result of a small and agile US force that toppled the Baath regime in just three weeks. The Bush administration argued that, if they had a longer war, the US would have had greater numbers in the theatre to maintain order, but this would have been strictly at the expense of American and Iraqi lives. As a result, sufficient US troops had not arrived in Iraq after Saddam fell.[174] Tommy Franks had considered this scenario before the war and described it as a 'catastrophic success'.[175] The PUK told the US that all Iraqi military, political, governmental and Baath Party institutions would collapse promptly, leaving a major administrative vacuum in Baghdad, submerging the country in looting, chaos and violence. Nawshirwan Mustafa Amin, Jalal Talabani's deputy on the Iraqi Governing Council, asserted that they made this point very clear to the Americans on numerous occasions before the war started. They advised Ryan Crocker, Zalmay Khalilzad and Garner about this likelihood.[176]

However, many officials perceived this as an exaggeration and underestimation of the Iraqi army.[177] The nature of the Iraq war militated against well-advanced planning due to the speed and nature of the process. The diplomacy conducted at the UN would have been jeopardised if relevant officials from US departments had been withdrawn for the post-hostilities planning. The occupation of Iraq was comparable to the US occupation of French North Africa in 1942 rather than to Germany in 1945, which was thought through well in advance.[178] The wrong questions were also asked before the invasion. Elliot Abrams, the National Security Council Middle East Affairs Director, told the president that two million people might be displaced as a result of the Iraq war. Preparations were being made to this end. Bush made it clear to his team that this effort should be conducted properly as a means of public diplomacy, providing a positive image of the US.[179]

5.3.3 Looting

Sustaining public order was a major factor towards the creation of stability in Iraq and also to instilling Iraqi confidence towards their liberators. Jalal Talabani, on a visit to Washington in August 2002, told senior administration officials about highly possible looting in Baghdad after the invasion. But when Garner took a proposal to the White House for US police advisors in Iraq to help secure law and order, the proposal was rejected. The US did not want US police to enforce law in Iraq.[180] Tony Blair stated the first assumption was that the coalition would be arriving to a fully functional civil service and that the Iraqi police would take internal security into their own hands. As Iraq was a highly brutalised state and the police heavily penetrated by Baathist elements, the Baathists naturally failed to show up for duty and other Iraqi police personnel, fearing retribution, did not go back to work. In addition, Iraqi police had a poor reputation and image due to their inherent corruption.[181] Frank Miller, on 10 March 2003, stated at an NSC meeting that the successful establishment of rule of law in the immediate post-conflict environment would be critical to ensuring stability, allowing for relief and reconstruction, and the rapid rebuilding of Iraqi society.[182]

After the US invasion of Panama, Richard Shultz argued: 'At the most general level, the first [lesson] is the need to recognise post-conflict situations as important and complex missions for the Department of Defense.' This was clearly not discerned in Panama. The US did not have, at the time of Operation Just Cause, a policy for the period following the use of force.[183] The same mistake was repeated in Iraq. Bremer acknowledges that the 40,000 US forces stationed in Baghdad in the immediate aftermath of Saddam's toppling had no orders to stop the looters.[184] The US failed to protect public property and maintain public order, since Secretary Rumsfeld and his senior aides did not think it was important.[185] The administration failed to fulfil its duty as an occupying power by not preventing the looting. It did not listen to regional experts and also overlooked guidance from its own State Department.[186] Meghan O'Sullivan, who was one of the senior US officials in Baghdad, confirms that 'lots of mistakes were made'. The first mistake she defined was allowing lawlessness to pervade after Saddam fled Baghdad. Part of the problem was insufficient number of troops; equally important was that they did not have the right guidelines to keep law and order and protect the rule of law.[187] When the US marines arrived in Baghdad, they were shocked with the level of looting. They had had no guidance to deal with the problem. All they managed to do was protect several hospitals and critical installations. However, they had no orders to shoot at the looters or restore order. They were focused on defeating the enemy.[188]

Looting, one of the most troublesome and damaging occurrences of the post-invasion period, was identified early on when ORHA was established. It was mentioned at the first major gathering of ORHA officials at the National Defense University in February 2003 during an exercise Garner described as a 'rock drill'. However, when the subject was brought up, CENTCOM officials attending the meeting were instructed not to address 'post-conflict issues', mostly due to the lack of enough troops to address them.[189] General Wesley Clark, former NATO military commander, argues that 'the ensuing disorder vitiated some of the boost in US credibility that was won on the battlefield, and it opened the way for deeper and more organised resistance during the following weeks'.[190] A senior CPA advisor acknowledged that US policy mistakes created the insurgency. The reluctance of the US to stop the looting, its lack of will to impose order, and finally Bremer's initial orders, led to the downward spiral.[191]

The Rumsfeld Doctrine, of minimal human force, along with the Turkish refusal to allow the US military to enter Iraq from the north, created the environment that allowed the looting to flourish.[192] In Panama, a huge looting spree started with the invasion. This came as a total surprise to the invading force. 'The looting [in Panama] created the impression that US troops were not managing the situation they had created by the intervention.' As a result of the Panama looting, precautions were integrated into future military planning to address this issue. However, with none of the following interventions was looting an issue.[193] The author asked a senior CPA official visiting Kurdistan shortly after the US invasion why the US failed to react, to which the official responded 'when allied troops entered Paris, Parisians didn't loot the Louvre'.[194]

The whole downward spiral of Iraq began with the looting. It showed how incompetent the US military was, how the US was not asserting order and how the Iraqi perception grew that the US could not be a serious fighting force.[195] Feith argues that before the invasion he asked Christopher Lamb, Deputy Assistant Secretary of Defense, to help prepare a paper on the establishment of civil order after major hostilities were over. Lamb produced a paper on 'maintaining public order in Iraq'. The premise of this analytical paper was that CENTCOM lacked focus on this important issue. It recognised that there was a lack of detailed planning that would affect public order in the post-Saddam environment. It emphasised the lack of cooperation between CENTCOM and ORHA that could lead to alarming consequences. ORHA believed CENTCOM would provide the necessary forces for maintaining post-invasion stability; meanwhile, the latter felt its forces had other priorities.[196] Feith and Lamb argued: 'Currently the fundamental planning assumption about maintaining order is that swift combat operations will limit large civil disturbances, [but] the same assumption was made in Operation Just Cause in Panama and proved wrong; massive civil disorder began almost immediately.'[197]

In an 18 October 2002 meeting, Feith had posed the question of post-war Iraq, to which he himself replied that the post-hostilities administration would fall to the Department of Defense. The intention of this question in General Franks' presence was to shed light on the lack of attention he saw in the general as regards his duty to running Iraq and establishing order after Saddam's toppling.[198] The major issue, according to Feith, was that CENTCOM relied heavily on CIA assessments in its preparation for the war. The CIA predicted that the Iraqi police force would remain largely intact. This was a contributing factor to help determine US troop levels by CENTCOM commanders in the run-up to the invasion, assuming the Iraqi police would be able to maintain public order after the invasion.[199] CENTCOM had relied heavily on CIA predictions that public order would be maintained through Iraq police force 'professionals'. Actions against looting, rioting and civil disorder were retained to the Iraqi police. This was a major intelligence flaw; an error that would not have required penetration of the inner circle of the Iraqi ruling elite. It demonstrated the scarcity of information the CIA had on Iraq; moreover, Feith asserts, the CIA dismissed challenges put forward by policy makers in favour of their own confident opinions.[200]

The initial period after an intervention is crucial in determining the future course of a state emerging from violent conflict. Mistakes made during this time have lasting effects, and the intervening power can often spend years 'undoing damages done'.[201] Many military interventions have shown that once the occupying power is not seen as in control and providing security, other militias will form to attack the foreign power. And the more anarchic the situation becomes, the more likely it is that the local population will tolerate another authoritarian armed group.[202] It is indeed ironic that the day the US won the war, it lost Iraq.

5.3.4 Outside interference

Tony Blair asserts that the second major flawed assumption driving the invasion mindset was the unexpected joint disruptive role of Iran and al-Qaeda.[203] The price the US and its foreign policy paid was substantial. Instead of sending a strong message to Iran and North Korea, it found itself tied up in a tedious process in Iraq. Instead of showing that the transition to democracy was viable, it showed it to be a very difficult process. Instead of encouraging further involvement by other nations, it left the British and the US alone.[204] The Sunni elites of the region despised the concept of a democratic Iraq, which would give way to a Shiite majority to rule the country. This paved the way for their deep dislike of the Iraqi externals. They would have preferred Saddam to have been replaced by another Sunni general.[205] Consequently they did not engage the new ruling elite in Iraq. There was also clear evidence of Iranian intervention in Iraq. Iran's objective was to hamper the development of a strong and unified Iraq, especially one where Sunnis had led a bloody war against Iran for eight continuous years. Second, Iran wanted to make regime change a pricy and bloody business for the US to deter any such consideration for Iran in the future.[206] Tony Blair told the Iraq Inquiry that the coalition had assumed that Iran would mostly watch and had 'no interest in destabilising Iraq'. However, as it turned out Iran did not want a Shiite majority democracy on its doorstep.[207]

Bremer told the *Sharq Al-Awsat* newspaper that Iran was uncooperative during his period as CPA administrator. However, Iran was not overly disruptive either. Only occasionally would the US find elements of the Revolutionary Guards working inside Iraq. The Americans would also find elements from their interior ministry and intelligence, but their contacts were with people of only a modestly senior level, as opposed to what happened afterwards. Syria also was a big problem from the beginning, he stressed. The CPA were able to know through those taken into custody that the 'majority of suicide bombers had come from Syria'. Bremer explained that they gradually came to learn that Syria plays a huge role in recruiting suicide bombers from Saudi Arabia, Yemen and North Africa. The suicide bombers involved in destabilising efforts were transferred to Syria, then moved onto Eastern Syria, and from there, crossed the border into Anbar and occasionally through Mosul. Bremer was adamant that Baathist Syria was involved as 'there is nothing that can happen in Syria without the government's knowledge, as Syria is a closed country'.[208]

5.4 Post-invasion phases

5.4.1 US occupation

5.4.1.1 ORHA: mentality of humanitarian assistance

Barbara Bodine, a senior ORHA (Office of Reconstruction and Humanitarian Relief) official, explains that the plan for post-war Iraq was for the US to be out of the country by the end of August 2003.[209] Lawrence Di Rita, a close aide to Donald Rumsfeld, at a meeting in Kuwait before the ORHA team left for Baghdad, stated that the US was not staying for more than three to four months after creating an interim government. He also emphasised that no more than 25,000 soldiers would remain by September 2003.[210] The basic assumptions of the war were, as a senior Pentagon official had noted, that it would be quick, easy, cheap and catalytic.[211]

Feith argues that, in the summer of 2002, he made several attempts to create a post-war planning office and designate someone to take up the task. To his dismay, he got nowhere. However, on 18 October 2002, Rumsfeld eventually asked Feith for a list of candidates for the position. This again had no outcome. Feith later learned from Stephen Hadley that the president was not willing to open such an office while diplomatic efforts were under way.[212] After Iraq's weapons declaration in December 2002, President Bush saw the war as inevitable. Now it was deemed possible to create an office to deal with post-war Iraq.[213] Due to the initial plans and expectations of US involvement in Iraq, the Pentagon chose Garner to lead the post-war effort.[214] This clearly indicated the US lack of will for nation-building and its focus on a humanitarian crisis as Garner had led Operation Provide Comfort in Iraqi Kurdistan to feed and repatriate displaced Kurds. ORHA was created on 20 January 2003 by the president.[215] It was considered part of CENTCOM, to help it with its civilian expertise in Phase IV of post-war reconstruction.[216] ORHA was a difficult organisation to make effective, due to its interagency structure as well as its objective of working with the military.[217] Making matters worse General Tommy Franks paid little attention to Phase IV of posthostilities planning. Franks submitted his resignation six weeks after the fall of Baghdad, evidence for his lack of commitment.[218]

Though Rumsfeld was against an occupation authority, he was also reluctant to hand over full authority to the Iraqis immediately after Saddam's overthrow, as was the case in Afghanistan. He believed that the Iraqi leaders were relatively unknown to ordinary Iraqis, possibly incompetent, corrupt and abusive of their new authority. The US government believed that Iraq was different to Afghanistan due to its substantial army and oil wealth. Rumsfeld wanted to strike a balance between immediate recognition like that of Afghanistan, and an outright occupation.[219] However, an early opposition conference, as opposed to the one held in December 2002 in London followed by several others, might have changed the post-Saddam political landscape in Iraq. It might have paved the way to an earlier transition of authority and avoided the occupation authority of the CPA that lasted more than a year.[220] Garner explained to the author that he did in fact bring to Baghdad leading Iraqi opposition leaders, Chalabi, Allawi, Pachachi, Barzani, Jalal Talabani and Hakim. He told them to set up operations, and he would make them into an interim government. Garner stressed that 'Bremer cancelled it'. In Garner's words the initial US plan was to create the IIA (Iraqi Interim Authority) to bring leaders forward 'to continue to have a liberation, not an occupation'.[221]

However, this changed; the acknowledgment of serious flaws in the post-war operations in Iraq made the administration rethink its strategy. They were unhappy with Garner's performance and replaced him with Paul Bremer.[222] Meghan O'Sullivan, who was in Baghdad at the time, explained that the US was not prepared for what actually transpired, but was operating on a set of assumptions that turned out not to be true. People did not expect that the structures of society would come apart so quickly. The assumption was that when Saddam was removed, institutions of government would be in place. When that turned out not to be true: 'we had a problem with public order, we had a problem with the rule of law, and no counterparts to work with'.[223] Rumsfeld had confirmed this assumption in February 2003: 'Iraq has a solid infrastructure with working networks of roads and [resources] and it has oil to help give free Iraq the means to get on its feet.'[224] ORHA was changed to CPA, as a realisation that the original construct for ORHA was narrower than what was needed in Iraq. ORHA had been initially created to deal with humanitarian assistance and some reconstruction. ORHA had a branch to alleviate displacement, and a lot of the planning was for that. However, that was not a consequence of war. What was perceived to be needed was a much more comprehensive effort to reconstruct the institutions of the state, as ORHA had too narrow a mission. The thinking was to get a new organisation that had the capacity, authority and capability to play a larger role to help rebuild Iraq.[225] Garner was informed of his replacement in late April 2003. The Pentagon claims that the replacement of Garner was part of the plan all along, but George Packer explains how the original plan was to send a civilian ambassador to support an interim Iraqi government.[226] Garner emphatically stressed that he 'did not expect to have a CPA, and thought he only would have ORHA deal with post invasion Iraq'.[227]

5.4.1.2 CPA: from liberators to occupiers

Upon his arrival, Bremer used Germany and Japan as examples for the scale of his new assignment. He affirmed to his aides, on his arrival date on 12 May 2003, that democracy cannot work unless the political structure is backed up with a civil society, which can only be assured with the presence of political parties, a free press, an independent judiciary and accountability in public spending.[228] Paul Bremer arrived in Iraq only after the military operation to overthrow Saddam Hussein had successfully concluded. Bremer stresses that he was assigned the difficult role of rebuilding a new Iraq. He summarises the challenges that faced the US-led coalition in three points: 'provide security for the Iraqi people, set Iraq on the path to a more open, humane and democratic society, and finally, reform Iraq's closed and moribund economy'. According to Bremer the first task was the responsibility of the coalition military, and the latter two of the Coalition Provisional Authority (CPA) that he led.[229]

With Paul Bremer's arrival, the policies of the US began to change dramatically, including those approved by Bush and those worked on by Garner. It was a complete reversal and change in strategy.[230] Brad Swanson, a CPA official, described the US presence in two phases. First, the arrogance phase, in which an under-manned, under-planned administration would take over the country then leave in six weeks with a functional government in place. This was followed by a hubris phase, which would involve great US involvement financially and in manpower. These were opposite strategies, and both were ideological responses.[231] A variety of issues had changed with Bremer's arrival, as there was no overarching coherent strategy for the Middle East, specifically for Iraq. Garner had taken steps to begin building a national government for Iraq. But the media had trumpeted the looting, rioting and gunfire. When Rumsfeld then said 'stuff happens', it painted a picture that no one was in control. Bremer was then sent over to get things under control. Hughes explained, 'The assumption was then all Iraqis would say yes. It was the kind of hubris that was totally unsubstantiated.'[232]

Bremer believed that with a solid political infrastructure to leave behind, the US had a greater chance of 'a success story' in Iraq. He wanted to emulate the

German and Japanese examples, otherwise, he stressed, it would descend into chaos, civil war or tyranny.[233] The two options available were: handing over authority to an unelected Iraqi government immediately; or retaining authority while following a slower, more deliberate political process towards restoration of sovereignty.[234] As a result of differing opinions on the transfer of power to the Iraqis, the US ended up with a long-term occupation authority. It resulted mainly from the desire to create a more inclusive political environment.[235] With the ongoing difficulties in Iraq, the Bush administration revised its original plans for the post-invasion period. No longer could nation-building be averted. The number of US forces increased, which led to more and aggressive patrols in Baghdad. In short, June 2003 saw an era of change in US policy towards Iraq, embracing an attempt to nation-build.[236]

Bremer asserts that he decided to create a plan of action as 'Washington's pre-war plans had been overtaken'.[237] Bremer refused to adopt the IIA plan due to his view that the Iraqi leadership lacked competence and that they were unrepresentative.[238] The creation of an Iraqi authority pre-invasion did not win support in the administration. But the creation of an Iraqi authority, known as the Iraqi Interim Authority, in the post-invasion era with power-sharing agreements incorporated was approved by the president and the National Security Council, but was delayed by Powell and Armitage, implemented by Garner and sidelined by Ambassador Bremer.[239] Feith blames the delay of the Iraqi political conference by almost a year as highly damaging to post-Saddam Iraq. Paul Bremer sidelined the Iraqis, on the basis that they showed no productive engagement to build the new Iraq, as the initial plan was to hand over immediately a substantial amount of power to the Iraqis. If further close interactions had been arranged among the Iraqis as a result of the conference this might not have occurred, Feith argues.[240]

As a consequence full US control in an American provisional occupation authority was adopted. The idea behind the 'Transitional Civil Authority' Armitage had proposed was that the externals be prevented from taking a major role in post-Saddam Iraq. When State Department and CIA officials were challenged they asserted that the externals lacked competence and legitimacy.[241] The State Department and the CIA may have had little sway at the table at National Security Council and Principals' meetings. However, State Department officials on the ground had substantial impact on Ambassador Bremer's views of the Iraqi externals. The CIA and State Department officers at CENTCOM also managed to belittle the military commanders' perceptions of the Iraqi externals. This also resulted in the commanders' opinion that training the Iraqi externals was a waste of time.[242] Even when Bremer created the IGC he decided to give no authority to the IGC independent of the CPA, thus no power-sharing arrangement.[243] On 13 July 2003 the CPA created the Iraqi Governing Council, composed of the six Iraqi leadership council members plus one internal as well eighteen others chosen by the CPA in a nationwide search.[244] However, the Iraqi Governing Council was rendered ineffective. Sumaidaie, a member of the twenty-five-member council, expressed the council's frustration. In the early stages the council needed to put its message to the people in respect to what the new Iraq was about and how it was proposed to take care of citizens' needs. The Ministry of Information had been disbanded. 'We the Governing Council were not given a channel to broadcast our ideas', explained Sumaidaie. As a result a big gap ensued. The Pentagon had assigned this task to a company called Science Applications International Corporation (SAIC). It became a serious defect for the IGC as the council was denied crucial access to the public. This could have prevented the building-up of the insurgency.[245]

During Garner's visit to Kurdistan in April 2003 he requested Barzani and Talabani to travel to Baghdad and help set up a new Iraqi administration. Garner requested that the G5 of friendly opposition groups expand their base to 20–25 by including new groups into the process, and from this organise a national conference inviting 300–500 Iraqi personalities to create the first post-Saddam Iraqi government under US supervision. This failed to materialise mostly due to the former opposition's inaction. Nawshirwan argues that the Supreme Council for the Islamic Revolution in Iraq (SCIRI) kept the talks going without allowing significant progress. And only after obstructing this request for three weeks did they approve the inclusion of the Islamic Dawa Party, led by Ibrahim Jaafari and the National Democratic Party, led by Naseer al-Chaderchi. This saga eventually led to the US disillusionment with the Iraqi opposition and encouraged its taking direct control of Iraq. It proposed UNSCR 1483 which was approved, and officially changed the US status from liberator to occupier of the country.[246] Bremer affirms this position. He states that when the group of exiles with which the US government had been in contact proved unable or unwilling to increase its representation, the CPA itself sought out Iraqi leaders who could broaden the group.[247]

Colin Powell and Richard Armitage were adamant about keeping power out of the hands of Iraqi 'externals' instead of transferring authority from the US to the Iraqis. Armitage, as mentioned earlier, had believed that the US would have to maintain control for a 'multi-year transitional period' since early summer of 2002. This belief originated from his deep distrust of all Iraqi externals, especially Chalabi, and a desire to create a 'credible' Iraqi leadership.[248] Bremer, also, was not happy with the skills of the Iraqi leadership. To him they lacked the dedication, diligence and necessary skills to govern. Accordingly he planned to run Iraq until he could establish a civil society, develop a democracy and cultivate a new leadership. The CPA would have to stay in power for several years until this could be achieved through the preparation of a new constitution and elections. Bremer's concept of legitimacy and the required work needed to this end was considered an open-ended commitment and unnecessary by Rumsfeld.[249] Bremer asserted: 'the exile leadership group did not reflect a balance of Iraq's population'. Bremer believed Sunnis were hardly represented, the Kurds overrepresented. The group included no women or members of important Iraqi minorities, such as Christians and Turkomen. Bremer states that the group was neither 'well-established' nor 'broadly representative'.[250]

Michael Rubin stated unequivocally that the 'neoconservatives were against the creation of the CPA'.[251] Before the war, there had been disagreements within the American government about the length of the occupation of Iraq. Some, including Feith, argued that as soon as Saddam was ousted, America should turn over sovereignty to a small group of Iraqi exiles with whom the US government had been in touch. However, officials at the State Department and CIA emphasised the deep divisions in Iraqi society caused by Saddam's long tyranny, and suggested the US would be obliged to undertake a long-term effort to put Iraq on the path to representative government. Bremer affirms that the president had agreed with the short-occupation version sometime in March.[252]

Feith criticises Paul Bremer for his claim of Iraqi reluctance to forward the political process. To him it was evident that Bremer could have made the Iraqi political figures advance if he wanted. Examples of this were the 15 November 2003 agreement, which led to the creation of the Transitional Administrative Law (TAL) and the dissolution of the Iraqi Governing Council and the creation of the interim government.[253] Bremer was constantly under pressure, intensifying in early October 2003, to hand over sovereignty as well as to give an increased role to the newly trained Iraqi police and army. Bremer was frustrated asserting 'if America cannot stand the heat after less than six months, we are going to have a very untidy century'.[254] Bremer had told Andrew Card that an early transfer of power to the Iraqis would 'make the president's vision of Iraq very difficult, if not impossible'. Bremer was conscious of the domestic implications of a prolonged occupation but insisted that the US 'do what's right for Iraq for five, ten, twenty years ahead'.[255]

Bremer was determined to create a blueprint to direct the CPA's efforts in Iraq. He had an 'ambitious vision' to transform a shattered country into a prosperous, equitable, peaceful and civil society.[256] Bremer announced his seven-step plan in the *Washington Post* article, entitled 'Iraq's Path to Sovereignty', on 8 September 2003. The CPA and the IGC, according to Bremer, had agreed that the first step was for the latter to convene a conference to draft a new constitution. This would have been ratified by the Iraqi people, leading to elections, a sovereign Iraqi government and the end of the occupation. This political sequence Bremer believes was outlined to top coalition leaders within weeks of the CPA's establishment.[257] However, Feith argues that Bremer's article in the *Washington Post* setting out seven steps to Iraqi sovereignty was a blatant deviation from the administration's IIA policy. It was effectively the State Department's multi-year occupation Transitional Civil Authority.[258] Bremer initially informed the Governing Council that the CPA plan for the return of sovereignty rested on the sequence below:

1 Writing a permanent constitution.
2 General referendum on the permanent constitution.
3 Holding general elections to elect a General Assembly and a cabinet recognised internationally.
4 Then returning sovereignty to Iraq.

For none of the steps above had Bremer suggested a timeline.[259] The Sistani 26 June 2003 *fatwa* rejecting a written constitution by CPA-appointed officials was one of many changes of course in Iraq.[260] Additionally, Rumsfeld wanted an agreed 'timetable for early recognition of Iraqi sovereignty, so that the Coalition could shed the "occupying power" label'. The US did not want to oppose nor appear to oppose elections.[261] As a result, and after the 15 November agreement, these major changes were agreed upon:

1   Partial elections for a transitional General Assembly allowing the creation of an interim government.
2   Dissolution of the Iraqi Governing Council and CPA.
3   Returning sovereignty to Iraq.
4   And then setting the stage for general elections, allowing the drafting of a permanent constitution.

However, for these stages, a fixed timeline was stipulated.[262]

Rumsfeld called Bremer on 13 September 2003 to advise him to hand over sovereignty to the Iraqi Governing Council or any other group of Iraqis.[263] Rumsfeld was committed to avoiding a prolonged US occupation of Iraq. Rumsfeld had proposed that an end date be declared for the termination of the CPA, preferably by the end of June 2004. The seven-step plan by Bremer was discarded as a result. Instead, an interim constitution was agreed upon, as elections would have prolonged the occupation.[264] Even Vice President Cheney was not happy with the mistakes made. He felt the establishment of the CPA and the appointment of Paul Bremer slowed down the transition process. In his mind, the creation of a provisional government before the invasion would have created grounds for a swifter transfer of power to the Iraqis.[265] The plan changed dramatically, due to objections from Sistani and Washington. So on 15 November 2003, with the approval of the US government, the CPA and the Governing Council laid out a new plan. The new plan was to work with Iraqi legal experts and the council to draft an interim constitution that would establish the framework for Iraq's politics and lead to elections. The agreement provided for an indirectly elected Iraqi government to assume sovereignty from the coalition. Al-Sistani objected to this aspect of the agreement. The CPA and the UN worked to answer his concerns and were able to gain a broad consensus on the transition process. All parties agreed that the TAL (interim constitution) would be drafted by the Governing Council and Iraqi legal experts in spring 2004, and that the CPA would then hand sovereignty to a non-elected, but representative, interim government by 1 July 2004.[266]

Bremer did not believe that the former Iraqi opposition deserved to govern. Qubad Talabani, the Kurdistan Regional Government's (KRG) former representative to Washington and son of Iraqi President Jalal Talabani, who was in Baghdad and involved in the negotiations of the TAL, stated that Bremer believed the 'Iraqis were hopeless'.[267] Bremer was convinced that the inability of this group 'to agree upon even the most basic questions' of its own internal functioning clearly showed that it was not ready to govern Iraq, or even to share substantially in such responsibilities.[268] The Iraqi Governing Council had far less power than the IIA was intended to have.[269] Bremer, though briefed before his departure about the creation of the IIA in Washington, set aside the IIA plan as he had developed his own views as regards his role in Iraq. He thought of the plan as merely a Pentagon one, and was convinced that he had greater flexibility as the man on the ground.[270] Even before he arrived in Iraq, Bremer had decided that an Iraqi leadership was incapable of receiving authority early on; he described the intention of the proponents of this attitude as a 'reckless fantasy'.[271] Bremer's goal in the TAL document was to create an Iraq that was unified, democratic and stable, which had a vibrant economy and a representative government.[272] Bremer wanted to create an Iraqi authority to show the Iraqis that the US was serious about political reform and transferring authority to the Iraqis. Bremer also emphasised that his intention was to broaden the political landscape to make it 'representative of all Iraqis'. This he also told the G7 of Iraqi opposition leaders in his first meeting.[273]

Bremer believed he had a direct mandate from the president. President Bush was adamant that the Iraq project had to be seen through vigorously, regardless of circumstances. He told Bremer that he was committed to bringing representative government to the Iraqi people and that he would not abandon them. Bush had asserted: 'We'll stay until the job is done. You can count on my support irrespective of the political calendar or what the media might say.'[274] At a 12 November 2003 NSC meeting in Washington, Bush stressed

> I believe in the inherent goodness of the Iraqi people. They have a basic instinct to live in peace, guided by universal values which are beyond politics ... It's important for everyone to know that we're going to stay the course and that I'm determined to succeed.[275]

Bremer argues that the interim constitution, or TAL, was the CPA's most important contribution to Iraq's political future.[276]

Rumsfeld's intervention halted the occupation of Iraq that would have lasted for several more years. However, Bremer's plan, according to Feith, did long-term strategic harm. First, it helped gain the insurgency public support. It confirmed their claims about the US desire for domination and exploitation. It also damaged the standing of the democratic opposition. It changed all Iraqi problems – political, social and economic – into US ones.[277] Nawshirwan stresses that if it were not for the isolation and international pressure from France, China, Russia and Germany, as well as the insurgency, the US would have disregarded Iraqi sentiments and would have mocked the possibility of transferring authority to the Iraqis and the restoration of Iraq's sovereignty.[278]

Bremer had already made it clear to his superiors in Washington that he had 'three red lines'. He wanted to leave behind a professional, incorrupt and human rights-conscious police force; second, an army not involved in internal affairs of Iraq; and finally to 'pass sovereignty to an Iraqi government elected on the basis of a constitution'.[279] Bremer was focused on paving the way to a new Iraq that enjoyed representative government, recognising that this was a 'complex challenge' requiring time, as Iraqis had little experience in 'self-rule and the institutions that supported it'. His ambition was to 'instil an understanding of democratic government'.[280] Wolfowitz had met with Bremer on 22 September 2003 to discuss the possibility of handing over sovereignty to the Governing Council. During this meeting, Bremer stressed the incompetence of the Iraqi Governing Council and its lack of representation. Bremer believed in Wolfowitz's notion that a democratic Iraq would revolutionise the region, but stressed that patience was a prerequisite if achieved.[281] Bremer's intention from his involvement in Iraq was not only to install democracy, but also to provide the social shock absorbers that guaranteed its sustainability. He was frustrated with certain administration officials he described as nation-building evaders.[282]

Feith explains that the US committed grave mistakes in Iraq, but he stresses that by far the greatest mistake was the mishandling of the transference of authority to the Iraqis after Saddam's overthrow. It opened up the perception that the US was not a liberator, but an occupier in the eyes of the average Iraqi. He explains 'it offended the personal dignity and national pride of many Iraqis, creating opportunities exploitable by hard-core Baathists, sectarian extremists, foreign jihadists, and Iraq's ill intentioned neighbours'.[283] Iraqi Foreign Minister Hoshyar Zebari stressed that the biggest mistake was to change the nature of the mission from liberation to occupation.[284] Feith asserts that the concept of liberation, not occupation, was an objective at the senior layers of government. President Bush had emphasised 'liberation, not occupation' as his guiding principle. There was general consensus before the invasion among all agencies of government that occupation would invite 'guerrilla warfare, terrorism, and political instability'.[285] George Packer, however, describes the replacement of Garner with Bremer as a rational departure in US strategy in an attempt to get Iraq under control, albiet with the mistaken assumption that Americans could run Iraq from the Green Zone with only nominal Iraqi participation.[286]

Even Bremer was losing patience. The CPA adjusted to the new realities on the ground. He asserted to a NSC meeting on 21 April 2004 that the more he has been in Iraq, the more he is 'attracted to the idea of returning sovereignty to them as quickly as possible'.[287] On 19 January 2004, Bremer met Kofi Annan in New York, where he emphasised that the Coalition would welcome the re-establishment of 'a long-term partnership with the UN' as well as to guarantee security for its officials upon returning to Iraq.[288] And on 23 April 2004, Bremer announced his relaxation of the strict de-Baathification policy by re-employing many army officers and teachers.[289]

Ali Allawi, a minister in the Iraqi Governing Council cabinet, identifies two blunders of this period that contributed immensely to the deteriorating situation in Iraq. First, the CPA made no effort in developing a new system of governance, as is the case in occupied territories, other than replacing the top echelons in government and replacing them with Iraqi expatriates. It was merely a continuation of the Baathist design of government. Second, the CPA did not have the mandate to directly administer the country and subsequently conduct such thorough reforms. This course of action clashed with the notion of liberation and added to the fear of a long-term commitment in Iraq that was not appealing to the US public.[290]

The CPA was predominantly 'about destroying the old Iraq', Nabil Al-Tikriti, Fellow at the US Institute of Peace, stressed.[291] Yet it had no desire to a commitment as difficult as rebuilding it. US goals changed in Iraq due to external (international) factors as well as internal factors. The internal factors were twofold: Washington and domestic US opinion, and Baghdad and domestic Iraqi opinion. Hughes explained how the objectives evolved. It was simple liberation as the president had described. But then it became more complex. The US wanted an Iraq that recognised the sovereignty of its neighbours, was not going to pose a threat to them, would participate in a free market economy, recognise humanitarian international law and have a representative government. This was eventually recognised as too stringent a list that could not be achieved, so it was scaled back. The goal then became an Iraq that could defend itself, govern itself and sustain itself. The standards were suddenly lowered.[292] Rubin describes it a typical case of 'mission creep', if you compare the stated objectives before and after the invasion.[293] Tommy Franks makes clear that his mission was restricted to two objectives. First, regime change and second to deprive Iraq of weapons conventional or WMD.[294] This was the most damaging as it denied it the necessary attention in Phase VI. Sumaidaie emphasised that in the early days the expectations were high; they were moderated in the light of reality, and reduced with reality.[295] Before creating the Iraqi Governing Council, Bremer issued the following orders, which had a dramatic impact on the events in the aftermath of the military invasion. Bremer eventually issued 100 orders during his administration of Iraq.

1   CPA Order Number 1: De-Baathification of Iraqi Society on 16 May 2003.
2   CPA Order Number 2: Dissolution of Entities on 23 May 2003.
3   CPA Order Number 3: Weapons Control on 23 May 2003. Overlooked as it could not be enforced.
4   CPA Order Number 4: Management of Property and Assets of the Iraqi Baath Party on 25 May 2003.
5   CPA Order Number 5: Establishment of the Iraqi De-Baathification Council on 25 May 2003.[296]

5.4.2 Towards sovereignty: the interim, transitional and permanent governments

The way in which the interim government was established was a reflection of a change in mood and perception in Washington. This was for two major reasons: first, the CPA proved incompetence in handling post-war Iraq; second, it reflected the deep flaws and ignorance of the neoconservative war camp in Washington as regards to the realities on the ground in Iraq. Because of the constant chaos in Iraq, the role of the neoconservative camp began to decline. The

State Department and the intelligence services began to gain further influence in the formulation of US Iraq policy.[297] The neoconservatives were losing ground to other power centres in Washington. With the empowerment of the interim government, arguments concerning stability and order in the Middle East began to resurface in Washington.[298] The interim government was used as a token to reconcile the Arab world and calm their fears. It was manifest of a new outlook for Iraq contrary to the neoconservative model. The Shiites had been profoundly marginalised, reducing fears of the Arab world regarding the emergence of a Shiite state that would be naturally allied to Iran.[299] The Shiite Islamist presence during the CPA was toned down in the interim government, with only one true Islamist minister, Adil Abd-al-Mahdi, who could be seen as more of a moderate than a radical. Power was being redistributed in Iraq with US interests in mind.[300] The continuing insurgency in Iraq also led to a reappraisal of previous Washington strategies. The violence in Iraq was no longer attributed to dead-enders and regime remnants. An acknowledgement was emerging of the Sunni rejection of the post-invasion order. Sunnis were encouraged and supported to become more influential in the new evolving order. Even Baathists who could contribute were accepted. The composition of the interim government reflected this new approach.[301] It was a twist in strategy that the Allawi interim government was determined to tackle. The de-Baathification order would be diluted only to the closest Saddam henchmen, and the senior officers of the previous regime would be accommodated to ensure more Sunni participation in an attempt to reverse the insurgency.[302] This was a reversal of strict de-Baathification and de-militarisation policies in order to appease the Sunnis, who were considered instrumental to the insurgency.[303] General Sanchez was relieved of his post as supreme commander and replaced by General Casey.[304] The UN was also being brought back centre-stage.

US strategy was changing. The constant and unrelenting violence created the circumstances for a major rethink of the Bush administration's policy towards Iraq. Having appointed an authoritarian Allawi, the neoconservative discourse was being sidelined in Washington. This new approach for Iraq was perceived to have merit.[305] The intention behind the structure and nature of the interim government was to limit Iraq's links with Iran and also to keep the pan-Arab appearance alive. Most of all, it was designed to keep Iraq in step with the US policy of isolating Iran.[306] During this period, the Kurds were also marginalised, treated as non-players. Allawi was portrayed as a strong man, although he did not have Saddam's 'fear factor'.[307] The interim government was used as a force for change and reconfiguration of previously pursued post-Saddam policies. It was a tool to bring back alienated Sunnis into the political process.[308] However, the rhetoric remained fairly consistent, with a further emphasis on democracy promotion. Failing to find WMD in Iraq after the war, the Bush administration focused its rhetoric to promoting democracy with no mention of the Baath regime's record or potential threats.[309]

Nevertheless, the appointed interim government performed its job in advancing the political process. It was mostly dominated by externals and no issue of legitimacy was raised during that period, Feith asks why the US government failed to install an Iraqi government for fourteen months, and imposed an occupation.[310] Bremer refutes this argument as unrealistic since 'such a government would have operated in a legal and political vacuum', answering to no-one, least of all to the people of Iraq. Bremer contents that in such a scenario, an interim Iraqi government would have assumed power with no constitution and not have accepted procedures for structuring or choosing a government, or for making decisions or passing and enforcing laws.[311]

However, this would change. Professor Juan Cole of the University of Michigan gave a concise description of the election outcome for the transitional National Assembly: 'This is a government that will have very good relations with Iran ... In terms of regional geopolitics this is not the outcome that the United States was hoping for.'[312] This explains why Zalmay Khalilzad arrived in Iraq in June 2005 with a new objective. Zalmay stated that 'I went to Iraq with a clear view that we needed to bring the Sunni Arabs into the political process.' The Sunnis had boycotted the elections for the transitional constitution-writing assembly that had taken place in January 2005 leading to Ibrahim Jaafari election as Prime Minister. Khalilzad had come to Baghdad as ambassador 'with a mission of bringing them [Sunnis] into the political process'.[313]

In November 2004 General George Casey also reviewed the US strategy in Iraq after General Ricardo Sanchez's departure. A new strategy was formulated in partnership with the British to ensure a counter-insurgency strategy with focus on the training of Iraqi security forces under the supervision of the US military. In February 2005 an unnamed official acknowledged that the senior leadership was contemplating an 'overarching counterinsurgency campaign plan'. After almost two years the US had finally recognised that the Iraq war was not over.[314] The 'Clear, Hold, Build' method was doctrinally established in FM 3–24 and endorsed by Secretary of State Condoleezza Rice in 2005: 'In short, with the Iraqi Government, our political-military strategy has to be to clear, hold, and build: to clear areas from insurgent control, to hold them securely, and to build durable, national Iraqi institutions.'[315] Casey took a different approach in dealing with the security crisis in Iraq. Casey focused on containing the insurgent violence, building up Iraqi security forces, rebuilding the economy, reaching out to the hostile Sunni community both through co-opting and coercion.[316]

However, this strategy proved flawed. US forces would clear, and then assign the role of holding the terrain to Iraqi forces which were lacking in quality and quantity.[317] The US was constantly returning to re-clear previously cleared terrain.[318] The basic problem with the approach was that US troop strength was inadequate to hold the terrain and subsequently secure the population.[319] President Bush had also recognised the failed US strategy in Iraq especially with the insurgency compounded by sectarian violence. The US had in 2006 both an insurgency and brewing civil war to deal with.

As it stands, the post-invasion period of Iraq was characterised by three major phases. The first phase immediately after the fall of Saddam's regime was a neo-conservative phase. The Bush administration pursued its idealistic and naïve perceptions of a post-war order with little success. The second phase was more sober, with a clear emphasis on security and stability, enshrined in the interim government of Ayad Allawi. In this period, the idealistic aspirations of the US for a new Iraq were abandoned for security. Former Baath and military elements were included in the security process. The third phase straddled the clear defeat of a pro-Western political order to a transitional government of Shiite dominance. This phase was characterised by great personal involvement of Zalmay Khalilzad in achieving further Sunni participation in the drafting of the constitution and the creation of a power balance to the excessive Shiite power in the post-Saddam era.[320] Battalion commander Lieutenant Colonel Dom Caraccilo described the different phases of the US invasion as follows: liberators, occupiers and counter-insurgents with no parallel to any other US enterprise in history. Caraccilo refutes any possible comparison with Germany, Japan, Vietnam and French Algeria. To him the insurgency had no organised structure, it was a confused mixture of various combining elements.[321] Matthew Stephenson of the State Department described US Iraq policy under President Bush having three distinct phases applying consistently to the political, military and economic levels of US interaction with Iraq. The first phase was a US managed operation, later transitioning into a joint US–Iraq effort, and finally by the end of the Bush administration a US-supported effort.[322] Stephenson described political evolution in Iraq; he divided the political timeline into three phases. Post Operation Iraqi Freedom the CPA had full sovereignty. The US then created an interim and a transitional government with sovereignty being transitioned during this period and Iraq only fully sovereign after the constitution was adopted and the constitutional permanent government elected.[323]

Khalilzad acknowledged that the US adapted. 'I think if you go in with very fixed ideas and do not have the agility to adjust, dealing with reality as you find them, I think that could be a constraint that could help cause failure.' He affirmed that as one of the few that knew the region, 'he could absorb the realities' of the region and he could advise leaders what sort of adjustments were required in US plans, in order to make progress and be successful.[324] Qubad Talabani uses personalities to describe the evolution in US policy after the invasion, 'you can gauge the US through characters'. Jay Garner was 'a sleeves-rolled-up official' working with his hands. Then you had 'a sharp, stern and serious Ambassador Bremer'. Negroponte he described as a reclusive figure, the US purposely taking the back seat to allow Iraqi sovereignty to flourish. Then Ambassadors David Satterfield and James Jeffrey who did not quite fill the void, followed by Khalilzad who was all about shuttle diplomacy.[325]

Bush made clear he was adjusting: 'stay the course means, let's get the job done, but it doesn't mean staying stuck on a strategy or tactics that may not be working'.[326] On 10 January 2007 Bush announced the surge. In a candid speech he stressed that 'it is clear that we need to change our strategy in Iraq'.[327] It is quite clear from the re-election of Bush for a second term that the policies of the Bush administration were far stronger than a handful of neoconservative intellectuals and the American Enterprise Institute. It was a national choice, and, even if a Kerry White House had been the outcome, the international circumstances would have left no choice but to continue existing policies. Therefore it could be argued that the very continuation of the policies of the Bush Doctrine explain that its principal themes correspond to American values, interests and capabilities.[328] On the eve of the fifth anniversary of 9/11 in 2006 President Bush took the opportunity to acknowledge mistakes made and also emphasised the necessity of continuity in the ongoing campaign in Iraq. He said:

> whatever mistakes have been made in Iraq, the worst mistake would be to think that if we pulled out, the terrorists would leave us alone. They will not leave us alone. They will follow us. The safety of America depends on the outcome of the battle in the streets of Baghdad.[329]

The adjustments made reflected changes in strategy, i.e. what to do, and tactics, i.e. how to do it. The principal policies remained the same.

Nevertheless, the second Bush term saw major changes as regards the Bush foreign policy team with several replacements in high-profile positions in the administration: Rice, Wolfowitz, Feith and later on Rumsfeld. The US showed greater warmth towards Europe. There were also attempts at showing more interest toward multilateralism as regards Iraq. The Bush administration pressed the UN into a greater role in Iraq with UNSCR 1770 allowing a greater political role with respect to promoting national reconciliation in the country.[330]

The National Security Strategy of 2006 perpetuated the notion of pre-emption and all other aspects of the Bush Doctrine, and in so doing echoed the already declared policy.[331] The Bush administration took its election for a second term as a mandate to continue its current policies.[332] Condoleezza Rice emphasised this attitude as mentioned in the previous chapter, in a 2005 statement in Cairo:

> For 60 years, my country, the United States, pursued stability at the expense of democracy in this region here, in the Middle East – and we achieved neither. Now, we are taking a different course. We are supporting the democratic aspirations of all people.

This is not to say after the continuous setbacks and discouragements on the ground in Afghanistan and especially with the insurgency in Iraq, as Philip Gordon states, a clear change in tone and style was not witnessed from the start of President Bush's second term in office, which Gordon defines as 'counterrevolution'; this time round multilateralism, alliances and consultation were given greater value. International institutions such as the ICC, which had had reluctant support during the first term, were given greater value as well as pledges to support the United Nations on certain issues; all became visible signs of retreat from previous policies.[333]

5.4.2.1   The mid-term elections 2006

The major change in Iraq came when the internal violence in Iraq reached unprecedented levels. The insurgency was compounded with signs of early phases of an all-out sectarian war between Iraq's Sunnis and Shiites. The November 2006 congressional elections were also a major indication of the decline in public support for the Bush administration and its Iraq war. The Democrats had promised a new approach to Iraq policy as their campaign slogan and had won Congress back. However, Bush was adamant that there would be no change of policy even with the recommendations of the Baker–Hamilton report in the pipeline.[334] The recognition of the deteriorating situation of Iraq was only publicly recognised in late 2006. The turning point seemed to be the statements made by Senator John Warner who said the 'situation is simply drifting sidewise' and that a 'change of course' should be considered if the situation had not changed by the end of 2006. Condoleezza Rice also visited Baghdad in October 2006 expressing her frustration with the Iraqi authorities due to their 'political inaction'.[335] The Iraqi Study Group co-chaired by James Baker and Lee Hamilton had already been commissioned on 15 March 2006 to assess the situation in Iraq. The study had seventy-nine recommendations. The boldest was that the US accelerate handing security to the Iraqi government and start withdrawal. The president, however, disagreed with this approach and was determined to see it through. Certain conservative and military figures intervened, advocating a new approach which eventually became known as the surge. Frederick Kagan, who was one of the leading architects of the surge, was a neoconservative, whereas cautious realists like Baker and Hamilton opposed it.[336] Even though the neoconservative agenda gained momentum as a result of 9/11, the marriage of convenience between realists, pragmatists and neoconservatives had begun to unravel in the mid second term of the Bush presidency as a result of the mounting troubles in Iraq.[337]

Congressman Christopher Van Hollen (D-MD) affirmed that in the lead-up to the war the Congress passed a resolution in the fall of 2002 authorising the president to use force in Iraq. It gave the president a 'blank cheque' and it did not require the president to come back to Congress. The Congress provided little oversight and continued its blank cheque until January 2007.[338] In 2006 and 2007 the US Congress re-established itself as an equal arm of government after many years of passiveness as a result of the 9/11 attacks.[339] With mid-term elections due in November 2006 and the presidential elections due in late 2008 no one in Washington was really prepared to ask for more troops. Both Republicans and Democrats wanted troop levels reduced.[340] When Democrats gained control of Congress in late 2006, there was more accountability in the development contracts. There was more accountability in terms of how effectively the training and equipping programme was going with the Iraqi military. The Congress held the administration accountable on benchmarks on which they had publicly stated the Iraqi government would be judged. Referring to the US Congress, Richard Kessler argued: when you influence something when it is pretty much under way, influence is diminished. Influence usually comes at the beginning when you try to articulate policy. But if you attempt to exert influence along the way, this will have diminished.[341] Until the Democrats took over in late 2006 after the mid-term elections, Congress did very little in the way of oversight because it had a Republican majority that was not going to be tough on its own administration. Congress really only began its job in early 2007. The Democratic takeover also led to the concentration of the minds in the Bush administration leading to the surge. Congress did not do a lot in the immediate aftermath of the war. It did not do a lot to question the Bush administration's moves. Bush had realised in 2006 it was a 'do or die situation', and the last chance to save the Iraq war. The administration knew that its back was against the wall and that there was a danger that the anti-war movement could grow, and be led by Congress.[342]

5.4.2.2 Bush's second term and the surge

As the insurgency began to build, General David Petraeus was assigned the role of reforming US military strategy to tackle the violence. This was almost a year after the invasion.[343] However, the actual change in Iraq came in the fall of 2006. General Peter Pace created a secret panel to review the Iraq strategy. The conclusions of the panel were briefed to the president on 13 December. The conclusion was to change the strategy from direct combat operations to a new supportive, training and advisory role. This was to be done through an initial increase of 20,000–30,000 troops to confront sectarian violence and increase security in Baghdad.[344] As a result in 2007 General George Casey's ineffective 'clear, hold and build' was replaced by a new strategy implemented by General Petraeus that focused on protecting the Iraqi populace.[345] Casey would 'clear' but not be able to 'hold' as the Iraqi forces assigned the role were incompetent to take on this responsibility. Petraeus took over the coalition forces command in Iraq on 10 February 2007 after he had demonstrated considerable success in his tour as head of the 101st Airborne division in 2003 in northern Iraq. The idea this time was to increase the US military presence in Baghdad and Anbar by 17,000 and 4000 troops respectively. Petraeus would establish thirty-six outposts across Baghdad where US and Iraqi forces would live and operate together. Iraqi troops would lead the way with US forces backing them as well as preventing sectarian violence. This new approach known as 'the surge', would also 'clear, hold and build' rather than embark upon the taking and re-taking of cities again and again as had been previously done and would focus on the protection of civilians, which in preceding years was at best a low priority.[346] The surge was helped by other internal factors. Frederick Kagan stated that Muqtada al-Sadr's truce was helpful, but that was less important than the Awakening (*sahwa*) movement that was facilitated by the surge.[347] Another major factor assisting the success of the surge was Iran's later adopted strategy; it allowed calm in Basra and southern Iraq to allow US and British withdrawal – a prime Iranian objective.

General Raymond Odierno was prominent in designing the surge. He and his staff did most of the military planning before Petraeus arrived in February 2007 although Petraeus was also involved. General Petraeus had authored the counter-insurgency manual which had laid out the template.[348] Kagan explained to the author that the strategy that the US pursued after it belatedly recognised it was facing an insurgency and a determined terrorist campaign in Iraq was based on two fundamental assumptions about counter-insurgency. One was that the presence of counter-insurgency forces is an irritant that fuels the insurgency, and therefore the number should be minimised and the profile of exogenous counter-insurgency forces should be minimised. The other assumption was that it is very important not to do things for the host government or security forces lest they become dependent on the external ally and fail to establish their own ability to defend themselves. These assumptions underlay General Abizaid's approach to the conflict throughout his tenure and also the assumption that guided General Casey as Iraq commander. The problem was, however, a third fact about counter-insurgency that the US military ignored. If the population is not provided with security then it does not matter if the profile of the external forces is minimised; if security is left to a host government incapable of providing adequate security, the latter is capable of deteriorating very rapidly to the point of total collapse.[349]

The situation that was developing in 2006, as the capabilities of the Iraqi government security forces were increasing steadily, was that violence was increasing exponentially. It looked as though there was no way the capabilities of the Iraq security forces were going to halt the deterioration in security in Iraq. So Frederick Kagan and others inside and outside the military proposed a change in strategy to prioritise providing security to the Iraqi population first, and worry about other things later. This was the origin of the shift in strategy in 2007, namely the surge. Executing that strategy required more forces. However, Kagan stressed that if the US had injected more forces into the previous strategy it would have failed. The need was not for more forces but for a change in strategy that needed more forces to work.[350] The surge was designed to provide security for the Iraqi people. This could not be done without controlling certain key terrain, but the purpose of the surge was not to control the terrain.[351]

Bush had always been sceptical of his successor's commitment to Iraq, which is why he hoped the surge would succeed. In early 2007 he stated that '(t)he danger is that the United States won't stay engaged'. He hoped for a longer presence of US forces in Iraq at the request of the Iraqi government. Bush asserted that 'the danger is, people come to office and say, "Let us promote stability – that's more important." The problem is that in an ideological war, stability isn't the answer to the root cause of why people kill and terrorise.'[352] Bush expressed his views on the escalating crises in Iraq on 1 December 2008. Regarding a possible pull-out of Iraq he argued that it would have 'compromised the principle that when you put kids into harm's way, you go in to win', Bush described his decision as 'a tough call', particularly 'since a lot of people were advising for me to get out of Iraq'. However, after listening to a lot of voices he ultimately decided, 'I'm not going to let your son die in vain; I believe we can win; I'm going to do what it takes to win in Iraq.'

There were no changes in policy. The policy was consistently 'don't get defeated'. This meant conclusive military victory and preventing the appearance of defeat.[353] Paul Pillar talked about these changes as more tactical in nature. He described as 'a lot of stumbling and fumbling' where a certain approach was pursued leading to failure then looking towards other alternatives.[354] Kagan described it as a kaleidoscope as the US alternately pursued very bad and good strategies. It is not very unusual in the way the US conducts wars and is common that America starts badly then rights itself after a period. 'I think we've done that in Iraq', Kagan asserted. He also affirmed that all US interests in addition to the moral obligation lead in the direction of standing by the Iraqi people.[355] Kagan stressed that US policy towards Iraq had been very consistent: 'changes in foreign policy no, our foreign policy has been very consistent, changes in military strategy, yes'.[356] Andrew Morrison of the State Department argued that US foreign policy is highly consistent. Morrison asserted that 'the same fundamental questions, the same fundamental issues lead to the same fundamental answers'.[357]

The US objective was to restore Iraq to stability. Former Congressman James Longley affirmed, 'I don't think the end objective has ever changed'. Another objective was to make Iraq a moderating influence in the Middle East, he asserted.[358] The State Department's Matthew Stephenson also argued that 'the end goal has always been the same'. The question has been how to reach that end goal. The goal has remained consistent with different routes attempted to get there. The US objective in Iraq is a democratic state at peace with its neighbours, which is economically strong and is not a haven for terrorists, a country that really is a place where political and economic growth can take place. The US, Stephenson asserted, was in the process of reaching such an objective: 'we're not there but we've made progress'.[359] The success of the surge cooled temperatures in Washington, a senior Congressional staffer explained.[360] This helped the US to pursue its goals in Iraq.

The truth, however, was that the Bush administration adjusted to realities on the ground in terms of its democracy agenda. Bush surrounded himself with pragmatists and problem solvers like Robert Gates and was not as strongly motivated by the ideology born after 9/11.[361] The new shift was managed by pragmatists and sceptics, those whose advice had been denounced and disregarded earlier.[362] During this transition the US became pragmatic and less idealistic. Stephenson explained, 'I think that's fair to say' that there had been a transition in US policy from idealistic aspirations to more realistic goals.[363] The administration dropped the policy to create a model Iraq for the region. The idea that it can be a fully fledged democracy diminished. The aim was to leave Iraq as a stable semi-democratic Iraq, not a democracy in the American or British sense of the word.[364] As policy is the art of the possible the goals were significantly narrowed as difficulties were encountered. The main US goal by the end of the Bush administration was to leave Iraq a stable place so that America did not have to go in again. The US initially thought much more broadly about democracy during the CPA. The broader goal through the CPA was to create a permanent democratic system for Iraq. During this first phase there were other clearly defined goals: eradicating WDM, disarming terrorists and restoring stability to Iraq. As violence was encountered the goal of creating a permanent democratic system decreased in importance to the White House and the focus was on stability.[365] Meghan O'Sullivan stressed that there was a shift towards a more pragmatic stance on a whole number of questions. The most obvious example of a movement towards pragmatism was working with the Awakening Councils. This idea of working with armed groups outside the Iraqi security forces had been rejected in earlier years as being at odds with the development of good security institutions. Supporting such groups, however, was eventually recognised as something that had inherent risks but overall had potentially more benefits; such risks were something that the US and Iraq would have to manage jointly.[366]

As the difficulties evolved and with steps taken to quell the insurgency, on 24 May 2007 Congress passed H.R. 2206 including eighteen benchmarks conditioning US support and funding for Iraq. This was signed into law by President Bush on 25 May 2007. One of the required benchmarks was the passing of a law for the reversal of de-Baathification. This law was passed in January 2008 by the Council of Representatives of Iraq. The law, however, did not satisfy Sunni demands helping towards national reconciliation. Another benchmark was the holding of provincial elections, a step designed to integrate the Sunnis back into the political process (they had boycotted the January 2005 elections). A provincial election law had been passed in February 2008 under US pressure. But after it was sent to the Iraqi presidency council, made up of the Iraqi president and the two vice presidents, it was vetoed by Adil Abdul-Mahdi, the Shiite vice president. It was only after the personal intervention of US Vice President Richard Cheney on a visit to Baghdad on 19 March 2008 that Abdul-Mahdi agreed to sign the bill. The provincial elections were eventually held in January 2009, allowing greater Sunni participation in the political process. This time there was no boycott from their side.

The third benchmark stipulated was the oil-revenue-sharing law. This law would allow the equitable distribution of oil revenues between Sunnis, Shiites and Kurds. This so far has not been passed by the Iraqi Council of Representatives, although a draft bill has been under discussion since 2007. The delay is due to Kurdish demands that 17 per cent of Iraqi oil revenues be allocated directly under the Kurdistan Regional Government's control and that the KRG maintain its freedom to develop existing and new fields on their territory and to directly sign contracts with international oil companies and export oil.

The fourth benchmark was to amend Iraq's constitution to allow the appeasement of the Sunni Arabs. The Bush administration believed that this was also a necessary step to bring the Sunnis back into the political process. This however remains unlikely to be achieved as the amendments demanded by the Sunnis infringe on Kurdish requirements to maintain their autonomy from Baghdad. A fifth benchmark that also failed to be implemented sufficiently was the fair distribution of reconstruction funds. This was due to sectarian discrimination against Iraq's Sunnis by the Shiite-led government.

As for the remaining thirteen benchmarks the results were mixed between largely unsatisfactory and partially achieved. Minority political parties' rights have been secured in the Iraqi constitution and Council of Representatives by-laws. Establishing support committees for the Baghdad security plan was largely successful. Neighbourhood security in Baghdad was also achieved. However, creating independent Iraqi security forces, disarming of militias, ensuring impartial law enforcement, keeping Iraqi forces free from partisan interference, addressing amnesty, the formation of new semi-autonomous regions and the purging of Iraq's defence and interior forces from sectarianism have not been met. As for the reduction of sectarian violence, providing military support in Baghdad and the empowerment of Iraqi security forces, the results have been partial.

The final concern of the Bush administration's Iraq policy was the future of the US military presence in the country. On 26 November 2007 both countries signed the US–Iraq Declaration of Principles for Friendship and Cooperation to allow a long-term relationship of cooperation and friendship between Iraq and the United States of America. This was to commit to begin negotiating the formal arrangements that will govern this relationship. The US and Iraq started to negotiate a mandate authorising the US presence after the expiration of UNSCR 1790 mandate on 31 December 2008.[367] It was a priority of the US negotiating team to stay in Iraq. The US wanted bases in Iraq, so it was willing to let the Iraqis make demands. From its point of view it was facing a new Cold War and a generational challenge against radical Islamic extremism for which bases were necessary in Iraq.[368] This did not materialise. On 27 November 2008 the Iraqi Council of Representatives approved a security pact that required the US military to end its presence in Iraq in the end of 2011. The pact, however, allowed the Iraqi government to negotiate with the United States to extend the presence of US troops if conditions on the ground were not stable beyond 2011. The purpose of restricting the Status of Forces Agreement (SOFA) to a timeline was primarily to show Iraqi constituents that Iraqi leaders were taking a stand against continued US presence. The Bush administration was anxious about the agreement slipping through to the Obama administration. After the agreement was reached, Bush stated: 'Two years ago, this day seemed unlikely but the success of the surge and the courage of the Iraqi people set the conditions for these two agreements to be negotiated and approved by the Iraqi parliament.' The security pact was composed of two major documents: the Status of Forces Agreement and a Strategic Framework Agreement allowing cooperation to take place on military and various other levels.[369] Thus, it could be argued that the transfer of sovereignty to Iraq did not happen until the end of 2008.[370] Iraq was now engaged with the US in a bilateral agreement removing Iraq from the mandate of the multi-national forces.

5.4.2.3 *The Obama administration and Arab Iraq*

When President Obama came to office an already identified foreign policy objective was to wind down the war in Iraq. An instinct for pragmatic government, realism, political caution and a renewed emphasis on diplomacy as a tool of US national security policy characterised his style of leadership. The Obama approach has been relatively non-ideological in practice but informed by an overarching sense of the United States' role in the world in the twenty-first century. At the beginning of the Obama presidency, Washington focused on securing its long-term strategic relationship with Iraqi Prime Minister Nouri Maliki, so that it could more easily withdraw US forces.[371] Following Bush's departure, the Obama administration was determined to allow the Security Pact signed during the Bush administration to take its course in Iraq without any alterations to the stipulated timeline. The administration was trying to manage and deter a growing Iraqi impatience with the US military presence; the Iraqis were asking for a hastened departure, a year in advance of the 2011 withdrawal deadline. On 1 September 2010, on Obama's orders, Operation Iraqi Freedom officially concluded with the initiation of Operation New Dawn. For this new phase US military objectives remained the pursuit of al-Qaeda and protection of the US embassy and personnel in Iraq; also, most crucially, the transition from combat operations to an advise and assist mission that was given to the 50,000-strong military contingency remaining in Iraq under the new name.[372]

Earlier, however, in accordance with the SOFA, removal of US forces from cities had been implemented, and it was completed by 30 June 2009; US troops ceased independently patrolling major Iraqi cities. The actual end of combat operations was on 19 August 2010 when the last combat soldier was withdrawn. Operation New Dawn proceeded on schedule and led to the final withdrawal of the last US soldiers on 18 December 2011. The negotiations for the extension of US forces' stay in Iraq beyond December 2011 had collapsed, after Iraq had refused to grant American troops legal immunity in Iraqi courts. The withdrawal was made public by President Barack Obama on 21 October 2011. The US military departure, however, was part of a larger Obama administration strategy to distance itself from the greater Middle East. The Obama administration put greater emphasis on Asia in 2011. The greater Middle East, it was believed, had come to dominate and distort American foreign and defence policy, and a course correction was called for. The Obama administration's vehicle for this correction was the announcement of a 'pivot' or 'rebalancing' toward Asia. A recognition that China was not just rising but becoming more assertive gave the pivot some urgency.[373]

The Obama administration was initially intent on keeping a residual force of around 10,000 troops after the expiry of the SOFA agreement. Many strategists believed that a continued US presence in Iraq, if it had been agreed, would have permitted a future Iraqi-American alliance serving as one of the linchpins of security in the strategically vital Middle East. US bases in Iraq would have allowed America to train the Iraqi forces, prepare them to carry out counter-terrorism missions, project power and influence in the Middle East, protect Iraqi airspace, damp down Arab–Kurd tensions, counter Iran and al Qaeda and possibly enable a more pro-Western direction. The extension of US forces' presence, however, required approval from the Iraqi Council of Representatives – a major feat, as it turned out, in such a fractured political atmosphere. Muqtada al-Sadr's continuous threats to resume his insurgency if US forces stayed beyond 2011 was a major obstacle for Prime Minister Nouri Maliki who led a coalition in which the Sadrists were a major component. The US presence was not popular among other Arab Iraqis either, making support from Sunni and Shiite politicians for the extension difficult. Additionally, the policy makers were concerned about sovereignty and Iranian pressure. Some Iraqis also acknowledged that the Iraqi army was in no position to maintain security. Regardless of Iraqi approval to allow a continued US military presence, America had decided to expand its embassy staff to 16,000 by 2012 – double the number it had in 2010, making it the largest embassy in the world. However, with reduced influence in the aftermath of the withdrawal and on the tenth anniversary of the invasion of Iraq in 2013 the State Department announced that they would cut the head count to 5500, of which over 4000 were contractors.

After the US military withdrawal, the US–Iraq Joint Coordination Committees approved in the 2008 Strategic Framework Agreement were activated to replace the US Provincial Reconstruction Teams to strengthen and continue bilateral partnership on a variety of initiatives including: political and diplomatic cooperation, defence and security, culture, economics and energy, health and environment, information technology and communications and law enforcement and judicial cooperation, to help transition to a long-term strategic relationship with Iraq. To this end, among the many areas of cooperation, in September 2011 Iraq signed a contract with America to purchase eighteen F-16 jet fighter aircraft, followed by a second deal in October 2012 to double that number.

The Obama administration remained thoroughly engaged with Iraq after the Bush presidency. After the second Iraqi general elections for a permanent government were held in March 2010, and following the lengthy stalemate in government formation, the US played a major role in helping to reach a political agreement among the various Iraqi electoral factions. The embassy team and senior officials from Washington shuttled among the parties for months. Even President Obama and Vice President Biden were deeply engaged. And when the deal was finally sealed in November, there were four people in the room: Prime Minister Maliki, *al-Iraqiyya* bloc leader Allawi, Kurdistan Region President Barzani – and the United States ambassador to Iraq, James Jeffrey. The United States backed Maliki for the post of prime minister over Allawi even though Allawi's party list had received more votes in the national elections held in March. US officials argued that only a Shiite Islamist had the credibility and legitimacy to serve as prime minister and disparaged any alternative to Maliki.

Regarding US success in achieving the objectives of its invasion, there are areas that reflect the fulfillment of some of its major goals. The US removed Saddam Hussein as a threat to its interests in the region. The termination of the potential threat posed by Iraqi WMD, ironically already absent due to Saddam Hussein's unilateral destruction, has been achieved and confirmed; additionally, Article 9 (Section E) of the permanent Iraqi Constitution has denied future Iraqi governments any aspirations to produce WMD. Finally, Iraq has a democracy; although immature and far from complete, it may hold the seeds of a mature democratic system in the heart of the Middle East. The US wants an Iraq that is unified, stable and able to police its internal affairs. It wants it to be able to defend its borders from outside aggression, be at peace with its neighbours and preferably a friend to the US. And it certainly does not want it to be a haven for al-Qaeda. However, in light of the difficult realities America faced in Iraq, issues such as the insistence on a robust democracy and the observation of human rights declined in significance in US Iraq policy considerations, as the likelihood has diminished that a future Iraq will remain unified.[374]

The post-invasion transition in Iraq proceeded in several stages. Initially the US was an occupying power, and the dominant military power in the country. With the new Iraqi governmental institutions becoming more capable and established, they slowly increased their capacity for independent decision-making, transitioning gradually towards sovereignty. From the first, appointed Allawi government, to the elected Maliki government formed after the national elections in December 2005, the transition was gradual but visible. Iraq, having an elected government and constitution in place, gained legitimacy and a capacity to take independent decisions. Samir Sumaidaie defined the evolution of US–Iraq relations as a 'relationship transformed from a subservient relationship in 2003 to something approaching the relationship of two sovereign countries each fending for their own interests'.[375]

As for the developments in US Iraq policy during the Obama administration, the foreign policy establishment, as under the Clinton administration, was led by career professionals and practitioners, primarily pragmatists, not ideologues. Obama appointed an ambassador to Iraq, Christopher Hill, who had no experience working in Iraq or serving anywhere in the Arab world. They were focused on furthering US national interests, preserving American power and dealing with problems as they came up. The Obama administration's approach caused some to question whether he had a strategy at all or merely responded to events. 'American policy is very weak', observed Fuad Hussein, the chief of staff to the president of the Kurdistan Region in Iraq. 'It is not clear to us how they have defined their interests in Iraq', Hussein stated. 'They are picking events and reacting on the basis of events. That is the policy.'[376] After its military withdrawal, the United States placed stability before democracy and strengthened Maliki's ability to maintain control and the unity of the country through the Iraqi military. And although the United States has withdrawn its troops from Iraq it still retained reduced leverage there. Iraq's leaders continued to strongly desire US engagement. The United States remained the indispensable broker, and was in daily contact with all the leading blocs. As much as Maliki desired to resist US efforts to rein him in, he still believed that the United States can help him rebuild Iraq. Iraqi forces were equipped and trained by Americans, and the country's leaders needed and expected US help. Secretary of State John Kerry signalled continued American engagement by making Iraq one of his first visits abroad in March 2013. Kerry also made it clear to Maliki during his visit that the US was unhappy with Iraq for letting Iran use its airspace to ship weapons and fighters to Syria. With no US air force support to patrol Iraqi airspace after its withdrawal in 2011, it was apparent that the United States' influence had diminished. Iran had gained greater influence in Iraq. Also during the Obama administration, the Iraq Oil Law was at the forefront of US concerns. On the US Vice President, Joseph Biden's, visit to Baghdad on 17 September 2009 he encouraged Iraqi leaders to pass an oil-revenue-sharing law, to allow the equitable distribution of oil revenues between Sunnis, Shiites and Kurds – but to no avail.[377] The Maliki government was also gradually gaining greater freedom. The day after the US military withdrawal, on 19 December 2011, Iraqi officials issued an arrest warrant for the Sunni Vice President Tariq al-Hashimi accusing him of involvement in overseeing paramilitary death squads.

This chapter and the preceding three addressed US Iraq policy at the national level, in other words US policy towards Arab Iraq. The chapter that follows, however, attempts to describe in detail a novel and highly neglected aspect of US foreign policy relating to the Kurds of Iraq. It focuses on a highly important aspect of US Iraq policy at the sub-national level, helping to give foreign policy analysts and students an insight into the position of the Kurds in US foreign policy discourse and helps illustrate Iraq's significance in US Middle East policy. But the US withdrawal had taken its toll. When Maliki met President Obama during a visit to Washington on 1 November 2013. The main purpose of the visit was to request US support amid escalating security concerns in Iraq. The US was simultaneously concerned with the rising terrorist activities of the Islamic State in Iraq and the Levant, and to this end agreed to consider Iraqi requests for intelligence assistance, training and weaponry. During the meeting the US stressed that Iraqi national elections be held by 30 April 2014 and that a more inclusive government with more Sunni participation be allowed. The White House again requested that Iraqi airspace be denied as an Iranian supply route to Syria.

Notes

1 Fred Dutton quoted in Jerel Rosati, *The Politics of United States Foreign Policy* (Australia: Wadsworth Publishing, 1999), p. 277.
2 Douglas Feith, *War and Decision: Inside the Pentagon at the Dawn of the War on Terrorism* (New York: HarperCollins Publishers, 2008), p. 272.
3 Richard Armitage quoted in Bob Woodward, *Plan of Attack* (London: Simon and Schuster, 2004), p. 414.
4 ORHA was created through national security directive NSD 24 on 20 January 2003. It was intended to act as a caretaker administration in Iraq until the creation of a democratically elected civilian government.
5 Michael Gordon and Bernard Trainor, *Cobra II: The Inside Story of the Invasion and Occupation of Iraq* (London: Atlantic Books, 2007), p. 182.
6 Donald Rumsfeld quoted in Woodward (2004), op. cit., pp. 14–15.
7 Feith (2008), op. cit., p. 370.
8 Ibid., p. 253.
9 Ibid., pp. 389–90.
10 Donald Rumsfeld, *Known and Unknown: A Memoir* (New York: Sentinel, 2011), p. 489.
11 Ibid., p. 372.
12 Ibid., p. 278.

13 Ibid.
14 Michael Rubin, Interview with Author, 7 July 2008, Washington, D.C.
15 Ibid., p. 435.
16 Ali Allawi, *The Occupation of Iraq: Winning the War, Losing the Peace* (USA: Yale University Press, 2007), p. 81.
17 Michael Rubin, Interview with Author, 7 July 2008, Washington, D.C.
18 Jay Garner, Telephone Interview with Author, 19 September 2008.
19 Samir Sumaidaie, Interview with Author, 24 July 2008, Washington, D.C.
20 Jay Garner, Telephone Interview with Author, 19 September 2008.
21 Peter Galbraith, Telephone Interview with Author, 18 July 2008.
22 Conrad Crane quoted in Thomas Ricks, *The Gamble: General David Petraeus and the American Military Adventure in Iraq, 2006–2008* (New York: The Penguin Press, 2009), p. 19.
23 Ibid.
24 Adam Garfinkle, Interview with Author, 7 August 2008, Washington, D.C.
25 Lawrence Wilkerson, Interview with Author, 26 August 2008, Washington, D.C.
26 Ibid.
27 Ibid.
28 Philip Wilcox, Interview with Author, 22 August 2008, Washington, D.C.
29 Jay Garner, Telephone Interview with Author, 19 September 2008.
30 Ibid.
31 Paul Hughes, Interview with Author, 29 July 2008, Washington, D.C.
32 Ibid.
33 Bob Woodward, *Bush at War* (London: Simon and Schuster, 2002), p. 322.
34 Richard Cheney quoted in Woodward (2004), op. cit., p. 126.
35 Woodward (2004), op. cit., p. 169.
36 Ivo Daalder and James Lindsay, *America Unbound: The Bush Revolution in Foreign Policy* (Maryland: The Brookings Institution, 2003), p. 198.
37 Allawi (2007), op. cit., p. 282.
38 Woodward (2004), op. cit., p. 150.
39 Gordon and Trainor (2007), op. cit., p. 537.
40 Zalmay Khalilzad. (2009). *Conversations with History: Responding to Strategic Challenges of the Post 9–11 World.* [University of California, Berkeley: Institute of International Studies] Available at: URL: http://globetrotter.berkeley.edu/people9/Khalilzad/Amb%20Khalilzad%20transcript.pdf Access Date: 15 July 2009.
41 George Packer, *The Assassins' Gate: America in Iraq* (New York: Farrar, Straus and Giroux, 2005), p. 214.
42 John Stuart Mill quoted in Ian Shapiro, *Containment: Rebuilding a Strategy against Global Terror* (Princeton: Princeton University Press, 2007), p. 38.
43 Ibid., p. xv.
44 Peter Galbraith, *The End of Iraq: How American Incompetence Created a War Without End* (New York: Simon and Schuster, 2006), p. 95.
45 Samir Sumaidaie, Interview with Author, 24 July 2008, Washington, D.C.
46 Thomas Ricks, *Fiasco: The American Military Adventure in Iraq* (London: Penguin Press, 2007), p. 65.
47 Ibid.
48 Allawi (2007), op. cit., p. 130.
49 Carole O'Leary, Interview with Author, 8 August 2008, Washington, D.C.
50 Ariel Cohen, Interview with Author, 25 August 2008, Washington, D.C.
51 Gordon and Trainor (2007), op. cit., p. 512.
52 Ricks (2009), op. cit., p. 5.
53 Ibid., p. 122.
54 Ricks (2007), op. cit., p. 253.

55 Gordon and Trainor (2007), op. cit., p. 571.
56 Samir Sumaidaie, Interview with Author, 24 July 2008, Washington, D.C.
57 Adam Garfinkle, Interview with Author, 7 August 2008, Washington, D.C.
58 Shapiro (2007), op. cit., p. 112.
59 Carole O'Leary, Interview with Author, 8 August 2008, Washington, D.C.
60 Ibid.
61 Ibid.
62 George W. Bush quoted in Woodward (2004), op. cit., p. 424.
63 Gordon and Trainor (2007), op. cit., p. 573.
64 Feith (2008), op. cit., p. 409.
65 Robert Draper, *Dead Certain: The Presidency of George W. Bush* (New York: Free Press, 2007), p. 188.
66 Woodward (2004), op. cit., p. 237.
67 George W. Bush quoted in Bob Woodward, *State of Denial: Bush at War, Part III* (London: Simon and Schuster, 2006), p. 187.
68 Woodward (2004), op. cit., p. 168.
69 Feith (2008), op. cit., p. 307.
70 Ibid., p. 436.
71 Ibid., pp. 406–7.
72 Adam Garfinkle, Interview with Author, 7 August 2008, Washington, D.C.
73 Lawrence Freedman, *A Choice of Enemies: America Confronts the Middle East* (New York: PublicAffairs, 2008), p. 429.
74 Ibid., p. 32.
75 Galbraith (2006), op. cit., p. 112.
76 George W. Bush. (1999a). *A Period of Consequences.* Available at: URL: www3.citadel.edu/pao/addresses/pres_bush.html Access Date: 20 December 2009.
77 Karin von Hippel, 'State-Building After Saddam: Lessons Lost', in *The Future of Kurdistan in Iraq*, ed. Brendan O'Leary and John McGarry *et al.* (Philadelphia: University of Pennsylvania Press, 2005), p. 252.
78 Condoleezza Rice, 'Campaign 2000: Promoting The National Interest', *Foreign Affairs* Vol. 79, No. 1 (2000): p. 53.
79 Packer (2005), op. cit., p. 42.
80 Woodward (2006), op. cit., p. 79.
81 Paul Bremer with Malcolm McConnell, *My Year in Iraq: The Struggle to Build a Future of Hope* (New York: Simon and Schuster, 2006), p. 151.
82 Gordon and Trainor (2007), op. cit., p. 174.
83 Feith (2008), op. cit., p. 158.
84 Ibid., p. 133.
85 Ibid., p. 149.
86 Donald Rumsfeld quoted in ibid., p. 101.
87 Ibid., p. 149.
88 Donald Rumsfeld. (2003). *Beyond Nation Building.* [US Department of Defense] Available at: URL: www.defense.gov/speeches/speech.aspx?speechid=337 Access Date: 20 June 2007.
89 Gordon and Trainor (2007), op. cit., p. 173.
90 von Hippel (2005), op. cit., p. 251.
91 Michael Cox, 'Empire by Denial: The Strange Case of the United States', *International Affairs* Vol. 81, No. 1 (2005): p. 19.
92 Gordon and Trainor (2007), op. cit., p. 578.
93 Feith (2008), op. cit., p. 129.
94 Senior Congressional Staffer, Interview with Author, 2 July 2008, Washington, D.C.
95 George W. Bush. (1999a). *A Period of Consequences.*
96 Woodward (2004), op. cit., p. 121.
97 Gordon and Trainor (2007), op. cit., p. 524.

98 Ibid., p. 538.
99 Feith (2008), op. cit., p. 88.
100 Paul Bremer *et al.*, 'Early Days in Iraq: Decisions of the CPA', *Survival* Vol. 50, No. 4 (2008): p. 53.
101 Feith (2008), op. cit., p. 333.
102 Woodward (2004), op. cit., p. 126.
103 Gordon and Trainor (2007), op. cit., p. 489.
104 Senior Congressional Staffer, Interview with Author, 2 July 2008, Washington, D.C.
105 Niall Ferguson, *Colossus: The Rise and Fall of the American Empire* (New York: Penguin, 2005), p. 208.
106 Brian Gifford quoted in Alastair Finlan, 'International Security', in *The Bush Doctrine and the War on Terrorism: Global Responses, Global Consequences*, ed. Mary Buckley and Robert Singh (Oxford: Routledge, 2006), p. 161.
107 Feith (2008), op. cit., p. 420.
108 Cox (2005), op. cit., p. 20.
109 Bremer (2006), op. cit., p. 106.
110 Ibid., p. 155.
111 Draper (2007), op. cit., p. 399.
112 Anthony Zinni. (2006). *Post-Saddam Iraq: The War Game.* [The National Security Archive: The George Washington University] Available at: URL: www.gwu.edu/~nsarchiv/NSAEBB/NSAEBB207/index.htm Access Date: 20 December 2009.
113 Woodward (2004), op. cit., p. 125.
114 Gordon and Trainor (2007), op. cit., p. 566.
115 Ricks (2007), op. cit., p. 64.
116 Woodward (2004), op. cit., p. 310.
117 Gordon and Trainor (2007), op. cit., p. 525.
118 Ibid., p. 131.
119 Feith (2008), op. cit., p. 367.
120 Gordon and Trainor (2007), op. cit., p. 236.
121 Packer (2005), op. cit., p. 133.
122 Douglas Feith quoted in Woodward (2004), op. cit., p. 343.
123 Packer (2005), op. cit., p. 129.
124 Paul Hughes, Interview with Author, 29 July 2008, Washington, D.C.
125 Ibid.
126 Ibid.
127 Ibid.
128 Ibid.
129 Bremer *et al.* (2008), op. cit., p. 27.
130 Paul Bremer. (2009). *Former US Civil Administrator to Iraq in an Extended Interview Recalls His Best and Worst Days in Baghdad* (Translated from Arabic by Author). [*Asharq Al-Awsat*] Available at: URL: www.aawsat.com/details.asp?section=4&issueno=11121&article=518522 Access Date: 20 December 2009.
131 Samir Sumaidaie, Interview with Author, 24 July 2008, Washington, D.C.
132 Feith (2008), op. cit., p. 367.
133 Gordon and Trainor (2007), op. cit., p. 582.
134 Jay Garner, Telephone Interview with Author, 19 September 2008.
135 Allawi (2007), op. cit., p. 283.
136 Ibid., p. 159.
137 Packer (2005), op. cit., p. 129.
138 Ibid., p. 198.
139 Paul Hughes, Interview with Author, 29 July 2008, Washington, D.C.
140 Bremer *et al.* (2008), op. cit., p. 30.
141 Samir Sumaidaie, Interview with Author, 24 July 2008, Washington, D.C.
142 Meghan O'Sullivan. (2009). *Charlie Rose: A Conversation with Meghan O'Sullivan.*

Available at: URL: www.charlierose.com/view/interview/9069 Access Date: 15 July 2008.
143 Meghan O'Sullivan, Telephone Interview with Author, 17 September 2008.
144 Robert Olson, *The Goat and the Butcher: Nationalism and State Formation in Kurdistan-Iraq since the Iraqi War* (California: Mazda Publishers, 2005), pp. 236–7.
145 Allawi (2007), op. cit., p. 173.
146 Woodward (2006), op. cit., p. 474.
147 Ibid., pp. 261–2.
148 Tony Blair. (2010). *Rt Hon Tony Blair Transcript.* [The Iraq Inquiry] Available at: URL: www.iraqinquiry.org.uk/media/45139/20100129-blair-final.pdf Access Date: 20 March 2010.
149 Ibid.
150 Feith (2008), op. cit., p. 415.
151 Gordon and Trainor (2007), op. cit., p. 586.
152 Feith (2008), op. cit., p. 407.
153 Ibid., p. 275.
154 Paul Pillar, Interview with Author, 15 July 2008, Washington, D.C.
155 Report of the Select Committee on Intelligence on Prewar Intelligence Assessments About Postwar Iraq. (2007). [US Senate] Available at: URL: http://intelligence.senate.gov/prewar.pdf Access Date: 20 March 2010.
156 Paul Pillar, Interview with Author, 15 July 2008, Washington, D.C.
157 Feith (2008), op. cit., p. 449.
158 Woodward (2006), op. cit., p. 296.
159 Ricks (2007), op. cit., p. 409.
160 Allawi (2007), op. cit., p. 133.
161 Ibid., p. 459.
162 Gordon and Trainor (2007), op. cit., p. 584.
163 Woodward (2006), op. cit., p. 184.
164 Ibid.
165 Bremer (2006), op. cit., pp. 105–6.
166 Ibid., p. 220.
167 Woodward (2006), op. cit., p. 297.
168 Ricks (2007), op. cit., p. 185.
169 Ibid., p. 378.
170 Woodward (2006), op. cit., p. 481.
171 Gordon and Trainor (2007), op. cit., p. 596.
172 Ibid., p. 168.
173 Michael Rubin, Interview with Author, 7 July 2008, Washington, D.C.
174 Peter Galbraith, *Unintended Consequences: How War in Iraq Strengthened America's Enemies* (New York: Simon and Schuster, 2008), p. 50.
175 Tommy Franks with Malcolm McConnell, *American Soldier* (New York: HarperCollins, 2004), p. 392.
176 Nawshirwan Mustafa Amin. (2007c). *My Memoirs from the Governing Council: Part 7* (Translated from Kurdish by Author). [Sbeiy.com] Available at: URL: www.sbeiy.com/ku/ArticleParts.aspx?PartID=8&ArticleID=182&AuthorID=36 Access Date: 20 June 2008.
177 Ibid.
178 Packer (2005), op. cit., p. 146.
179 George W. Bush quoted in Woodward (2004), op. cit., pp. 276–8.
180 Gordon and Trainor (2007), op. cit., p. 180.
181 Blair (2010), op. cit.
182 Frank Miller quoted in Woodward (2004), op. cit., p. 339.
183 Richard Shultz quoted in von Hippel (2005), op. cit., pp. 264–5.
184 Bremer (2006), op. cit., p. 14.
185 Galbraith (2006), op. cit., p. 113.

186 Ibid., p. 111.
187 Meghan O'Sullivan, Telephone Interview with Author, 17 September 2008.
188 Gordon and Trainor (2007), op. cit., p. 489.
189 Packer (2005), op. cit., p. 123.
190 von Hippel (2005), op. cit., p. 255.
191 Packer (2005), op. cit., p. 196.
192 von Hippel (2005), op. cit., p. 253.
193 Ibid., p. 254.
194 CPA Official – Baghdad, personal communication with author.
195 Packer (2005), op. cit., p. 138.
196 Douglas Feith and Christopher Lamb quoted in Feith (2008), op. cit., pp. 362–4.
197 Ibid., p. 364.
198 Ibid., p. 319.
199 Ibid., p. 363.
200 Ibid., p. 365.
201 von Hippel (2005), op. cit., p. 253.
202 Ibid., pp. 261–2.
203 Blair (2010), op. cit.
204 Gordon and Trainor (2007), op. cit., p. 582.
205 Feith (2008), op. cit., p. 372.
206 Gordon and Trainor (2007), op. cit., p. 592.
207 Blair (2010), op. cit.
208 Bremer (2009), op. cit.
209 Packer (2005), op. cit., p. 132.
210 Ibid., p. 133.
211 Ricks (2009), op. cit., p. 15.
212 Feith (2008), op. cit., p. 316.
213 Ibid., p. 347.
214 Packer (2005), op. cit., p. 121.
215 Feith (2008), op. cit., p. 349.
216 Ibid., p. 349.
217 Ibid., p. 350.
218 Ibid., p. 291.
219 Ibid., p. 402.
220 Ibid., p. 381.
221 Jay Garner, Telephone Interview with Author, 19 September 2008.
222 Daalder and Lindsay (2003), op. cit., p. 153.
223 Meghan O'Sullivan, Telephone Interview with Author, 17 September 2008.
224 Rumsfeld (2003), op. cit., *Beyond Nation Building Speech.*
225 Meghan O'Sullivan, Telephone Interview with Author, 17 September 2008.
226 Packer (2005), op. cit., p. 144.
227 Jay Garner, Telephone Interview with Author, 19 September 2008.
228 Bremer (2006), op. cit., p. 19.
229 Bremer *et al.* (2008), op. cit., p. 21.
230 Packer (2005), op. cit., p. 190.
231 Ibid., p. 187.
232 Paul Hughes, Interview with Author, 29 July 2008, Washington, D.C.
233 Bremer (2006), op. cit., p. 205.
234 Bremer *et al.* (2008), op. cit., p. 33.
235 Galbraith (2006), op. cit., p. 116.
236 Daalder and Lindsay (2003), op. cit., p. 154.
237 Bremer (2006), op. cit., p. 125.
238 Feith (2008), op. cit., pp. 445–6.
239 Ibid., p. 375.

240 Ibid., p. 282.
241 Ibid., p. 279.
242 Ibid., p. 370.
243 Ibid., p. 447.
244 Ibid., p. 447.
245 Samir Sumaidaie, Interview with Author, 24 July 2008, Washington, D.C.
246 Nawshirwan Mustafa Amin. (2007d). *My Memoirs from the Governing Council: Part 8* (Translated from Kurdish by Author). [Sbeiy.com] Available at: URL: http://sbeiy.com/ku/ ArticleParts.aspx?PartID=9&ArticleID=182&AuthorID=36 Access Date: 20 June 2008.
247 Bremer *et al.* (2008), op. cit., p. 36.
248 Feith (2008), op. cit., p. 370.
249 Ibid., p. 458.
250 Paul Bremer. (2008). *Facts for Feith: CPA History.* [Nationalreview Online] Available at: URL: http://article.nationalreview.com/?q=NDIwN2MzOTljOTNlODdiMD IzZWQ5ZmZjZTQyZjQ5NzM= Access Date: 15 May 2008.
251 Michael Rubin, Interview with Author, 7 July 2008, Washington, D.C.
252 Bremer (2008), op. cit.
253 Feith (2008), op. cit., p. 448.
254 Bremer (2006), op. cit., p. 189.
255 Ibid., p. 206.
256 Ibid., p. 115.
257 Bremer *et al.* (2008), op. cit., p. 38.
258 Feith (2008), op. cit., p. 453.
259 Amin (2007c), op. cit., *My Memoirs from the Governing Council: Part 7* (Translated from Kurdish by Author).
260 Allawi (2007), op. cit., p. 211.
261 Feith (2008), op. cit., p. 467.
262 Amin (2007c), op. cit., *My Memoirs from the Governing Council: Part 7* (Translated from Kurdish by Author).
263 Bremer (2006), op. cit., p. 167.
264 Feith (2008), op. cit., p. 464.
265 Draper (2007), op. cit., p. 387.
266 Bremer *et al.* (2008), op. cit., p. 39.
267 Qubad Talabani, Interview with Author, 31 July 2008, Washington, D.C.
268 Bremer *et al.* (2008), op. cit., p. 37.
269 Feith (2008), op. cit., p. 447.
270 Ibid., p. 437.
271 Ibid., pp. 440–1.
272 Bremer (2006), op. cit., p. 115.
273 Ibid., p. 78.
274 George W. Bush quoted in ibid., p. 12.
275 George W. Bush quoted in ibid., p. 227.
276 Bremer *et al.* (2008), op. cit., p. 39.
277 Feith (2008), op. cit., p. 516.
278 Amin (2007c), op. cit., *My Memoirs from the Governing Council: Part 7* (Translated from Kurdish by Author).
279 Bremer (2006), op. cit., p. 203.
280 Ibid., p. 116.
281 Ibid., p. 171.
282 Ibid., p. 12.
283 Feith (2008), op. cit., p. 500.
284 Hoshyar Zebari quoted in Robert Pollock, 'The Voice of Iraq', *The Wall Street Journal* (2006, 24 June), p. A10.
285 Feith (2008), op. cit., p. 368.

286 Packer (2005), op. cit., p. 144.
287 Bremer (2006), op. cit., p. 343.
288 Ibid., p. 281.
289 Ibid., p. 342.
290 Allawi (2007), op. cit., p. 161.
291 Nabil Al-Tikriti, Interview with Author, 18 June 2008, Washington, D.C.
292 Paul Hughes, Interview with Author, 29 July 2008, Washington, D.C.
293 Michael Rubin (2009), Email communication with author.
294 Franks (2004), op. cit., pp. 330–1.
295 Samir Sumaidaie, Interview with Author, 24 July 2008, Washington, D.C.
296 Nawshirwan Mustafa Amin. (2007b). *My Memoirs from the Governing Council: Part 2* (Translated from Kurdish by Author). [Sbeiy.com] Available at: URL: www.sbeiy.com/ku/ArticleParts.aspx?PartID=2&ArticleID=182&AuthorID=36 Access Date: 20 June 2008.
297 Allawi (2007), op. cit., p. 281.
298 Ibid., p. 337.
299 Ibid., p. 296.
300 Ibid., p. 289.
301 Ibid.
302 Ibid., p. 337.
303 Ibid., p. 289.
304 Ricks (2007), op. cit., p. 391.
305 Allawi (2007), op. cit., p. 337.
306 Ibid., p. 299.
307 Qubad Talabani, Interview with Author, 31 July 2008, Washington, D.C.
308 Allawi (2007), op. cit., p. 289.
309 Feith (2008), op. cit., p. 521.
310 Ibid., p. 496.
311 Bremer *et al.* (2008), op. cit., p. 35.
312 Juan Cole quoted in Allawi (2007), op. cit., p. 289.
313 Khalilzad (2009), op. cit.
314 Packer (2005), op. cit., p. 446.
315 Condoleezza Rice. (2005). *Clear, Hold, Build: Modern Political Techniques in COIN.* [Available at: www.dtic.mil/cgi-bin/GetTRDoc?AD=ADA495007&Location =U2&doc=GetTRDoc.pdf Access Date: 20 December 2007.
316 Ricks (2007), op. cit., p. 393.
317 Ricks (2009), op. cit., p. 51.
318 Ibid., p. 55.
319 Ibid., p. 103.
320 Allawi (2007), op. cit., pp. 398–9.
321 Packer (2005), op. cit., p. 302.
322 Matthew Stephenson, Interview with Author, 10 June 2008, Washington, D.C.
323 Ibid.
324 Khalilzad (2009), op. cit.
325 Qubad Talabani, Interview with Author, 31 July 2008, Washington, D.C.
326 George W. Bush. (2006). *Press Conference by the President.* [The White House] Available at: URL: http://georgewbush-whitehouse.archives.gov/news/releases/2006/11/ 20061108–2.html Access Date: 20 June 2008.
327 George W. Bush. (2007a). *President's Address to the Nation.* [The White House] Available at: URL: http://georgewbush-whitehouse.archives.gov/news/releases/2007/ 01/20070110–7.html Access Date: 20 January 2008.
328 Robert Singh, 'The Bush Doctrine', in *The Bush Doctrine and the War on Terrorism: Global Responses, Global Consequences*, ed. Mary Buckley and Robert Singh (Oxford: Routledge, 2006), p. 24.

329 George W. Bush quoted in Draper (2007), op. cit., p. 391.
330 Caroline Kennedy-Pipe, 'American Foreign Policy After 9/11' (pp. 401–19), in *US Foreign Policy*, ed. Michael Cox and Doug Stokes (Oxford: Oxford University Press, 2008), p. 417.
331 Timothy Lynch and Robert Singh, *After Bush: The Case for Continuity in American Foreign Policy* (Cambridge: Cambridge University Press, 2008), p. 179.
332 Stephen Ryan, 'The United Nations', in *The Bush Doctrine and the War on Terrorism: Global Responses, Global Consequences*, ed. Mary Buckley and Robert Singh (Oxford: Routledge, 2006), p. 187.
333 Philip Gordon, 'The End of the Bush Revolution', *Foreign Affairs* Vol. 85, No. 4 (2006): p. 81.
334 Allawi (2007), op. cit., p. 454.
335 Ricks (2007), op. cit., p. 442.
336 Michael Rubin, Interview with Author, 7 July 2008, Washington, D.C.
337 Kennedy-Pipe (2008), op. cit., p. 404.
338 Christopher Van Hollen, Telephone Interview with Author, 18 July 2008, Washington, D.C.
339 Ricks (2007), op. cit., p. 451.
340 Gordon and Trainor (2007), op. cit., p. 596.
341 Richard Kessler, Interview with Author, 2 July 2008, Washington, D.C.
342 Senior Congressional Staffer, Interview with Author, 2 July 2008, Washington, D.C.
343 Freedman (2008), op. cit., p. 246.
344 Ricks (2007), op. cit., p. 446.
345 Lynch and Singh (2008), op. cit., p. 182.
346 Ricks (2007), op. cit., pp. 444–5.
347 Frederick Kagan, Interview with Author, 25 July 2008, Washington, D.C.
348 Ibid.
349 Ibid.
350 Ibid.
351 Ibid.
352 George W. Bush quoted in Draper (2007), op. cit., p. 418.
353 Adam Garfinkle, Interview with Author, 7 August 2008, Washington, D.C.
354 Paul Pillar, Interview with Author, 15 July 2008, Washington, D.C.
355 Frederick Kagan, Interview with Author, 25 July 2008, Washington, D.C.
356 Ibid.
357 Andrew Morrison, Interview with Author, 21 August 2008, Washington, D.C.
358 James Longley, Interview with Author, 22 July 2008, Washington, D.C.
359 Matthew Stephenson, Interview with Author, 10 June 2008, Washington, D.C.
360 Senior Congressional Staffer, Interview with Author, 2 July 2008, Washington, D.C.
361 Sam Parker, Interview with Author, 27 June 2008, Washington, D.C.
362 Ricks (2009), op. cit., p. 128.
363 Matthew Stephenson, Interview with Author, 10 June 2008, Washington, D.C.
364 David Pollock, Interview with Author, 17 July 2008, Washington, D.C.
365 Michael Rubin, Interview with Author, 7 July 2008, Washington, D.C.
366 Meghan O'Sullivan, Telephone Interview with Author, 17 September 2008.
367 United Nations Security Council Resolution 1790 was adopted unanimously by the United Nations Security Council on 18 December 2007, extending the mandate of the multinational force in Iraq until 31 December 2008. The mandate had been established in 2004 by Security Council resolution 1546 and previously extended by resolutions 1637 and 1723.
368 Sam Parker, Interview with Author, 21 July 2008, Washington, D.C.
369 Sudarsan Raghavan, 'Security Accord Approved In Iraq', *The Washington Post* (2008, 28 November), p. A01.
370 Richard Fenning. (2009). *Analysis: A New Iraq?* [BBC Radio 4] Available at: URL:

http://news.bbc.co.uk/nol/shared/spl/hi/programmes/analysis/transcripts/15_06_09. txt Access Date: 20 September 2009.

371 Ned Parker, 'The Iraq We Left Behind: Welcome to the World's Next Failed State', *Foreign Affairs* Vol. 91, No. 2 (2012): p. 96.

372 Ricks (2009), op. cit., p. 308.

373 Richard N. Haass, 'The Irony of American Strategy: Putting the Middle East in Proper Perspective', *Foreign Affairs* Vol. 92, No. 3 (2013): p. 59.

374 Ricks (2009), op. cit., p. 316.

375 Samir Sumaidaie, Interview with Author, 24 July 2008, Washington, D.C.

376 Michael R. Gordon. 'Failed Efforts and Challenges of America's Last Months in Iraq', *The New York Times* (2012, 23 September), p. A1.

377 On the same visit Biden also urged Iraqi leaders to pass an election law to allow general elections in January 2010. The elections were eventually held, however, on 7 March 2010. His final message was to ask the Iraqi parliament to pass foreign investment laws providing sufficient protection to overseas companies interested in investing in Iraq.

6 The Iraqi Kurds in US foreign policy

From Kennedy to Obama

> The Turkish portion of the present Ottoman Empire should be assured a secure sovereignty, but the other nationalities which are now under Turkish rule should be assured an undoubted security of life and an absolutely unmolested opportunity of autonomous development...
>
> Woodrow Wilson, Fourteen Points Speech, 8 January 1918[1]

Introduction

The preceding chapters of this book are largely focused on US Iraq policy at the national level. As such the previous chapters are restricted to US interaction with Arab Iraq and its largest ethnicity – the Arabs. What contemporary scholarship largely fails to address is US relations with Iraq's Kurds, the second largest ethnicity in Iraq, who were largely absent from government in Baghdad until the toppling of Saddam Hussein in 2003. This chapter attempts to describe and address this sub-national interaction, perceiving it as the second limb of US Iraq policy. This chapter attempts to deal with US policy, or lack thereof, towards the Kurds of Iraq. It aims to identify various phases of interaction and non-interaction, resulting mostly from the evolution of regional and international political events. The chapter attempts to tackle US relations with Iraq's Kurds, starting from 1961, when the Kurdish nationalist movement in Iraq ignited and first sought US support under the Kennedy administration. It will follow through the various stages, highlighting the most important interactions, but will primarily concentrate on the George W. Bush administration, as his time in office was rich in events and political developments, following on into US-Kurdish interaction during the Obama administration. Subsequently, a rigorous understanding of continuity and change in US Iraq policy at the sub-national level is gained.

6.1 Historical overview

The Kurds of the Middle East are caught up, reluctantly, in the strategic geopolitical calculations of the various influential actors of the region. With the creation of the post-colonial order, both superpowers and regional powers have fought relentlessly for domination of the Middle East. The Kurds, a substantial ethnicity in the Middle East, with nationalistic aspirations at heart, have had to struggle in a hostile political environment to promote their cause. As a result, and at their peril, the stateless Kurds have had to play at both regional and international levels to advance their ethnic struggle. Following the onset of the Cold War, the Kurds have been embroiled in the superpowers' competition for dominance in the Middle East. Their first major shock came in the context of the very initial phases of the Cold War, when the Soviet-supported Kurdish Republic of Mahabad collapsed in December 1946, due to US demands for Moscow's withdrawal from northern Iran. They were, perhaps, among the first victims of the Cold War.

The Kurds, initially promised a nation of their own in the 1920 Sevres Treaty, ended up as major losers in the 1923 Treaty of Lausanne. Their nationalist aspirations were crushed by the powerful regional player, Turkey. Since the collapse of the Ottoman Empire, the Kurds, deprived of a nation state of their own, were subjugated by the nations of the region. They found themselves divided among superior regional adversaries – Iraq, Iran, Turkey and Syria – who have constantly sought their suppression. Regardless of the circumstances, they have continued to fight continuously for the right to self-determination. Despite these inherent difficulties, they have managed to sustain their struggle.

Moreover, the stateless Kurds, though not a primary actor in the region in a state-centric international system, have had considerable influence on the evolution of political events in the Middle East. To advance their cause they have had to play at both the complex interdependent regional and international systems, attempting to maximise their power vis-à-vis existing regional rivalries and superpower interests. As a result, they have found themselves politically undermined in the severest ways. At both levels they have found themselves enmeshed in complicated political situations, and exploited as a tool to advance the interests of regional and international powers.

6.2 The Kurds: victims of the Cold War

6.2.1 The Kurds ignored: 1961–1972

The US gradually gained influence in the Middle East with the decline of the British Empire; and soon the United States started to show interest in the Kurds, a substantial ethnicity in the Middle East and sizable minority in Iraq. One of the earliest-documented signs of such interest came in a memo sent by Edward Crocker II, the first US ambassador to Baghdad, on 10 April 1950. Crocker sent a cable from Baghdad to the State Department eight months after the publication of a new Kurdish language news bulletin, *Aga u Rudawe Hefteyiyekan*, prepared weekly by the US Information Service at the American embassy in Baghdad. Crocker described the venture as strictly directed at Iraqi Kurds with the sole intention as 'an effort to fill the gap in the democratic information activity countering Soviet propaganda to the Kurds'.[2] A second publication with the same anti-communist message by the name of *Payam* was published from 1954 to 1958 by the US embassy in Baghdad. The US interest in the Iraqi Kurds at this time served two purposes. First, it was an attempt at keeping the Kurds from Soviet influence. Second, it was to help the pro-Western Iraqi monarchy keep the Kurds under control. In a declassified telegram from the US embassy in Tehran, Henry Grady encouraged the broadcast of VOA (Voice of America) in Kurdish; he also emphasised that it should in no way encourage Kurdish political nationalism, but rather promote Kurdish support for the central Iranian government.[3] This would largely apply to Iraq as it, too, was ruled by a friendly pro-Western monarch. After the collapse of the Soviet-backed Kurdish republic of Mahabad in December 1946, Defence Minister Mustafa Barzani and around five hundred of his followers crossed into the Soviet Union and remained there for twelve years and only returned to Iraq in 1958 on the invitation of the new revolutionary Iraqi government of Abdul Karim Qasim. Barzani's exile to the Soviet Union for twelve years convinced US officials that he had been influenced by the communist ideology. He was even erroneously denounced as the Red Mulla, although he led the Kurdistan Democratic Party and had never sympathised with Marxist ideology. Another reason for US suspicion of the Kurdish leadership was that several of the leaders of the Iraqi Communist Party were Kurds.

With the September Revolution of 1961 under the leadership of Mustafa Barzani, the Kurds of Iraq tried to reach out to the outside world. The objective was, first, to gain recognition for their national cause; and, second, to obtain military and financial support to continue their armed struggle. The Kurds knew that without an outside power on their side, their national struggle had little chance of success; and, they thought, no power was better suited to perform this role than the US. The image of the US as a beacon of freedom and democracy was not lost on the Kurds. Woodrow Wilson's fourteen points, among them (in point twelve) the right to self-determination for ethnicities living under the crumbling Ottoman Empire, had considerable influence on the Kurds. Iraq had also started to drift away from the West after the 1958 revolution, and signs of its friendship with the Soviet Union were becoming apparent. Thus, on a practical level, the US seemed the most attractive ally.

To this end, the Kurdish leadership made attempts to develop contacts with the US. It appears that Barzani's attempts to establish links with the US were based on strategic calculations relevant to that era – Iraq had gained the enmity of the US after the 1958 revolution. The incoming Qassim government restored relations with the Soviet Union, permitted Iraqi Communist Party influence and suppressed pro-Western party activities.[4] Three years earlier, it overthrew the pro-Western Iraqi monarchy. Qassim had also withdrawn from the pro-Western Baghdad Pact of 1955 and the 1937 Saadabad Pact, intended to curtail Soviet influence.[5] Moreover, it was a nationalist regime with pan-Arab aspirations and disdain for Western colonial influence. After Qassim overthrew the British-installed monarchy in 1958, the US grew anxious about the new regime in Baghdad, which it perceived as a largely radical nationalist entity, developing ties with Moscow. The Qassim government further offended the Kennedy administration's sensitivities by its attempts to nationalise the Iraqi oil installations, which were owned by US and British interests. For these reasons the US embassy in Baghdad established links with dissident officers in the Iraqi army. In 1963 a second coup, led by these officers, replaced Qassim before the nationalisation was achieved.[6] With the overthrow of Qassim in 1963, the US was happy with the nature of the new regime; declassified US documents describe the new 1963 Iraqi government as a 'moderate regime'.[7]

The earliest reports of US-Kurdish relations suggest that the first serious contacts made were in the early 1960s. Mustafa Barzani appears to have started seeking support in earnest from the US during this period, coinciding with the beginning of the Kurdish revolt under his leadership in September 1961. Barzani, however, had made earlier attempts at establishing relations with the US. In a visit to the US embassy in Baghdad in February 1944 which had achieved no results, Barzani had requested to meet Loy Henderson, US ambassador to Baghdad, but was only received by a junior diplomat based at the embassy.[8] Asad Khailany, the KDP's Baghdad branch head, had initially made contact with the US embassy in Baghdad in 1960; this was before the 1961 revolution and the start of hostilities with Qassim's regime. He was the first Kurdish official to do so on behalf of the Kurdish movement. His first serious approach, however, on behalf of the KDP for political support, was to the First Political Secretary James Akins in 1962 after the hostilities started. The US had very little information on the Kurds at the time. In Khailany's words 'most of them were ignorant about the [Kurdish] case'. In 1964, Akins invited Khailany to meet with Under Secretary of State Philip Talbot in Baghdad. Talbot was interested to know more about Iraq and the Kurdish plight, because the Kurds were emerging as a significant force in the country and the US had little information about them. Khailany asked Under Secretary Talbot to give him one good reason why the US did not support Kurdish nationalist rights; to which he responded, 'It's not in my hands, that's politics.' The US continued to show sympathy, but no material support, for the Kurdish cause. State Department policy was not to recognise Kurdish nationalist rights; however, they backed human rights.[9] In a 1962 interview in the *New York Times*, Barzani told Dana Adams Schmidt, 'Let the Americans give us military aid, openly or secretly, so that we can become truly autonomous, and we will become your loyal partners in the Middle East.'[10] Barzani seems to have believed that the Kurds could play a significant role in the region as a strategic US ally. They wanted to attract American support in return for becoming a loyal regional partner. The Kurds, a non-Arab ethnicity, believed that they could play the role of a significant client to counter pan-Arab and Islamist tendencies in the region. However, the US did not seem to lack strategic allies in the region. On a strictly realpolitik assessment of the region, the US had more to gain from regional allies like Turkey and the Shah's Iran than from the stateless Iraqi Kurds.

In a March 1972 memo (declassified on 21 June 2006), NSC official Harold Saunders reported a request from SAVAK, the Iranian intelligence service, for

US assistance to Mustafa Barzani. Saunders stated that 'similar approaches have been made over the last ten years and have been turned down'. He also made clear that 'there is nothing absolutely needed from us except that they want to involve us'. Moreover, he contended that 'the odds are against the Kurds succeeding'. Saunders also stated that US involvement in this issue 'could be regarded by the Soviets as a move directed against them'.[11] In 1968 Barzani made a visit to Israel to nurture a relationship that, he thought, would eventually help advance the Kurdish cause. Barzani knew that Israel's relations with the US were unique and, for this reason, wanted to enlist Israel's support. Barzani had initiated contacts with Israel in 1963, and military cooperation had begun in 1965. Barzani did not trust Israel, but sought Israeli attention, hoping it would attract US support. This was to no avail. Harold Saunders advised against US involvement, for he believed that 'any assistance that may be needed by Barzani is fully within the capability of Iran or Israel to provide'.[12]

US-Iraqi diplomatic relations were totally suspended over the Six-Day War of 1967. Following this, in 1968, the Baath Party ascended to power in a coup, for the second time making the US uneasy; a radical, nationalist and pan-Arab party was a cause for concern in Washington. Although there were no diplomatic relations, the US described the new Baathist government as 'a little harder to deal with than the old'.[13] The Baath ideology of Arab socialism was by default closer to Soviet communism. The Baathists, eager to establish strong roots in the country they had lost once in November 1963, were able to advance their regime economically with the nationalisation of the Iraq Petroleum Company in 1972. They also managed to secure a strategic security relationship with the Soviet Union in April, 1972 – all the more reason for the US to be concerned about Iraq.

Mustafa Barzani enjoyed the backing of the Soviet Union, until the Treaty of Friendship between Iraq and the Soviets was signed in 1972;[14] this appears to be another reason why Barzani aspired to further support to from the opposite pole, the US. The Kurds believed in the possibility of greater US attention to the Kurdish revolt as a counter-balance to the Soviet alliance with Iraq. However, two calls for US support, in 1971 and 1972, were totally ignored. The Pike Congressional Report[15] asserts that both requests were deemed destabilising, as they would create the opportunity for Soviet intervention in both Iran and Turkey, both US allies, which had large Kurdish populations.[16]

The US continued to ignore Kurdish requests for support for their nationalist movement. The negative US reaction to this appeal was based on several concerns, as shown by declassified US documents. The US felt that a Barzani-dominated regime would have difficulty surviving in the face of what would, doubtless, become consolidated Arab opposition to it, from both inside and outside Iraq. Second, the Soviets were so well established economically in Iraq that, even if Barzani succeeded in overthrowing the Baathists, it was unlikely that Barzani could break Iraq's ties with Moscow, unless the US were prepared to step in with immediate and substantial assistance. Furthermore, US support, for a coup operation which was perceived to be ill-organised, would be difficult to conceal; thus the US would risk further strain on its relations with the other Arab states because of support for a non-Arab movement, backed by other non-Arab states (Iran and Israel), against the Arabs. Fourth, facilitating the coming to power of a Kurdish-supported government in Baghdad also risked raising Kurdish expectations in neighbouring Iran and Turkey, causing concern, at least in Turkey if not Iran. Additionally, any encouragement to the Kurds, from the US point of view, would give further impetus to Kurdish nationalist aspirations which aimed, eventually, to establish a separate state of Kurdistan. Such a step, they believed, would be retrogressive, in that it would represent further fragmentation in an already fragmented area.[17] Moreover, the US was wary of committing itself to a guerrilla campaign, the greatest success of which could only be a standoff with the government in Baghdad and preservation of Kurdish autonomy. The US knew that if the battle turned against the Kurds, it would neither have the assets nor the interest to provide decisive support. Financially the US government emphasised that the resources necessary were available in Saudi Arabia and Iran; the US felt that this should be a regional effort, rather than one for which it would provide direct support. Finally, the US considered the implications of supporting the Kurds in the context of the Moscow summit talks of May 1972. It knew that the Soviets had made a recent effort to persuade the Kurds to join the Baath Party in a national unity government in Baghdad; hence it believed that support for the Kurds would be read politically as a direct anti-Soviet move.[18] As a consequence of these perceptions the Kurds continued to be ignored by the United States.

6.2.2 The Kurds as pawns: 1972–1975

Few Kurds at that time lived in the United States, so Mustafa Barzani asked Mohammed Dosky (a Kurd and a former Iraqi diplomat) to make contacts on his behalf and report back. Before him Shafiq Qazaz in 1965 had been appointed by Barzani as the first Kurdish representative to Washington, who, faced with numerous challenges, had managed to present the plight of the Kurds. Dosky arrived in Washington in 1972, and made the rounds of Congress and the State Department. He developed contact with Senator Henry (Scoop) Jackson (D-WA), and with Jackson's young assistant, Richard Perle; and with influential labour leader George Meany. However, the first documented and confirmed evidence of covert US support for the Kurds, going back to July 1972, appeared in the leaked Pike House Committee hearings. It started with the Shah requesting President Nixon and Henry Kissinger's help in aiding the Kurds.[19] On 30 May 1972, President Nixon and Secretary Kissinger visited the Shah in Tehran. The twenty-two-hour visit culminated in their approval of the Shah's request for covert support to the Kurdish movement in Iraq.[20] The Pike Report asserted that 'the project was initiated as a favour to our ally, who had cooperated with US agencies and had come to feel menaced by his neighbour'.[21] Through the arrangements made by the Shah of Iran, Idris Barzani and Mahmoud Osman, personal representatives of Kurdish leader Mullah Mustafa Barzani, met on 30

June 1972 with CIA Director Richard Helms, Colonel Richard Kennedy of the NSC and a CIA officer. On 31 July 1972 President Nixon approved support for the Kurdish struggle, and with this started the first relationship with the United States. This relationship, however, was official but covert.

In a memo to Nixon, Kissinger explained why the US should support Iran:

> The Shah of Iran is an island of stability in an otherwise unstable area ... the Shah's foreign policy, while increasingly flexible, is openly based on a special relationship with the US. From our viewpoint, he is a good friend.[22]

The Shah intended, with this support, to use the Kurdish revolt as a bargaining chip to increase pressure on Iraq.[23] The Pike Report quoted CIA memos which characterised the Kurds as 'a uniquely useful tool for weakening (our ally's enemy's) potential for international adventurism'.[24] The US was not a totally disinterested party either, as the prolongation of the Kurdish revolt was directly related to its efforts to advance the Middle East peace process. When Kissinger was asked by Israeli Ambassador Simcha Dinitz on 21 March 1974 to support the Kurdish plight, he responded that the US already was as 'it is in our interest to keep the Iraqis distracted while we are working on the Syrians'.[25] The shift in US strategy had very little to do with support for the Kurdish struggle per se. Nor did it have anything to do with US recognition of the Kurds as of any political significance or of particular strategic value. The secretive nature of the support, a CIA covert operation, suggests that it was only one of numerous typical CIA operations. So the Kurds gained significant US support in 1972, solely on the basis of the Shah's request, which advanced both US and Iranian interests. The Kurds were considered an effective pawn to destabilise Iraq. Brent Scowcroft expressed the US view of the time, stating: 'The Kurds were derivative. The Shah was a good ally. And he was having this problem with Iraq. We were emotionally supporting the Kurds, but it wasn't a big deal.'[26]

Moreover, Nixon and Kissinger saw Iraq as a Soviet client; to topple the Baath regime would have been a significant blow in the Cold War.[27] During the Nixon administration, Iraq had become a pawn in the Cold War. To achieve this, Nixon awarded the Kurdish liberation movement in Iraqi Kurdistan 5 million USD for supplies and weapons through the CIA. Britain, Israel and Iran also paid 7 million USD collectively to fund the Kurdish revolt. Kissinger, then Secretary of State, recommended by 1973 that the funding be increased, since Iraq's role as a chief Soviet ally was becoming more detrimental. Iraq was also blocking an Israeli-Palestinian peace deal and 'continued to finance terrorist organisations'.[28] Additionally, oil seems to have played a role in America's reversal of its non-interaction policy with the Kurds. US cooperation only came two weeks after the Iraq Petroleum Company was nationalised by the Baathist government in Baghdad.[29] According to American journalist Aron Latham, the Kurdish rebellion in Iraq would, it was hoped, be the equivalent of the truckers' strike in Chile. It was intended to topple Saddam Hussein, as had been the case with Salvador Allende, and bring about a friendlier regime. Nixon and Kissinger thought that the US could then, possibly, regain access to the Iraqi oil fields.[30]

Moreover, the CIA station chief in Tehran sent a cable to Washington stating 'only a few Kurdish leaders knew that until recently they had our secret support for their military resistance because it diverted Iraq from Israel'.[31] Kissinger, with brutal candour, later stated in his book *White House Years*, 'the benefit of Nixon's Kurdish decision was apparent in just over a year: only one Iraqi division was available to participate in the October 1973 Middle East War'.[32] Two of Barzani's visits to Tel Aviv, in 1968 and 1973, also confirmed that Israel's help for the Kurdish movement was not based on genuine support for the cause itself; Israel's support for the Kurdish struggle was only to contain and weaken Iraq. It also failed to produce the special relationship with the US, which Barzani sought. Israel never genuinely supported the Kurdish cause because of its unique relationship with Turkey. It avoided damaging relations with its only ally in the Middle East for strategic, political and military reasons, as well as for historical considerations: at a time when Jews residing under the Ottoman Empire were being persecuted with the 'blood libel', Suleiman the Magnificent had declared the 'blood libel' illegal in 1554.

In a memorandum to Henry Kissinger, only partly declassified in 2006, Harold Saunders of the National Security Council stated that the United States could support the Kurdish movement on the basis of three major calculations. Saunders believed that, if it permitted or encouraged the Kurds to remain a source of instability in Iraq, this would thwart the Soviet effort to promote a national unity government as a sounder base for the Soviet position. Also supporting the Kurds would be a means of tying down Iraqi forces since the security of Iran, Jordan and the Israel was in the US interest. Finally, domestic instability in Iraq would lessen the prospect of active Iraqi meddling in the Gulf.[33]

6.2.3 The Kurds betrayed: 1975

Lee Dinsmore, a former US Consul in Kirkuk, explains that the Kurds were assured by the US government, through the CIA officials in Baghdad, that they would continue to receive aid through Iran.[34] However, with the signing, in 1975, of the Algiers Agreement between Saddam Hussein and the Shah, all promises of continued support for the Kurdish military offensive against the Baath regime came to an end. Barzani had rejected the 1974 self-rule offered by the Baath government, due to promises he had received from the US and Iran of military assistance. He told US officials in Iran, 'This is what they have to use against us. If you will give us arms to match those arms, we will fight. Otherwise, we will make peace. We don't want to be massacred.' Barzani told Edmund Ghareeb from the American University in an interview in 1976: 'Without American promises, we would not have acted the way we did. Were it not for the American promises, we would never have become trapped and involved to such an extent.'[35] In 1970 Barzani and Saddam had made a deal. The Shah, who was backing Barzani, did not like the deal, because he was using the Kurds as a tool against Iraq. Barzani believed that, because the US was involved, he had a real commitment; however, the following year, on 6 March 1975,

Saddam and the Shah signed the Algiers Accord and the US simply went along with them. Kissinger betrayed the Kurds, by allowing the Shah to use the Kurds with a total disregard of human costs.[36] The US broke its promise of support to the Kurdish movement. The Pike report also confirmed this view: the US 'acted, in effect, as guarantor that the insurgent group would not be summarily dropped by the foreign head of state (the Shah)'.[37] But this all changed; the Shah managed to secure genuine concessions from Iraq in the Algiers Accord and, with it, all US and Iranian support to the Kurds ceased.

The deliberate termination of US support to the Kurdish struggle shows that it was never intended to succeed. Nixon, Kissinger and the Shah, according to the Pike report, hoped that 'our client [Barzani] would not prevail'. They preferred instead to sap the resources of 'our ally's neighbouring country [Iraq]'. This policy was not imparted to the Kurds, who were encouraged to continue fighting. The report concluded, 'Even in the context of overt action, ours was a cynical enterprise.'[38] Iran and the White House were only interested in prolonging the Kurdish insurgency and not in its success, because of the effect success would have on US allies, Turkey and Iran.[39] Ambassador William Eagleton argues that the basis of US support for the Kurdish movement in 1972 'was a desire to respond positively to the Shah's request, which was apparently based on Barzani's insistence that some kind of big power support was needed to balance Iraq's Soviet connection'.[40] Brent Scowcroft explained the US position and attitude:

> In 1975, quite suddenly the Shah made a deal with Iraq. And so he had no further interest in fomenting trouble up there in Kurdistan. As a matter of fact he had a disinterest, because there are a lot of Kurds up there in Iran. So then he wanted us to stop supporting them, and then we had no practical way to support them. We ended our support – it was just small potatoes. It wasn't really an issue at the time that I recall.[41]

The possibility of interruption of oil flow from Iraq to the West seems to have influenced US considerations; the 1973 oil embargo was still a fresh memory at the time. Above all, the American ally, Iran, had achieved considerable success in its venture of exploiting the Kurds. The Algiers Agreement provided the Shah with many of the concessions to which he aspired. Additionally, the US support for the Kurdish movement not only achieved the containment of Iraq, it also helped weaken Iraq significantly.

Furthermore, by 1975 Anwar Sadat of Egypt had already signed the Sinai Agreement and the possibility of a peaceful solution to the Arab-Israeli conflict was being considered. Syria had refused to join the negotiations, in which Kissinger was deeply involved. Baathist Syria, a rival of Iraq, was hostile to the US ally, Israel. Therefore a weakened Iraq, in the face of a hostile Syria, was not favourable to US interests. On the contrary, a strong Iraq was considered as an effective tool to encourage Syria's agreement to these talks. Moreover, the continuation of US support to the Kurds would have provided an excuse for further Soviet involvement in the region; both Turkey and Iran had substantial Kurdish communities that could have been mobilised through Soviet support.[42] The US saw no need for the continuation of a Kurdish insurgency to weaken Iraq at a time when the Arab-Israeli peace process was gaining ground and a strong Iraq was counterbalancing its rival Syria, which strongly opposed any rapprochement with Israel.

In a statement to the Pike investigation, Henry Kissinger explained, with brutal frankness, his role in the abrupt termination of support to the Kurdish movement: 'covert action should not be confused with missionary work'.[43] After the Algiers Agreement, the US took no particular interest in the Kurdish cause. For American officials, their ally, Iran, had achieved significant concessions in the accord; any support for the Kurdish cause would only have aggravated their Turkish and Iranian allies, with their substantial Kurdish minorities. The US betrayal of the Kurds went unnoticed.

So the Kurds were left largely ignored by the US. Barzani was finally allowed to travel to the United States, arriving on that steamy afternoon in August 1975. When Barzani travelled to the US for the second time, in June 1976, he was even, initially, denied a visa. The State Department stipulated that his visit would be conditional upon his committing himself not to meet with the media or make political statements. Joseph Sisco, Undersecretary of State for Political Affairs, visited Barzani, having been instructed by Kissinger to 'Hear Barzani out and let him blow off steam, nothing more.' Sisco explained to Barzani that the United States had come in to help the Kurds at the request of the Shah; and now, at the request of the Shah it was pulling out.[44] The US did grant around a thousand of his followers asylum in the US, a trivial humanitarian gesture when taking into account the gravity of the collapse of the Kurdish movement. Barzani eventually died in Georgetown University Hospital in 1979.[45] This episode was indicative of the degree to which the Kurds were no more than a pawn of the Cold War in the Middle East region. The Kurds were simply abandoned from the late 1970s until the early 1990s.

6.3 The Kurds in the US Iraq tilt: 1979–1990

6.3.1 Saddam's adventure in Iran: 1980–1988

The US tilt towards Iraq after the Shah's overthrow was described in detail in Chapter 2: Iraq gained favour as an ally against revolutionary Iran. This ensured the continuation, by the US government, of the institutional neglect of the Iraqi Kurds. In mid 1983, Iranian complaints surfaced of Iraq's use of chemical weapons on the battlefield; and, on 5 March 1984, the US State Department condemned Iraq's use of mustard gas. This was before Donald Rumsfeld's second visit to Saddam;[46] it was partly in response to Iranian complaints to the international community and partly the US paying lip service to the Geneva Protocol and conventions, to which it was signatory – otherwise, the Reagan administration was willing to ignore Iraqi use of chemical weapons against the Iranians and its own civilian Kurds. The Reagan administration continued to believe that

Iraq's behaviour could be moderated and that, as a strategic asset, it could protect US interests in the region.[47] The Kurds were absolutely ignored before the First Gulf War. When the Anfal and Halabja massacres were committed by Iraq against the Kurds, the US did not react, apart from verbal condemnation. The State Department ignored it, since the policy was to deal with Iraq at the national level. Hikmat Bamarni, the KDP's North America branch head, explained that the US had no intention of dealing with the Kurds, because it was considered an internal Iraqi matter and intervention was seen as not in the interest of the US.[48]

During this period, the Kurds gained no significant recognition at the political level – subjected to various means of genocide, they were neglected in the ongoing conflict. The only signs of US attention to the Kurds came towards the end of the Iran–Iraq war. In September 1987, Haywood Rankin, a political counsellor at the US embassy in Baghdad, travelled to Iraqi Kurdistan with Congressional staffer Peter Galbraith. Both saw the atrocities of the Anfal Campaign against the Kurds. Rankin produced a twenty-seven-page document recounting his observations, which was circulated at the State Department and other Reagan administration agencies. Galbraith also produced a report published by the Senate Foreign Relations Committee entitled 'War in the Persian Gulf: The US Takes Sides' recounting these atrocities.[49] On his return to Washington Galbraith reported this; it was the beginning of his efforts to advance the Kurdish cause in the US.[50]

During the gas attacks on the Kurds, which had actually started in March 1987, the Reagan administration remained indifferent: it issued no public statement denouncing these actions.[51] The brutality of Saddam's regime continued, with few in the US taking notice. After the international public outrage at the Halabja gassing, Senator George Mitchell introduced a non-binding resolution, denouncing the attacks made by Iraq.[52] But the Reagan administration was not interested. US State Department spokesman Charles Redman even stated, with regard to the Iraqi use of chemical weapons on the Kurdish town of Halabja on 23 March 1988: 'There are indications that Iran may also have used chemical artillery shells in this fighting.'

In April 1988, shortly after the Halabja gassing and before the end of the Iran–Iraq war, Kurdish leader, Jalal Talabani, made his first visit to the US, hoping to obtain weapons and support for autonomy. He gave a talk at the Wilson Forum and met informally with some White House officials and with Senator Claiborne Pell (Rhode Island Democrat and Chairman of the Senate Foreign Relations Committee from 1987 to 1994).[53] Peter Galbraith managed to arrange a meeting with the director of the State Department's Northern Gulf Affairs, Larry Pope. However, only a few days later the Turkish President, Kenan Evren, protested to Secretary George Shultz over this meeting with 'Kurdish terrorists'. This meeting, unknown to Secretary Shultz, resulted in a rebuke for Pope.[54] The Iraqis, too, complained about these meetings. As a result, the State Department declared a ban on meetings with the Iraqi opposition, the Kurds included;[55] so, the Kurds' attempt to establish contact with the US failed to produce a positive response.

In August 1988 the Iraqi government carried out a second wave of chemical attacks on Kurdish villages in the Dohuk Governorate, bordering Turkey. In response, on 8 September, Secretary of State George Shultz during a meeting with Iraq's Deputy Prime Minister, Saadoun Hammadi, and denounced as 'unjustified and abhorrent'[56] Iraq's use of chemical weapons.[57] The US Senate passed a bill, sponsored by Senator Claiborne Pell, to impose sanctions on Iraq. The bill was titled 'The Prevention of Genocide Act of 1988'; it was passed unanimously on 9 September 1988. A congressional investigation into Iraq's use of chemical weapons against its Kurdish population was conducted by Galbraith and Christopher Van Hollen, to help secure the House's support.[58] However, the House of Representatives refused to pass the bill, except in a watered-down version.[59] The Prevention of Genocide Act failed because of a number of US interests: expanding trade in rice and other grain between US farmers and Iraq, the desire to contain Iran and unwillingness to antagonise Turkey superseded any other considerations.[60] Charles Redman, on 14 September, described the Act as 'premature'.[61] This was a clear indication of the United States' refusal to accept Iraq as a threat or to reject it as a strategic asset. Even after the Anfal Campaign and its gas attacks, the US continued to show next to no interest in the Kurds.

Galbraith argues that the Reagan administration failed to recognise that the Iraqi regime was in no way a reliable US partner, nor a source of stability in the region. In consequence, it overlooked the gassing of the Kurds. The Reagan White House continued to believe that the Baath regime would moderate its behaviour and eventually be a US strategic asset.[62]

6.3.2 Saddam's adventure in Kuwait: 1990

Jalal Talabani, now Foreign Relations representative of the Kurdistan Front, visited Washington, D.C. again on 10 August 1990, a week after Saddam occupied Kuwait. He offered US officials military intelligence and cooperation against Baghdad in return for military, financial and political support to the Kurds.[63] In a statement published in the *Washington Post*, hoping to induce US support, he declared that 'If President Bush approves, I will send 10,000 of my men to fight side by side with the US military in Kuwait against the Iraqi army.'[64] This, too, came to nothing. Even after Saddam occupied Kuwait, the US policy of no contact with the Iraqi opposition had not changed;[65] no one from the Bush administration agreed to meet him.[66] He did, through journalists sympathetic to the Kurds, manage to meet a junior State Department official in a café; but the official told him bluntly, 'America at this time has no intention of making contact with the Iraqi opposition.'[67] Former Deputy Assistant Secretary of State, David Mack, explained that, prior to the beginning of hostilities between US and Iraq, the US was very careful how it associated with people from the Iraqi opposition, the reason for that he stressed was that 'we had every reason to believe that they would be of very little help to us in the goal of the operation which was the liberation of Kuwait'. Moreover, as regards the US goal of change inside Iraq the US believed that it was far more likely to come from within the Iraqi regime than it was to come from London, 'that was why when Jalal Talabani came to Washington he was seen outside the State Department at a level lower than mine'.[68]

6.4 The Kurds noticed: 1991–2000

6.4.1 *Operation Provide Comfort: 1991*

The Kurds caught a break in 1991, but this came at great cost. Even after the US-led coalition had ejected Iraq from Kuwait, there was no change towards the Iraqi opposition or the Kurds. It seemed that the US, although uncomfortable with Saddam's behaviour, did not want to upset the status quo. After Galbraith's intervention, and only a week before the Kurdish uprising of spring 1991, on 28 February, the State Department agreed to meet a Kurdish delegation already in Washington. They had been scheduled to meet Richard Schifter, Assistant Secretary of State for Human Rights. But when they arrived at the State Department, they were taken to a coffee shop outside the building and received by two junior State Department officials. Galbraith argues that 'Turkish sensibilities [were] a main reason for the cold shoulder in Official Washington'.[69]

However, in the Senate Foreign Relations Committee room, on 27 February 1991, Senator Pell and Peter Galbraith had chaired an Inter-Parliamentary Consultation on the Kurds. Many Kurdish leaders were present including Talabani and Zebari. During their meeting with the US senators, the Kurds emphasised their pro-American sentiment and the likelihood of an uprising.[70] The Kurds' quest for the fulfilment of their nationalist aspirations had turned them towards the US – a Kurdish perception that it was the land of freedom and self-determination. Up to this point, every attempt had ended in failure, as US political interests overrode any chance of full support. However, this was about to change with the two Bush presidencies, the first in 1991 and the second in 2003.[71]

On 1 March 1991, Galbraith tried to contact Richard Haass, the National Security Council's director for the Middle East, after Talabani had told him of an uprising in Iraqi Kurdistan in the 27 February meeting. Failing to reach him, Galbraith spoke to his deputy, Sandy Charles. Charles angrily told Galbraith that he was meddling at a sensitive time. Galbraith argued that it was US policy to get rid of the regime, to which Charles replied: 'Our policy is to get rid of Saddam Hussein, not his regime.'[72] Yet on 15 February 1991, President George H. W. Bush had delivered a speech in Andover, Massachusetts, asking the Iraqi people to overthrow the regime; he had stated:

> And there's another way for the bloodshed to stop, and that is for the Iraqi military and the Iraqi people to take matters into their own hands and force Saddam Hussein, the dictator, to step aside, and then comply with the United Nations resolutions and rejoin the family of peace-loving nations.[73]

But the true intention of the administration was to secure a clean overthrow of Saddam Hussein, without the involvement of the diverse Iraqi opposition. The

US had no interest in creating a new regime, only to rid Iraq of Saddam Hussein and his inner circle; this, it was hoped, would come through a military coup, bringing a new leadership that would sustain Iraq's territorial integrity and unity, but without creating problems for US allies in the region, such as Egypt, Turkey and Saudi Arabia.[74] A Kurdish victory in 1991 would have meant the possible partition of Iraq and instability in the region – especially in Turkey, which was waging its own war against the PKK. The other countries in the region, such as Saudi Arabia, Egypt and the Gulf states, feared the emergence of a Shiite-dominated regime in Baghdad.[75] During the popular uprising of 1991, the Bush administration refrained from interference in the conflict. The White House Press Secretary, Marlin Fitzwater, stated on 16 March 1991: 'We don't intend to involve ourselves in the internal affairs of Iraq.'[76] President Bush's assessment of the 1991 uprising is described in Brent Scowcroft's memoir as follows:

Occasionally, he [Bush] indicated the removal of Saddam would be welcome, but for very practical reasons there was never a promise to aid an uprising. While we hoped that a popular revolt or coup would topple Saddam, neither the United States nor the countries of the region wished to see the break-up of the Iraqi state. We were concerned about the long term balance of power at the head of the gulf. Breaking up Iraq would pose its own destabilising problems. While Ozal put the priority on Saddam and had a more tolerant view of the Kurds than other Turkish leaders before or since, Turkey – and Iran – objected to the suggestion of an independent Kurdish state. However admirable self-determination for the Kurds or Shiites might have been in principle, the practical aspects of this particular situation dictated the policy. For these reasons alone, the uprisings distressed us...[77]

Nevertheless, under Ozal's leadership, Turkey now changed its hostile non-negotiating posture towards the Kurds. On 8 March 1991 it officially received Jalal Talabani and Mohsin Dizai.[78] This meeting, before the uprising, was the beginning of change. After this visit Talabani explained that the most significant result of the meeting was: 'Turkey lifting its objection to the establishment of direct relations between the Kurdish front in Iraq and the United States.'[79] Moreover, after the suppressed uprising of 1991 and the mass exodus of the Kurds, at the request of France, Turkey and Iran, the UN Security Council passed a Security Council resolution (UNSCR 688), demanding that Iraq stop repressing its domestic population 'including most recently in Kurdish populated areas'.[80] As a result a No-fly zone, sponsored by the US, UK and France, was enforced to protect the Kurds; this enabled flights for reconnaissance and to monitor disarmament.[81] It should be pointed out that this resolution was in clear contradiction of Article 2(7) of the UN Charter, which prohibits interference in internal affairs.[82] UNSCR 688 was a significant resolution, for two major reasons. It was the second of its kind – after the League of Nations 1926 annexation of *Mosul Vilayet* – to mention the Kurds in an international document; second, it was the first case of the United Nations insisting on the right of intervention in the internal affairs of a sovereign state.[83] The US intervention in Iraqi Kurdistan was also the first of its kind based on the humanitarian grounds that became one of the hallmarks of US foreign policy in the 1990s. This event allowed the Kurds to govern and control substantial portions of Iraqi Kurdistan leading to the 'territorialisation' of Kurdish nationalism – an important development in the state formation process.[84]

After Secretary of State James Baker's visit to the Iraqi-Turkish border, where thousands of Kurds were stranded, Baker called President Bush, requesting a change in US policy.[85] Operation Provide Comfort initially started as a humanitarian effort to relieve those fleeing Iraq after the crushing of the 1991 uprising against Saddam's regime. It started off with a US-protected enclave under the command of Anthony Zinni, a Marine brigadier general at the time, to protect the Kurds from potential harm. Zinni argued that 'we were saddling ourselves with an open-ended commitment to protect them in that environment'.[86] The UN resolution which led to 'Operation Provide Comfort' was initially established on the initiative of UK Prime Minister John Major who, at an EC summit on 8 April 1991, asked that UN-protected enclaves be established to protect the Kurds (this had been suggested to him by Turkish President Turgut Ozal).[87] President Bush senior explained the US intervention in 1991: 'We simply could not allow 500,000 to a million people to die up there in the mountains.'[88] Jay Garner, the commanding general of the operation, described to the author Operation Provide Comfort as the 'highlight of the military career of those involved'. Moreover, he stressed that though humanitarian in nature it did not lack a political element. The political element pushed primarily by John Major was that at least Britain and the US should keep the Kurds from dying as 'Bush senior had encouraged a rebellion that was left to collapse in an intolerant public and politically damaging atmosphere'.[89]

Qubad Talabani described the 1991–1998 period as insignificant in US-Kurdish relations. The Kurds were in his words 'just a blip on the radar screen'. Even in 1992, when the Kurds held elections, there was no support for them from Washington. In fact, Deputy Assistant Secretary of State at the time, David Mack, strongly discouraged Najmaldin Karim, then the sole representative of the Kurds in Washington, from holding these elections. When congressional staffers wanted to go and monitor the elections, Mack chastised them, urging them not to go and telling them that it was sending the 'wrong messages'. Qubad Talabani described this period as one of humanitarian operation and nothing more; he went on to claim that, in fact, the humanitarian intervention itself was not an American-led initiative; it was John Major's and President François Mitterand's initiative – they were the ones who forced it upon the Americans. It was only after James Baker's flight to the region that he was able to come back and say, 'we need to do something here'. It was a reluctant intervention; nobody in the decision-making process in the US during 1991–1992, which set up Operation Provide Comfort, the Safe Haven, and eventually the No-fly zone, thought that this US-led intervention would create what exists today in Kurdistan. The US had no idea that it would evolve into the Kurdistan Regional Government, the

Iraqi Kurdistan Parliament flags, a constitution and the Peshmarga.[90] On 16 April 1991, President George Bush senior declared that US forces would enter Iraqi territory to establish refugee camps, to help feed and shelter Kurdish refugees stranded on the Iraqi-Turkish border. He stated:

> The approach is quite simple: if we cannot get adequate food, medicine, clothing and shelter to the Kurds living in the mountains along the Turkish-Iraq border, we must encourage the Kurds to move to areas in northern Iraq where the geography facilitates, rather than frustrates, such large-scale relief effort. Consistent with UNSC Resolution 688 and working closely with the United Nations and other international organisations and with European partners, I have directed the US military to begin immediately to establish several encampments in northern Iraq where relief supplies for these refugees will be made available in large quantities and distributed in an orderly manner ... adequate security will be provided at these temporary sites by US, British and French air and ground forces, again consistent with United Nations Security Council Resolution 688 ... all we are doing is motivated by humanitarian concerns.[91]

On 6 April, Operation Provide Comfort I began. Joint Task Force Provide Comfort was formed and deployed to Incirlik Air Base, Turkey, to conduct humanitarian operations in northern Iraq; the task force dropped its first supplies to Kurdish refugees on 7 April. Air units operating from Incirlik enforced a No-fly zone above the thirty-sixth parallel. General Jay Garner led a 20,000-strong military force to push the Iraqi army southwards. It was considered an example of the success of a military humanitarian mission.[92] Provide Comfort I ended on 24 July 1991 and, on the same day, Provide Comfort II began. It was a show of force to deter new Iraqi attacks on the Kurds, and had only limited humanitarian aspects to its mission. It ended on 31 December 1996. The No-fly zones were also indicative of a new post-Cold War American unilateralism. John Pilger asked Boutros Boutros-Ghali, Secretary General of the UN, about the legality of these zones. 'The Security Council never approved or in any way ratified these zones', Boutros-Ghali stated.[93]

However, the No-fly zone wasn't really aimed at the Kurds, but at Saddam. The US no longer trusted Saddam and so wanted to contain him as a regional power. It certainly had a humanitarian element, to protect the Kurds. However, in reality, it was less about humanitarianism and more about pure politics. The US now considered Iraq a nuisance; the objective was now to keep it in check. The No-fly zones were one way of weakening Saddam as part of this containment policy.[94]

After the negotiations between Baghdad and the Kurdish leadership broke down in 1991, the Baath regime withdrew its authority from the major Kurdish areas and imposed its sanctions.[95] It was after these events that the US started to see the Kurds as a useful tool against Saddam's regime.[96] The Kurdish safe haven, established in Northern Iraq through the No-fly zone, became part of the US attempt to contain the Iraqi regime.[97] The US saw the Kurdish client as a useful weapon against Baghdad. The US had again, for the second time, become pro-Kurdish for reasons not too dissimilar to the 1972–1975 period.[98]

The Kurds managed to hold on to the three predominantly northern governorates after the Baathists withdrew. They started to create their own administrative institutions and held elections to this end. The US welcomed the 1992 parliamentary elections in the Kurdish region after Baghdad withdrew its administration – even though it was an unintended consequence. On 15 May 1992 the State Department expressed verbal support; spokeswoman Margaret Tutwiler stated that the US hoped the elections would

> help lead to a better life for all the people of northern Iraq ... [it] welcome[d] public and private assurances by the Iraqi Kurdish leadership [that the elections would deal] only with local administrative issues [and did not] represent a move towards separatism.[99]

When the Kurdistan Regional Government was initially formed, after the first election, the bulk of US interests was served as a follow-up to the First Gulf War, where the US had helped sustain and create the No-fly zone. The American sense was that the elections were local issues, not issues the US wanted to deal with in great depth; its major connection to Iraqi Kurdistan was via the INC and humanitarian concerns.[100]

The Kurds were officially received, for the first time, in Washington on 7 October 1991 by Assistant Secretary Edward Djerejian. The State Department stated that the meeting with the Iraqi Kurdistan Front delegation took place within the context of broadening US government contacts with a wide range of groups opposed to Saddam Hussein and the then Iraqi regime. It also asserted that the US did not back any particular opposition faction, nor did it aim to shape a government to succeed Saddam Hussein. This was a matter for the Iraqi people. The United States, it said, 'supports peaceful political reform within Iraq, not Iraq's breakup'.[101]

Gradually a new US Iraq policy started to take root. In the early 1990s US policy towards Iraq changed in the context of dual containment of Iran and Iraq. Ayal Frank, senior advisor to the Kurdistan Regional Government, explained US policy towards Iraq needed to be understood in the context of Iran. Frank stressed that Iraq, for the most part, was seen as a lesser evil than Iran; but both needed to be contained, particularly after the Gulf War. The Iraqi opposition therefore was seen by the US government only within the context of Saddam's Iraq. In this context the Iraqi opposition from the American point of view had less significance than Saddam's Iraq, Iran, Iraq–Iran rivalry or US interests in the region.[102] During this period the US government saw the Kurds as one player within the Iraqi opposition; not the most important, but equal to others. In any case that opposition only carried a certain amount of weight in the larger context of US policy towards Iraq and the even larger context of US policy towards Iraq and Iran.[103] In the 1990s, Kurdish leaders were always received at a higher level if they were part of a larger Iraqi opposition delegation.[104]

The US did not interfere in the day to day details of running the Kurdistan Region. When the Oil for Food Programme started, the US made sure that the UN would set aside a share for the Kurdish north. Andrew Morrison of the State Department explained that it was very much the US which was behind the negotiations with the UN, which led to a 13 per cent allocation for the Kurds.[105]

However, although the Kurds constituted part of the opposition, they were arguably in a very different category than the rest of that opposition. The Kurds were by far the most organised and most legitimate opposition group and had substantial forces on the ground. They had intelligence organisations and capabilities. The Kurdish parties had a sophisticated infrastructure, relative to other Iraqi opposition groups; they were able to house many of the other Iraqi opposition groups and leaders and that carried a certain *gravitas*. So when Kurdish leaders were speaking to the Americans, it was not only as a key element of the Iraqi opposition but also as one that represented a genuine constituency.[106]

6.4.2 The Washington Accord: 1998

As the civil war between the PUK and KDP was escalating, the US was becoming uncomfortable with its repercussions. The lethal character of the conflict was unprecedented, leading eventually to the Iraqi army being invited by the KDP to repress PUK advances on the KDP and consequently to retake the Kurdish capital, Erbil. In late January 1995 President Clinton sent a US delegation with a letter to both Kurdish leaders, stating: 'We will no longer cooperate with the other countries to maintain security in the region if the clashes continue.'[107] The civil war led to political instability and this created a serious power vacuum, giving regional and international powers an opportunity to become involved.[108] The US was not happy about this; nor was it comfortable with Iranian mediation efforts to end the Kurdish civil war. David Litt, Country Director for Northern Gulf Affairs at the State Department, at a talk given at the Washington Institute for Near East Policy on 8 February 1995, cautioned both the Kurdish parties to reject the assistance of the Iranian government, as it was 'not a disinterested or neutral observer ... and its objectives are not at all consonant with those of the Iraqis or the US government'.[109] Litt had visited Kurdistan between 24 and 27 January of that year, meeting with the KDP, the PUK and the INC, as well as the prominent Kurdish politician Nawshirwan Mustafa Amin; he threatened that, if the fighting did not stop, and if Iranian intervention was accepted, the US would halt Operation Provide Comfort, stop protecting the Kurds and leave the Kurds to Saddam.[110] On 11 January 1995, Jalal Talabani sent Nawshirwan a note in which he stated that the 'US has threatened to sever relations and says we will be "crossing the red line" if we accept Iranian involvement. Dr. Chalabi also says that the US may withdraw and we [Kurds] will be left to Saddam.'[111]

Andrew Morrison explained that the US was concerned about the fighting at the time. There had already been a first Iraqi army incursion and the US was worried that it might happen again, if the fighting continued and grew worse, with a potentially very aggressive Iraqi force of two divisions on the Kurdistan border.[112] The

US was frustrated and dissatisfied that it had not convinced the two parties to set aside their differences and stop the fighting; the KDP–PUK civil war had the potential to become a disaster, with fighting in major Kurdish cities, and with Turkey or Iraq getting involved.[113] Morrison pointed out that when the fighting broke out again after the Iraqi incursion of August 1996 the US thought it was hazardous. The US was also concerned about the potential for a humanitarian crisis, and worked intensively to ensure the civil war did not get out of hand.[114]

During this period, and fearful of Iraq's retribution on US employees, in September 1996 the State Department received presidential approval for a voluntary evacuation. The US launched Operation Pacific Haven evacuating more than 6000 Kurds, leading to their legal emigration to the US.[115]

The civil war was not in the US interest. Iran was becoming more involved in Kurdish issues, providing military support to the PUK, and Turkey was taking the KDP's side, ensuring air support for advancing KDP forces. The safe haven created in northern Iraq was falling into the hands of regional powers, a prospect the US did not relish. The US therefore made an unprecedented effort to stop the fighting; Deputy Assistant Secretary of State David Welch visited Kurdistan from 17 to 20 July 1998 to negotiate a settlement.

The US had not been successful in previous attempts to solve the crisis within the framework of the Ankara Process. The first US-sponsored attempts at reconciliation, held in two rounds at Drogheda, just north of Dublin, Ireland, in August and September 1995, had ended in failure. This time Welch extended invitations to both Kurdish leaders to visit Washington to negotiate a final settlement and sign a reconciliation agreement; and this time it led to a peaceful resolution, concluded in the Washington Agreement, signed by Barzani and Talabani under State Department sponsorship on 17 September 1998. Before Barzani and Talabani visited Washington, on 8 September 1998 State Department spokesman James Rubin stated:

> We also want to listen to the real voices of the Iraqi people. Both of these leaders [Barzani and Talabani] represent the interests of millions of Iraqi Kurds. In extraordinarily difficult circumstances they are working to cooperate with the international community and we hope that they will have a chance to talk to a wide spectrum of people in Washington and real leaders will be heard from.[116]

Mack explained that the purpose behind bringing the Kurdish leaders to Washington for reconciliation was linked to US support for all Iraqi opposition groups based on the fundamental desire to isolate and weaken the government of Saddam and prevent him from being a threat to regional security. He stressed that 'it wasn't because we favoured Kurdish separatism'.[117] During the signing ceremony Secretary of State Madeleine Albright stated:

> And, as today's meeting reflects, we are intensifying our efforts to help Iraqis – whether Arab or Kurd, Shiite or Sunni – to develop a deeper sense

of common purpose and a more effective strategy for achieving their future in a democratic and pluralist Iraq.[118]

There was a gradual progression in the US-Kurdish relationship, starting from the mid 1990s when the Iraqi opposition movement was becoming more active, and then also during the infighting between the KDP and the PUK. The US involvement evolved from considering the Kurds as part of the Iraqi opposition movement, to stopping them from fighting, and regrouping them once again. The Kurdish movement was able to stop the internal fighting, unify their efforts and then become a leading element of the Iraqi opposition movement.[119] The US was always involved in Iraqi Kurdistan throughout the 1990s but not in the details of everyday governance of the region.[120] From 1998 to 2003, there was a sharp increase in cooperation, assistance and support from the US.[121] From the US perspective, Kurdistan was the sole window into Iraq and this was not to be disturbed. The agreement, at least in theory, was good, as it rejected any invitation or provocation of outside interference.[122]

There was further US interest in the Kurdish question; a congressional hearing was held to assess the use of chemical weapons by the Iraqi regime. Professor of Medical Genetics from Liverpool University, Christine Gosden, a researcher of the Halabja gas attack, testified to the US Senate in April 1998.[123] The Senate hearing was titled 'Chemical and Biological Weapons Threats to America: Are We Prepared?', testimony to an already recognised threat of the potential harm WMD could do to the United States. Gosden advised the Senate Judiciary Subcommittee on Technology, Terrorism, and Government Information and the Senate Select Committee on Intelligence that the US should take three steps to tackle this issue. First, develop a national plan to respond to WMD attacks, immediately treat victims of the attacks not only to save lives but to prevent genetic disorders in future generations and finally revive and maintain national medical programmes to deal with potential civilian and military casualties of chemical attacks.[124]

Moreover, one of the articles of the Washington Accord stressed that both parties would endeavour to create a united, pluralistic and democratic Iraq that would ensure the political and human rights of the Kurdish people in Iraq and of all Iraqis on a political basis decided by all the Iraqi people. It also stressed that both parties aspired to an Iraq reformed on a federal basis that would maintain the nation's unity and territorial integrity. The clause ended 'we understand that the US respects such aspirations for all the Iraqi people'.[125] Additionally, the US maintained it would continue to support UNSCR 688 condemning the repression of the Iraqi population.[126] Included in the Accord was a statement that 'UN Security Council Resolution 688 noted the severe repression of the Iraqi people, particularly the Kurdish people in Iraq. The potential for repression has not eased since 1991, when the resolution was passed.'[127]

In a letter to Congress on 5 November 1998, titled 'Status of Efforts to Obtain Iraq's Compliance with UN resolutions', President Clinton declared:

Both Barzani and Talabani have made positive, forward-looking statements on political reconciliation. We will continue our efforts to reach a permanent reconciliation through mediation in order to help the people of northern Iraq find the permanent, stable settlement which they deserve, and to minimise the opportunities for Baghdad and Tehran to insert themselves into the conflict and threaten Iraqi citizens in this region.[128]

Matthew Stephenson from the State Department stressed that the US considered the Kurds 'close friends and strong allies'. During Saddam Hussein's time, it was widely held that the Kurds were fighting Saddam and the US supported those efforts.[129]

By 1998 the Clinton administration was becoming entangled in the Lewinsky scandal and Congress was dominated by the Republicans. Seizing the opportunity created by the weakness of President Clinton, the Republicans in agreement with Democrats managed to pass the Iraq Liberation Act. The act authorised the president to designate Iraqi opposition groups for military assistance to achieve its goal. On 4 February 1999 President Clinton chose seven groups to pursue this goal; three of them were Kurdish political parties, including the KDP and the PUK. However, the Clinton administration remained focused on the policy of containment: in a statement on 28 December 1998 President Clinton asserted that:

The No-fly zones have been and will remain an important part of our containment policy ... because we effectively control the skies over much of Iraq, Saddam has been unable to use air power to repress his own people or to lash out again at his neighbours.[130]

6.5 The Kurds, a valuable asset: 2001–2003

6.5.1 The Kurdish model

In a Deputies' meeting on 13 July 2001 under the George W. Bush administration, Paul Wolfowitz already suggested empowering the Iraqis towards regime change. He suggested excluding Iraqi Kurdistan from the UN economic sanctions. This, he argued, would be a step towards freeing Iraq. However, he was conscious that such a step would antagonise Turkey, which had its own sizable Kurdish population; Turkey would object to an internationally recognised Kurdish enclave, which could pave the way to an independent Kurdistan. This led him to suggest the creation of a second free Iraqi enclave in Southern Iraq on the border with Kuwait.[131]

The Kurds continued to be seen as an asset in the US, if only to help contain Iraq. Their function as a thorn in the side of and a source of humiliation for Iraq's regime was paramount to US interests in the region. However, this all changed; the attacks of 9/11 were a watershed in US relations with both Iraq and its Kurds. 9/11 transformed the prospects of Iraqi Kurdistan, giving it significant value. The Kurdish leadership had already developed close ties with Bush administration neoconservatives. They knew that a US invasion of Iraq was imminent.[132]

The Kurds were also used to enlist the US public. The Kurds were 'an excellent example of Saddam's brutality' that Bush could pull out in front of America, saying: 'Saddam Hussein gassed his own people – the Kurds'. The Kurds were used as an emotional lever and, for some Americans who were on a knife's edge about going to war, the Kurds helped to clinch the argument. If the potential threat of WMD in a post-9/11 world was not enough reason, Saddam's gassing of his own people helped change their minds. It was a scary thing for Americans that reminded them of the Holocaust and, for some, conjured up horrific 'Last Days' scenarios.[133] Saddam Hussein's treatment of the Kurds was one of the contributing factors, one of the paragraphs of indictment of Saddam Hussein. In making the case for war the genocidal activity by Saddam Hussein even if not politically or legally convincing, was morally and psychologically effective in shaping American attitudes to his regime. It provided both a humanitarian and a political justification.[134]

Furthermore, Iraqi Kurdistan was providing a model for Iraqis who did not live in the northern zone, of how good life could be for Iraqis *not* living under Saddam Hussein.[135] If any questions were raised before the invasion about democracy and freedom in Iraq, the Americans and those who supported them, could point to the Kurds in the north and their successes. These were reasons for the US to value the Kurds;[136] another reason was their availability. Considering that the US objective was to project the image of liberator rather than occupier, the US wanted to show that that it genuinely wanted to help the Iraqis rid themselves of Saddam Hussein. The only Iraqis available for such partnership were the 'externals': the Kurds and the Iraqi exiles.[137]

In the first weeks of February 2002, the initial phases of the regime-change plan came into effect, when the president signed an Executive Finding that gave the go-ahead for CIA and SOF to start covert activities, inside Iraq,[138] to destabilise Saddam Hussein.[139] The *Washington Post* reported that on 16 February 2002 the new top secret order for regime change in Iraq directed the CIA to support the US military in overthrowing Saddam and granted it authority to support opposition groups and conduct sabotage operations inside Iraq.[140]

By the second week of July 2002, the first CIA operatives made their way through Turkey into Iraqi Kurdistan; each member was assigned a Turkish officer as a minder. They were eight in number but divided into two teams of four. The first team made its way to a CIA base close to Turkey and the second to one on the outskirts of Sulaimani City. The objective of these CIA teams was to develop an operational base for further covert action.[141] These CIA operatives were later supplemented with a special operations force. A senior Kurdistan Regional Government official on condition of anonymity clarified to the author that the first advanced team of American SOF elements arrived in Kurdistan in November 2002. Their mission was to evaluate the situation on the ground and start upgrading the capacities available of their Kurdish allies. However, the bulk of US SOF brigades started arriving in late January and early February 2003 gradually adding to their numbers.[142]

The Kurds, however, mindful of their past experiences with the US, were in no hurry to take the role of the Afghan Northern Alliance. They knew that the American plans for post-Saddam Iraq would determine the future of their autonomous region in northern Iraq; the Kurdish leadership was adamant that they would not cooperate unless they received assurances from the US regarding their security, and their status in post-Saddam Iraq.[143] In April 2002, Barzani and Talabani had been invited to the US secretly in a private plane.[144] This time they were hosted at the CIA training base in Virginia, known as 'The Farm' where they met CIA director George Tenet and a host of other senior US officials.[145] The main purpose of the visit was for the Americans to assure the Kurds that the US's intention to topple the regime was real; but, also, the US wanted to ask them 'are you on board for this effort?'[146] Most American participants knew that such an operation required full Kurdish support.[147] Qubad Talabani stated that he did not think the US could have launched Operation Iraqi Freedom 'without the buy-in of the Kurds'.[148]

The Kurds, having felt betrayed by the US on previous occasions, were worried about their security. They feared two possible outcomes of Saddam's overthrow: first that their American-sponsored freedom would end, second that the regime's demise would result in the domination of Kurdistan by Baghdad.[149] When in April 2002 the US brought the Kurdish leadership to Washington, the US conceded to the Kurds the security guarantees necessary to get them on board; they agreed to change their policy from responding 'at a time and place of our choosing', to an immediate response if Saddam moved against the Kurds. Qubad Talabani stated that 'that was enough for the Kurds buy-in. Some of the other things we asked for we are still waiting for.'[150] From that time Kurdish leaders Masoud Barzani and Jalal Talabani were enthusiastic supporters of the US drive to topple Saddam's regime. Since they knew that they could not influence Bush's decision, they deemed it a strategic move to be completely on the US side.[151]

In terms of future political gains, the US promised the Kurds 'nothing, except one thing and – even that wasn't a real promise'. In the fall of 2002 the Kurds were told, at the highest levels of the US government, that if they played it right, kept silent about nationalist aspirations, stood by the US, supported American goals in Iraq and didn't make trouble, 'you will come out of this holding what you have going in to it'.[152] Kurdish fears were further eased when, on 6 March 2003, Bush stated: 'Iraq will provide a place where people can see that the Shiite and the Sunni and the Kurds can get along in a federation. Iraq will serve as a catalyst for change, positive change.'[153] This statement was what the Kurds were looking for, after many years of fighting with the central government in Baghdad. It gave federalism distinct recognition. However, prior to this, State Department officials had deliberately avoided support for federalism, due to Turkish sensitivities.[154]

But from the summer of 2002 the US was also seeking Turkish cooperation. The US briefed the Turkish military staff on the Iraq war plan. The US recognised that Turkey had suffered financially as a result of the 1991 Gulf War and had also accepted hundreds of thousands of Kurdish refugees. In the light of this, the US prepared a generous aid package.[155] In July 2002 Paul Wolfowitz visited Turkey to start negotiating the Turkish role in the possible US invasion of Iraq. Turkey, fearing the revival of nationalist aspirations among its more than 15 million Kurds, requested that an independent state of Iraqi Kurdistan should not be created and the US assured Ankara that this would not be the case.[156]

On 3 December 2002, Paul Wolfowitz led negotiations with Turkey again. This time Turkey agreed to allow the use of its airspace and bases, providing a second UNSCR resolution was obtained authorising military action. US and Turkish officials met again in Ankara in February 2003; by this time the second Security Council resolution was of no significant importance to the Turks. Turkey requested that Turkish forces be allowed into Iraqi Kurdistan; otherwise US troops would not be allowed access. They also requested US assurances that the Kurdish Peshmarga would enter neither Kirkuk nor Mosul; the US agreed. The Turks also promised that their forces would not enter any Kurdish city or town; they would stay away from Mosul and Kirkuk unless the Peshmarga entered.[157]

Turkey was concerned that any action in Iraq would affect its own territorial integrity: that war in neighbouring Iraq would lead to Kurdish independence and Turkey's fracture along ethnic lines. The US reassured the Turkish officials that their strategic interests would be respected in Iraq. US officials also told them that they shared Turkey's concerns that Iraq's disintegration would lead to instability in the region; the US would give the Turks a substantial say in the post-Saddam reconstruction policy.[158] The Kirkuk oil fields and the possibility of them falling into Kurdish hands was another major concern to Turkey; it believed that such a development would provide enough financial and political leverage to establish an independent Kurdistan.[159] Moreover, the emergence of a Shiite state in Iraq was alarming to both the Kemalist secularists and the Sunni-dominated Justice and Development Party; a Shiite state closely aligned with Iran in the vicinity challenged the former's secularism and the latter's Sunnism.[160] Turkey's unrelenting opposition to Kurdish nationalism, and its solid alliance with the US, dating back to the Truman Doctrine in 1947, still are the principal factors preventing an independent Kurdistan. Although the US has given occasional verbal support to the Kurds, it has always tilted towards its strategic NATO ally Turkey; to its former ally, the Shah, in Iran; and prior to 1990 to its tacit ally Saddam Hussein.[161] American geostrategic interests in central Eurasia have made Washington value its alliance with Turkey, which it has seen as a force to balance both Iran and Russia.[162] Consolidating its position as regards the likely invasion through Turkey, the foreign ministry issued a statement:

> The Turkish army will enter the region to prevent an exodus, to prevent the Kurds from establishing a free Kurdistan, to prevent them entering Kirkuk and Mosul, and also to protect the Turcomans. We don't want a clash between Turkey and the Kurds, and for that reason we are sending lots of troops to the region as a warning.[163]

6.5.2 Operation Iraqi Freedom

Coming after these negotiations and agreements, the refusal of the Turkish parliament to allow access to the US 4th Infantry Division (ID), created a crisis in US-Turkish relations. It also angered many neoconservatives who valued Turkish relations with the US.[164] President Bush was concerned about Turkey's position against allowing a northern front to be opened; however, he was more concerned about the possibility of a Turkish incursion into the Kurdish north.[165] During the war, Zalmay Khalilzad was asked to stay in Ankara to use his diplomatic skills to prevent a Turkish incursion into Northern Iraq aimed at pre-empting any Kurdish move for independence.[166] Richard Cheney had spoken to the Turkish leaders as well, before the war, telling them in no uncertain terms that their participation would not be needed. 'I think they'll behave. We've got to keep a lid on the Kurds too', he affirmed.[167] The neoconservatives detested Saddam Hussein and wanted to get rid of him; they wanted to establish a pluralistic and democratic Iraq. According to Najmaldin Karim, governor of Kirkuk, just before the US invaded, the neoconservatives were willing to forget about the Kurds and deal with Turkey, allowing the Turkish army to come in. The neoconservatives (Wolfowitz and Khalilzad) were involved in negotiations to reduce Kurdish involvement.[168]

In the initial planning for the US invasion of Iraq, NATO ally Turkey had senior status over rival Kurds south of their border in Iraq. The US deemed it inappropriate to embark on this venture without Turkish blessing and co-operation. The Iraqi Kurdish officials were so convinced that the Turkish relationship with America would take precedence over their own concerns, that they asked the Pentagon: first, to limit the Turkish presence in Iraq to certain supply corridors in northern Iraq; second, to ensure that a substantive Turkish contingent would operate only in areas south or east of Tikrit – areas of operation that Erbil felt would limit Turkish influence in the disputed city of Kirkuk.[169] However, after the Turkish parliament refused to allow the US invasion of Iraq from Turkey, US-Kurdish relations started to improve. On 25 March 2003, after the final US negotiations with Turkey failed, the US turned to the Kurds as a major contributing force for the military operation. On the night of 26 March more than a thousand members of the 173rd Airborne Brigade arrived in Iraqi Kurdistan through an airdrop over the Kurdish airfield at Harir.[170]

The closer the US got to Operation Iraqi Freedom, the more Kurdish influence became evident. In the build-up to OIF, the fact that there was a smaller northern front than the US had expected created a much greater level of dependency on the Kurds. Had the 4th ID been present in the north, it might have been that they would not have needed the Kurdish Peshmarga as much; but, in the event, both in Operation Viking Hammer and also in the areas of Kirkuk and Mosul, they only had Special Forces troops there. This created a strong operational bond, not just a political and strategic bond, between the US military and Kurdish forces. The Turkish parliament's rejection of a US northern front from Turkey created a dynamic that reflected positively on the Kurds. According to

Qubad Talabani this all came 'on the back of a Turkish rejection'. Turkey, a strategic ally and NATO partner, did not let the Americans in and yet 'here are these Kurds with their Kalashnikovs and unsophisticated machinery that are really so passionate about fighting alongside Americans'.[171] As the Kurdish political parties had military components, General Tommy Franks was willing to appoint liaison officers to the Kurdish opposition groups in northern Iraq but was refusing to do the same for the INC; however, he eventually conceded under Wolfowitz's pressure.[172] The Kurds had two assets of value in the run-up to the war. The first was their command of a military component, the Peshmarga, numbering close to 100,000 men. Second, there was the presence in Iraqi Kurdistan of an al-Qaeda-associated Islamist group, *Ansar al-Islam*, providing a link to the US War on Terror.[173]

When the war started, the Kurds suddenly became what the Northern Alliance was for the Americans in Afghanistan – a dependable ally with which cooperation could be built.[174] From 2003 the Kurds of Iraq fought with US forces – both Special Forces and others – and fought well; over time an appreciation grew within the military establishment in Iraq that the Kurds were good fighters, and reliable as well.[175]

So, the Turkish refusal to allow the passage of the 4th ID to northern Iraq dramatically damaged US-Turkish relations and, at the same time, created unprecedented leverage for the Iraqi Kurds, forcing the Pentagon to re-plan its northern front with greater emphasis on its Kurdish allies. The Peshmarga, numbering almost 100,000 and a small group of Special Forces, constituted a new front in the invasion.[176] The Kurds effectively led the march into Kirkuk and Mosul, a prospect unthinkable if Turkey had been a member of the coalition.[177] As resistance in Kirkuk crumbled, Kurdish forces rushed in to fill the vacuum.[178] Talabani arrived in Kirkuk on 10 April 2003, the very day the Iraqi resistance disappeared, and used the opportunity to give a speech. He was suddenly interrupted whilst on the microphone by a special operations officer who took him to a room where head of the Military Coordination and Liaison Command Lieutenant General Pete Osman was waiting. General Osman told Talabani of the risk he was creating for a Turkish military intervention and asked Talabani and his Peshmargas to leave Kirkuk immediately – Talabani reluctantly agreed. This caused a major problem for the US – the Kurds were trying to expand their sphere of influence, which was a potential trigger for Turkish troops to push into northern Iraq. Colin Powell subsequently spoke to his counterpart in Ankara, assuring him that Kirkuk would return to normal.[179]

This resembled US policy in Afghanistan. In a Deputies' meeting on 9 October 2001 both Richard Armitage and John McLaughlin advised against a Northern Alliance incursion into Kabul. They believed that it could lead to civil war between the Pashtuns and the invading force;[180] Wolfowitz added that the US should try to create an international force to take over Kabul, to show that it was not trying to favour one Afghan group over the other.[181] In the same way, to prevent a civil war and/or a Turkish incursion, the Kurds were advised not to take over in Kirkuk and Mosul; the United States believed that a Kurdish takeover would send a message to the rest of Iraq that the US was biased towards the Kurds. Restraining the Kurds, however, would ensure US neutrality. Empowering the Kurds to take the reins of power in both cities, the US also believed, would allow acts of Kurdish retribution against Arab residents in the city. This would have the potential to develop into all-out civil war between Arabs and Kurds. In a policy paper, drafted by Feith's policy shop and produced on 15 October 2001, entitled 'Military Strategy in Afghanistan' the Northern Alliance was advised to refrain from dominance in Kabul; it stressed that

> [T]he future of Kabul must be decided by a political process and not military action alone. We expect you to declare, as soon as possible, that your goal is not to establish dominion over the entire country, but to get a political process started that will reflect the interests of all the Afghan peoples.[182]

The same concerns determined US Iraq policy after the invasion: the US refused to take sides on the highly contentious Kirkuk issue, where the Kurds wanted to reverse decades of Arabisation.

Operation Iraqi Freedom also involved the largest US SOF force since the Vietnam War, with a significant SOF presence in Northern Iraq. Coalition personnel worked with Kurdish fighters against the regime. SOF forces helped bring in the 173rd Airborne Brigade, and marked and called in coalition air power on regime targets; they were also responsible for attacking a number of specific targets, such as airfields, weapons of mass destruction sites and command and control headquarters.[183] The 10th Special Forces Group (Airborne), elements of Joint SOF Command and CIA Special Activities Division paramilitary officers linked up and were the first to enter Iraq prior to the invasion. Their efforts, under the code name 'Operation Viking Hammer', organised the Kurdish Peshmarga to defeat *Ansar al-Islam*; this involved a battle for control of a territory in north-eastern Iraq that was occupied by *Ansar al-Islam*.[184] With a larger challenge and greater military operation for regime change awaiting, the US did not want its Kurdish allies to be distracted and engaged with these Islamist militants.[185] In the North, the 10th Special Forces Group (10th SFG) had the mission of aiding the PUK and the KDP, and employing them against the thirteen Iraqi divisions located in the vicinity of Kirkuk and Mosul.[186]

Turkey had originally officially banned any Coalition troops from using their bases or airspace, so lead elements of the 10th SFG had to make a detour for infiltration; their flight was supposed to take four hours but instead took ten. However, only hours after the first of these flights, Turkey did allow the use of its airspace and the rest of the 10th SFG infiltrated accordingly. After Operation Viking Hammer, concurrent and follow-on missions involved attacking and thus tying down Iraqi forces in the north, preventing their deployment to the southern front and the main theatre of the invasion. The SOF forces present in northern Iraq had two roles, one military and the other political. The military role was to defeat the 150,000 Iraqi troops on the border of the de facto Kurdish enclave. The political role was to keep the Peshmarga in line, preventing the Kurds from taking Kirkuk, reason enough for a Turkish intervention. It was in the interest of the US to maintain peace between rival Kurdish factions and also prevent them from upsetting the status quo.[187]

6.6 The Kurds in the new Iraq: 2003–2014

6.6.1 The Coalition Provisional Authority

When the United States invaded Iraq in 2003, another window opened for the Kurds. With Saddam's regime gone, the Iraqi Kurds, along with returning Iraqi exiles, had the rare chance to forge a new Iraq: democratic, pluralistic and decentralised. After the fall of Saddam's regime, the Coalition Provisional Authority (CPA) awarded five seats out of the twenty-five seats of the Iraqi Governing Council to the Kurds. They also had two seats on the rotating presidency of nine Iraqi leaders.[188] This was the first sign of a reduction in Kurdish influence after Saddam was toppled. The Kurdish quota in the Iraqi opposition had been one-quarter, as opposed to the one-fifth imposed by the United States.[189] After the invasion Jay Garner was even instructed not to mention federalism with the Kurdish leaders although he had done so privately.[190] Paul Bremer, US Administrator of Iraq from May 2003 to June 2004, expected the Kurds to relinquish a measure of the autonomy they had achieved between the First Gulf War and the liberation of Iraq.[191] The Kurds were given the key to the Iraqi Foreign Ministry in the first Governing Council cabinet; however, signs of US discontent with the Kurds became obvious with the establishment of the CPA. The Kurds' perception was that they were starting to devalue within the context of the new Iraq. After an article critical of the CPA appeared in the *New York Times* based on an interview with Jalal Talabani, Bremer told Talabani that the US could not work with his group if confidential issues and disagreements with the CPA were voiced in the media after disagreements he had had were made public.[192] Bremer also talks critically about a 'G7' (seven leading opposition groups) meeting in June 2003, with a Talabani initiative, for a 'handpicked national conference' to establish a new government to avoid the creation of the Governing Council.[193] On 25 June 2003 Bremer visited Talabani at his headquarters in Iraqi Kurdistan; he assured Talabani of the US determination to create a federal Iraq. Talabani was pleased that the US was accommodating this Kurdish objective.[194] During this visit Talabani approved a request by Bremer to serve on the Iraqi Governing Council.[195] The next day Bremer made the same request to Masoud Barzani, who also agreed.[196] Michael Rubin, former OSP and CPA official, stressed that the US support for federalism came from its support for Kurdistan.[197] This mollified the Kurdish leadership enough for them to consent to political participation in Baghdad. The CPA however was unequivocal on Iraq's territorial unity. Bremer had told Tony Blair that he had told the Kurds that the Coalition 'would not tolerate actions that provoked the break up of Iraq' as well as telling them that he needed full cooperation from them on drafting the interim constitution, the Transitional Administrative Law (TAL).[198]

The invasion was the watershed in US-Kurdish relations. After the invasion, for the first time in recent living memory, the Kurds of Iraq were playing an ever-increasing role in Baghdad. The US government was relying on the Kurds to serve their interests in Baghdad, to be their advocates within internal Iraqi deliberations and decisions as they related to Iraq's relations with the US.[199] The Kurds constantly supported the US under the CPA,[200] and so played a significant role in rebuilding Iraq. It is ironic that the Kurds, who are the only major group in Iraq that despise the Iraqi identity, took on this role. The US was dependant on the assistance of the Kurds to stabilise Iraq.[201] America's failure to predict the Iraqi resistance compelled them to depend on Iraqi army brigades solely composed of Kurdish soldiers (Peshmarga).[202]

Following Operation Iraqi Freedom came the necessity for greater US-Kurdish interaction. There was a need for the US to get the Kurds involved in Baghdad; this was to ensure the formation of a future government, pass pieces of legislation and craft the TAL. The Kurds, Qubad Talabani affirmed, 'were able to take our level of sophistication and organisation to Baghdad with us', and they managed to negotiate most of what was important to Kurdistan, in their negotiations with the rest of the country. This, at times, Talabani emphasised, 'put a strain on US-Kurdish relations', particularly in the final hours of drafting the TAL, when the Kurds staged a walkout and threatened to boycott the process because they were holding firm on a key article (61c) of that law.[203] This article served Kurdish concerns allowing a rejection of the permanent Iraqi constitution if deemed unfavourable to Kurdish interests. Qubad Talabani and the other Kurdish negotiators demanded that the permanent Iraqi constitution be rendered void if two-thirds of the population in three Iraqi provinces voted negative against ratifying the constitution. The CPA negotiators had initially insisted on four provinces but after the delegation's walk-out made calls to Washington to seek approval and eventually gave way to the Kurdish demand.

The US was not favourable to all Kurdish demands during the drafting of TAL.[204] The Kurds were anxious about the prospect of a permanent constitution that did not reflect their concerns. They wanted a specific clause that gave the Kurds a veto if this was to occur. Initially Bremer declined to concede this Kurdish request. However, later on he came to understand the 'tyranny of the majority' as the Shiites pursued their religious agenda.[205] The eventual document did not include many of the Kurdish demands. The Kurdish leadership had to make concessions. The CPA was adamant that a strong central government be created in Baghdad – this, of course, was contrary to Kurdish requests for *less* central control. After the TAL was signed, the new Security Council Resolution was due to be passed to enforce the end of occupation and restoration of sovereignty. However, Kurdish demands for reference to the TAL in UNSCR 1546 were disregarded at the request of Grand Ayatollah Sistani.[206]

Among the former Iraqi opposition, the Kurdish leadership were the only ones with a recognised constituency, which was heavily pro-US. They continued to have influence; however as the Kurdish element became diluted within the overall context of a new Iraq, they gradually lost their special status. The US position started to adapt to the new situation; the change in US-Kurdish relations started after 2003, as America's interests in Iraq broadened. The US had interests in Baghdad's position and in the Iraqi state as a whole. This meant that the Kurds ranked lower on the American priority list. The Kurds became 'no longer the most important interlocutor in Iraqi politics'; rather it became one of a number of important interlocutors in Iraqi politics.[207]

Initially, on 27 January 2004, Bremer proposed a framework for the Kurdish region: the Kurdistan Region would be recognised as a federal unit, but with few powers. The central government would have authority over the region's security, natural resources, economy and borders.[208] The first draft of the TAL, called the Pachachi Plan after the then president of the Iraqi Governing Council, had very little in it for the Kurds.[209]

Then, following new instructions from Washington on 6 February 2004, Bremer informed the Kurdish leadership that the White House wanted to eliminate the mention of Kurdish as an official language in the provisional constitution. Moreover, the Kurdistan Region would not be mentioned in the document, and Iraq's federal structure would be based on the eighteen governorates, rather than the existing structure of Kurdish, Sunni Arab and Shiite Arab territories.[210] As regards the Peshmarga, Bremer wanted to disband them. This was drafted in the TAL according to Bremer's terms, after he threatened to disregard other Kurdish requests.[211] During the process of writing the TAL, Bremer threatened the Kurdish leadership with severing their 'special relationship' when they voiced objections.[212]

The reason for the US desire to dismantle the Kurdish regional government was to create an Iraq based on geographical units, reflecting the non-ethnic structure of US states: a concept based on ideals rather than reality. Moreover, the intention of excluding Kurdish as an official language came from the desire to make Arabic the common communication language for the whole nation.[213] Turkey might have been influential, as well, in forming this policy. The furthest Turkish officials and intellectuals were willing to go was the acceptance of a form of 'geographic federalism' based on the previously drawn boundaries of the eighteen governorates of Iraq. This was to dilute the ethnic composition as well as to break up the Kurdish region, and subsequently create a non-ethnic provincial identity.[214] The Kurdish leadership was worried about American pressure. Galbraith advised the Kurdish negotiators in Kurdistan:

> The United States, I pointed out, needed the Kurds at least as much as the Kurds needed the Americans ... The Bush administration might not like the Kurds insisting on their rights, I said, but it would respect them for doing so.[215]

Nawshirwan believes that the Kurdish leadership, in its pursuit of special party interests and 'to please the United States', failed to make the most of this opportunity.[216] Najmaldin Karim believes that the Kurdish leadership lacked assertiveness and aggression; Karim compared the Kurds with the Sunnis, who are comparable in numbers, but more vocal in their requests. The Kurds, he argued, were suffering from 'The Battered Child Syndrome' mentality.[217] The Kurdish proposals for inclusion of a Kurdistan chapter in the TAL were received with discomfort by the CPA negotiators; they perceived the Kurdish requests as opposing the US desire for a united Iraq.[218]

6.6.2 The Kurds: towards a sovereign Iraq

During the Interim Government period, as a gesture to reassure the Sunni Arabs that the post-Baath period would not change the essential character of the Iraqi state, the presidency was not to be given to the Kurds.[219] Bremer told Talabani, 'For too long they [Sunni Arabs] have felt underrepresented in the new Iraq.'[220] Kurdish leaders Jalal Talabani and Masoud Barzani sent a joint letter on 1 June 2004 to President Bush expressing their discontent with the US position that Kurds would be allowed neither the premiership nor presidency of Iraq. For most of 2004, the Kurds were non-players in Iraq; it was only when the constitutional drafting process began that they suddenly became players again.[221]

After Allawi's interim government expired with the election of the constitution drafting National Assembly in January 2005, Ibrahim Jaafari was nominated for Prime Minister for the transitional period. His nomination, however, was not welcomed by Washington. In response, the US aimed to counterbalance a probable Islamist agenda with more Kurdish power in the new transitional government.[222] The first Kurdish president in Iraq's history was democratically elected in the January 2005 elections. Iraq's Deputy Prime Minister and Foreign Minister were also Kurds; and, during Jaafari's premiership, the Kurdish leadership managed to advance its aspirations during the drafting of the permanent constitution. The result was a much weaker central government, compared to the TAL, which gave greater power to the central government in Baghdad. The Kurds during this period also supported Zalmay Khalilzad's attempts to prevent Jaafari's candidacy for the premiership after the general elections of December 2005 for the permanent government.[223] The State Department and CIA assessments of the Kurds' role in Iraq post-Saddam, externals versus internals, was another example of flawed analysis. Both agencies had argued that the Kurds would have no significant national role beyond the boundaries of northern Iraq. This was turned out to be incorrect, as many Kurdish leaders played significant roles in the appointed and elected governments.[224]

Khalilzad was US ambassador to Iraq from June 2005 to March 2007. When he arrived in Iraq he may have thought that the administration's goal of a 'democratic, federal, pluralist, and unified Iraq' was viable. However, as he started his shuttle diplomacy between the different Iraqi factions, to assist in the creation of the permanent constitution, it was clear that he was not exercising the art of nation-building, but rather 'negotiation of a tripartite peace treaty'.[225] The permanent constitution essentially reversed all Kurdish concessions in the TAL for central government control on many issues.[226] The US seems to have woken up to the unrealistic nature of its aspirations for a non-ethnic and non-sectarian Iraq.

Congressman Christopher Van Hollen (D-MD), also a former congressional Foreign Relations Committee staffer, stated that the US government's position was that Iraqis should have strong regional autonomy. The region controlled by Iraqi Kurds should therefore have a high degree of autonomy and independent decision-making powers, all within the overall framework of a united Iraq. Van Hollen asserted that there were some in the US government who would have liked to reduce that degree of autonomy, but he believed that most people supported a large degree of autonomy within the Kurdish areas.[227] It was an arrangement that would keep Iraq together and address Kurdish rights. Christopher Straub, Deputy Assistant Secretary of Defense, asserted that the US supported the idea of a federal Iraq saying that a federal Iraq 'seems to us to make sense'.[228]

While the Kurds were trying to pursue their own agenda of maximal autonomy, America was trying to enforce a different direction. The US policy during the appointments of its successive political representatives – Bremer, Negroponte, Khalilzad, Crocker, Hill, Jeffrey and Beecroft – was consistent in seeking to build a strong central government. America was extremely unclear and inconsistent on where it stood with reference to the Iraqi Constitution and its support for what was, essentially, ethnic federalism.[229] Inside the State Department, the Iraqi Constitution was rejected and ignored, as if it had never been written. Very few officials or career officers gave any credence whatsoever to the Constitution as it was considered by many at State level and in the administration as non-representative of the realities on the ground.[230] The US was actually working against Kurdish interests in Baghdad.[231]

The US did not want oil-rich Kirkuk to go to the Kurdistan Regional Government, because it believed that this would lead to Kurdish independence. The reason the US does not support Kurdish independence is that it supports Turkish integrity and believes that a Kurdish declaration of independence will cause a war in the region. Furthermore, with Kurdish independence, there would be blowback in Turkey among its large Kurdish population, leading to the destabilisation of the country.[232] The US government is very attuned to Turkish sensitivities, and that will always be an inhibiting factor – that is the main reason US policy will aim to keep Iraq one country.[233] David Mack explained that 'regional stability' and the stability of 'our NATO ally Turkey' are major considerations in Washington when it comes to the Kurdish issue.[234] Peter Galbraith stressed: 'Turkey is the only reason there is no independent Kurdistan.'[235]

When in 2006 the PKK, the Turkish Kurdish military group, and Iranian Kurdish groups, primarily the PJAK, conducted raids into Turkey and Iran, both countries retaliated by bombing and carrying out air strikes against guerrilla hideouts inside Iraqi Kurdish territory. The US, however, warned Turkey against any such attacks in the future in Iraqi Kurdistan and appointed former NATO commander Joseph Ralston in August 2006 as special coordinator to Ankara to deal with the PKK problem.[236] In 2007, Turkey was threatening an incursion into northern Iraq. 'We are making it very clear to Turkey that we don't think it is in their interests to send troops into Iraq', Bush said at a White House press conference on 17 October 2007.[237] On the same day Geoff Morrell, the chief spokesman of the Pentagon, said that the US government was sympathetic to Turkey, which was suffering PKK terrorist attacks; but the best way to deal with this threat was through diplomatic means. 'We have urged the Turks to show restraint', Morrell said. 'We understand their frustration, we understand their anger, but we are urging them not to engage in cross-border operations.'[238] There was tension in US-Kurdish relations after the Americans eventually agreed to an incursion by Turkey into northern Iraq in December 2007. Masoud Barzani was scheduled to go to Baghdad to take part in a meeting with Condoleezza Rice and other officials, but then refused to go, in protest against the American position on the incursion and bombings by Turkey. Kurdistan Region Prime Minister, Nechirvan Barzani, stated that it was 'unacceptable' that the United States, 'in charge of monitoring our airspace, authorised Turkey to bomb our villages'.[239] Turkey entered Iraqi Kurdistan territory again on 21 February 2008. On 28 February 2008, Bush urged Turkey to 'move quickly, achieve their objective and get out' and, after their incursion, they did withdraw on 29 February.[240] US-Turkish relations tremendously affected the Iraqi Kurds. When Turkish troops entered Iraqi Kurdistan, the Kurds protested against US silence on this issue of Kurdistan's security. The United States responded by stating that it could not stop the Turks from entering northern Iraq, because 'they have interests with Turkey and it would affect their relationship'.[241] A National Security Council official explained to the author, however, that the US continued to work with both the Kurds and Turkey on confidence-building measures as the US aim is to prevent raids from both sides of the border.[242]

In late 2008, the Iraqi Kurds and the Turks experienced some rapprochement; on 14 October 2008, a special envoy from Turkey, Murad Ocalik, visited Kurdistan Region President Masoud Barzani in Baghdad, to work towards an easing of relations. The Turks thus seemed to have modified their hostile stance towards the Iraqi Kurds. As regards the US strategic alliance with Turkey, initially the US swung towards the Kurds on some occasions and back to Turkey on others. The US, eventually, came to a point where it could actually have a relationship with both sides. Qubad Talabani explained that the Kurds told the United States from the beginning that this did not have to be a zero-sum game and that the US could have relations with the two entities at the same time. As US policy gradually evolved, the US became mindful of both Turkey's and the Iraqi Kurds' sensitivities.[243]

'Turkey's concerns matter to the US very much' because Turkey is a NATO ally, explained Christopher Straub. Turkey is a long-term ally of the US, bilaterally as well as through NATO; America shares Turkey's concerns about the fact that elements of the PKK are located on Iraqi soil. The US considers the PKK to be a terrorist organisation and the US has been at war, since 11 September, against terrorist movements. America agreed with Turkey that it was absolutely not permissible for a country to give safe havens to a terrorist movement. The US spoke about this to the Iraqi Kurdistan Regional Government, and also to the Iraqi government in Baghdad. However, the US recognised the practical difficulties faced, due to the terrain, by the Iraqi government, and the Iraqi Kurdistan government. The US continued to urge the Iraqi Kurds to continue to take measures to weaken the PKK and eventually to expel it from Iraqi Kurdistan. The US approved of improvements in Turkish-Iraqi-Iraqi Kurdish economic and political relations, apart from the contentious issue of PKK. In 2008 America noted, with interest, that relations between Turkey and Iraq were growing closer. Turkey's relations with the Kurdistan Regional Government (KRG) were also growing closer; financially, Turkey was the biggest investor in Iraqi Kurdistan. In 2012 the volume of trade between Iraq and Turkey had reached 12 billion USD, of which 70 per cent was between the Kurdistan Region and Turkey.[244] Turkey and the KRG, once at odds because of Ankara's fears over Kurdish political aspirations, have found themselves in 2014 largely aligned in their alarm at the Shiite-led government of Iraqi Prime Minister Maliki, its tilt towards Iran especially after the US withdrawal in December 2011, and his aggressive attempts at unilateralism and consolidation of power. Ironically, these latest developments in Turkish-KRG relations have raised alarm in Washington about the possible disintegration of Iraq.

Another significant factor in US geopolitical calculations is Iran. The United States believes that, eventually, it will restore a US-Iranian alliance, and the Iranians, too, are fiercely against federalism; not so much because of their 8–9 per cent Kurdish population, but because of the Azeris, who represented 30–40 per cent of their population. If the Azeris were to achieve federalism, it would be the end of the Iranian state.[245] The ultimate missing piece for American foreign policy in the Middle East is Iran. America has never recovered from the loss of its alliance with Iran; its alliance with Turkey has never compensated for that loss; and the US ultimately wants it back. The US is reluctantly in alliance with the Sunni Arab world, since it does not believe that the Arab world will ever accept Israel. The US wants an alliance with the main power in the region, Iran; this possible future ally has oil and gas and so can balance Sunni influence in the region. Turkey cannot play this role in the same way Iran did historically, because Turkey does not have the oil and gas of Iran. Iran also has the strategic asset of 70 million relatively educated people. With the end of the hostile Islamic regime in Iran, the Americans hope to regain that alliance and are willing to sacrifice alliances with Arab states in order to do so.[246]

Moreover, it is in the US interest to have a united Iraq as a united and strong country on the western flank of Iran to act as buffer to Iranian expansion and influence.[247] The US also opposes an independent Kurdistan out of the conviction that a divided Iraq cannot be successful, and that, as a landlocked state, an independent Kurdistan has nowhere to sell its oil. The US believes it would be in a similar situation to Armenia, leading to regional problems and instability rather than stability.[248] The sentiment in Washington towards the Kurds was very much opposed to their independence. The break-up of Iraq beyond the current federal status is believed not to be in the US interest nor in the interest of the Kurds. Frederick Kagan was unequivocal in stating, 'America's strategic interests are invested much more heavily in Arab Iraq' than in Kurdistan. He advised the

Kurdish leadership to be very careful to recognise that if it looked as if Arab Iraq was to succeed, America's interests lay much more in making sure that that happened than in taking care of the Kurds.[249]

Moreover, the US government from President Bush downwards had no real sympathy with ethnic federalism.[250] The reason is the administrative structure of the US; the fifty American states are geographical administrative units rather than ethnic entities.[251] American nationalism was not based on language and common blood – it was not an ethno-linguistic nationalism like European nationalism.[252] The European concept of ethnic nationalism was transferred to post-colonial states – such as Iraq itself – after the collapse of the Ottoman Empire, which was mostly divided on the basis of tribal and sectarian loyalties.[253] Furthermore, the dominant US perspective was that the needs of people were not met only by having governments of their own ethnicity.[254] The US, however, supported the humanitarian concerns of Iraqi Kurdistan. David Mack stressed that the US essentially supported the rights of Kurds to have the rights that all Iraqis should have at managing their own political affairs and having a greater say in how their country was run 'but we do not support a Kurdish state'.[255]

In that context, the Kurds were unimportant and even an inconvenience. The US assumed that Kurds would behave as good Iraqis and that they did not want independence. On the Kurdish side, the Kurdish leaders, notably Barham Salih and to a lesser extent Jalal Talabani, encouraged the belief that the Kurds would be just good Iraqis. Salih and Talabani kept talking about the 'liberation of Iraq', and referring to themselves as 'we Iraqis' in order to encourage the US invasion. They left the impression that the Kurds would behave as the Bush administration wanted.[256] The Kurdish leadership were very much aware of Turkish sensitivities and the red lines for the Turks. This represented a substantial self-deterring factor.[257] For these reasons, the independence of Kurdistan was never seriously considered in Washington before the invasion. There was no debate or agonising in the administration about the possible issue of Kurdish self-determination.[258] Paul Pillar made clear that 'you won't find anything in US policy to declare itself in support of an independent Kurdistan'.[259] US support for self-determination (when and if afforded) was not entirely a product of 'pure idealism' as the creation of new nations was strategically calculated to be at the expense of other empires, weakening US rivals and increasing their own power.[260] Thus in light of the points made above the creation of an independent Kurdistan and support for such an enterprise would conflict with US strategic priorities and interests.

US policy towards the Iraqi Kurds is part of American policy towards Iraq, which is part of US policy towards the Middle East, which is part of US foreign policy in general. A State Department official explained to the author: 'When we think of a policy we think of it as something that stands on its own. How can you have a policy towards a part of a country?' The US does however see the Kurdistan Regional Government as a separate federal entity within the context of Iraq as provided for in the Iraqi constitution.[261] The US supports a regional administration that has the Kurdistan Regional Government as part of the nation of Iraq.[262] Throughout Iraq, the US encouraged a process of developing democracy, with provincial councils and regional groups running some of their affairs. However, the US also believed in a system of national government which brought the whole country together. To the degree that the Kurdish people worked through the regional and national instruments of democracy, they were working through the constitution that was created for the entire country; Matthew Stephenson, at the US Department of State, stressed that 'we support that constitution'.[263] The United States had never supported the Kurds in Iraq concerning Kurdish nationalist aspirations. For America it was merely support for 20 per cent of the Iraqi population that was actively fighting Saddam. That is a critical distinction. The idea was that Kurds would be direct beneficiaries as free people in an autonomous region in a federal republic of Iraq.[264]

US Iraq policy at the sub-national level is not a policy of independence and separatism. It is a policy of sympathy and support for the welfare of Kurds.[265] There is respect and sympathy for the Iraqi Kurds that did not exist before, based on what was achieved in the late 1990s. Many in Washington were surprised by how well things went at the time. Even after the invasion there was considerable goodwill towards Kurdistan as it was perceived as the calmest region of Iraq.[266] Kurdistan is also seen as a model for the rest of Iraq. Considering that one of the purposes of the invasion of Iraq was to create a model for the Middle East, and since Arab Iraq had yet to be perceived to meet that standard, Iraqi Kurdistan had been presented as a model for Iraq and subsequently the rest of the Middle East. State Department Official Matthew Stephenson, who worked in the Office for Iraqi Economic Affairs and Assistance Coordination and was responsible for private sector development, banking reform and helping to channel finance into Iraq, explained that the US saw Kurdistan as a prime example of economic success within the country. The US appreciated how the Kurds had achieved that success and wanted the construction, opportunities and stability to be used as a model which other parts of Iraq could replicate and draw investment to improve the quality of life for their people.[267]

After the security situation in Iraq deteriorated in 2006, Democratic Senator Joseph Biden championed the idea of a loose confederation of states as the only path to peace. This was, of course, an attractive prospect for the Kurds.[268] As mentioned in the previous chapter, the first indications of this appeared in the *New York Times* article by Senator Biden and Leslie Gelb on 1 May 2006.[269] This eventually led to a non-binding, so-called Sense of the Senate resolution passed on 26 September 2007 which called upon the Bush administration to pursue federalist, semi-autonomous regions in Iraq – Sunni, Shiite and Kurdish entities – with a modest federal government located in Baghdad. This was received with great relief by the Kurds. 'I think the resolution passed by the Senate is a very good one', Jalal Talabani said on CNN's 'Late Edition' program. 'It is insisting on the unity of Iraq, of the security of Iraq, of the prosperity of Iraq, of national reconciliation and asking our neighbours not to interfere in the internal affairs of Iraq.'[270] However, this argument lost favour as the 'surge' started to improve the security situation[271] and so from the Kurdish perspective, things took another turn for the worse with the 'surge'. As part of its renewed commitment to making things work in Iraq, the United States began empowering Sunni Arabs to stand up to the insurgents and pressed the Kurds into power-sharing deals. Washington's position was that the Kurds should help preserve Iraqi unity by learning to work with the government in Baghdad.[272]

There has been no change in US perceptions of the Kurds. The US has always seen the Kurds as part of Iraq. The US appreciates the fact that Iraq is free to make its own arrangements and Iraq is clearly determined on a federal status for the Kurdistan Region. This, Christopher Straub explained, has been a 'long standing tradition in Iraq', 'it just hasn't been honoured before'. He stressed that there is 'really no change in US policy towards Iraqi Kurdistan'. The US supports what Iraqi people work out for themselves. The US does not want to be 'accused of interfering in somebody else's internal affairs'.[273] The major departure seemed to be that the US acknowledged the structure of Iraqi society and felt it could address the various components, while trying not to antagonise the others. There was no US policy towards Iraqi Kurds; there was an Iraq policy in which the Kurds were a component. America had finally become sophisticated enough to deal with the different components of Iraqi society, separately from each other.[274]

The US was reluctant to involve itself in the details of domestic Iraqi politics. Rumsfeld had made this clear in a 16 January 2004 Principals' meeting. He stated that 'on all but a few key points of strategic importance ... the US has no interest in pushing ideas on the Iraqis [because] Iraq is their country, and the Iraqis should make political arrangements that best suit them'. This was in response to a debate at the meeting on Bremer's disagreements with Sistani as regards elected delegates for the drafting of a new constitution and elections for a new legislative council.[275] Similarly, in a stand-off in Afghanistan between Karzai and the warlord Pacha Khan the Bush administration refused to intervene, to avoid involvement in domestic Afghan politics.[276] US policy was merely to continuously encourage a peaceful and legitimate resolution of the Kirkuk issue, support federation and for Kurdistan to stay within Iraq. The US supported the Iraqi constitution but perceived the application of Article 140 as a domestic Iraqi issue.[277] It is worth noting that the US involved the United Nations Assistance Mission for Iraq and its special representative, Staffan de Mistura, in 2007 (and onwards) to tackle Article 140 as it wanted both to delay it and to avoid taking sides.[278] After the invasion, the Kurds were expected to be helpful to the US and not a source of instability. The Americans recognised the Iraqi constitution but were still 'uncomfortable' with parts of it. Kenneth Katzman, a senior Middle East analyst in the US Congress, asserted that the US had worked to persuade the Kurds to mute their aspirations, especially by delaying Article 140 in order to avoid irritating the largely stable north.[279]

The US looked at the Kurds in the light of the US concerns as regards Iraqi unity and avoiding problems with Turkey; in particular, it did not want the Turks to invade northern Iraq. The US does not want to risk bad relations with the Turks, because it needs them. So the presence of the PKK in Iraqi Kurdistan was an issue. The US had done nothing to get rid of the PKK; one reason for this was that the US did not have enough forces in Iraq and another was that the American public would not accept more casualties from fighting other peoples' wars.[280]

The major change in US-Kurdish relations came as the Kurds took on an official position in Baghdad after April 2003. Kurds became leaders of Iraq in addition to being leaders of Iraqi Kurdistan. The Bush administration dealt with them as genuine and legitimate Iraqis, particularly after the first elections in January 2005. This was the beginning of an overt and institutionalised relationship.[281] And, since the referendum on the Iraqi constitution and the official acceptance of federalism, the US has dealt with Kurdistan as an entity. Every time US officials went to Baghdad, they made a point of going to Kurdistan. Before April 2003 they dealt with the KRG separately from Baghdad. The same relationship existed after April 2003, but with a different emphasis; the KRG was seen as, and treated as, an established entity.[282] After being officially elected as the president of the Kurdistan Region on 12 June 2005, and after the Iraqi constitution, which recognised federalism, was approved in the referendum of 15 October 2005, Masoud Barzani was officially invited to the White House. He was received on 25 October 2005 by President Bush; it was the first meeting of this nature in Kurdish history. It was heralded as a major achievement by the Kurds, a once oppressed and overlooked nation. President Bush met once again with Barzani on a further official visit to the White House on 29 October 2008. During this meeting Bush praised the Kurdish role in supporting the strategic security agreement between Iraq and the US. So, again, during the last days of the Bush administration, the Kurds regained value; when the Security Accord saw setbacks in Arab Iraq, the Kurds were used as a proxy to advance the agreement, which was eventually signed. In the same visit to Washington and during a talk at the Centre for Strategic and International Studies, Barzani even referred to the possibility of basing US forces in Kurdistan: 'if the United States asks for its forces to be based in the Kurdistan region, I am confident that the Kurdistan regional parliament and the people of Kurdistan region and the Kurdistan regional government would welcome that'.[283] But, as the US had lessened its dependency on the Kurds, it was only natural that they did not hold the status they held at the beginning of Operation Iraqi Freedom.

The Kurdish leadership was invited to Washington on several occasions. During Prime Minister Nechirvan Barzani's visit to Washington in May 2008, he met with a wide range of senior US officials, members of Congress, and business leaders. Most significant were his meetings with President Bush, Vice President Cheney, Secretary of Defense Gates and National Security Advisor Hadley. He emphasised that the Kurds are true friends and allies of the United States, but asked that the US strengthen and support the democratic process that had started in the region and for commitment to the Iraqi constitution. Accordingly, he asked for continued US engagement and support for the political process in Iraq and the Kurdistan Region, and specifically for help in resolving the unresolved issues with Baghdad.[284] The main concerns that were expressed by the United States had to do with the obvious issue of the overall stability and unity of Iraq. Prime Minister Barzani firmly communicated that the KRG has no hidden agenda. Barzani told the Americans that Iraqi Kurdish leadership are committed to a federal, democratic and pluralistic Iraq. He told them that the KRG was determined to solve the outstanding problems: Kirkuk and the disputed territories, oil and gas contracts, status of the Peshmarga and the regional budget. The Prime Minister also asserted that the KRG would do its best to improve its relationship with Turkey because it is an important neighbour. Barzani expressed his concern that the US policy towards Iraq overall was unclear, and its policy towards the Kurdistan Region even more so. Barzani confirmed the Kurds' commitment to Iraq but asked what the commitment of Federal Iraq and the United States is to the Kurdistan Region.[285]

The Kurds are vulnerable; their status has not changed as regards the international context of the Middle East. When needed, as a pawn they gain value, when redundant they are insignificant, but overall they remain an asset to the US in a hostile region. The place of the Iraqi Kurds in US foreign policy ends up being re-negotiated all the time. It is an ongoing subject of negotiation; based partly on what is happening in Baghdad, partly on regional alliances, partly on how the US sees its long-term role in Iraq and the Gulf. In many ways the policy towards the Kurds has been, in political science terms, a 'dependant variable'. US-Kurdish relations primarily depend on what else is going on. There is a recognition in Washington that, in a region with a variety of problems, where a lot of people are seen as problems, the Kurds are an asset. The US recognises that with the Kurds things get done and promises are kept. Iraqi Kurdistan is seen as a place where the US can work with the people rather than a problem that America wants to wish away.[286]

The US also benefits from sustaining the Kurdistan Region entity in Iraq as a potential source of pressure on Turkey. The US wants more Turkish compliance as regards its regional interests, especially Turkish disassociation from Iran and greater Turkish influence on the Turkic nations of Central Asia that are growing closer to Russia.[287] However, the Kurds seem to have had no particular strategic importance in US national interest calculations in the Middle East. The US at the bipartisan level, however, appreciated the value of a special relationship with the Kurds, so they then worked backwards, rather than having a US strategic interest in Iraqi Kurdistan per se – a principle which had no relevance in International Relations.[288] Kurdistan is not a place that the US government has a specific policy towards. US policy is always an extension, a function of Turkish policy and/or of Iraq policy. There is no policy towards Iraqi Kurdistan. There is no such thing as 'Kurdistan policy'.[289] There is a confidence and comfort in the Kurdish relationship, but no desire to do anything that would make the US have to take action to defend the Kurds.[290]

Regardless of the tensions and clashes of interests, there still appears to be recognition of US-Kurdish friendship. Some in the US describe it as sympathy, others as strategic. The relationship changes, as regards US demands on the Kurds, with the nature of US interests. The Kurdish side has consistently sustained its friendship with the US as it deems it strategic for its protection and survival. But, since the Kurds are in a partnership that is heavily weighted towards the US and its interests, this partnership remains shaky. The Kurds seemed to have a fluctuating status in the new Iraq; generally they have considerable sympathy but, when it comes to actual partnership, there seems to be reluctance. The US does see Kurdistan as an ally, albeit in an unofficial capacity; Qubad Talabani stated that, in this 'game', it was not really about friendship but interests. If Kurdistan can serve America's interests for a given issue, then the Kurds are allies. However, if the Kurds are an impediment to US interests on a certain issue, 'we're maximalist, a problem, overreaching Kurds'. When the Kurds are compared to groups hostile to the Americans, they are considered as allies; the Kurds are not hostile to the US and the US knows and appreciates that.[291] The State Department's Matthew Stephenson explained that the Kurds and the US are still seen as close friends. Additionally, the US continues to support the Kurdish successes in northern Iraq, including the economic resurgence.[292] The US is allied with the Iraqi Kurds; however, not in an official way nor a formal way. The US recognises the good feeling between Americans and Iraqi Kurds, and that is 'important', Deputy Assistant Secretary of Defense, Christopher Straub, told the author. He also emphasised that it is as important as relations between nations, and that is important for the Kurds to remember. There is sympathy because of the victimisation by Saddam and the way the Kurds rallied against him. But there is no 'separate policy about Iraqi Kurdistan compared to Iraq', he continued. Straub stressed that the US dreams of a good outcome for Iraq where Iraq's Kurds are content in Iraqi Kurdistan; content in an Iraq that has peace and a representative government, and that is economically prosperous and federal.[293] Andrew Morrison argued that the US does not have mutual defence pacts with Israel and Kuwait, and Kuwait was not even designated as a major non-NATO ally of the US until 2004; but the US relationship with both countries had been and is characterised by intense cooperation and so the absence of a formal pact does not diminish its depth and strength.[294] Morrison stressed that although the US cannot have a treaty of alliance with the Iraqi Kurds, this has not detracted from the strength of the relationship. [295]

6.6.3 The Kurds and the Obama administration

President of the Kurdistan Region, Masoud Barzani, met with US President Barack Obama in Baghdad on 7 April 2009. This was President Obama's first trip to Iraq since his inauguration in January 2009. President Obama expressed his pleasure that relations between the Kurdistan Region and Turkey had been improving. Barzani on his part asked for US support and commitment to the Iraqi constitution. Later that year after Kurdish officials rejected a deal that would increase the total number of seats in the Iraqi Council of Representatives in a newly drafted election law, President Obama and Vice President Biden called Barzani on 6 December 2009 to urge a Kurdish compromise and allow the passing of the law. The conversation paved the way for Barzani to accept the compromise number of seats allocated to the Kurds in the elected council that followed in 2010. Barzani only agreed to this after reassurances were given by both leaders concerning US support for the

Iraqi constitution. The Kurds were further mollified by a White House statement the following day, on 7 December, stressing US commitment to Iraq's constitution, including Article 140. Robert Gates also in a visit to Erbil on 12 December 2009 thanked Barzani for the compromise on the Iraqi election law and assured the Kurdish leadership of continued US friendship and support for their security and development. Stressing clearly, however, not for Kurdish independence but rather support only within the confines of a united Iraq. President Barzani visited Washington for the third time, but the first during the Obama administration, meeting President Obama on 25 January 2010 at the White House. The vice president also participated in the meeting. In his discussion with President Barzani, President Obama reaffirmed strong US support for and engagement with a secure, prosperous and autonomous Kurdistan Region within a united, federal Iraq, and lauded the contribution of the KRG to Iraq's development. President Obama encouraged President Barzani to take constructive action on issues that divide Iraq in order to consolidate security gains and to unlock Iraq's potential as a regional political and economic leader. The president extended US good offices to help Iraqis move forward in forging a broad political consensus to resolve outstanding disagreements between the Kurdistan Regional Government and the Government of Iraq, in accordance with the Iraqi constitution and working closely with the United Nations in these efforts.[296] During this meeting, President Barzani highlighted the significance of Iraq's general elections on 7 March 2010 and reaffirmed the Kurdistan Region's commitment to a federal, democratic and pluralistic Iraq. Moreover, he emphasised the importance of a strategic and long-term US engagement with Iraq and the Kurdistan Region.[297]

The US maintained neutrality during the domestic disturbances between the major ruling Kurdish parties (KDP and PUK) and the opposition groups, namely the Gorran Movement, that started on 17 February 2011 and lasted sixty-two days. Their intention was to avoid giving out the wrong signals. To the ruling parties, a violent crackdown on the dissent was unacceptable, as was the continuation of unrest by the opposition in a largely stable Kurdistan Region. The US continuously encouraged the KDP and PUK to take steps forward towards reform and good governance, fighting corruption and tolerance of legitimate opposition. Moreover, the US did not want to alienate the major parties as their friendship and alliance were instrumental to advancing US interests in Iraq, neither did they want Kurdistan, a model for the rest of Iraq, to see disruption and disorder. During these disturbances on 8 April 2011 Defense Secretary Robert Gates visited President Barzani in Erbil, making no mention of the domestic disturbances, but rather encouraging the Kurdish leadership to exert its influence on Baghdad to complete the formation of the Baghdad government by appointing the key security ministers whose positions were still vacant. The second US request from the Kurds was to pressure the Baghdad government into extending US military presence beyond December 2011 when the SOFA agreement expired. The Kurds were the only ones to publicly express a need for US soldiers to stay in Iraq. To support this US request, Babakir Zebari, Chief of Staff of the Iraqi army and a Kurd, publicly stressed that the Iraqi army would not be ready to control Iraq until 2020.

US-Kurdish relations were further strengthened and institutionalised after a proposal submitted in 2009 to open a US consulate was passed. The resolution, H.R. 873, passed the House of Representatives by a voice vote on 19 May 2010, sponsored by Congressman Dana Rohrabacher (R-CA) and Lincoln Davis (D-TN). On 10 July 2011 the US officially opened its first consulate in Erbil, the capital of the Kurdistan Region of Iraq. The president of the Kurdistan Region, Masoud Barzani, described the opening of the consulate as an 'historic day for the US-Iraqi Kurdistan relations'. The event was attended by both Thomas Nides, Deputy Secretary of State, and James Jeffrey, US ambassador to Iraq. Furthermore, on 3 September 2013 the US and the KRG signed an agreement for the construction of a permanent compound on land allocated for a new Consulate General in Erbil.

The Kurds continued to play a role welcomed by Washington in influencing events in Baghdad, especially so after the stalemate in government formation after the March 2010 elections. After these elections the US saw signs of a drift toward authoritarianism under Prime Minister Maliki. Exploiting the US-Kurdish friendship, on 4 November 2010 President Obama attempted to persuade the Kurdish Iraqi president, Jalal Talabani, to give up his post to secular Shiite leader Ayad Allawi, as his bloc enjoyed broad Sunni support, in the hope that a more inclusive government would check Maliki's power. He failed.[298] On 10 November 2010, Maliki and Allawi reached a power-sharing agreement, at a meeting hosted in Erbil and sponsored by the US, in which Maliki was to relinquish his direct command of the security forces and his tight grip on the cabinet and most ministries.

Kurdish leader Masoud Barzani once again visited Washington and was met by President Obama on 4 April 2012. Obama administration officials pressed Barzani to re-engage with Baghdad as relations between leaders in the autonomous Kurdistan region and the central government had soured over payments to the international oil companies. The US remained fully engaged with Iraq albeit with reduced influence after the US withdrawal. Antony Blinken, Deputy National Security Advisor, had stated, on 16 March 2012, that '[d]uring the most recent political standoff, the United States remained the indispensable honest broker and the only one trusted by, and in regular communication with, all of the leading blocs'. The White House commented on the Obama–Barzani meeting: 'The United States is committed to our close and historic relationship with Kurdistan and the Kurdish people, in the context of our strategic partnership with a federal, democratic and unified Iraq.' Also discussed were the steps the US would take to expand the services offered at the US consulate in Erbil. As a result, the US consulate in Erbil started issuing US visas from 25 June 2013.

A further development in this relationship was the establishment of the United States Kurdistan Business Council in April 2012 with President Obama's former National Security Advisor James Jones as its CEO. The idea behind this step was to strengthen US-Kurdish relations based on economic and trade interests. Two major US oil giants ExxonMobil and Chevron had already signed lucrative deals in 2011 and 2012 respectively with the KRG, giving them substantial stakes in Kurdistan. On the cultural level, US-Kurdish relations took a major step forward with the establishment in October 2007 of 'The American University of

Iraq, Sulaimani' in the Kurdistan Region. The first group of (mostly Kurdish) students graduated in 2010.

The Kurdish community in the US also has a presence at the lobbying level through individuals and through the Kurdish National Congress of North America. This was established in 1988 with the encouragement of Jalal Talabani after his visit to Washington to highlight the gas attack on the town of Halabja by Saddam's regime. Later other organisations were also founded that lobby for and raise awareness of the Kurdish cause; these are the American Kurdish Information Network, the Washington Kurdish Institute, Kurdish Human Rights Watch, the American Kurdish Council, the American Society for Kurds and the Kurdish American Society.

This evolving friendship was also enhanced by the establishment of a congressional caucus. On 25 May 2008 the Kurdish-American Congressional Caucus was inaugurated. According to the director of the Washington Kurdish Institute the establishment of the caucus, which initially had fourteen members, was another 'big step' towards enhancing American-Kurdistan relations, in addition to its importance for the 50,000 Kurdish Americans.[299] During the inauguration of the bi-partisan caucus, Congressman Lincoln Davis (D-TN) stated that he hoped that it would 'stand as a symbol of continued friendship and cooperation between the United States and Iraq's Kurdish people' in America's effort to bring 'peace and stability to a federated Iraq'.[300] However, he carefully clarified on a different occasion in July that the establishment of the caucus was not an attempt to 'help Kurds form their own independent state'.[301] By 2014 the caucus had fifty-three congressional members, illustrating the significant progress in relations and further recognition of the Kurdish issue. This changed the Kurds' standing in Washington.

The Kurdistan Regional Government also has active and highly effective representation in Washington that did not exist until 1997. This representation was officially recognised in February 2007 and has managed to develop a wide range of contacts and relations with various agencies and influential figures in the US. It has also spent in excess of 8.5 million USD (2003–2014) on lobbying and public relations.

Relations between Ankara and Baghdad deteriorated against the background of the Sunni-Shiite rivalry in the region, Iraqi Prime Minister Nouri Maliki's tilt toward Iran and his tacit support for Syrian President Bashar al-Assad, and the sharp personal antipathy between Turkish Prime Minister Recep Tayyip Erdogan and Maliki. All of this weakened Ankara's 'commitment' to the almost sacred notion of Iraqi unity and emboldened it to expand bilateral ties with the KRG. If there is one country that has helped build a strong Kurdish entity in Iraqi Kurdistan, it is Turkey. This seems paradoxical, in view of Ankara's traditional opposition to autonomous Kurdish power in Iraq and the well-known pressures it exerted on its allies, especially the United States, not to support Iraqi Kurdish aspirations lest success spill over to Turkey's own restive Kurds. On the other hand, Ankara did its best to reap the economic fruits of its relations with the emerging entity, as Turkey became the sixteenth largest economy in the world. The Kurdistan region hosted many Turkish companies, over a thousand in 2014 alone, giving many Turks vested interests in the KRG and thus further tightening the connection between Turkey and the KRG. Turkey is seen as the KRG's gateway to the West and indeed, has become the KRG's main lifeline to the world. A stunning example of Ankara's new policy is the surprising pipeline deal it cut with the KRG on 20 May 2012, without Baghdad's approval. This agreement envisages two pipelines, one for oil and one for gas, running from KRG territory to Turkey. The oil pipeline would be able to export more than 1 million bpd by the end of 2015 and 2 million bpd by 2019. These pipelines will answer Turkey's need for oil and gas, but they may also further boost Kurdish aspirations for independence. These aspirations, however, have been discouraged by the US. America believes this newly founded Turkish-KRG alliance will only further alienate Baghdad from the West, and encourage 'more violent conflict and disintegration within Iraq'.[302] And although the US values greater oil flow to world markets, it wants the KRG to funnel these revenues into the Iraqi budget for the benefit of all Iraqis, and not for Kurdistan only. America was also concerned that KRG oil exports through Turkey would exclude Turkey from 100% of Iraq's oil exports and restrict it to only 20% of Iraq's oil situated in the Kurdistan region. The US wanted Turkey's Cehan terminal to become an alternative to the Strait of Hormuz in transporting oil to world markets. The US withdrawal from Iraq had the opposite effect on the Kurds. Not only did it not weaken the KRG, as the Kurds feared it would; it actually reinforced its strategic importance. The severe rivalry that developed between Iran and Turkey increased the KRG's significance in both American and Turkish eyes.[303]

In April 2012, at the same time as opposition to Maliki's autocratic style was growing, the KRG suspended oil exports through the Iraqi pipeline as a result of Baghdad refusing to pay international oil companies based in the Kurdistan Region their due fees. In the same month President Barzani hosted a meeting of Maliki's opponents, all nominal partners in the coalition government. Their intent was to unseat the prime minister through a vote of no confidence if he continued to renege on the power-sharing promises he had made when he formed his government in December of 2010 after being elected to a second term. They failed to dethrone Maliki, who enjoyed the tacit support of both Iran and the United States. By early August 2012, the Obama administration, concerned that reduced oil exports from Iraq could push up gasoline prices, was pressuring the Kurds to end their stand. Without winning any concessions on payments to the oil companies from Baghdad, the KRG caved in and reopened the valves. By mid-September, the two sides had reaffirmed their original deal of 2010, in which Baghdad had agreed to pay fees due to international oil companies.[304]

The Kurdistan Region, however, was pursuing a discreet agenda to build an independent Kurdistan, actively working to weaken the central federal structure and strengthening its internal institutions. In August 2008, for instance, when tensions arose between Arabs and Kurds in the northern Iraqi governorate of Diyala, and then several months later in Kirkuk and Neynawa, Prime Minister Nouri Maliki attempted to assert control of these areas by moving Iraqi forces into those areas causing a crisis with the Kurds. The two sides came close to armed conflict over control of disputed territories in northern Iraq, which the Kurdistan Regional Government was seeking to incorporate within its federal region. This brought the Arab-Kurd dispute to the attention of the US military and policy makers. At the request of Maliki and Masoud Barzani, commander of US forces in Iraq General Odierno devised a system of cooperation among the Iraqi Security Forces, the Peshmarga and US troops in operational centres, at checkpoints and during patrols.[305] In August 2009 Odierno proposed joint patrols in disputed territories. The tripartite force was named the Golden Lions and launched on 13 January 2010. This helped establish relationships between the leaders of the various forces, building mutual trust and confidence and restoring stability to the disputed territories. But soon after the US withdrawal in late 2011 that system fell apart.

Through intense diplomacy, the US remained thoroughly engaged in fractious Iraqi politics after its military withdrawal. Following the escalating tension between Baghdad and the KRG after the Iraqi army's build-up of the Dijla Forces, in November 2012 on the borders of the disputed territories historically claimed by the Kurdish liberation movement, the US played a significant role in de-escalating the tension, and encouraged a return to the negotiation table. Biden told Maliki that armed clashes with Kurdish Peshmarga constitute a 'red line', even offering a redeployment of the US military to ensure there are no clashes between both sides. The US also remained engaged in the internal affairs of the Kurdistan Region. The US State Department responded when tension erupted on 30 June 2013 when in a parliamentary vote the joint parliamentary faction of the KDP and PUK extended the presidency of Masoud Barzani for an additional two years, beyond his stipulated tenure. On 3 July 2013 US State Department spokesperson Jen Psaki implicitly expressed American dissatisfaction with the postponement of due elections: 'The United States supports regular, free and democratic elections as fundamental to ensuring the will of the people.'[306]

The US initially lacked understanding of Iraq's composition and ethnic makeup; while the educational process has been slow, considerable progress has indeed been made. Washington now understands the size and complexity of the Kurdish problem in Iraq and the region in general. From this understanding it now has a more sophisticated approach in dealing with Iraq as a whole. It is able to deal with Iraq at the national and sub-national levels with a sophistication that was lacking in the early 1960s at the beginning of the Kurdish revolt. With US acknowledgement of the 'special case' of the Kurds, for this reason it also endorses federalism. US support for the autonomous region is a means to protect it from being overrun by Baghdad. This allows for the preservation of Kurdish identity without the US needing to endorse a separate state. From the start of Operation Provide Comfort, interaction between US officials and the Kurdish leadership increased. Many visits by US officials, diplomats and military personnel from Washington, enhanced by the friendliness and appreciation of the Kurdish people, have helped establish a broad understanding of the distinctness of Iraq's Kurds. It has also helped nurture an admiration for Kurdish achievements and an appreciation of their informal alliance with the United States.

The US sees the Kurds of Iraq strictly within the dimensions of the political structure of the region. It is bound by the state-centricity of the international system and the policy makers and practitioners in Washington are profoundly committed to preserving this system. Any modification of the geographical boundaries of the neighbouring states is considered politically risky. The US has no stomach for protecting the Kurds in the likely scenario of Iranian or Turkish invasion, and the US public has neither awareness of, nor interest in the Kurdish issue. Thus it would be difficult for any administration to commit American blood and treasure to such a prospect. The argument in Washington as regards Kurdish independence has constantly rotated around the instability produced if it was achieved. Since the 2003 war, the Kurds have been seen favourably in US foreign policy as one component of the new Iraqi government and the new Iraqi way of life, as long as they do not seek independence. The Kurds, in US eyes, had been doing the right thing and were playing a constructive role for the most part. They were considered a good model for the new Iraq. Most people in the US government – in both the executive branch and legislative branch – know that.[307]

A real interest in Kurdish independence has never emerged on the US agenda for various reasons. Nationalism in the United States was defined by creed and a sense of mission and not based on ethnicity, which was largely associated with European nations and the Treaty of Westphalia of 1648. The very nature and structure of the US denies any such sentiment significant value. The US, a nation of ethnic pluralism, was established by immigrants from all corners of the earth and as such no ethnic national identity has been established. Thus any attempts to carve out ethnic nation states from post-colonial nation states hold little merit in US foreign policy. This also explains the Americans' early proposal for geographic federalism, based on the eighteen provincial boundaries of Iraq, which was only overruled because of Kurdish protests. Furthermore, the US has demonstrated no genuine interest in national liberation movements whose aims do not coincide with furthering US national interests.

US rhetoric supports the right to self-determination as a concept, but in practice there is no evidence to further this claim. The US maintained and supported ethnic strife during the Cold War in efforts to weaken the Soviets and their allies. The US supported the Kurds from 1972 to 1975 to weaken Soviet ally Iraq and support its own ally, Iran. The US had maintained this policy not only during the Cold War, but as far back as Theodore Roosevelt's administration, when it supported Colombian separatists, leading to the creation of Panama in exchange for US control over the Panama Canal. The US, however, has a constant tendency rhetorically to support human rights as timeless and universal values. The US consistently defends the human rights of political dissidents, religious and ethnic minorities, rhetorically at least, even within friendly nations. This is especially the case when members of those groups' diaspora communities have a large presence in the US and use their numbers to effectively lobby policy makers.

US national interest has overridden any regard or consideration for national liberation movements abroad. The fact that any support for self-determination would encroach on the national interest and sovereignty of other states has made such support inappropriate. As the ultimate guiding moral principle of a state is its survival, the US has only encouraged and supported these movements where US national interest has been at stake. The risk of breaching the national interest of another state, where little US interest has been at stake, is out of bounds in US foreign policy. Any support for Kurdish independence in the near future falls squarely within this formula. Any attempt at advancing Kurdish separatism based on US support has been, and will be, met by a negative response as it touches on US interests with NATO ally Turkey, potential and former ally Iran, Arab Iraq and a large number of friendly Arab nations.

The US does not support nor envisage an independent Kurdistan, but will likely help the secession of Kurdistan if its association with Iraq leads to instability in the country and the region or if the Sunni and Shiite components of Iraq maintain irreconcilable differences with each other. This US support, however, would come with the caveat of Kurdish appreciation for Turkish and US regional concerns. In a hostile region like the Middle East, where the US cannot afford to antagonise friends, the Iraqi Kurds are now perceived as a valuable political asset. Interestingly, the US has no formal policy of denying the Kurds an independent state.

Kurdistan cannot achieve independence right now, as there is no support for such a move in Washington, but the ground has been prepared. Washington understands this is what Iraqi Kurdistan really wants. Washington is also psychologically accepting that Iraq has the potential of breaking up; given previous American thinking that an independent Kurdistan is impossible, that barrier has been crossed and this is a huge step forward. The United States used to be against Kurdish independence, full stop. American administrations opposed it in part because Kurdish independence was thought to be a short-term ploy of the Soviet government after the Second World War, designed to hurt Iran and Turkey, both American allies at the time. But the reasons for this opposition no longer remain. Also, the old order in the Middle East is quickly disappearing and the Arab Spring is evolving at considerable speed. The transition is still in its early phases, and what will follow (and when) is uncertain. Some borders, however, are likely to be redrawn, and some new states may even emerge as a result. Right now, however, the international environment is not suitable for independence. An independent Kurdistan in the future is likely to be achieved through some sort of Velvet Divorce between Arab Iraq and the Kurdistan Region, akin to the dissolution of the former Czechoslovakia in 1993. The US may play a role in negotiating this secession. Kurdistan is already self-sufficient with its own army and is developing its own oil resources.

The major obstruction to an independent Kurdistan is US sensitivity to the interests of regional powers, particularly Turkey. US rhetoric commonly argues that an independent Kurdistan would invite instability, a concept that could be refuted by citing the recent developments inside Turkey. These include, for example, Turkey's gradual relaxation of restraints on Kurdish cultural and linguistic rights in the country, beginning with the first television broadcast in the Kurdish language in June 2004. Also, Turkey's increasing rapprochement with the Kurdistan Regional Government including the opening of a consulate general in Erbil in 2010, its attempts in October 2012 to start reaching an agreement with the PKK and the substantial volume of trade between the Kurdistan Region and Turkey are all testimony to the possibility of friendly relations based on mutual respect and cooperation. Most important to highlight is how little impact Kurdish nationalism has had on destabilising and weakening regional powers with sizable Kurdish minorities. This means an independent Kurdistan is indeed possible as a viable and logical entity, becoming a source of stability, enhancing security and alleviating insecurity in a region plagued otherwise with tensions and conflict. Essentially a sovereign state of Kurdistan can play the crucial role of both a US and Turkish ally in the region, advancing their interests in exchange for credible security guarantees.

Many prerequisites for Kurdistan's independence already exist although the Kurdish leadership has chosen not to pursue it. The Kurdish leadership, however, must be clear in Washington about the Kurdish people's desire for independence. They should also state clearly that as pragmatic leaders they have no intention of declaring independence right now, but as democratic leaders this is inevitable since this is what Kurdish people really want. Internally, the KRG must demonstrate that an independent Kurdistan will be a viable entity; this can be demonstrated through good governance and economically sound policies by the KRG. The Americans will certainly support the Kurds if they feel that they are committed to democracy and the rule of law. Kurdistan must establish a democratic government of institutions; externally, the KRG must guarantee that regional stability will be maintained and that an independent entity will not upset regional US allies and threaten their territorial integrity. This can be achieved through security agreements and the establishment of excellent trade and diplomatic relations with regional states.

US Kurdish policy has transitioned through four stages over the period covered in this book; starting initially with 'contacts' (1961–1971) to a 'covert relationship' (1972–1975) to an 'overt relationship' (1991–2004) and finally evolving into an overt 'institutionalised relationship' (2005–2014) embodied in an official but undeclared US Kurdish policy. Masoud Barzani has met with US presidents Bush and Obama seven times in total since assuming the presidency of the Kurdistan Region in June 2005. This clearly demonstrates the gradual increase in sophistication of US foreign policy. The evolution in US interaction with the Kurds, from humanitarian assistance to strategic partnership, as a non-state ally and an asset, is testimony to the enhanced role of the Kurds as a non-state actor in international relations of the Middle East.[308] The US's inadvertent favouring of one ethnic group in a multi-ethnic and bi-sectarian state contributed significantly to the likelihood of state formation by the Kurds.[309]

There has been a gradual evolution in US-Kurdish relations; from 1991 to 1998 the premise of US interaction with the Kurds was mostly a humanitarian operation with the containment of Saddam in mind. From 1998 to 2003, there was a very sharp increase in cooperation, assistance and support due to the public policy of regime change. From 2003 to 2014, there was a more steady and gradual improvement in relations.[310] There was a time when Kurdistan was at the centre of US attention, especially during Operation Iraqi Freedom and the immediate aftermath of

Saddam's overthrow. Under the Obama administration, however, Kurdistan is seen as something of a distraction, undermining its official 'one Iraq' policy. Although the Kurdistan Region prides itself on its peace and security compared with the rest of Arab Iraq. (However, although not one American soldier has died in the Kurdish region, compared to more than 4488 in Arab Iraq, the State Department in 2014 applied the same travel advisory for Kurdistan as for the rest of Iraq.) US policy towards the Iraqi Kurds has always been a dependent variable, inseparable from the US policy towards Iraq as a whole, Turkey and Iran. As described above, the events that changed the political landscape in Iraq have developed in such a way as to give Iraqi Kurds, almost as if by accident under the George W. Bush administration, the opportunity to realise many of their aspirations, and to achieve political and economic advances unprecedented in centuries of Kurdish history.

Notes

1 Woodrow Wilson. (1918). *Primary Documents – Woodrow Wilson's 'Fourteen Points' Speech, 8 January 1918.* [firstworldwar.com] Available at: URL: www.firstworldwar.com/source/fourteenpoints.htm Access Date: 20 June 2007.
2 Edward Crocker. (1950). *United States Embassy, Iraq Cable from Edward S. Crocker II to the Department of State. 'Recent Developments in Connection with the Kurdish-Language News Bulletin', April 10, 1950.* [The National Security Archive: The George Washington University] Available at: URL: www.gwu.edu/~nsarchiv/NSAEBB/NSAEBB78/propaganda%20002.pdf Access Date: 20 December 2007.
3 Henry Grady. (1951). *United States Embassy, Iran Cable from Henry F. Grady to the Department of State. [Kurdish Voice of America Broadcasts], August 6, 1951.* [The National Security Archive: The George Washington University] Available at: URL: www.gwu.edu/~nsarchiv/NSAEBB/NSAEBB78/propaganda%20027.pdf Access Date: 20 December 2007.
4 Michael Gunter, *The Kurds of Iraq: Tragedy and Hope* (New York: St Martin's Press, 1992), p. 26.
5 The Baghdad Pact was created in 1955 by the United Kingdom, Iraq, Turkey, Iran and Pakistan with the aim of strengthening regional defence and preventing the infiltration of the Soviet Union into the Middle East. The Saadabad Pact was a non-aggression pact signed by Turkey, Iran, Iraq and Afghanistan on 8 July 1937. The treaty was signed in Tehran's Saadabad Palace and was part of an initiative for greater Middle Eastern-Oriental relations spearheaded by King Mohammed Zahir Shah of Afghanistan.
6 Toby Dodge, 'US Foreign Policy in the Middle East', in *US Foreign Policy*, ed. Michael Cox and Doug Stokes (Oxford: Oxford University Press, 2008), p. 232.
7 Robert Strong. (1964). *Airgram from the Embassy in Iraq to the Department of State.* [US Department of State: Office of the Historian] Available at: URL: http://history.state.gov/historicaldocuments/frus1964–68v21/d162 Access Date: 20 December 2007.
8 Aziz Barzani, E-mail Interview with Author, 14 September 2011.
9 Asad Khailany, Telephone Interview with Author, 5 July 2009.
10 Mustafa Barzani quoted in Edmund Ghareeb, *The Kurdish Question in Iraq* (New York: Syracuse University Press, 1981), p. 44.
11 Harold Saunders. (1972a). *Memorandum from Harold Saunders of the National Security Council Staff to the President's Deputy Assistant for National Security Affairs (Haig), Washington, March 27, 1972.* [US Department of State: Office of the Historian] Available at: URL: http://history.state.gov/historicaldocuments/frus1969–76ve04/media/pdf/d301.pdf Access Date: 20 December 2009.

12 Ibid.
13 John Foster. (1968). *Memorandum from John W. Foster of the National Security Council Staff to the President's Special Assistant (Rostow).* [US Department of State: Office of the Historian] Available at: URL: http://history.state.gov/historical-documents/frus1964–68v21/d200 Access Date: 20 December 2009.
14 Kerim Yildiz, *The Kurds In Iraq: The Past, Present and Future* (London: Pluto Press, 2004), p. 22.
15 This is the unauthorised publication of US House of Representatives Pike Committee Report investigating the CIA, published on 16 February 1976 in *The Village Voice* under the title 'The Report on the CIA that President Ford Doesn't Want You to Read', pp. 70–92. The part dealing with the Kurds is entitled 'Case 2: Arms Support', pp. 85–8.
16 Ghareeb (1981), op. cit., pp. 139–40.
17 Andrew Killgore. (1972). *Memorandum from Andrew Killgore of the Bureau of Near Eastern and South Asian Affairs to the Assistant Secretary for Near Eastern and South Asian Affairs (Sisco), Washington, April 3, 1972.* [US Department of State: Office of the Historian] Available at: http://history.state.gov/historicaldocuments/frus1969–76ve04/media/pdf/d304.pdf Access Date: 20 December 2009.
18 Harold Saunders. (1972b). *Memorandum from Harold Saunders of the National Security Staff to the President's Assistant for National Security Affairs (Kissinger), Washington, June 7, 1972.* [US Department of State: Office of the Historian] Available at: URL: http://history.state.gov/historicaldocuments/frus1969–76ve04/media/pdf/d313.pdf Access Date: 20 December 2009.
19 Ghareeb (1981), op. cit., p. 139.
20 Peter Galbraith, *The End of Iraq: How American Incompetence Created a War Without End* (New York: Simon and Schuster, 2006), p. 147.
21 Ghareeb (1981), op. cit., p. 141.
22 Henry Kissinger quoted in Quil Lawrence, *Invisible Nation: How The Kurds' Quest for Statehood is Shaping Iraq and the Middle East* (New York: Walker Publishing Company, 2008), p. 25.
23 Ibid., p. 24.
24 Ghareeb (1981), op. cit., p. 141.
25 Henry Kissinger. (1974). *Meeting with Israeli Ambassador Dinitz: Secret, Memorandum of Conversation, Washington, March 21, 1974.* [The National Security Archive: The George Washington University] Available at: http://gateway.proquest.com/openurl?url_ver=Z39.88–2004&res_dat=xri:dnsa&rft_dat=xri:dnsa:article:CKT01078 Access Date: 1 December 2008.
26 Brent Scowcroft quoted in Lawrence (2008), op. cit., p. 25.
27 Ghareeb (1981), op. cit., p. 141.
28 Bob Woodward, *Plan of Attack* (London: Simon and Schuster, 2004), pp. 69–70.
29 Ghareeb (1981), op. cit., p. 140.
30 Aron Latham quoted in Ghareeb (1981), op. cit., p. 141.
31 Ibid., p. 144.
32 Henry Kissinger, *White House Years* (Boston: Little, Brown and Company, 1979), p. 1265.
33 Saunders (1972b), op. cit.
34 Ghareeb (1981), op. cit., p. 159.
35 Mustafa Barzani quoted in ibid.
36 Peter Galbraith, Telephone Interview with Author, 8 August 2008.
37 Ghareeb (1981), op. cit., p. 140.
38 Ibid.,
39 Ibid., p. 141.
40 Gunter (1992), op. cit., p. 27.
41 Brent Scowcroft quoted in Lawrence (2008), op. cit., p. 28.

42 Edmund Ghareeb, Interview with Author, 22 August 2008, Washington, D.C.
43 Galbraith (2006), op. cit., p. 147.
44 Joseph Sisco quoted in David Korn. (1994). *The Last Years of Mustafa Barzani.* [The Middle East Quarterly] Available at: www.meforum.org/220/the-last-years-of-mustafa-barzani Access Date: 20 December 2007.
45 Ibid.
46 Lawrence (2008), op. cit., p. 33.
47 Galbraith (2006), op. cit., p. 34.
48 Hikmat Bamarni, Interview with Author, 16 July 2008, Washington, D.C.
49 Galbraith (2006), op. cit., p. 27.
50 Lawrence (2008), op. cit., p. 40.
51 Galbraith (2006), op. cit., p. 27.
52 Ibid., p. 28.
53 Jalal Talabani quoted in Khadduri and Ghareeb (1997), op. cit., p. 205.
54 Galbraith (2006), op. cit., p. 41.
55 Ibid.
56 George Shultz quoted in Galbraith (2006), op. cit., p. 33.
57 Yildiz (2004), op. cit., p. 31.
58 Peter Galbraith and Christopher Van Hollen. (1988). *Chemical Weapons Use in Kurdistan: Iraq's Final Offensive* (Committee Print 100–148). Washington, D.C.: Senate Committee on Foreign Relations.
59 Galbraith (2006), op. cit., pp. 30–4.
60 Lawrence (2008), op. cit., p. 41.
61 Charles Redman quoted in Galbraith (2006), op. cit., p. 33.
62 Ibid., p. 34.
63 Khadduri and Ghareeb (1997), op. cit., p. 201.
64 Nawshirwan Mustafa Amin. (2010). *From Comradeship to Treachery* (Translated from Kurdish by Author). [Sbeiy.com] Available at: URL: http://sbeiy.com/ku/article_detail.aspx?ArticleID=2561&AuthorID=36 Access Date: 20 January 2010.
65 Galbraith (2006), op. cit., p. 41.
66 Ibid., p. 40.
67 Amin (2010), op. cit.
68 David Mack, Interview with Author, 27 August 2008, Washington, D.C.
69 Galbraith (2006), op. cit., p. 46.
70 Ibid.
71 Lawrence (2008), op. cit., p. 3.
72 Galbraith (2006), op. cit., p. 46.
73 George H. W. Bush. (1991a). *Remarks to Raytheon Missile Systems Plant Employees in Andover, Massachusetts.* Available at: URL: http://bushlibrary.tamu.edu/research/public_papers.php?id=2711&year=1991&month=2 Access Date: 15 December 2009.
74 Khadduri and Ghareeb (1997), op. cit., p. 205.
75 Ibid., p. 205.
76 Marlin Fitzwater quoted in ibid., p. 204.
77 George H. W. Bush and Brent Scowcroft, *A World Transformed* (New York: Vintage Books, 1999), p. 489.
78 Michael Gunter, 'Turkey's New Neighbor, Kurdistan', in *The Future of Kurdistan in Iraq*, ed. Brendan O'Leary and John McGarry et al. (Philadelphia: University of Pennsylvania Press, 2005), p. 223.
79 Michael Gunter, *The Kurdish Predicament in Iraq: A Political Analysis* (Pennsylvania: Macmillan, 1999), p. 28.
80 Yildiz (2004), op. cit., p. 38.
81 Douglas Feith, *War and Decision: Inside the Pentagon at the Dawn of the War on Terrorism* (New York: HarperCollins Publishers, 2008), p. 186.

82 Yildiz (2004), op. cit., p. 39.
83 David McDowall, *A Modern History of the Kurds* (New York: I.B.Tauris, 2004), pp. 373–5.
84 Robert Olson, *The Goat and the Butcher: Nationalism and State Formation in Kurdistan-Iraq since the Iraqi War* (California: Mazda Publishers, 2005), p. 233.
85 Lawrence (2006), op. cit., p. 55.
86 Thomas Ricks, *Fiasco: The American Military Adventure in Iraq* (London: Penguin Press, 2007), p. 9.
87 Yildiz (2004), op. cit., p. 40.
88 George H. W. Bush quoted in Gunter (1992), op. cit., p. 57.
89 Jay Garner, Telephone Interview with Author, 19 September 2008.
90 Qubad Talabani, Interview with Author, 31 July 2008, Washington, D.C. Peshmarga is the term used by Kurds to refer to armed Kurdish fighters. It literally means 'those who face death'.
91 George H. W. Bush. (1991b). *Remarks on Assistance for Iraqi Refugees and a News Conference.* Available at: URL: http://bushlibrary.tamu.edu/research/public_papers. php?id=2882&year=1991&month=4 Access Date: 16 December 2009.
92 Bob Woodward, *State of Denial: Bush at War, Part III* (London: Simon and Schuster, 2006), p. 104.
93 John Pilger. (2000). *Labour Claims its Actions are Lawful While it Bombs Iraq, Starves its People and Sells Arms to Corrupt States.* Available at: URL: www.john-pilger.com/page.asp?partid=308 Access Date: 16 December 2009.
94 Ayal Frank, Interview with Author, 11 June 2008, Washington, D.C.
95 Woodward (2006), op. cit., p. 210.
96 Gunter (2005), op. cit., p. 225.
97 Lawrence (2008), op. cit., p. 4.
98 Nabil Al-Tikriti, Interview with Author, 18 June 2008, Washington, D.C.
99 Yildiz (2004), op. cit., p. 44.
100 Andrew Morrison, Interview with Author, 21 August 2008, Washington, D.C.
101 *Meeting with Iraqi Kurdistan Front – statement on Assistant Secretary of State Edward Djerejian's meeting with a delegation – Transcript.* (1991). Available at: URL: http://findarticles.com/p/articles/mi_m1584/is_n40_v2/ai_11555741/ Access Date: 17 December 2009.
102 Ayal Frank, Interview with Author, 11 June 2008, Washington, D.C.
103 Ibid.
104 Najmaldin Karim, Interview with Author, 8 July 2008, Washington, D.C.
105 Andrew Morrison, Interview with Author, 21 August 2008, Washington, D.C.
106 Qubad Talabani, Interview with Author, 31 July 2008, Washington, D.C.
107 Gunter (1999), op. cit., p. 81.
108 Ibid., p. 111.
109 David Litt. (1995). *The Situation in Northern Iraq: Problems and Prospects.* [The Washington Institute for Near East Policy] Available at: www.washingtoninstitute. org/templateC05.php?CID=2862 Access Date: 20 December 2007.
110 Nawshirwan Mustafa Amin. (2009). *Dream or Nightmare, The Inside Story of Iraqi Kurdistan 1992–2002: Part 2* (Translated from Kurdish by Author). [Sbeiy.com] Available at: URL: www.sbeiy.com/ku/ArticleParts.aspx?PartID=34&ArticleID=15 39&AuthorID=36 Access Date: 20 June 2008.
111 Jalal Talabani quoted in ibid.
112 Andrew Morrison, Interview with Author, 21 August 2008, Washington, D.C.
113 Ibid.
114 Ibid.
115 Herbert Friedman. (2004). *Operation Provide Comfort.* Available at: URL: www. psywarrior.com/ProvideComfort.html Access Date: 17 December 2009.
116 James Rubin. (1998). *US Department of State Department: Daily Press Briefing.*

Available at: URL: www.fas.org/news/iraq/1998/09/980908db-1.html Access Date: 17 December 2009.
117 David Mack, Interview with Author, 27 August 2008, Washington, D.C.
118 Madeline Albright. (1998). *Transcript: Albright, Talabani, Barzani Remarks*, 9/27/98. Available at: URL: www.fas.org/news/iraq/1998/09/980908db-1.html Access Date: 17 December 2009.
119 Qubad Talabani, Interview with Author, 31 July 2008, Washington, D.C.
120 Andrew Morrison, Interview with Author, 21 August 2008, Washington, D.C.
121 Qubad Talabani, Interview with Author, 31 July 2008, Washington, D.C.
122 Lawrence (2008), op. cit., p. 91.
123 Yildiz (2004), op. cit., p. 223.
124 Christine Gosden. (1998). *Congressional Testimony: Hearing of the Senate Judiciary Subcommittee on Technology, Terrorism and Government and the Senate Select Committee on Intelligence:* Washington, D.C.
125 Gunter (1999), op. cit., p. 102.
126 Ibid., p. 108.
127 Ibid., p. 105.
128 Bill Clinton. (1998). *A Report on the Status of Efforts to Obtain Iraq's Compliance with the Resolutions Adopted by the UN Security Council* (105th Congress, 2nd Session: House Document 105–212). Washington, D.C.: The White House.
129 Matthew Stephenson, Interview with Author, 10 June 2008, Washington, D.C.
130 Bill Clinton quoted in Yildiz (2004), op. cit., p. 89.
131 Feith (2008), op. cit., p. 208.
132 Peter Galbraith, 'Kurdistan in a Federal Iraq', in *The Future of Kurdistan in Iraq*, ed. Brendan O'Leary and John McGarry *et al.* (Philadelphia: University of Pennsylvania Press, 2005), p. 270.
133 Carole O'Leary, Interview with Author, 8 August 2008, Washington, D.C.
134 Daniel Pipes, Interview with Author, 23 July 2008, Washington, D.C.
135 Ibid.
136 Paul Pillar, Interview with Author, 15 July 2008, Washington, D.C.
137 Feith (2008), op. cit., p. 369.
138 *US led forces entered Iraq two months prior JHS Res.114.* (2005). Available at: URL: www.downingstreetmemo.com/2005/08/us-led-forces-entered-iraq-two-months.html Access Date: 17 December 2009.
139 Kenneth Katzman. (2003). *Iraq: US Regime Change Efforts, the Iraqi Opposition, and Post-War Iraq* (Order Code RL31339). Washington, D.C.: Congressional Research Service.
140 Bob Woodward, 'With CIA Push, Movement to War Accelerated', *The Washington Post*, (2004, 19 April), p. A01.
141 Woodward (2004), op. cit., pp. 140–1.
142 Senior KRG official, Telephone Interview with Author, 20 May 2010.
143 Yildiz (2004), op. cit., p. 103.
144 Qubad Talabani, Interview with Author, 31 July 2008, Washington, D.C.
145 Lawrence (2008), op. cit., p. 117.
146 Qubad Talabani, Interview with Author, 31 July 2008, Washington, D.C.
147 Lawrence (2008), op. cit., p. 117.
148 Qubad Talabani, Interview with Author, 31 July 2008, Washington, D.C.
149 Galbraith (2006), op. cit., p. 157.
150 Qubad Talabani, Interview with Author, 31 July 2008, Washington, D.C.
151 Galbraith (2006), op. cit., p. 158.
152 Carole O'Leary, Interview with Author, 8 August 2008, Washington, D.C.
153 George W. Bush quoted in Galbraith (2005), op. cit., p. 271.
154 Ibid.
155 Feith (2008), op. cit., pp. 394–5.

156 Yildiz (2004), op. cit., pp. 104–5.
157 Ibid., p. 106.
158 Feith (2008), op. cit., p. 395.
159 Sophia Wanche, 'Awaiting Liberation: Kurdish Perspectives on a Post-Saddam Iraq', in *The Future of Kurdistan in Iraq*, ed. Brendan O'Leary and John McGarry *et al.* (Philadelphia: University of Pennsylvania Press, 2005), p. 191.
160 Ali Allawi, *The Occupation of Iraq: Winning the War, Losing the Peace* (USA: Yale University Press, 2007), p. 315.
161 Gunter (2005), op. cit., pp. 224–5.
162 Ibid., p. 227.
163 Yildiz (2004), op. cit., p. 106.
164 Galbraith (2006), op. cit., p. 158.
165 Woodward (2004), op. cit., p. 369.
166 Michael Gordon and Bernard Trainor, *Cobra II: The Inside Story of the Invasion and Occupation of Iraq* (London: Atlantic Books, 2007), p. 358.
167 Richard Cheney quoted in Woodward (2004), op. cit., p. 370.
168 Najmaldin Karim, Interview with Author, 8 July 2008, Washington, D.C.
169 Michael Rubin. (2008). *Is Iraqi Kurdistan a Good Ally?* [AEI Middle Eastern Outlook] Available at: URL: www.meforum.org/1822/is-iraqi-kurdistan-a-good-ally Access Date: 15 February 2008.
170 Yildiz (2004), op. cit., p. 110.
171 Qubad Talabani, Interview with Author, 31 July 2008, Washington, D.C.
172 Feith (2008), op. cit., p. 397.
173 Yildiz (2004), op. cit., p. 130.
174 Henri Barkey, Interview with Author, 21 August 2008, Washington, D.C.
175 Ayal Frank, Interview with Author, 11 June 2008, Washington, D.C.
176 Galbraith (2005), op. cit., p. 271.
177 Gunter (2005), op. cit., p. 225.
178 Galbraith (2006), op. cit., p. 158.
179 Gordon and Trainor (2007), op. cit., pp. 514–15.
180 Feith (2008), op. cit., p. 97.
181 Ibid.
182 Ibid., p. 105.
183 *Operation Iraqi Freedom.* (2005). Available at: URL: www.globalsecurity.org/military/ops/iraqi_freedom.htm Access Date: 17 June 2007.
184 Linda Robinson, *Masters of Chaos: The Secret History of the Special Forces* (New York: PublicAffairs, 2004), p. 308.
185 Qubad Talabani, Interview with Author, 31 July 2008, Washington, D.C.
186 Robinson (2004), op. cit., p. 308.
187 Gordon and Trainor (2007), op. cit., pp. 386–7.
188 Galbraith (2005), op. cit., pp. 278–9.
189 Nawshirwan Mustafa Amin. (2007a). *My Memoirs from the Governing Council: Part 1* (Translated from Kurdish by Author). [Sbeiy.com] Available at: URL: http://sbeiy.com/ku/ArticleParts.aspx?PartID=1&ArticleID=182&AuthorID=36 Access Date: 20 June 2008.
190 Peter Galbraith, Telephone Interview with Author, 8 August 2008.
191 Bremer, Paul, James Dobbins and David Gompert, 'Early Days in Iraq: Decisions of the CPA', *Survival* Vol. 50, No. 4 (2008): pp. 21–56.
192 Paul Bremer III with Malcolm McConnell, *My Year in Iraq: The Struggle to Build a Future of Hope* (New York: Simon & Schuster, 2006), p. 83.
193 Ibid., p. 87.
194 Ibid., p. 92.
195 Ibid.
196 Ibid., p. 93.

197 Michael Rubin, Interview with Author, 7 July 2008, Washington, D.C.
198 Bremer (2006), op. cit., p. 269.
199 Ayal Frank, Interview with Author, 11 June 2008, Washington, D.C.
200 Galbraith (2006), op. cit., p. 215.
201 Marianna Charountaki, *The Kurds and US Foreign Policy: International Relations in the Middle East since 1945* (Oxford: Routledge, 2011), p. 234.
202 Olson (2005), p. 243.
203 Qubad Talabani, Interview with Author, 31 July 2008, Washington, D.C.
204 Ibid.
205 Galbraith (2005), op. cit., p. 275.
206 Noah Feldman. (2005). *The Democratic Fatwa: Islam and Democracy in the Realm of Constitutional Politics.* [Oklahoma Law Review] Available at: URL: http://adams.law.ou.edu/olr/articles/vol. 58/feldman581.pdf Access Date: 18 December 2009.
207 Nabil Al-Tikriti, Interview with Author, 18 June 2008, Washington, D.C.
208 Galbraith (2005), op. cit., pp. 163–4.
209 Najmaldin Karim, Interview with Author, 8 July 2008, Washington, D.C.
210 Galbraith (2006), op. cit., p. 165.
211 Ibid., p. 135.
212 Ibid., p. 140.
213 Ibid., p. 166.
214 Gunter (2005), op. cit., p. 226.
215 Galbraith (2006), op. cit., pp. 162–3.
216 Nawshirwan Mustafa Amin. (2008). *A Historic Opportunity Lost!* (Translated from Kurdish by Author). [Sbeiy.com] Available at: URL: www.sbeiy.com/ku/article_detail.aspx?ArticleID=800&AuthorID=36&AspxAutoDetectCookieSupport=1 Access Date: 20 January 2009.
217 Najmaldin Karim, Interview with Author, 8 July 2008, Washington, D.C.
218 Galbraith (2005), op. cit., p. 273.
219 Allawi (2007), op. cit., p. 280.
220 Bremer (2006), op. cit., p. 143.
221 Qubad Talabani, Interview with Author, 31 July 2008, Washington, D.C.
222 Allawi (2007), op. cit., p. 393.
223 Galbraith (2006), op. cit., p. 215.
224 Feith (2008), op. cit., p. 495.
225 Galbraith (2006), op. cit., p. 193.
226 Ibid., p. 170.
227 Christopher Van Hollen, Telephone Interview with Author, 18 July 2008.
228 Christopher Straub, Interview with Author, 14 July 2008, Virginia (The Pentagon).
229 Carole O'Leary, Interview with Author, 8 August 2008, Washington, D.C.
230 Ibid.
231 Ibid.
232 Ibid.
233 Paul Pillar, Interview with Author, 15 July 2008, Washington, D.C.
234 David Mack, Interview with Author, 27 August 2008, Washington, D.C.
235 Peter Galbraith, Telephone Interview with Author, 8 August 2008.
236 Gordon and Trainor (2007), op. cit., p. 594.
237 George W. Bush. (2007b). *Press Conference by the President.* [The White House] Available at: URL: http://georgewbush-whitehouse.archives.gov/news/releases/2007/10/20071017.html Access Date: 20 June 2008.
238 Geoff Morrell quoted in Jim Garamone. (2007). *Spokesman Cites Diplomacy as Preferred Course for Turk-PKK Issue.* [Department of Defense] Available at: URL: www.firstworldwar.com/source/fourteenpoints.htm Access Date: 20 December 2007.
239 Nechirvan Barzani quoted in *Iraq's Kurdish Leader Snubs Rice.* (2007). [BBC

News] Available at: URL: http://news.bbc.co.uk/1/hi/world/europe/7150355.stm Access Date: 17 May 2008.

240 George W. Bush quoted in *Bush Urges Turks to End Offensive in Iraq Quickly.* (2008). [Reuters] Available at: URL: www.defense.gov/news/newsarticle.aspx?id=47832 Access Date: 17 May 2008.

241 Senior Iraqi Diplomat II, Interview with Author, 31 July 2008, Washington, D.C.

242 National Security Council Official, Interview with Author, 11 July 2008, Washington, D.C.

243 Qubad Talabani, Interview with Author, 31 July 2008, Washington, D.C.

244 Christopher Straub, Interview with Author, 14 July 2008, Virginia (The Pentagon).

245 Carole O'Leary, Interview with Author, 8 August 2008, Washington, D.C.

246 Ibid.

247 Henri Barkey, Interview with Author, 21 August 2008, Washington, D.C.

248 Jon Alterman, Interview with Author, 26 August 2008, Washington, D.C.

249 Frederick Kagan, Interview with Author, 25 July 2008, Washington, D.C.

250 Carole O'Leary, Interview with Author, 8 August 2008, Washington, D.C.

251 Ibid.

252 Ibid.

253 Ibid.

254 David Mack, Interview with Author, 27 August 2008, Washington, D.C.

255 Ibid.

256 Peter Galbraith, Telephone Interview with Author, 8 August 2008.

257 Paul Pillar, Interview with Author, 15 July 2008, Washington, D.C.

258 Ibid.

259 Ibid.

260 Michael Cox, 'The Imperial Republic Revisited: The United States in the Era of Bush', in *The War on Terrorism and the American 'Empire' after the Cold War*, ed. Alejandro Colas and Richard Saull (Oxford: Routledge, 2006), p. 121.

261 State Department Official, Interview with Author, 18 June 2008, Washington, D.C.

262 Matthew Stephenson, Interview with Author, 10 June 2008, Washington, D.C.

263 Ibid.

264 Jason Gluck, Interview with Author, 27 June 2008, Washington, D.C.

265 Paul Pillar, Interview with Author, 15 July 2008, Washington, D.C.

266 Daniel Pipes, Interview with Author, 23 July 2008, Washington, D.C.

267 Matthew Stephenson, Interview with Author, 10 June 2008, Washington, D.C.

268 Lawrence (2008), op. cit., p. 321.

269 Joseph Biden and Leslie Gelb, 'Unity Through Autonomy in Iraq', *The New York Times* (2006, 1 May), p. ED19.

270 Jalal Talabani. (2007). *CNN Late Night Edition with Wolf Blitzer.* Available at: URL: http://transcripts.cnn.com/TRANSCRIPTS/0710/07/le.01.html Access Date: 18 December 2009.

271 National Security Council Official, Interview with Author, 11 July 2008, Washington, D.C.

272 Joost R. Hiltermann, 'Revenge of the Kurds: Breaking Away from Baghdad', *Foreign Affairs* Vol. 91, No. 6 (2012): p. 18.

273 Christopher Straub, Interview with Author, 14 July 2008, Virginia (The Pentagon).

274 Qubad Talabani, Interview with Author, 31 July 2008, Washington, D.C.

275 Feith (2008), op. cit., p. 467.

276 Ibid., p. 146.

277 Article 140 is the article which was re-introduced from the TAL (Article 58) into the permanent constitution. It deals specifically with Kurdish claims to territories previously under Baghdad's control before OIF, a major point of contention with the rest of Arab Iraq. The article requires 'normalisation [reversal of Arabisation] and a census, and concludes with a referendum in Kirkuk and other disputed territories'.

278 Henri Barkey, Interview with Author, 21 August 2008, Washington, D.C.
279 Kenneth Katzman, Interview with Author, 10 July 2008, Washington, D.C.
280 Henri Barkey, Interview with Author, 21 August 2008, Washington, D.C.
281 Charountaki (2011), op. cit., pp. 181–7.
282 Najmaldin Karim, Interview with Author, 8 July 2008, Washington, D.C.
283 Masoud Barzani. (2008). *The Kurdistan Region and the Future of Iraq.* [Centre for Strategic and International Studies] Available at: URL: http://csis.org/event/kurdistan-region-and-future-iraq Access Date: 15 July 2009.
284 Falah Bakir, E-mail Interview with Author, 12 May 2011.
285 Ibid.
286 Jon Alterman, Interview with Author, 26 August 2008, Washington, D.C.
287 Aijaz Ahmed. (2007). *The Real News.* [The Real News Network] Available at: URL: www.youtube.com/watch?v=W5mRygvDmwI Access Date: 15 July 2009.
288 Marc Lynch, Interview with Author, 24 June 2008, Washington, D.C.
289 Henri Barkey, Interview with Author, 21 August 2008, Washington, D.C.
290 Jon Alterman, Interview with Author, 26 August 2008, Washington, D.C.
291 Qubad Talabani, Interview with Author, 31 July 2008, Washington, D.C.
292 Matthew Stephenson, Interview with Author, 10 June 2008, Washington, D.C.
293 Christopher Straub, Interview with Author, 14 July 2008, Virginia (The Pentagon).
294 Israel was only designated a US major non-NATO ally in 1989.
295 Andrew Morrison, Interview with Author, 21 August 2008, Washington, D.C.
296 Barack Obama. (2010). *Readout of the President's Meeting with the President of Iraq's Kurdistan Region Masoud Barzani.* [The White House] Available at: URL: www.whitehouse.gov/the-press-office/readout-presidents-meeting-with-president-iraqs-kurdistan-region-masoud-barzani Access Date: 22 August 2011.
297 Masoud Barzani. (2010). *President Barzani Concludes Successful Washington Visit.* [Kurdistan Regional Government] Available at: URL: www.krg.org/articles/detail.asp?rnr=223&lngnr=12&smap=02010100&anr=33605 Access Date: 20 August 2011.
298 Michael R. Gordon, 'Failed Efforts and Challenges of America's Last Months in Iraq', *The New York Times* (2012, 23 September), p. A1.
299 Shwan Ziad, Interview with Author, 20 August 2008, Washington, D.C.
300 Lincoln Davis quoted in *PM Barzani Attends Launch of Kurdish-American Caucus.* (2008). [Kurdistan Regional Government] Available at: URL: www.krg.org/articles/detail.asp?smap=02010100&lngnr=12&asnr=&anr=24345&rnr=223 Access Date: 20 June 2008.
301 Lincoln Davis quoted in *New Congressional Caucus Meets with Local Kurds.* (2008). [Nashville Public Radio] Available at: URL: http://wpln.org/?p=2606 Access Date: 20 June 2008.
302 Francis Ricciardone quoted in *US Warns of Chaos, Disintegration in Iraq.* (2013). [Hurriyet Daily News] Available at: URL: http://www.hurriyetdailynews.com/us-warns-of-chaos-disintegration-in-iraq.aspx?PageID=238&NID=40575&NewsCatID=359 Access Date: 20 March 2013.
303 Ofra Bengio. (2012). *Will the Kurds Get Their Way.* [The American Interest] Available at: URL: www.the-american-interest.com/article.cfm?piece=1323 Access Date: 10 July 2013.
304 Hiltermann (2012), op. cit., pp. 20–1.
305 Emma Sky, 'Iraq, From Surge to Sovereignty', *Foreign Affairs* Vol. 90, No. 2 (2011): p. 124.
306 Jen Psaki. (2013). *US Department of State Department: Daily Press Briefing.* Available at: URL: www.state.gov/r/pa/prs/dpb/2013/07/211535.htm Access Date: 4 July 2013.
307 Ayal Frank, Interview with Author, 11 June 2008, Washington, D.C.
308 Charountaki (2011), op. cit., pp. 256–7.
309 Olson (2005), p. 244.
310 Qubad Talabani, Interview with Author, 31 July 2008, Washington, D.C.

7 Conclusion

Now, Iraq is not a perfect place. It has many challenges ahead. But we're leaving behind a sovereign, stable and self-reliant Iraq, with a representative government that was elected by its people. We're building a new partnership between our nations. And we are ending a war not with a final battle, but with a final march toward home.

Barack Obama, 14 December 2011[1]

This book has addressed America's Iraq policy at three major levels: the supra-national, the national and the sub-national, in order to assess US foreign policy as one of continuity or change. The national level (the second level of this study) has been restricted to US policy towards Arab Iraq; the third level, however, has addressed US Iraq policy at the sub-national level, focusing on US-Kurdish relations.

At the supra-national level (the first level of this study), US foreign policy is directly a function of US Grand Strategy. The period covered presents visible departures in that Grand Strategy, which reflect constantly on US policy towards Iraq at both the national and sub-national levels. For the 1961–2014 timeline covered in this book, US Iraq policy corresponds neatly to the three Grand Strategies transcending the period. Phase I (1961–1990) was Cold War influenced. Phase II (1991–2000) was influenced by a Liberal Internationalist Grand Strategy; and Phase III (2001–2014) was influenced by the War on Terror. These distinct transitions in Grand Strategy are highly relevant for testing consistencies and departures in US Iraq policy. As the overarching global guiding tool, Grand Strategy is supreme above any other considerations in US foreign policy. As a superpower, America adapted effectively to these different periods of its Grand Strategy, affecting subsequently its regional and bilateral interactions. Since Grand Strategy takes precedence over regional geostrategic foreign policy calculations and bilateral foreign policy interactions, US Iraq policy fell naturally into these three different realms.

The first phase of US Iraq policy covered in this book conformed to the Cold War Grand Strategy. This era of US Iraq policy was defined by the broader policy parameters prescribed to this period. During the Cold War era America's grand strategic purpose was predominantly defined as the containment and deterrence of the ideological spread of communism.[2] Cold War presidents shared the conviction that public and elite support for foreign policy could be most effectively built on a strategic framework of global, anti-communist containment. This strategy of containment represented the best way to stop further Soviet and Soviet-sponsored expansion.[3] Within this context the primary objective was to contain Iraq, limiting any advances made towards its special relationship with the Soviet Union. This era was characterised by the use of the Iraqi Kurds as a pawn to contain the Soviet ally Iraq. In July 1972, the CIA sponsored the Kurdish movement in order to assist the Shah's Iran in its fight to contain Soviet influence penetrating the Middle East through its proxy Iraq. Iran was one of the pillars in America's fight to contain the Soviet Union, and Iraq was becoming a threat to US interests and allies in the region. To the US then, Iraq's April 1972 strategic agreement with the Soviet Union meant it had to be contained. Ironically, history later repeated itself when this containment strategy was revived after Iraq's occupation of Kuwait, with the Kurds involved in containing and weakening the Baath regime in Baghdad.

With the end of the Cold War, the foreign policy strategy of President George H. W. Bush was one of post-Cold War order-building. This was based on building and strengthening institutions – essentially a Liberal Internationalist Grand Strategy. Bush wanted the US to recreate a New World Order under US leadership and in pursuit of its goals use multilateralism to achieve them. Following the collapse of the Soviet Union the Bush senior administration put on course and articulated steps with the objective of expanding NATO, establishing greater interaction with the European Community and widening the role of the Conference on Security Cooperation in Europe. On the regional level, the Bush administration pushed for the North American Free Trade Agreement and in East Asia helped create the Asia-Pacific Economic Cooperation.[4] With this new mindset the US dealt with Saddam's aggression on Kuwait through the UN. An international consensus to liberate Kuwait from Saddam Hussein's regime was built through the UN Security Council. The liberation of Kuwait, as well as the multilateral approach that was exhausted in achieving the goal, was hailed as a major victory for a New World Order.

Continuing this trend, the Clinton administration pursued its strategy of 'enlargement' through institution-building. This strategy involved using multilateral institutions to integrate and stabilise new and emerging market democracies into the democratic Western world. The Clinton administration went to great lengths to make the World Trade Organization a reality, a major step towards establishing international trade law. As Clinton's National Security Advisor Anthony Lake noted, the idea was to 'foster and consolidate new democracies and market economies where possible'.[5] Within this context and in this international environment, the Clinton administration pursued and made possible the continuation of Security Council consensus to endorse the UN-mandated sanctions regime on Iraq.

This strategy of 'enlargement' was followed by the third era of Grand Strategy, described as the War on Terror. In terms of continuity with the previous administration, the Bush presidency was already in continuance with that of President Clinton. Unilateralism was already on the agenda from the mid 1990s onward, mainly due to the Republican takeover of Congress in January 1995 after the mid-term elections, and to the emergence of the United States as an unrivalled international military and economic power.[6] The increasing terrorist attacks on US interests in Africa and the Middle East were the third factor. The flexibility enjoyed by the Clinton administration in its early years had diminished by 1995. In 1998 the US retaliated against Afghanistan and Sudan for harbouring al-Qaeda. In Sudan, the US destroyed a pharmaceutical plant it claimed was producing chemical weapons. This attack was a precursor to the US invasion of Iraq, with the same intention of destroying production facilities for WMD. It was also a precedent for the 2001 invasion of Afghanistan, where a terrorist-associated nation was attacked without the authorisation from the UN Security Council. Other contemporary examples of US unilateralism, endorsed by a 'coalition of the willing', include the 1999 US intervention in Kosovo which had no explicit UN resolution. Operation Desert Fox in Iraq in 1998, executed by the Clinton administration and similar to Operation Iraqi Freedom in 2003, had no Security Council authorisation other than the numerous resolutions condemning Iraqi non-compliance. An older example of the US unilateral tradition is the 1948 Berlin airlift under President Truman which had no UN mandate.[7]

The end of the Cold War brought positive and negative consequences for the Middle East. Of the positive, the most important was the end to superpower rivalry and interference associated with vital strategic interests in the region. However, the most immediate negative repercussion of the Cold War's conclusion was the perceived relaxation of political impediments, which led to Saddam Hussein's invasion of Kuwait. This result gave rise to the 'jihadist' struggle of Osama Bin Laden and other Islamist factions and provided a new thrust to Political Islam in the Middle East.[8] The US-led military campaign to expel Iraq from Kuwait brought major US military bases to Saudi Arabia that remained in the country long after the Iraqi defeat. Saddam's invasion of Kuwait had brought a sense of insecurity to the oil-rich, security-deficient and US-dependent Gulf States. This in turn invited a Western presence that perhaps contributed to the attacks on 9/11, for the presence of these US bases fuelled Islamic extremists, destabilised Saudi Arabia and led to a full-fledged insurrection against the US. Islamic jihadists already believed they had defeated the Soviets in Afghanistan in 1989, and thus they were determined to force a US withdrawal from Muslim lands.

Although the foreign policy of George W. Bush was continuing an already established unilateral trend before the 9/11 attacks, it was characterised by a sharp departure in US Grand Strategy, a shift from the Liberal Internationalist agenda pursued by Clinton. The attacks on 9/11 and the seriousness of Islamic extremism had essentially done what the Soviet threat had achieved during the Truman administration: it encouraged a rethinking of US strategy. Bush's September 2002 National Security Strategy argued for a dramatic rethinking of the international order and condemned the fact that it had taken 'almost a decade' to 'comprehend the true nature of this threat' – that threat being the bloody and dramatic nature of Islamic extremism. The US had already suffered major terrorist attacks on its interests during the Clinton presidency: the bombings of the Khobar Towers in Saudi Arabia (1996), US embassies in Tanzania and Kenya (1998) and the *USS Cole* in Yemen's port of Aden (2000). The Bush administration's policy was a return to America's nineteenth century policies of unilateralism, as opposed to its role as 'multilateral alliance leader and institution builder' of the twentieth century.[9] Essentially, Bush's 2002 NSS Grand Strategy for a War on Terror was on a par both in terms of significance as well as in substance to Truman's National Security Council Report 68 in 1950, which advocated a Cold War Grand Strategy of globalised containment.

Moreover, US unilateral intervention and the promotion of democracy were on the US foreign policy agenda long before George W. Bush's accession to power. An early instance of such a venture was the US invasion of foreign territory during the Spanish America war in 1898, in which demands for Cuban self-determination and the subjugation of natives in Spanish colonies were cited as a cause for concern, in addition to the alleged and still disputed sinking of the *USS Maine* by a Spanish mine. The very same scenario was repeated during the invasion of Iraq when the chemical attacks on the Kurds and human rights abuses of the Baath regime, plus Iraq's alleged possession of stocks of WMD, were invoked as a cause for intervention. The Vietnam War is also consistent with this theme where the Gulf of Tonkin incident in 1964 was used to justify drawing the US into the conflict after two alleged attacks by North Vietnamese torpedo boats.

US foreign policy is predominantly characterised by its consistency. US foreign policy may veer left and right, but always pulls back toward the centre as a result of a political gravity reasserting itself.[10] US foreign policy is characterised by a consistent four-stage repetitive cycle. This can be applied to most US interventions throughout history. The first stage is the 'shock' stage where the US finds itself subject to aggression. The British provocations associated with the war of 1812, the sinking of the *USS Maine*, the attack on Pearl Harbor, the Gulf of Tonkin incident and the attacks of 9/11 were all received with shock in response to acts of unprovoked aggression. The second phase, which is repeated throughout these incidents, is a two-stage reaction. The first is a 'realist' reaction, addressing the problem in order to prevent it from reoccurring, and restabilising the status quo. This stage is concerned with bringing the perpetrators to justice. The second stage of the reaction is the 'metaphysical' stage, at which point the need for retribution, 'forced upon' the US to carry out, becomes an act of ending tyranny and evil. It becomes an attempt at defeating oppression and bringing freedom to the people. The third stage of this oft-repeated cycle is 'overreach'. During this stage, mission creep becomes a constant feature of these US military interventions, with the US adopting a goal that exceeds both its capabilities and its commitment threshold. Finally, these three steps end with the 'holdback' stage, a return to cautious realism, as was the case with the US military withdrawal from Iraq under the Obama administration.[11]

This is not to say the US invasion of Iraq is common practice for America. In only two other instances in America's military history did the US veer out of the Western hemisphere when no immediate threat was posed to US national security. One parallel to the Iraq invasion, smaller in scale but also not mandated by the UN, was the Cambodian campaign of May–June 1970, in which the American military launched several incursions into sovereign Cambodian territory as part of the Vietnam War. A second example would be the US invasion of North Korea in 1950. This too had no explicit UN authorisation, despite the wider Korean War being fought under UN auspices. Though both examples show remarkable resemblance to the Iraq venture, they do not in any shape or form reflect the scale and objectives of the US campaign in Iraq and the relatively lengthy occupation of the country.

The objectives of democracy-promotion and respect for human rights have been guiding points of influence on US foreign policy since the country's founding in 1776. The Declaration of Independence, the preamble of the US constitution and the Bill of Rights are the foundation stones of US foreign policy idealism. The importance of these values and the belief in their universality are unique to the United States. Thus the promotion of democracy and the defence of human rights abroad is inherently a US principle and is by no means a concept introduced by the George W. Bush administration, his predecessors or the Obama administration or any of the future successors. The heightened emphasis of this attribute under the Bush administration was instead only a reaction, one based on a belief that genuine stability could not be achieved unless these principles were planted in Iraq and elsewhere in the Middle East.

The US then has a long history of intervening in sovereign states primarily, of course, in the Western hemisphere, without international authorisation to achieve regime change and promote democracy. One of the most recent of these was the invasion of Grenada in October 1983, under the Reagan administration, controversially conducted to overthrow Marxist revolutionaries and install democratic rule. Another example is the US invasion of Panama to depose General Manuel Noriega in December 1989. One of the reasons given for the invasion was to defend democracy and human rights in Panama. After the invasion the democratically elected Guillermo Galimany was sworn into the presidential office. Under the Clinton administration in July 1994, the UN Security Council issued resolution 940 authorising a US-led military campaign, codenamed 'Operation Uphold Democracy', to restore the democratically elected government of Jean-Bertrand Aristide in Haiti.

As regards the US policy of regime change in Iraq, this has remained constant since Iraq's occupation of Kuwait. Indeed, this was a policy objective first devised by President George H. W. Bush and signed in October 1991, in an authorised presidential 'lethal finding' authorising the CIA to facilitate the overthrow of Saddam Hussein.[12] This policy continued into the Clinton administration, in addition to the already pursued sanctions-based containment, which essentially became known as 'containment-plus'. It was also the Clinton administration that signed the Iraq Liberation Act into law, making it a declared US policy to topple Saddam's regime. Bush senior had anticipated regime change after his re-election in late 1992; neither of these goals materialised but the policy remained intact. After the Iraq defeat and expulsion from Kuwait in 1991, UN Security Council resolution 686 set out the terms of the ceasefire, signed by both US General Norman Schwarzkopf and Iraqi General Sultan Hashim on 3 March 1991 in Iraq near the Kuwaiti border. The war and the resolution that followed had achieved the initial stated goal of returning Kuwait sovereignty. However, UNSCR 686 was soon augmented and succeeded by resolution 687. Section I (paragraph 33) of resolution 687 stated the conditionality of the ceasefire, contingent upon Iraq's dismantling and destruction of all proscribed WMD. Iraq failed to achieve this numerous times (the last being during the last round of inspections in November 2002), in other words failing to satisfy US suspicions over its claims of total destruction. As a result of heightened fears following 9/11 and the US government's genuine belief at the time that Saddam Hussein had accumulated stockpiles of WMD, it was logical that the 'conditional ceasefire' be invoked to settle the Iraq issue permanently.

Following Saddam's occupation of Kuwait, the economic sanctions imposed initially in resolution UNSCR 661 and then drafted in 687 were only reintroduced to further pressure the Iraqi regime, in the hope that this would accelerate its downfall. This is despite the fact that the sanctions initially were a tool only to bring about Iraq's withdrawal from Kuwait, and with no relevance to a post-liberation environment. UNSCR 687 was essentially a UN-mandated but US-designed document for regime change. Indeed, the US had no intention whatsoever of allowing these sanctions to be lifted and permitting Iraq a return to normality. The economic sanctions imposed on the regime had very little to do with the disarmament demanded of Iraq. The sanctions were instead merely an attempt to weaken the regime with the objective of its eventual downfall, rather than an exercise in punishment for non-compliance with articles of resolution 687. As the nature of resolution 687 was strict and did not correspond to its initial objective of liberating Kuwait, the US made its ratification possible by introducing paragraph 14, purportedly to allow for the creation in the Middle East of 'a zone free from weapons of mass destruction', only to mollify reluctant Security Council members.[13] This paragraph was considered a 'throwaway' paragraph by US policy makers, who had no intention of implementing it.[14]

Secretary of State Madeleine Albright, in a speech delivered at Georgetown University on 26 March 1996, stated that the sanctions against Iraq would not be lifted as long as Saddam Hussein remained in power. This was two years before the passage of the Iraq Liberation Act, which called for replacing Saddam with a democratic government. During the campaign of George W. Bush, Condoleezza Rice asserted in 2000 that Saddam had 'no useful place in international politics'. The policy of regime change was a constant in US policy, reiterated throughout the presidencies of three successive administrations and therefore neither new nor novel as a US policy objective. Secretary of State James Baker had disclosed US views vividly and unequivocally on 23 May 1991 when he stated that the US could have a 'formal ceasefire but no genuine peace' as long as Saddam remained in power, and that Iraq would not join the international community until there was a 'change in regime'.[15]

The end of the First Gulf War was only an end to major conventional kinetic warfare and by no means an end of hostilities. The very nature of the conditionality made the continuation of peace between the US and Iraq dependent on the implementation of the operative paragraphs of resolution 687. As a result, the US and Iraq were at a constant state of war from 1991 onwards, well in advance of the actual regime change and before the declaration of the Bush Doctrine in 2002. In early August 2002, while briefing the NSC on the military's plan to invade Iraq, General Tommy Franks, CENTCOM commander, informed the president that Iraqi air defences had that year targeted US aircraft or violated the No-fly zones fifty-two times, double the number of 2001.[16] In 1999 and 2000 Saddam's forces had fired seven hundred times at US pilots patrolling the No-fly zones.[17] The US was also retaliating for these attacks. In this light it is evident that the Iraq war was not pre-emptive in many senses. The US had been carrying out an ongoing military campaign in Iraq through continued airstrikes since 1991. The very fact that the US was containing Iraq – itself a form of military action – through the enforcement of No-fly zones is another testament to this argument. Additionally, pre-emption itself was not a new concept in US military policy. Brent Scowcroft argued that this had always been a valid resort in US policy. The use of pre-emptive force was only viewed as an innovation because it had never been made public in any official US document or presidential statements.[18]

With regard to US interests in Iraq at the national level, there are five major areas of concern that have dominated US–Iraq relations since 1979 and beyond:[19] a secure supply of oil, concerns about Iraqi sponsorship of terrorism, the proliferation of WMD, the containment of Iran and Iraq's role in the Arab-Israeli dispute. Iraq has had a history of being seen by the US as a potential source of threat through its WMD programmes. The earliest of these concerns was raised in 1973 with Congressman Robert Huber's (R-MI) floor speech to the US Congress on possible Soviet supplies of chemical weapons to Iraq.[20] The issue of WMD was also discussed, however casually, in Donald Rumsfeld's first and second encounters with Iraqi officials in the early 1980s. With respect to terrorism, as early as 1979 Iraq was a member of the US State Department's first state sponsors of terrorism list. All these issues during Saddam's reign (some even preceding Saddam Hussein's presidency) have constantly and continuously directed US Iraq policy.

Worth noting also is since the US inception to superpower status, Iraq has always been seen as a function of US policy towards Iran. During the Kurdish revolt of 1974, American covert support for the Iraqi Kurds was provided in the context of helping Iran. In the first instance the Kurds were used as pawns to weaken a hostile Iraq, whilst following the overthrow of the Shah, Iraq was used to weaken Iran and, ideally, create out of Iraq the long-needed ally lost in the Shah's Iran. The US has seen Iraq through the lenses of its interests and the geopolitical significance of Iran. During the Shah's reign Iraq was seen as a rogue element affecting Iran's regional interests. After the Shah was overthrown, it was seen as a check on Iranian influence in the region. A 6 May 1965 State Department document sent to the US embassy in Baghdad makes clear that it was seen to be in the interests of both the US and Iran that Iraq and Iran improve their bilateral relations.[21] The US containment strategy of Iraq in the 1990s likewise included Iran in the calculus. The strategy of neutrality, pursued during the early years of the Iran–Iraq war in the 1980s, was also implemented to achieve the same goal. Years later, the toppling of Saddam and the creation of a democratic state in neighbouring Iraq would, in the eyes of American policy makers at least, serve as a catalyst in Iran, helping to dethrone the theocratic regime.

The five factors mentioned above are constants in US Iraq policy that have remained to this day. The only departures have been in the strategies pursued in achieving them. These five constants are also a function of three regional constants defining US Middle East policy: access to oil resources, the security of Israel and intense US opposition to the emergence of potential regional powers. At the regional level, US policy towards the Middle East has been surprisingly clear and consistent. What distinguishes the Middle East from the rest of the world (compared to Africa, Latin America and Asia) is America's unwillingness to soften, much less renounce, its hegemonic role; or even more significantly, its willingness to act in such opposition to world public opinion with respect to a fair resolution of the Israel/Palestine conflict.[22] These three US regional concerns, in addition to the five above-mentioned national concerns, have consistently guided US policy and consequently have been pursued within US global Grand Strategy.

US Iraq policy has been one of consistency as opposed to new departures. Seen as a rogue state and considered a threat to Israel and oil supplies for many years, Iraq was first perceived as a threat to US interests after the overthrow of the monarchy in 1958, until February 1963 when a coalition of Baathists and nationalists gained power. However, the Baathist rhetoric during this period then too became a source of US concern. The US saw the removal of the Baath Party from power in November 1963 as being favourable to the revival of healthy US–Iraq relations. Iraq however then broke off diplomatic relations with the US in response to its support for Israel in the Six-Day War of 1967. The positive US attitude changed once again with the Baath Party's resumption of power in a 1968 coup. From that time until 2003 Iraq was not looked upon favourably as an ally or friend by the United States. Even as the US supported Saddam during the Iran–Iraq war, one of its objectives was to allow the weakening of both hostile regimes. Iraq was used as a pawn to contain Iran, and to maintain the regional balance of power.

A policy is a vision, a view and a goal. US foreign policy towards Iraq has been for the most part consistent in its goals. What has happened is that different issues have gained heightened attention at different times. The goals mentioned above have been amplified or reduced in relative importance based on the geopolitical context of the era. What could also be argued is that different strategies have been pursued, adopted and then adjusted to achieve these goals. In essence what has changed are the strategies (what to do) and tactics (how to do it) when it has come to issues of US foreign policy relating to Iraq.

As for the 2003 US-led military campaign in Iraq, if taken within a broader historical context, it becomes remarkably similar to the British invasion of Iraq in November 1914. The British occupation forces experienced two phases after the fall of Baghdad in 1917. The same history of the British occupation repeated itself for the US in Iraq after the 2003 invasion. The first phase would involve full engagement in the country in order to bring about fundamental change in the way Iraq was governed. This would require immense resources and time to achieve. The second would be to facilitate the creation of a new Iraqi government, one that would bring order to the country and respect the strategic regional interests of the occupying power, eventually allowing withdrawal from the country. The second phase would mean recognising the existing power structure in Iraq. The occupying power, when faced by internal resistance and significant loss of lives and treasure, would avoid a state-building project and take the second route, and disengage from Iraq's internal affairs. In this case, it would favour lesser risks and costs, preferring the short-term advantages of sustainable social transformation.[23] The US did exactly this. Upon claiming the role of occupying power, the United States engaged in a highly ambitious project of reforming and transforming Iraq. Highly progressive and liberal market rules were introduced, and a bill of rights was drafted on a par with Western democracies. The US, however, was confronted with major obstacles: growing internal public resentment, an insurgency, hostility of regional and international powers and the lack of support from previous opposition groups. This environment drove the US to opt for the second option, where the creation of an Iraqi government was eventually chosen.

The second major dimension of this study was US Iraq policy at the sub-national level. In particular it has focused on the US-Kurdish relationship from 1961 onwards, a highly important area of US foreign policy but one that, for the most part, has been ignored in contemporary scholarship. The same can be said for consistency in US policy towards Kurdish Iraq under George W. Bush, his predecessors and the Obama administration that followed. A Circular Airgram sent from the State Department on 2 March 1963, shortly after the inception of Kurdish revolt in 1961, defines the US policy position as one of finding a political solution within Iraq's national boundaries. It was US policy that the Iraqi government and the Kurds would be able to 'come promptly to a mutually satisfactory agreement'.[24] The US did not contemplate a policy towards the Kurds that could allow for an independent state. Its policy towards the Kurds was always one in which the Kurds were part of a greater Arab Iraq, with Baghdad as its capital. This remained a constant policy objective throughout the George W. Bush and Obama administrations, as the US under Bush and Obama dealt with the Kurdish nationalist movement and the KRG within the confines of Iraq. Second, the 1963 document stipulates that the Kurdish issue is 'strictly an internal Iraqi matter'. This US policy of neutrality has also remained largely unaltered since the US avoided taking sides with the Kurds after the overthrow of Saddam Hussein. An area of major departure under Bush, however, was the actual US occupation of Iraq. The 'strictly hands-off policy' that the 1963 document prescribed changed after the 2003 overthrow due to direct US influence in Iraq. The third constant, detailed in a 6 August 1963 declassified State Department document, was also highly consistent with Bush's and Obama's policy towards Iraq's Kurds. It saw validity and legitimacy in their demands merely on sympathetic grounds, not on the grounds of vital US interests.[25] The position described in a US State Department telegram to the US Embassy in Baghdad on 5 April 1963 defines two other policies that remained largely intact under Bush and later the Obama administration.[26] The fourth constant: the US perceived its relations and interests with Arab Iraq as being far superior to its sympathies for Kurdish nationalist aspirations. The fifth constant, a position both Presidents Bush and Obama continued – considered Kurdish nationalist aspirations as maximalist; the same document reflected the same attitude towards Kurdish aspirations and advised compromise on their demands for autonomy. A sixth factor was the US interest in maintaining stability in Iraq and the Middle East. The US advised the Kurds to avoid being used as 'agents for interests of others' in a 16 December 1964 US embassy telegram.[27] America urged the Kurdish movement to use restraint in its opposition to the government in Baghdad. This has also remained the same throughout the intervening years and during the Bush presidency and the Obama administration that followed.

Notes

1 Barack Obama. (2011). *Remarks by the President and First Lady on the End of the War in Iraq.* The White House. Available at: URL: www.whitehouse.gov/the-press-office/2011/12/14/remarks-president-and-first-lady-end-war-iraq Access Date: 20 May 2013.
2 Steven Wright, *Analysing United States Foreign Policy Towards the Middle East 1993–2003: Origins and Grand Strategies.* PhD thesis, University of Durham, 2005, p. 4.
3 Richard Melanson, *American Foreign Policy Since the Vietnam War: The Search for Consensus from Richard Nixon to George W. Bush* (New York: M.E. Sharpe, 2005), pp. 4–8.
4 John Ikenberry, *After Victory: Institutions, Strategic Restraint, and the Rebuilding of Order After Major Wars* (Princeton: Princeton University Press, 2001), p. 234.
5 Ibid., pp. 235 and 244.
6 John Dumbrell, 'Unilateralism and "America First"? President George W. Bush's Foreign Policy', *The Political Quarterly* Vol. 73, No. 3 (2002), p. 282.
7 Condoleezza Rice, *No Higher Honor: A Memoir of My Years in Washington* (New York: Crown Publishers, 2011), p. 204.
8 Richard Falk, 'The Global Setting: US Foreign Policy and the Future of the Middle East', in *The Iraq War and Democratic Politics*, ed. Alex Danchev and John Macmillan *et al.* (Oxford: Routledge, 2005), p. 24.
9 Daniel Deudney and Jeffrey Meiser, 'American Exceptionalism', in *US Foreign Policy*, ed. Michael Cox and Doug Stokes (Oxford: Oxford University Press, 2008), p. 40.
10 Walter Russell Mead. (2003). *US Foreign Policy and the American Political Tradition.* [University of California, Berkeley: Institute of International Studies] Available

at: URL: http://globetrotter.berkeley.edu/people3/Mead/mead-con4.html Access Date: 15 March 2008.

11 Adam Garfinkle, Interview with Author, 7 August 2008, Washington, D.C.

12 Scott Ritter, *Iraq Confidential: The Untold Story of America's Intelligence Conspiracy* (London: I.B. Tauris, 2005), pp. 47 and 128.

13 Ibid., p. 4.

14 Ibid., p. 5.

15 James Baker. (1991). *Congressional Testimony: Hearing of the Subcommittee of the Committee on Appropriations on Foreign Operations, Export Financing and Related Agencies Appropriations for Fiscal Year 1992.* Washington, D.C.

16 Tommy Franks with Malcolm McConnell, *American Soldier* (New York: Harper-Collins, 2004), p. 388.

17 George W. Bush, *Decision Points* (New York: Crown Publishers, 2010), p. 228.

18 Brent Scowcroft quoted in Ivo Daalder and James Lindsay, *America Unbound: The Bush Revolution in Foreign Policy* (Maryland: The Brookings Institution, 2003), p. 126.

19 Lawrence Freedman, *A Choice of Enemies: America Confronts the Middle East* (New York: PublicAffairs, 2008), p. 158.

20 Lokman Meho, *The Kurdish Question in US Foreign Policy: A Documentary Sourcebook* (Connecticut: Praeger Publishers, 2004), p. 29.

21 Ibid., p. 462.

22 Falk (2005), op. cit., p. 23.

23 Charles Tripp. (2003). *Iraq: The Imperial Precedent.* [Le Monde Diplomatique] Available at: URL: www.globalpolicy.org/component/content/article/169/36402.html Access Date: 20 June, 2008.

24 Meho (2004), op. cit., p. 445.

25 Ibid., p. 451.

26 Ibid., p. 450.

27 Ibid., p. 460.

Bibliography

1 List of interviews

Name	Date	Location	Position
Academics			
Dr Aziz Barzani	14 September 2011	From the Kurdistan Region of Iraq by e-mail	Lecturer in History at the Department of History in the University of Salahaddin in Erbil, Kurdistan Region, Iraq.
Dr Mary-Jane Deeb	30 June 2008	Washington, D.C. Audio recording of the interview retained.	Chief of the African and Middle Eastern Division, Library of Congress in Washington, D.C. Middle East expert and former editor of *The Middle East Journal*.
Professor Edmund Ghareeb	22 August 2008	Washington, D.C. Copy of notes taken during the interview retained.	Mustafa Barzani Scholar of Global Kurdish Studies at the Centre for Global Peace and Adjunct Professor of Middle East History and Politics at the School of International Service in the American University in Washington, D.C.
Dr Marc Lynch	24 June 2008	Washington, D.C. Audio recording of the interview retained.	Associate Professor of Political Science and International Affairs and Director of the Institute for Middle East Studies at The Elliot School of International Affairs, The George Washington University in Washington, D.C.

continued

Name	Date	Location	Position
Professor Carole O'Leary	8 August 2008	Washington, D.C. Audio recording of the interview retained.	Programme Director and Scholar-in-Residence at the Centre for Global Peace and Research Professor at the School of International Service in the American University in Washington, D.C.
Think tank scholars			
Dr Jon Alterman	26 August 2008	Washington, D.C. Audio recording of the interview retained.	Director and Senior Fellow, Middle East Programme at the Centre for Strategic and International Studies in Washington, D.C. Former member of the Policy Planning Staff at the US Department of State and Special Assistant to the Assistant Secretary of State for Near Eastern affairs.
Dr Nabil Al-Tikriti	18 June 2008	Washington, D.C. Audio recording of the interview retained.	Jennings Randolph Fellow at the US Institute of Peace in Washington, D.C. and Assistant Professor of History at the University of Mary Washington in Virginia.
Dr Ariel Cohen	7 August 2008 25 August 2008	Washington, D.C. Audio recording of the interviews retained.	Senior Research Fellow, The Kathryn and Shelby Cullom Davis Institute for International Studies at The Heritage Foundation in Washington, D.C.
Jason Gluck	27 June 2008	Washington, D.C. Audio recording of the interview retained.	Senior Rule of Law Adviser at the Rule of Law Centre of Innovation at the United States Institute of Peace in Washington, D.C.
Professor James Goldgeier	10 July 2008	Washington, D.C. Audio recording of the interview retained.	Whitney Shepardson Senior Fellow for Transatlantic Relations at the Council on Foreign Relations and Professor of Political Science and International Affairs at The Elliot School of International Affairs, The George Washington University in Washington, D.C.

Name	Date	Location	Position
Dr Frederick Kagan	25 July 2008	Washington, D.C. Audio recording of the interview retained.	Resident Scholar and Director of the Critical Threats Project at the American Enterprise Institute in Washington, D.C. He is also one of the intellectual architects of the 'surge' strategy in Iraq.
Dr Phebe Marr	19 June 2008	Washington, D.C. Audio recording of the interview retained.	Senior Fellow at the United States Institute of Peace in Washington, D.C. Former expert advisor to the Political Development Group of the Iraq Study Group which prepared the *Baker–Hamilton Report*.
Sam Parker	27 June 2008 21 July 2008	Washington, D.C. Audio recording of the interviews retained.	Iraq Programme Officer in the Centre for Post-Conflict Peace and Stability Operations at the United States Institute of Peace in Washington, D.C.
Dr Daniel Pipes	23 July 2008	Washington, D.C. Audio recording of the interview retained.	Director of the Middle East Forum and Taube distinguished visiting fellow at the Hoover Institution of Stanford University.
Dr David Pollock	17 July 2008 24 July 2008	Washington, D.C. Audio recording of the interviews retained.	Senior Fellow at the Washington Institute for Near East Policy in Washington, D.C.
Shwan Ziad	20 August 2008	Washington, D.C. Audio recording of the interview retained.	Director, Washington Kurdish Institute in Washington, D.C.
Government and political figures			
Anonymity Requested	18 June 2008	Washington, D.C. Audio recording of the interview retained.	State Department Official in Washington, D.C.
Anonymity Requested	2 July 2008	Washington, D.C. Audio recording of the interview retained.	Senior Professional Staff Member, US Congress, House Foreign Affairs Committee.
Anonymity Requested	9 July 2008	Washington, D.C. Copy of notes taken during the interview retained.	Senior Iraqi Diplomat I, Iraqi Embassy in Washington, D.C.
Anonymity Requested	11 July 2008	Washington, D.C. Audio recording of the interview retained.	National Security Council Official, The White House.

continued

Name	Date	Location	Position
Anonymity Requested	31 July 2008	Washington, D.C. Audio recording of the interview retained.	Senior Iraqi Diplomat II, Iraqi Embassy in Washington, D.C.
Anonymity Requested	8 August 2008	Washington, D.C. Copy of notes taken during the interview retained.	Former foreign policy advisor and personal representative of Member to the Senate Foreign Relations Committee.
Falah Bakir	12 May 2011 24 May 2011	From the UK by e-mail	Head of the Kurdistan Regional Government's Department of Foreign Relations (minister) – Erbil, Iraqi Kurdistan.
Hikmat Bamarni	16 July 2008	Washington, D.C. Audio recording of the interview retained.	Head of the Kurdistan Democratic Party's 7th Branch for North America and Consul General of the Republic of Iraq to the United States.
Professor Henri Barkey	21 August 2008	Washington, D.C. Audio recording of the interview retained.	Bernard L. and Bertha F. Cohen Professor at Lehigh University in Pennsylvania. Former member of the Policy Planning Staff at the US Department of State.
Ayal Frank	11 June 2008	Washington, D.C. Audio recording of the interview retained.	Senior advisor to the Kurdistan Regional Government's Representation to the United States. Former Senior Legislative Assistant to member of House of Representatives.
Ambassador Peter Galbraith	18 July 2008 8 August 2008	From Washington, D.C. by Telephone Audio recording of the interviews retained.	Former Senior Professional Staff Member for the US Senate Committee on Foreign Relations and first US Ambassador to Croatia.
Dr Adam Garfinkle	7 August 2008	Washington, D.C. Audio recording of the interview retained.	Editor of *The American Interest* magazine. Former Speechwriter to US Secretaries of State Colin Powell and Condoleezza Rice.

Name	Date	Location	Position
Lieutenant General Jay Garner (US Army-Ret.)	19 September 2008	From the UK by Telephone Audio recording of the interview retained.	Director of the Office for Reconstruction and Humanitarian Assistance (ORHA) in 2003 and Commanding General Operation Provide Comfort in northern Iraq (1991).
Colonel Paul Hughes (US Army-Ret.)	29 July 2008	Washington, D.C. Audio recording of the interview retained.	Director of Iraq programs in the Centre for Post-Conflict Peace and Stability Operations at the United States Institute of Peace in Washington, D.C. Former senior staff officer for ORHA and later with the Coalition Provisional Authority (CPA) in Iraq.
Dr Najmaldin Karim	8 July 2008	Washington, D.C. Audio recording of the interview retained.	Governor of Kirkuk Province since 29 March 2011. President of the Washington Kurdish Institute in Washington, D.C. and founding member of the Kurdish National Congress of North America, served as its President from 1991 to 1999. Former member of the Iraqi Council of Representatives.
Dr Kenneth Katzman	10 July 2008	Washington, D.C. Audio recording of the interview retained.	Senior Middle East analyst at the Congressional Research Service in the US Congress in Washington, D.C. Former CIA Officer and Professional Staff Member, US Congress, House Foreign Affairs Committee.
Dr Richard Kessler	2 July 2008	Washington, D.C. Audio recording of the interview retained.	Subcommittee Staff Director at the US Senate Committee on Homeland Security and Governmental Affairs. From November 2008, Staff Director, Committee on Foreign Affairs at US House of Representatives.

continued

Name	Date	Location	Position
Dr Asad Khailany	5 July 2009	From the UK by Telephone Audio recording of the interview retained.	Former senior member and head of the 5th branch of the Kurdistan Democratic Party in Baghdad and founder and first president of the Kurdish National Congress of North America.
Congressman James Longley Jr	22 July 2008	Washington, D.C. Audio recording of the interview retained.	Former Lieutenant Colonel, US Marine Corps (Ret.). Major US Marine Corps during Operation Provide Comfort in northern Iraq (1991), and former member of the US House of Representatives (R-ME).
Ambassador David Mack	27 August 2008	Washington, D.C. Audio recording of the interview retained.	Vice President of the Middle East Institute. Former Deputy Assistant Secretary of State for Near Eastern Affairs.
Andrew Morrison	21 August 2008	Washington, D.C. Audio recording of the interview retained.	Senior State Department official at the UN political office of the Bureau of International Organization Affairs. Former head of the State Department's Iraq desk (1997–1999) and senior CPA official in Iraq.
Dr Meghan O'Sullivan	17 September 2008	From the UK by Telephone Audio recording of the interview retained.	Jeane Kirkpatrick Professor of the Practice of International Affairs, Harvard Kennedy School. Former Special Assistant to President George W. Bush and Deputy National Security Advisor for Iraq and Afghanistan. Former ORHA official and political adviser and assistant to Paul Bremer in the CPA. And prior to that member of the Policy Planning Staff at the US Department of State.

Name	Date	Location	Position
Richard Perle	24 September 2008	From the UK by Telephone Audio recording of the interview retained.	Former Chairman of the Defense Policy Board Advisory Committee (2001–2003) and Assistant Secretary of Defense for International Security Policy (1981–1987).
Professor Paul Pillar	15 July 2008	Washington, D.C. Audio recording of the interview retained.	Professor of Security Studies at Georgetown University in Washington, D.C. Former National Intelligence Officer for the Near East and South Asia (2000–2005), and Deputy Director of the Counterterrorist Center at the Central Intelligence Agency.
Lieutenant Colonel Richard Raftery (US Marines-Ret.)	27 June 2008	Washington, D.C. Audio recording of the interview retained.	Executive Vice President at Innovative Analytics and Training in Washington, D.C. Major US Marine Corps (intelligence officer) during Operation Provide Comfort in northern Iraq (1991).
Dr Michael Rubin	7 July 2008	Washington, D.C. Audio recording of the interview retained.	Resident Scholar at the American Enterprise Institute in Washington, D.C. Former Staff assistant on Iran and Iraq in the Office of Special Plans in the Defense Department (2002–2003) and Political Advisor to the CPA in Baghdad (2003–2004).
Matthew Stephenson	10 June 2008	Washington, D.C. Audio recording of the interview retained.	State Department Official at the Bureau of Near Eastern Affairs in Washington, D.C.
Christopher Straub	14 July 2008	The Pentagon, Arlington, Virginia. Audio recording of the interview retained.	Deputy Assistant Secretary of Defense for Near East and South Asian affairs. Former, Office of Special Plans official, Senior Professional Staff Member, US Congress, Senate Intelligence Committee and Lieutenant Colonel (US Army-Ret.).

continued

Name	Date	Location	Position
Ambassador Samir Sumaidaie	24 July 2008	Washington, D.C. Audio recording of the interview retained.	Ambassador of the Republic of Iraq to the United States. Former Member of the Iraqi Governing Council, Minister of Interior in the Interim Iraqi government and Iraq's Permanent Representative to the United Nations.
Qubad Talabani	31 July 2008 20 May 2010	Washington, D.C. From the UK by Telephone Audio recording of the interviews retained.	Head of the Kurdistan Regional Government's Department of Coordination and Follow-Up (minister). Former Representative of the Kurdistan Regional Government of Iraq to the United States (2004–2012) and former member of the Kurdish delegation negotiating the Transitional Administrative Law with the CPA in Baghdad in 2004.
Congressman Christopher Van Hollen (D-MD)	18 July 2008	From Washington, D.C. by Telephone Audio recording of the interview retained.	Member of the United States House of Representatives. Former senior professional staff member for the US Senate Committee on Foreign Relations.
Ambassador Philip Wilcox	22 August 2008	Washington, D.C. Audio recording of the interview retained.	President of the Foundation for Middle East Peace. Former Principal Deputy Assistant Secretary of State for Intelligence and Research.
Colonel Lawrence Wilkerson (US Army-Ret.)	26 August 2008	Washington, D.C. Audio recording of the interview retained.	Professorial Lecturer in the Honours Program at the George Washington University in Washington, D.C. Former Chief of Staff to US Secretary of State Colin Powell.

2 Primary documents

Declassified governmental documents

Bush, George H. W. (1989). *National Security Directive 26.* [Federation of American Scientists: Intelligence Resource Program] Available at: URL: www.fas.org/irp/offdocs/nsd/nsd26.pdf Access Date: 20 December 2007.

Crocker, Edward. (1950). *United States Embassy, Iraq Cable from Edward S. Crocker II to the Department of State. 'Recent Developments in Connection with the Kurdish-Language News Bulletin', April 10, 1950.* [The National Security Archive: The George Washington University] Available at: URL: www.gwu.edu/~nsarchiv/NSAEBB/NSAEBB78/propaganda%20002.pdf Access Date: 20 December 2007.

Dole, Bob, 'US Senators Chat with Saddam' (pp. 58–60) in *The Iraq War Reader: History, Documents, Opinions*, ed. Micah Sifry and Christopher Cerf (New York: Touchstone, 2003).

Foster, John. (1968). *Memorandum from John W. Foster of the National Security Council Staff to the President's Special Assistant (Rostow).* [US Department of State: Office of the Historian] Available at: URL: http://history.state.gov/historicaldocuments/frus1964–68v21/d200 Access Date: 20 December 2009.

Grady, Henry. (1951). *United States Embassy, Iran Cable from Henry F. Grady to the Department of State. [Kurdish Voice of America Broadcasts], August 6, 1951.* [The National Security Archive: The George Washington University] Available at: URL: www.gwu.edu/~nsarchiv/NSAEBB/NSAEBB78/propaganda%20027.pdf Access Date: 20 December 2007.

Hussein, Saddam, 'The Glaspie Transcript: Saddam Meets the US Ambassador' (pp. 61–71), in *The Iraq War Reader: History, Documents, Opinions*, ed. Micah Sifry and Christopher Cerf (New York: Touchstone, 2003).

Hussein, Saddam. (2004a). *Interview Session 4, Conducted by George Piro: Baghdad Operations Centre: Federal Bureau of Investigation.* [The National Security Archive: The George Washington University] Available at: URL: www.gwu.edu/~nsarchiv/NSAEBB/NSAEBB279/05.pdf Access Date: 20 December 2009.

Hussein, Saddam. (2004b). *Casual Conversation, June 11, 2004: Baghdad Operations Centre: Federal Bureau of Investigation.* [The National Security Archive: The George Washington University] Available at: URL: www.gwu.edu/~nsarchiv/NSAEBB/NSAEBB279/24.pdf Access Date: 20 December 2009.

Killgore, Andrew. (1972). *Memorandum from Andrew Killgore of the Bureau of Near Eastern and South Asian Affairs to the Assistant Secretary for Near Eastern and South Asian Affairs (Sisco), Washington, April 3, 1972.* [US Department of State: Office of the Historian] Available at: http://history.state.gov/historicaldocuments/frus1969–76ve04/media/pdf/d304.pdf Access Date: 20 December 2009.

Kissinger, Henry. (1974). *Meeting with Israeli Ambassador Dinitz: Secret, Memorandum of Conversation, Washington, March 21, 1974.* [The National Security Archive: The George Washington University] Available at: http://gateway.proquest.com/openurl?url_ver=Z39.88–2004&res_dat=xri:dnsa&rft_dat=xri:dnsa:article:CKT01078 Access Date: 1 December 2008.

Kissinger, Henry. (1975). *Discussion with Iraqi Foreign Minister Saadoun Hammadi: Secret, Memorandum of Conversation, December 17, 1975.* [The National Security Archive: The George Washington University] Available at: http://gateway.proquest.com/

openurl?url_ver=Z39.88–2004&res_dat=xri:dnsa&rft_dat=xri:dnsa:article:CKT01856 Access Date: 1 December 2008.

Meho, Lokman, *The Kurdish Question in US Foreign Policy: A Documentary Source-book* (Connecticut: Praeger Publishers, 2004).

Report of the Select Committee on Intelligence on Prewar Intelligence Assessments About Postwar Iraq. (2007). [US Senate] Available at: URL: http://intelligence.senate.gov/prewar.pdf Access Date: 20 March 2010.

Saunders, Harold. (1972a). *Memorandum from Harold Saunders of the National Security Council Staff to the President's Deputy Assistant for National Security Affairs (Haig), Washington, March 27, 1972.* [US Department of State: Office of the Historian] Available at: URL: http://history.state.gov/historicaldocuments/frus1969–76ve04/media/pdf/d301.pdf Access Date: 20 December 2009.

Saunders, Harold. (1972b). *Memorandum from Harold Saunders of the National Security Staff to the President's Assistant for National Security Affairs (Kissinger), Washington, June 7, 1972.* [US Department of State: Office of the Historian] Available at: URL: http://history.state.gov/historicaldocuments/frus1969–76ve04/media/pdf/d313.pdf Access Date: 20 December 2009.

Strong, Robert. (1964). *Airgram from the Embassy in Iraq to the Department of State.* [US Department of State: Office of the Historian] Available at: URL: http://history.state.gov/historicaldocuments/frus1964–68v21/d162 Access Date: 20 December 2007.

Teicher, Howard. (1995). *United States District Court Southern District of Florida.* [The National Security Archive: The George Washington University] Available at: URL: www.gwu.edu/~nsarchiv/NSAEBB/NSAEBB82/iraq61.pdf Access Date: 20 December 2007.

Zinni, Anthony. (1999). *Post-Saddam Iraq: The War Game.* [The National Security Archive: The George Washington University] Available at: URL: www.gwu.edu/~nsarchiv/NSAEBB/NSAEBB207/index.htm Access Date: 20 December 2009.

Public governmental and official documents

Baker, James. (1991). *Congressional Testimony: Hearing of the Subcommittee of the Committee on Appropriations on Foreign Operations, Export Financing and Related Agencies Appropriations for Fiscal Year 1992*, Washington, D.C.

Blair, Tony. (2010). *Rt Hon Tony Blair Transcript.* [The Iraq Inquiry] Available at: URL: www.iraqinquiry.org.uk/media/45139/20100129-blair-final.pdf Access Date: 20 March 2010.

Bowen, Stuart Jr, *Hard Lessons: The Iraq Reconstruction Experience* (USA: US Independent Agencies and Commissions, 2009).

Clinton, Bill. (1998). *A Report on the Status of Efforts to Obtain Iraq's Compliance with the Resolutions Adopted by the U.N. Security Council* (105th Congress, 2nd Session: House Document 105–212). Washington, D.C.: The White House.

Ehrenberg, John, J. Patrice McSherry, José Ramón Sánchez and Caroleen Marji Sayej, ed. *The Iraq Papers* (Oxford: Oxford University Press, 2010).

Galbraith, Peter and Christopher Van Hollen. (1988). *Chemical Weapons Use in Kurdistan: Iraq's Final Offensive* (Committee Print 100–148). Washington, D.C.: Senate Committee on Foreign Relations.

Gosden, Christine. (1998). *Congressional Testimony: Hearing of the Senate Judiciary Subcommittee on Technology, Terrorism and Government and the Senate Select Committee on Intelligence*, Washington, D.C.

Iraq Liberation Act of 1998 (Enrolled Bill (Sent to President)). (n.d.). [Iraq Watch] Available at: URL: www.iraqwatch.org/government/US/Legislation/ILA.htm Access Date: 17 December 2008.

Katzman, Kenneth. (2000). *Iraq's Opposition Movements* (Order Code 98–179 F). Washington, D.C.: Congressional Research Service.

Katzman, Kenneth. (2003). *Iraq: US Regime Change Efforts, the Iraqi Opposition, and Post-War Iraq* (Order Code RL31339). Washington, D.C.: Congressional Research Service.

Office of the Iraq Programme: Oil for Food. (2010). Available at: URL: www.un.org/Depts/oip/background/scrsindex.html Access Date: 11 March 2008.

Powell, Colin. (2002). *The President's International Affairs Budget Request for FY 2003.* [Committee on International Relations: House of Representatives] Available at: URL: www.globalsecurity.org/military/library/congress/2002_hr/77532.pdf Access Date: 20 December 2007.

Prados, Alfred. (2002). *Iraq: Former and Recent Military Confrontations with the United States* (Order Code IB94049). Washington, D.C.: Congressional Research Service.

Public Law 106–113 106th Congress. (1999). Available at: URL: http://frwebgate.access.gpo.gov/cgi-bin/getdoc.cgi?dbname=106_cong_public_laws&docid=f:publ113.106.pdf Access Date: 17 December 2008.

Rice, Condoleezza. (2005). *Clear, Hold, Build: Modern Political Techniques in COIN.* Available at: URL: www.dtic.mil/cgi-bin/GetTRDoc?AD=ADA495007&Location=U2&doc=GetTRDoc.pdf Access Date: 20 December 2007.

The White House. (2002). *The National Security Strategy of the United States of America: September 2002,* Washington, D.C.

The White House. (2006). *The National Security Strategy of the United States of America: March 2006,* Washington, D.C.

Wolfowitz, Paul. (2003). *Department of Defense Budget Priorities for Fiscal Year 2004.* [Committee on the Budget: House of Representatives] Available at: URL: http://usiraq.procon.org/sourcefiles/WolfowitzTestimonyHBC.pdf Access Date: 20 December 2007.

Speeches, statements and media interviews

Ahmad, Aijaz. (2007). *The Real News.* [The Real News Network] Available at: URL: www.youtube.com/watch?v=W5mRygvDmwI Access Date: 15 July 2009.

Albright, Madeleine. (1998). *Transcript: Albright, Talabani, Barzani Remarks, 9/27/98.* Available at: URL: www.fas.org/irp/news/1998/09/98091707_nlt.html Access Date: 17 December 2009.

Barzani, Masoud. (2008). *The Kurdistan Region and the Future of Iraq.* [Centre for Strategic and International Studies] Available at: URL: http://csis.org/event/kurdistan-region-and-future-iraq Access Date: 15 July 2009.

Barzani, Masoud. (2010). *President Barzani concludes successful Washington visit.* [Kurdistan Regional Government] Available at: URL: www.krg.org/articles/detail.asp?rnr=223&lngnr=12&smap=02010100&anr=33605 Access Date: 20 August 2011.

Benn, Tony. (2007). *Documentary: 'I Knew Saddam.'* Available at: URL: www.youtube.com/watch?v=oEH4sBsazGg&feature=channel Access Date: 20 December 2008.

Bush, George H. W. (1990). *Address Before a Joint Session of the Congress on the Persian Gulf Crisis and the Federal Budget Deficit.* Available at: URL: http://bushlibrary.tamu.edu/research/public_papers.php?id=2217&year=1990&month=9 Access Date: 15 December 2009.

Bush, George H. W. (1991a). *Remarks to Raytheon Missile Systems Plant Employees in Andover, Massachusetts.* Available at: URL: http://bushlibrary.tamu.edu/research/public_papers.php?id=2711&year=1991&month=2 Access Date: 15 December 2009.

Bush, George H. W. (1991b). *Remarks on Assistance for Iraqi Refugees and a News Conference.* Available at: URL: http://bushlibrary.tamu.edu/research/public_papers.php?id=2882&year=1991&month=4 Access Date: 16 December 2009.

Bush, George W. (1999a). *A Period of Consequences.* Available at: URL: www3.citadel.edu/pao/addresses/pres_bush.html Access Date: 20 December 2009.

Bush, George W. (1999b). *Governor George W. Bush, 'A Distinctly American Internationalism', Ronald Reagan Presidential Library, Simi Valley, California, November 19, 1999.* Available at: URL: www.mtholyoke.edu/acad/intrel/bush/wspeech.htm Access Date: 20 December 2009.

Bush, George W. (2001). *Address to a Joint Session of Congress and the American People.* [The White House] Available at: URL: http://georgewbush-whitehouse.archives.gov/news/releases/2001/09/20010920–8.html Access Date: 20 June 2009.

Bush, George W. (2002a). *President Delivers State of the Union Address.* [The White House] Available at: URL: http://georgewbush-whitehouse.archives.gov/news/releases/2002/01/20020129–11.html Access Date: 20 June 2008.

Bush, George W. (2002b). *President Bush, Prime Minister Blair Hold Press Conference.* [The White House] Available at: URL: http://georgewbush-whitehouse.archives.gov/news/releases/2002/04/20020406–3.html Access Date: 20 June 2008.

Bush, George W. (2002c). *President Bush Meets with French President Chirac.* [The White House] Available at: URL: http://georgewbush-whitehouse.archives.gov/news/releases/2002/05/20020526–2.html Access Date: 20 June 2008.

Bush, George W. (2002d). *President Bush Delivers Graduation Speech at West Point.* [The White House] Available at: URL: http://georgewbush-whitehouse.archives.gov/news/releases/2002/06/20020601–3.html Access Date: 20 June 2008.

Bush, George W. (2002e). *President's Remarks at the United Nations General Assembly.* [The White House] Available at: URL: http://georgewbush-whitehouse.archives.gov/news/releases/2002/09/20020912–1.html Access Date: 20 June 2009.

Bush, George W. (2002f). *Bush Calls Saddam 'The Guy Who Tried to Kill My Dad'.* [CNN.com/Inside Politics] Available at: URL: http://archives.cnn.com/2002/ALLPOLITICS/09/27/bush.war.talk/ Access Date: 17 June 2008.

Bush, George W. (2003a). *President Delivers 'State of the Union'.* [The White House] Available at: URL: http://georgewbush-whitehouse.archives.gov/news/releases/2003/01/20030128–19.html Access Date: 20 June 2008.

Bush, George W. (2003b). *President Bush Meets with Prime Minister Blair.* [The White House] Available at: URL: http://georgewbush-whitehouse.archives.gov/news/releases/2003/01/20030131–23.html Access Date: 20 June 2008.

Bush, George W. (2003c). *President Discusses the Future of Iraq.* [The White House] Available at: URL: http://georgewbush-whitehouse.archives.gov/news/releases/2003/02/20030226–11.html Access Date: 20 June 2008.

Bush, George W. (2003d). *President Bush Addresses the Nation.* [The White House] Available at: URL: http://georgewbush-whitehouse.archives.gov/news/releases/2003/03/20030319–17.html Access Date: 20 June 2008.

Bush, George W. (2003e). *President Addresses the Nation.* [The White House] Available at: URL: http://georgewbush-whitehouse.archives.gov/news/releases/2003/09/20030907–1.html Access Date: 20 May 2008.

Bush, George W. (2003f). *President Bush: Address to The Heritage Foundation.* [The

Heritage Foundation] Available at: URL: www.heritage.org/Press/Commentary/bush 111103.cfm Access Date: 20 March 2008.

Bush, George W. (2004). *Joint Press Conference: President Bush and PM Sharon.* [Israel Ministry of Foreign Affairs] Available at: URL: www.mfa.gov.il/MFA/Government/S peeches+by+Israeli+leaders/2004/Bush-Sharon+Press+Conference+14-Apr-2004.htm Access Date: 20 June 2007.

Bush, George W. (2006). *Press Conference by the President.* [The White House] Available at: URL: http://georgewbush-whitehouse.archives.gov/news/releases/2006/11/ 20061108–2.html Access Date: 20 June 2008.

Bush, George W. (2007a). *President's Address to the Nation.* [The White House] Available at: URL: http://georgewbush-whitehouse.archives.gov/news/releases/2007/01/ 20070110–7.html Access Date: 20 January 2008.

Bush, George W. (2007b). *Press Conference by the President.* [The White House] Available at: URL: http://georgewbush-whitehouse.archives.gov/news/releases/2007/10/ 20071017.html Access Date: 20 June 2008.

Bush, George W. (2008). *President George Bush Interview by Charles Gibson – ABC News.* Available at: URL: http://cloudfront.mediamatters.org/static/video/2008/12/02/ media-20081202-bush.mov Access Date: 20 December 2008.

Bush, George W. (2009). *President Bush Delivers Farewell Address to the Nation.* [The White House] Available at: URL: http://georgewbush-whitehouse.archives.gov/news/ releases/2009/01/20090115–17.html Access Date: 20 June 2009.

Carter, Jimmy. (1980). *State of the Union Address 1980.* Available at: URL: www.jim-mycarterlibrary.org/documents/speeches/su80jec.phtml Access Date: 14 December, 2009.

Clinton, Bill. (1998a). *Statement on Signing the Iraq Liberation Act of 1998.* Available at: URL: http://findarticles.com/p/articles/mi_m2889/is_45_34/ai_53414246/ Access Date: 15 January 2009.

Clinton, Bill. (1998b). *Statement by the President: The Oval Office.* [The White House] Available at: URL: http://clinton2.nara.gov/WH/New/html/19981216–3611.html Access Date: 20 June 2008.

Clinton, Bill. (2000). *Statement by the President.* [The White House] Available at: URL: http://clinton6.nara.gov/2000/12/2000–12–31-statement-by-president-on-signature-the-icc-treaty.html Access Date: 20 June 2008.

Fenning, Richard. (2009). *Analysis: A New Iraq?* [BBC Radio 4] Available at: URL: http://news.bbc.co.uk/nol/shared/spl/hi/programmes/analysis/transcripts/15_06_09.txt Access Date: 20 September 2009.

Garamone, Jim. (2007). *Spokesman Cites Diplomacy as Preferred Course for Turk-PKK Issue.* [Department of Defense] Available at: URL: www.firstworldwar.com/source/ fourteenpoints.htm Access Date: 20 December 2007.

Khalilzad, Zalmay. (2009). *Conversations with History: Responding to Strategic Challenges of the Post 9–11 World.* [University of California, Berkeley: Institute of International Studies] Available at: URL: http://globetrotter.berkeley.edu/people9/Khalilzad/Amb%20 Khalilzad%20transcript.pdf Access Date: 15 July 2009.

Letter to President Bush on the War on Terrorism. (2001). [Project For The New American Century] Available at: URL: www.newamericancentury.org/Bushletter.htm Access Date: 20 June 2009.

Mann, James. (2005). *Conversations with History: The Bush War Cabinet.* [University of California, Berkeley: Institute of International Studies] Available at: URL: http://globe-trotter.berkeley.edu/people5/JMann/jmann-con3.html Access Date: 15 March 2008.

Mead, Walter Russell. (2003). *US Foreign Policy and the American Political Tradition.* [University of California, Berkeley: Institute of International Studies] Available at: URL: http://globetrotter.berkeley.edu/people3/Mead/mead-con4.html Access Date: 15 March 2008.

Meeting with Iraqi Kurdistan Front – Statement on Assistant Secretary of State Edward Djerejian's Meeting with a Delegation – Transcript. (1991). Available at: URL: http://findarticles.com/p/articles/mi_m1584/is_n40_v2/ai_11555741/ Access Date: 17 December 2009.

New Congressional Caucus Meets with Local Kurds. (2008). [Nashville Public Radio] Available at: URL: http://wpln.org/?p=2606 Access Date: 20 June 2008.

Obama, Barack. (2010). *Readout of the President's Meeting with the President of Iraq's Kurdistan Region Masoud Barzani.* [The White House] Available at: URL: www.whitehouse.gov/the-press-office/readout-presidents-meeting-with-president-iraqs-kurdistan-region-masoud-barzani Access Date: 22 August 2011.

Obama, Barack. (2011). *Remarks by the President and First Lady on the End of the War in Iraq.* [The White House] Available at: URL: www.whitehouse.gov/the-press-office/2011/12/14/remarks-president-and-first-lady-end-war-iraq Access Date: 20 May 2013.

O'Sullivan, Meghan. (2009). *Charlie Rose: A Conversation with Meghan O'Sullivan.* Available at: URL: www.charlierose.com/view/interview/9069 Access Date: 15 July 2008.

Perle, Richard. (2003). *Truth, War & Consequences: Interview Richard Perle.* [Frontline] Available at: URL: www.pbs.org/wgbh/pages/frontline/shows/truth/interviews/perle.html Access Date: 20 December 2008.

Pipes, Daniel. (2004). *Conversations with History: Militant Islam.* [University of California, Berkeley: Institute of International Studies] Available at: URL: http://globetrotter.berkeley.edu/people4/Pipes/pipes-con4.html Access Date: 15 March 2008.

PM Barzani Attends Launch of Kurdish-American Caucus. (2008). [Kurdistan Regional Government] Available at: URL: www.krg.org/articles/detail.asp?smap=02010100&lngnr=12&asnr=&anr=24345&rnr=223 Access Date: 20 June 2008.

Psaki, Jen. (2013). *US Department of State Department: Daily Press Briefing.* Available at: URL: www.state.gov/r/pa/prs/dpb/2013/07/211535.htm Access Date: 4 July 2013.

Rice, Condoleezza. (2005). *Condoleezza Rice's Remarks from her Cairo Speech at AUC.* [The Arabist] Available at: URL: www.arabist.net/blog/2005/6/20/condoleezza-rices-remarks-from-her-cairo-speech-at-auc.html Access Date: 15 July 2009.

Rubin, James. (1998). *US Department of State Department: Daily Press Briefing.* Available at: URL: www.fas.org/news/iraq/1998/09/980908db-1.html Access Date: 17 December 2009.

Rumsfeld, Donald. (2003). *Beyond Nation Building.* [US Department of Defense] Available at: URL: www.defense.gov/speeches/speech.aspx?speechid=337 Access Date: 20 June 2007.

Talabani, Jalal. (2002). *Jalal Talabani: 'No Grounds for a Relationship with Baghdad'.* [Middle East Forum] Available at: URL: www.meforum.org/126/jalal-talabani-no-grounds-for-a-relationship-with Access Date: 20 June 2007.

Talabani, Jalal. (2007). *CNN Late Night Edition with Wolf Blitzer.* Available at: URL: http://transcripts.cnn.com/TRANSCRIPTS/0710/07/le.01.html Access Date: 18 December 2009.

Wilson, Woodrow. (1918). *Primary Documents – Woodrow Wilson's 'Fourteen Points' Speech, 8 January 1918.* [firstworldwar.com] Available at: URL: www.firstworldwar.com/source/fourteenpoints.htm Access Date: 20 June 2007.

Wolfowitz, Paul. (2001). *DoD News Briefing – Deputy Secretary Wolfowitz.* Available at: URL: www.dartmouth.edu/~govdocs/docs/iraq/dod.htm Access Date: 17 February 2008.

3 Newspapers and news magazines

A Brief History of a Long War (Iraq, 1990–2003). (2006). Available at: URL: www.mud-villegazette.com/2006_09.html Access Date: 21 February 2009.

Aita, Judy. (1999). *US Pledges Support for Iraqi Opposition.* Available at: URL: www.fas.org/news/iraq/1999/11/991101-iraq-usia.htm Access Date: 20 June 2008.

Arons, Nicholas. (2001). *US-Supported Iraqi Opposition.* [Washington, D.C.: Institute for Policy Studies] Available at: URL: www.iraqwatch.org/perspectives/for-pol-in-focus-iraqoppo.pdf Access Date: 20 December 2009.

Bengio, Ofra. (2012). *Will the Kurds Get Their Way.* [The American Interest] Available at: URL: www.the-american-interest.com/article.cfm?piece=1323 Access Date: 10 July 2013.

Biden, Joseph and Leslie Gelb. 'Unity Through Autonomy in Iraq', *The New York Times* (2006, 1 May), p. ED19.

Bookman, Jay. 'The President's Real Goal in Iraq', *The Atlanta Journal-Constitution*, (2002, 29 September), p. 1F.

Borger, Julian. (2002). *US Big Guns Silent on 'Regime Change'.* [guardian.co.uk] Available at: URL: www.guardian.co.uk/world/2002/feb/13/worlddispatch.usa Access Date: 20 June 2007.

Bremer, Paul. (2008). *Facts for Feith: CPA History.* [Nationalreview Online] Available at: URL: http://article.nationalreview.com/?q=NDIwN2MzOTljOTNlODdiMDIzZWQ5Zm ZjZTQyZjQ5NzM= Access Date: 15 May 2008.

Bremer, Paul. (2009). *Former US Civil Administrator to Iraq in an Extended Interview Recalls his Best and Worst Days in Baghdad* (Translated from Arabic by Author). [*Asharq Al-Awsat*] Available at: URL: www.aawsat.com/details.asp?section=4&issuen o=11121&article=518522 Access Date: 20 December 2009.

Bumiller, Elizabeth. 'Traces of Terror: The Strategy; Bush Aides Set Strategy to Sell Policy on Iraq', *The New York Times* (2002, 7 September), p. ND1.

Bush Urges Turks to End Offensive in Iraq Quickly. (2008). [Reuters] Available at: URL: www.reuters.com/article/idUSANK00037420080228 Access Date: 17 May 2008.

Cohn, Robert. (2008). *Best of Bob: Presidents and Precedents.* [jewishinstlouis.org] Available at: URL: www.jewishinstlouis.org/page.aspx?id=125519&page=8 Access Date: 20 June 2009.

Erikson, Marc. (2002). *Iraq: In All but Name, the War's on.* [Asia Times Online] Available at: URL: www.atimes.com/atimes/Middle_East/DH17Ak03.html Access Date: 15 July 2008.

Events Leading Up to the 2003 Invasion of Iraq. (n.d.). [History Commons] Available at: URL: www.historycommons.org/timeline.jsp?timeline=complete_timeline_of_the_ 2003_invasion_of_iraq&startpos=100 Access Date: 17 December 2008.

Everest, Larry. (n.d.). *1980–1988, Iran-Iraq: Helping Both Sides Lose the War.* Available at: URL: http://coat.ncf.ca/our_magazine/links/issue51/articles/51_30–31.pdf Access Date: 20 June 2007.

Everest, Larry. (2003). *Four Questions for Saddam – and the US.* [New America Media] Available at: URL: http://news.pacificnews.org/news/view_article.html?article_id=c33 335175cc184e56416dbb1d1ebc595 Access Date: 20 June 2009.

Feith, Douglas. 'Why We Went to War in Iraq', *The Wall Street Journal* (2008, 3 July), p. 13.

Friedman, Herbert. (2004). *Operation Provide Comfort.* Available at: URL: www.psy-warrior.com/ProvideComfort.html Access Date: 17 December 2009.

Friedman, Thomas. 'The Long Bomb', *The New York Times* (2003, 2 March), p. ED13.

Gordon, Michael R. 'Failed Efforts and Challenges of America's Last Months in Iraq', *The New York Times* (2012, 23 September), p. A1.

Hoagland, Jim. 'How CIA's Secret War on Saddam Collapsed; A Retired Intelligence Operative Surfaces with Details and Critique of US Campaign', *The Washington Post* (1997, 26 June), p. A21.

Iraq's Kurdish Leader Snubs Rice. (2007). [BBC News] Available at: URL: http://news.bbc.co.uk/1/hi/world/europe/7150355.stm Access Date: 17 May 2008.

Kagan, Robert. 'Democracies and Double Standards', *Commentary* Vol. 104, No. 2 (1997, August), pp. 19–26.

Kagan, Robert and William Kristol, 'What to Do about Iraq', *The Weekly Standard* Vol. 7, No. 18 (2002, January), pp. 23–6.

Khalilzad, Zalmay and Paul Wolfowitz, 'Overthrow Him', *The Weekly Standard* Vol. 3, No. 12 (1997, December), p. 14.

Knowledgerush: April Glaspie. (2005). Available at: URL: www.knowledgerush.com/kr/encyclopedia/April_Glaspie/ Access Date: 17 December 2008.

Krauthammer, Charles. 'The New Unilateralism', *The Washington Post* (2001, 8 June), p. A29.

Layne, Ken. (2002). *Saddam Pays 25K for Palestinian Bombers.* [Fox News] Available at: URL: www.foxnews.com/story/0,2933,48822,00.html Access Date: 20 June 2009.

Lobe, Jim. (2004). *So, Did Saddam Hussein Try to Kill Bush's Dad?* Available at: URL: www.commondreams.org/headlines04/1019–05.htm Access Date: 15 July 2008.

Mason, Barnaby. (2001). *Powell's New Plans for Iraq.* [BBC News] Available at: URL: http://news.bbc.co.uk/1/hi/world/middle_east/1192815.stm Access Date: 20 September 2008.

Mearsheimer, John and Stephen Walt, 'An Unnecessary War', *Foreign Policy* (2003, Jan/Feb), pp. 51–9.

Mearsheimer, John and Stephen Walt. (2006). *The Israel Lobby.* [London Review of Books] Available at: URL: www.lrb.co.uk/v28/n06/john-mearsheimer/the-israel-lobby Access Date: 20 June 2008.

Mylroie, Laurie. (2001). *The United States and the Iraqi National Congress.* Available at: URL: www.mail-archive.com/ctrl@listserv.aol.com/msg78634.html Access Date: 15 January 2009.

Operation Iraqi Freedom. (2005). Available at: URL: www.globalsecurity.org/military/ops/iraqi_freedom.htm Access Date: 17 June 2007.

Perle, Richard. 'Why the West Must Strike First Against Saddam Hussein', *The Daily Telegraph* (2002, 9 August), p. 22.

Pilger, John. (2000). *Labour Claims its Actions are Lawful While it Bombs Iraq, Starves its People and Sells Arms to Corrupt States.* Available at: URL: www.johnpilger.com/page.asp?partid=308 Access Date: 16 December 2009.

Plett, Barbara. (2001). *Analysis: Will 'Smart' Sanctions Work?* [Amman: BBC] Available at: URL: http://news.bbc.co.uk/1/hi/world/middle_east/1366201.stm Access Date: 20 September 2008.

Podhoretz, Norman. 'Neoconservatism: A Eulogy', *Commentary* (1996, Vol. 101, No. 3), pp. 19–27.

Pollock, Robert. 'The Voice of Iraq', *The Wall Street Journal* (2006, 24 June), p. A10.

Raghavan, Sudarsan. 'Security Accord Approved In Iraq', *The Washington Post* (2008, 28 November), p. A01.

Rice, Condoleezza. 'Why We Know Iraq Is Lying', *The New York Times* (2003, 23 January), p. ED25.

Sciolino, Elaine. 'CIA Asks Congress for Money to Rein In Iraq and Iran', *The New York Times* (1995, 12 April), p. FD8.

Stansfield, Gareth. (2003). *Can the Iraqi Opposition Unite?* [Royal Institute of International Affairs] Available at: URL: www.guardian.co.uk/world/2003/mar/23/iraq.theworldtodayessays Access Date: 20 June 2007.

Thomas, Evan, Christopher Dickey and Gregory Vistica, 'Bay of Pigs Redux', *Newsweek* Vol. 131, No. 12 (1998, 23 March), pp. 36–44.

Tripp, Charles. (2003). *Iraq: The Imperial Precedent.* [Le Monde Diplomatique] Available at: URL: www.globalpolicy.org/component/content/article/169/36402.html Access Date: 20 June 2008.

Tyler, Patrick. 'Congress Notified of Iraq Coup Plan', *The New York Times* (1992, 9 February), p. FD1.

UN Approves Iraq Sanctions Review. (2001). [BBC News] Available at: URL: http://news.bbc.co.uk/1/hi/world/middle_east/1364434.stm Access Date: 17 June 2008.

UNSCOM Chronology of Main Events. (1999). Available at: URL: www.un.org/Depts/unscom/Chronology/chronologyframe.htm Access Date: 19 February 2009.

US Led Forces Entered Iraq Two Months Prior JHS Res.114. (2005). Available at: URL: www.downingstreetmemo.com/2005/08/us-led-forces-entered-iraq-two-months.html Access Date: 17 December 2009.

US Warns of Chaos, Disintegration in Iraq. (2013). [Hurriyet Daily News] Available at: URL: http://www.hurriyetdailynews.com/us-warns-of-chaos-disintegration-in-iraq.aspx?PageID=238&NID=40575&NewsCatID=359 Access Date: 20 March 2013.

Woodward, Bob. 'Behind Diplomatic Moves, Military Plan Was Launched', *The Washington Post* (2004, 18 April), p. A01.

Woodward, Bob. 'With CIA Push, Movement to War Accelerated', *The Washington Post* (2004, 19 April), p. A01.

4 Memoirs

Amin, Nawshirwan Mustafa. (2007a). *My Memoirs from the Governing Council: Part 1* (Translated from Kurdish by Author). [Sbeiy.com] Available at: URL: http://sbeiy.com/ku/ArticleParts.aspx?PartID=1&ArticleID=182&AuthorID=36 Access Date: 20 June 2008.

Amin, Nawshirwan Mustafa. (2007b). *My Memoirs from the Governing Council: Part 2* (Translated from Kurdish by Author). [Sbeiy.com] Available at: URL: www.sbeiy.com/ku/ArticleParts.aspx?PartID=2&ArticleID=182&AuthorID=36 Access Date: 20 June 2008.

Amin, Nawshirwan Mustafa. (2007c). *My Memoirs from the Governing Council: Part 7* (Translated from Kurdish by Author). [Sbeiy.com] Available at: URL: www.sbeiy.com/ku/ArticleParts.aspx?PartID=8&ArticleID=182&AuthorID=36 Access Date: 20 June 2008.

Amin, Nawshirwan Mustafa. (2007d). *My Memoirs from the Governing Council: Part 8* (Translated from Kurdish by Author). [Sbeiy.com] Available at: URL: http://sbeiy.com/ku/ArticleParts.aspx?PartID=9&ArticleID=182&AuthorID=36 Access Date: 20 June 2008.

Amin, Nawshirwan Mustafa. (2008). *A Historic Opportunity Lost!* (Translated from Kurdish by Author). [Sbeiy.com] Available at: URL: http://sbeiy.com/ku/article_detail. aspx?ArticleID=800&AuthorID=36 Access Date: 20 January 2009.

Amin, Nawshirwan Mustafa. (2009). *Dream or Nightmare, The Inside Story of Iraqi Kurdistan 1992–2002: Part 2* (Translated from Kurdish by Author). [Sbeiy.com] Available at: URL: http://sbeiy.com/ku/ArticleParts.aspx?PartID=34&ArticleID=1539 &AuthorID=36 Access Date: 20 June 2008.

Amin, Nawshirwan Mustafa. (2010). *From Comradeship to Treachery* (Translated from Kurdish by Author). [Sbeiy.com] Available at: URL: http://sbeiy.com/ku/article_detail. aspx?ArticleID=2561&AuthorID=36 Access Date: 20 January 2010.

Baer, Robert, *See No Evil: The True Story of a Ground Soldier in the CIA's War on Terrorism* (London: Arrow Books, 2002).

Bush, George H. W. and Brent Scowcroft, *A World Transformed* (New York: Vintage Books, 1999).

Bush, George W., *Decision Points* (New York: Crown Publishers, 2010).

Bremer, L. Paul III with Malcolm McConnell, *My Year in Iraq: The Struggle to Build a Future of Hope* (New York: Simon and Schuster, 2006).

Brzezinski, Zbigniew, *Power and Principle: Memoirs of the National Security Advisor 1977–1981* (London: Weidenfeld and Nicolson, 1983).

Cheney, Dick with Liz Cheney, *In My Time: A Personal and Political Memoir* (New York: Threshold Editions, 2011).

Feith, Douglas, *War and Decision: Inside the Pentagon at the Dawn of the War on Terrorism* (New York: Harper Collins Publishers, 2008).

Franks, Tommy with Malcolm McConnell, *American Soldier* (New York: HarperCollins, 2004), p. xiv.

Gates, Robert M., *Duty: Memoirs of a Secretary at War* (New York: Knopf Publishing Group, 2014).

Kissinger, Henry, *White House Years* (Boston: Little, Brown and Company, 1979).

Powell, Colin with Joseph E. Persico, *My American Journey* (New York: Ballantine Books, 2003).

Rice, Condoleezza, *No Higher Honor: A Memoir of My Years in Washington* (New York: Crown Publishers, 2011).

Ritter, Scott, *Iraq Confidential: The Untold Story of America's Intelligence Conspiracy* (London: I.B. Tauris, 2005).

Rumsfeld, Donald, *Known and Unknown: A Memoir* (New York: Sentinel, 2011).

Tenet, George with Bill Harlow, *At the Center of the Storm: My Years at the CIA* (New York: HarperCollins, 2007).

5 Books

Ahmed, Mohammed M. A., *America Unravels Iraq: Kurds, Shiites and Sunni Arabs Compete for Supremacy* (California: Mazda Publishers, 2010).

Ahmed, Mohammed M. A., *Iraqi Kurds and Nation Building* (New York: Palgrave Macmillan, 2012).

Allawi, Ali, *The Occupation of Iraq: Winning the War, Losing the Peace* (USA: Yale University Press, 2007).

Baylis, John, Steve Smith and Patricia Owens, ed., *The Globalization of World Politics: An Introduction to International Relations* (Oxford: Oxford University Press, 2008).

Chandrasekaran, Rajiv, *Imperial Life in the Emerald City: Inside Iraq's Green Zone* (New York: Alfred A. Knopf, 2006).

Charountaki, Marianna, *The Kurds and US Foreign Policy: International Relations in the Middle East since 1945* (Oxford: Routledge, 2011).

Daalder, Ivo and James Lindsay, *America Unbound: The Bush Revolution in Foreign Policy* (Maryland: The Brookings Institution, 2003).

Dobbins, James, Seth Jones, Benjamin Runkle and Siddharth Mohandas, *Occupying Iraq: A History of the Coalition Provisional Authority* (Santa Monica: RAND Corporation, 2009).

Dodge, Toby, *Iraq's Future: The Aftermath of Regime Change* (Oxford: Routledge, 2005).

Dodge, Toby, *Iraq – From War to a New Authoritarianism* (Oxford: Routledge, 2013).

Draper, Robert, *Dead Certain: The Presidency of George W. Bush* (New York: Free Press, 2007).

Ferguson, Niall, *Colossus: The Rise and Fall of the American Empire* (New York: Penguin, 2005).

Freedman, Lawrence, *A Choice of Enemies: America Confronts the Middle East* (New York: PublicAffairs, 2008).

Frum, David and Richard Perle, *An End To Evil: How To Win the War on Terrorism* (USA: Random House, 2003).

Galbraith, Peter, *The End of Iraq: How American Incompetence Created a War Without End* (New York: Simon and Schuster, 2006).

Galbraith, Peter, *Unintended Consequences: How War in Iraq Strengthened America's Enemies* (New York: Simon and Schuster, 2008).

Gerges, Fawaz A., *The End of Americas Moment?: Obama and the Middle East* (New York: Palgrave Macmillan, 2012).

Ghareeb, Edmund, *The Kurdish Question in Iraq* (New York: Syracuse University Press, 1981).

Gordon, Michael and Bernard Trainor, *Cobra II: The Inside Story of the Invasion and Occupation of Iraq* (London: Atlantic Books, 2007).

Gordon, Michael and Bernard E. Trainor, *The Endgame: The Inside Story of the Struggle for Iraq, from George W. Bush to Barack Obama* (London: Atlantic Books, 2012).

Gunter, Michael, *The Kurds of Iraq: Tragedy and Hope* (New York: St Martin's Press, 1992).

Gunter, Michael, *The Kurdish Predicament in Iraq: A Political Analysis* (Pennsylvania: Macmillan, 1999).

Haliday, Fred, *The Middle East in International Relations: Power, Politics and Ideology* (Cambridge: Cambridge University Press, 2005).

Halper, Stefan and Jonathan Clarke, *America Alone: The Neo-Conservatives and the Global Order* (New York: Cambridge University Press, 2004).

Herring, Eric and Glen Rangwala, *Iraq in Fragments: The Occupation and its Legacy* (New York: Cornell University Press, 2006).

Hiltermann, Joost R., *A Poisonous Affair: America, Iraq, and the Gassing of Halabja* (New York: Cambridge University Press, 2007).

Hurst, Steven, *The United States and Iraq since 1979: Hegemony, Oil, and War* (Edinburgh: Edinburgh University Press, 2009).

Ikenberry, John, *After Victory: Institutions, Strategic Restraint, and the Rebuilding of Order After Major Wars* (Princeton: Princeton University Press, 2001).

Jentleson, Bruce, *American Foreign Policy: The Dynamics of Choice in the 21st Century* (New York: W. W. Norton and Company, 2004).

Khadduri, Majid and Edmund Ghareeb, *War in the Gulf, 1990–91: The Iraq-Kuwait Conflict and Its Implications* (New York: Oxford University Press, 1997).

Lawrence, Quil, *Invisible Nation: How The Kurds' Quest For Statehood Is Shaping Iraq and The Middle East* (New York: Walker Publishing Company, 2008).

Lynch, Timothy and Robert Singh, *After Bush: The Case for Continuity in American Foreign Policy* (Cambridge: Cambridge University Press, 2008).

Mann, James, *Rise of the Vulcans: The History of Bush's War Cabinet* (New York: Penguin Group, 2004).

McDowall, David, *A Modern History of the Kurds* (New York: I.B.Tauris, 2004).

Melanson, Richard, *American Foreign Policy Since the Vietnam War: The Search for Consensus from Richard Nixon to George W. Bush* (New York: M.E. Sharpe, 2005).

Norton, Ann, *Leo Strauss and the Politics of American Empire* (USA: Yale University Press, 2004).

Olson, Robert, *The Goat and the Butcher: Nationalism and State Formation in Kurdistan-Iraq since the Iraqi War* (California: Mazda Publishers, 2005).

Packer, George, *The Assassins' Gate: America in Iraq* (New York: Farrar, Straus and Giroux, 2005).

Power, Samantha, *A Problem from Hell: America and the Age of Genocide* (New York: Basic Books, 2002).

Ricks, Thomas, *Fiasco: The American Military Adventure in Iraq* (London: Penguin Press, 2007).

Ricks, Thomas, *The Gamble: General David Petraeus and the American Military Adventure in Iraq, 2006–2008* (New York: The Penguin Press, 2009).

Robinson, Linda, *Masters of Chaos: The Secret History of the Special Forces* (New York: PublicAffairs, 2004).

Rosati, Jerel, *The Politics of United States Foreign Policy* (Australia: Wadsworth Publishing, 1999).

Shapiro, Ian, *Containment: Rebuilding a Strategy against Global Terror* (Princeton: Princeton University Press, 2007).

Tanner, Stephen, *The Wars of the Bushes: A Father and Son as Military Leaders* (Pennsylvania: CASEMATE, 2004).

Woodward, Bob, *Bush at War* (London: Simon and Schuster, 2002).

Woodward, Bob, *Plan of Attack* (London: Simon and Schuster, 2004).

Woodward, Bob, *State of Denial: Bush at War, Part III* (London: Simon and Schuster, 2006).

Woodward, Bob, *The War Within: A Secret White House History 2006–2008* (London: Simon and Schuster, 2008).

Yildiz, Kerim, *The Kurds In Iraq: The Past, Present and Future* (London: Pluto Press, 2004).

6 Book chapters

Cox, Michael, 'The Imperial Republic Revisited: The United States in the Era of Bush' (pp. 114–30), in *The War on Terrorism and the American 'Empire' after the Cold War*, ed. Alejandro Colas and Richard Saull (Oxford: Routledge, 2006).

Cox, Michael, 'The Imperial Republic in an Age of War: The United States from September 11 to Iraq' (pp. 57–82), in *Understanding Global Terror*, ed. Christopher Ankersen (Cambridge: Polity Press, 2007).

Deudney, Daniel and Jeffrey Meiser, 'American Exceptionalism' (pp. 24–42), in *US Foreign Policy*, ed. Michael Cox and Doug Stokes (Oxford: Oxford University Press, 2008).

Dodge, Toby, 'US Foreign Policy in the Middle East' (pp. 213–35), in *US Foreign Policy*, ed. Michael Cox and Doug Stokes (Oxford: Oxford University Press, 2008).

Dumbrell, John, 'Bush's War: The Iraq Conflict and American Democracy' (pp. 33–44), in *Iraq War and Democratic Politics*, ed. Alex Danchev and John MacMillan (Oxford: Routledge, 2005).

Dumbrell, John, 'The Neoconservative Roots of the War in Iraq' (pp. 19–39), in *Intelligence and National Security Policymaking on Iraq: British and American Perspectives*, ed. James Pfiffner and Mark Phythian (Manchester: Manchester University Press, 2008a).

Dumbrell, John, 'America in the 1990s: Searching for Purpose' (pp. 88–104), in *US Foreign Policy*, ed. Michael Cox and Doug Stokes (Oxford: Oxford University Press, 2008b).

Ehteshami, Anoushiravan, 'The Middle East: Between Ideology and Geo-politics' (pp. 104–20), in *The Bush Doctrine and the War on Terrorism: Global Responses, Global Consequences*, ed. Mary Buckley and Robert Singh (Oxford: Routledge, 2006).

Falk, Richard, 'The Global Setting: US Foreign Policy and the Future of the Middle East' (pp. 19–32), in *The Iraq War and Democratic Politics*, ed. Alex Danchev and John MacMillan (Oxford: Routledge, 2005).

Finlan, Alastair, 'International Security' (pp. 150–63), in *The Bush Doctrine and the War on Terrorism: Global Responses, Global Consequences*, ed. Mary Buckley and Robert Singh (Oxford: Routledge, 2006).

Galbraith, Peter, 'Kurdistan in a Federal Iraq' (pp. 268–81), in *The Future of Kurdistan in Iraq*, ed. Brendan O'Leary, John McGarry and Khaled Salih (Philadelphia: University of Pennsylvania Press, 2005).

Gunter, Michael, 'Turkey's New Neighbor, Kurdistan' (pp. 219–34), in *The Future of Kurdistan in Iraq*, ed. Brendan O'Leary, John McGarry and Khaled Salih (Philadelphia: University of Pennsylvania Press, 2005).

Indyk, Martin, 'The Postwar Balance of Power in the Middle East' (pp. 83–112), in *After the Storm: Lessons from the Gulf War*, ed. Joseph Nye and Roger Smith (Maryland: Madison Books, 1992).

Kagan, Robert and William Kristol, 'Introduction: National Interest and Global Responsibility' (pp. 3–24), in *Present Dangers: Crisis and Opportunity in American Foreign and Defense Policy*, ed. Robert Kagan and William Kristol (USA: Encounter Books, 2000).

Kennedy-Pipe, Caroline, 'American Foreign Policy After 9/11' (pp. 401–19), in *US Foreign Policy*, ed. Michael Cox and Doug Stokes (Oxford: Oxford University Press, 2008).

Ryan, Stephen, 'The United Nations' (pp. 173–88), in *The Bush Doctrine and the War on Terrorism: Global Responses, Global Consequences*, ed. Mary Buckley and Robert Singh (Oxford: Routledge, 2006).

Schmidt, Brian, 'Theories of US Foreign Policy' (pp. 7–23), in *US Foreign Policy*, ed. Michael Cox and Doug Stokes (Oxford: Oxford University Press, 2008).

Singh, Robert, 'The Bush Doctrine' (pp. 12–31), in *The Bush Doctrine and the War on Terrorism: Global Responses, Global Consequences*, ed. Mary Buckley and Robert Singh (Oxford: Routledge, 2006).

Tripp, Charles, 'Iraq' (pp. 186–215), in *The Cold War and the Middle East*, ed. Yezid Sayigh and Avi Shlaim (Oxford: Oxford University Press, 2003).

Vanly, Ismet Sheriff, 'Kurdistan in Iraq' (pp. 139–93), in *A People Without a Country: The Kurds and Kurdistan*, ed. Gerard Chaliand (New York: Olive Branch Press, 1993).

von Hippel, Karin, 'State-Building After Saddam: Lessons Lost' (pp. 251–67), in *The*

Future of Kurdistan in Iraq, ed. Brendan O'Leary, John McGarry and Khaled Salih (Philadelphia: University of Pennsylvania Press, 2005).

Wanche, Sophia, 'Awaiting Liberation: Kurdish Perspectives on a Post-Saddam Iraq' (pp. 186–94), in *The Future of Kurdistan in Iraq*, ed. Brendan O'Leary, John McGarry and Khaled Salih (Philadelphia: University of Pennsylvania Press, 2005).

7 Academic articles

A Clean Break: A New Strategy for Securing the Realm. (1996). [The Institute for Advanced Strategic and Political Studies] Available at: URL: www.iasps.org/strat1. htm Access Date: 20 December 2007.

Bradley, Curtis (2002). *US Announces Intent Not to Ratify International Criminal Court Treaty*. [The American Society of International Law] Available at: URL: www.asil.org/ insigh87.cfm Access Date: 20 December 2009.

Bremer, Paul, James Dobbins and David Gompert, 'Early Days in Iraq: Decisions of the CPA', *Survival* Vol. 50, No. 4 (2008): pp. 21–56.

Carothers, Thomas, 'Promoting Democracy and Fighting Terror', *Foreign Affairs* Vol. 82, No. 1 (2003): pp. 84–97.

Cox, Michael, 'Empire by Denial: The Strange Case of the United States', *International Affairs* Vol. 81, No. 1 (2005): pp. 15–30.

Cox, Michael, 'Why Did We Get the End of the Cold War Wrong', *The British Journal of Politics and International Relations* Vol. 11, No. 2 (2009): pp. 161–76.

Dumbrell, John, 'Unilateralism and "America First": President George W. Bush's Foreign Policy', *The Political Quarterly* Vol. 73, No. 3 (2002): pp. 279–87.

Dumbrell, John, 'Evaluating the Foreign Policy of President Clinton – Or, Bill Clinton: Between the Bushes', *The Second Eccles Centre for American Studies Plenary Lecture* given at the British Association of American Studies Annual Conference, 2005.

Feldman, Noah. (2005). *The Democratic Fatwa: Islam and Democracy in the Realm of Constitutional Politics*. [Oklahoma Law Review] Available at: URL: http://adams.law. ou.edu/olr/articles/vol. 58/feldman581.pdf Access Date: 18 December 2009.

Fisher, Louis, 'Deciding on War Against Iraq: Institutional Failures', *Political Science Quarterly* Vol. 118, No. 3 (2003): pp. 389–410.

Gaddis, John L., 'Grand Strategy in the Second Term', *Foreign Affairs* Vol. 84, No. 1 (2003): pp. 2–15.

Garnham, David, *Clinton's Foreign Policy* (Nablus: Centre for Palestinian Research and Studies, 1994).

Gordon, Philip, 'The End of the Bush Revolution', *Foreign Affairs* Vol. 85, No. 4 (2006): pp. 75–86.

Haass, Richard N., 'The Irony of American Strategy: Putting the Middle East in Proper Perspective', *Foreign Affairs* Vol. 92, No. 3 (2013): pp. 57–67.

Hiltermann, Joost R., 'Revenge of the Kurds: Breaking Away from Baghdad', *Foreign Affairs* Vol. 91, No. 6 (2012): pp. 16–22.

Jervis, Robert, 'Understanding the Bush Doctrine', *Political Science Quarterly* Vol. 118, No. 3 (2003): pp. 365–88.

Kagan, Robert. (1999). *Distinctly American Internationalism*. [Carnegie Endowment for International Peace] Available at: URL: www.carnegieendowment.org/publications/ index.cfm?fa=view&id=237 Access Date: 20 June 2008.

Kagan, Robert, 'America's Crisis of Legitimacy', *Foreign Affairs* Vol. 83, No. 2 (2004): pp. 65–87.

Korn, David. (1994). *The Last Years of Mustafa Barzani*. [The Middle East Quarterly] Available at: www.meforum.org/220/the-last-years-of-mustafa-barzani Access Date: 20 December 2007.

Krauthammer, Charles, 'The Unipolar Moment', *Foreign Affairs* Vol. 70, No. 1 (1990/1991): pp. 23–33.

Krauthammer, Charles, 'The Unipolar Moment Revisited: America, The Benevolent Empire', *The National Interest* Vol. 70 (Winter 2002): pp. 5–17.

Leffler, Melvyn, '9/11 and the Past and Future of American Foreign Policy', *International Affairs* Vol. 79, No. 5 (2003): pp. 1045–63.

Litt, David. (1995). *The Situation in Northern Iraq: Problems and Prospects*. [The Washington Institute for Near East Policy] Available at: www.washingtoninstitute.org/templateC05.php?CID=2862 Access Date: 20 December 2007.

Marshall, Joshua, 'Remaking the World: Bush and the Neoconservatives', *Foreign Affairs* Vol. 82, No. 6 (2003): pp. 142–6.

Mazarr, Michael, 'George W. Bush, Idealist', *International Affairs* Vol. 79, No. 3 (2003): pp. 503–22.

Mead, Walter Russell, 'God's Country?' *Foreign Affairs* Vol. 85, No. 5 (2006): pp. 24–43.

Nye, Joseph, 'US Power and Strategy After Iraq', *Foreign Affairs* Vol. 82, No. 4 (2003): pp. 60–73.

Nye, Joseph, 'Transformational Leadership and US Grand Strategy', *Foreign Affairs* Vol. 85, No. 4 (2006): pp. 139–48.

Parker, Ned, 'The Iraq We Left Behind: Welcome to the World's Next Failed State', *Foreign Affairs* Vol. 91, No. 2 (2012): pp. 94–110.

Rebuilding America's Defenses: Strategy, Forces and Resources for a New Century. (2000). [The Project for the New American Century] Available at: URL: www.newamericancentury.org/RebuildingAmericasDefenses.pdf Access Date: 20 December 2007.

Rice, Condoleezza, 'Campaign 2000: Promoting the National Interest', *Foreign Affairs* Vol. 79, No. 1 (2000): pp. 45–62.

Roosevelt, Franklin D. (2005). *2005 Topical Symposium Prospects for Security in the Middle East April 20–21, 2005.* [National Defense University] Available at: URL: www.ndu.edu/inss/Symposia/Topical2005/Agenda.htm Access Date: 20 June 2009.

Ross, Dennis, 'The Middle East Predicament', *Foreign Affairs* Vol. 84, No. 1 (2005): pp. 61–74.

Rubin, Michael. (2008). *Is Iraqi Kurdistan a Good Ally?* [AEI Middle Eastern Outlook] Available at: URL: www.aei.org/outlook/27327 Access Date: 15 February 2008.

Rubinoff, Edward L., Wynn H. Segall and Heidi L. Gunst Akin. (2001). *New U.N. Debate on Iraq: The 'Smart' Sanctions Approach.* [The Metropolitan Corporate Counsel] Available at: URL: www.akingump.com/files/Publication/2dbd5b91–6cda-40e5-b6c4-f34cff9b8c9b/Presentation/PublicationAttachment/19872f31–1584–4a1d-8524-f629ce3bdbf0/236.pdf Access Date: 20 December 2008.

Sky, Emma, 'Iraq, From Surge to Sovereignty', *Foreign Affairs* Vol. 90, No. 2 (2011): pp. 117–27.

Stansfield, Gareth. *Iraqi Kurdistan: An Analysis and Assessment of the Development and Operation of the Political System*. PhD thesis, University of Durham, 2001.

Wanche, Sophia. *Identity, Nationalism and the State System: The Case of Iraqi Kurdistan*. PhD thesis, University of Durham, 2002.

Wright, Steven. *Analysing United States Foreign Policy Towards the Middle East 1993–2003: Origins and Grand Strategies*. PhD thesis, University of Durham, 2005.

Index